LATINO POLITICS IN MASSACHUSETTS

T0346686

LATINO POLITICS IN MASSACHUSETTS

STRUGGLES, STRATEGIES, AND PROSPECTS

EDITORS

CAROL HARDY-FANTA

JEFFREY N. GERSON

Routledge
Taylor & Francis Group

NEW YORK AND LONDON

Published in 2002 by
Routledge
711 Third Avenue
New York, NY 10017

Published in Great Britain by
Routledge
2 Park Square, Milton Park,
Abingdon, Oxfordshire, OX14 4RN

First issued in paperback 2016

Routledge is an imprint of the Taylor & Francis Group, an informa business

Library of Congress Cataloguing-in-Publication Data
Latino politics in Massachusetts : struggles, strategies, and prospects /
editors Carol Hardy-Fanta and Jeffrey Gerson.
p. cm. — (Race and politics)
Includes bibliographical references and index.
ISBN 0-8153-3142-8
1. Hispanic Americans—Massachusetts—Politics and government. 2.
Massachusetts—Political and government—3. Political participation—
Massachusetts. I. Hardy-Fanta, Carol, 1948–
II. Gerson, Jeffrey, 1951–. III. Series
F75.S75 L37 2001
323.1'1680744—dc21

20001016009

ISBN 13: 978-1-138-97943-7 (pbk)
ISBN 13: 978-0-8153-3142-1 (hbk)

To my mother, Sue M. Hardy, and in loving memory of my father, Eldon A. Hardy.

CHF

In loving memory—*a mi abuela,* Olivia Lamberty Arlequin, and *tío,* Francisco Alfonso Lamberty.

JNG

Table of Contents

List of Maps and Figures

MAPS

FIGURES

List of Tables

Series Editor Preface

The Routledge series "Race and Politics" encompasses scholarly studies on the dynamics of American politics from a broad perspective. As political science moved from primarily an institutional approach to one which incorporated behavioral dimensions new questions were raised about the political implications of the post 1960's wave of immigrants, the role of naturalized American voters, the influence of the media on elections, and the changing nature of federalism. Two events, the Civil Rights Movement and increased non-European immigration were pivotal in spurring social science research on the political dimensions of race and ethnicity.

With new voters entering the political system questions on participation strategies for incorporation and political empowerment had to be revisited. The Hardy-Fanta and Gerson volume, *Latino Politics in Massachusetts: Struggles, Strategies and Prospects* expands Latino scholarship by looking these issues. As Latinos become the largest minority group in the U.S. displacing African Americans increased attention must be given to the political impact of changing demographics. Although Massachusetts does not have one of the highest concentrations of Latinos, it is becoming an increasingly diverse state. In order to understand the changes that are taking place in a New England context the authors present two approaches: one is an overview of efforts of political inclusion in Massachusetts cities and the second focuses on the building blocks of political empowerment such as creating coalitions, promoting Latino voter registration, and developing feasible civil rights strategies.

This study does not end with a simplistic prescription to merely increase Latino turnout. Rather as the articles illustrate attaining a piece of the pie entails multiple strategies—mobilizing behind a viable candidate, building coalitions across cultures, and developing young leaders, both male and female. Past electoral success in Springfield, Lawrence, and Boston offer a political succession model for other communities. Cultural and political struggles will continue, as Latinos at the local level attain greater electoral success by addressing the obstacles of unresponsive school systems, at-large systems of voting, and divisions within the diverse Latino community which have hindered more rapid progress.

Latino Politics in Massachusetts presents a fresh analytical look at the micro level. The impact of new political actors at the in local politics has been a neglected area of research. National and regional studies on Latinos so dominate political science that it is easy to forget that states can be laboratories for addressing issues that will become trends in national electoral politics. This volume is merely a harbinger of future studies of Latino politics from the state perspective.

Acknowledgments

The goal of this book is to offer a first look at the history of Latino politics in a state that, until recently, has not been considered of prime importance in the study of Latino political representation or influence. In tracing the path to writing this book, one moment stands out: when one of the authors called a national Latino political think-tank a few years ago to urge greater attention to Latino politics in this state, the organization's representative replied, "Well, we don't care about Massachusetts." From that point on, this book had to be written. The reason is that Latino candidates, Latino community residents, and Latino communities as a collective whole *do* care. The book had to be written to document the struggles and strategies, the barriers and the successes—the prospects for a future of Latino political power in a small northeastern state like Massachusetts.

This book is also needed because Latinos living in Massachusetts are part of communities that are remarkably diverse. Although there is more diversity by country of origin in southwestern states such as California, Texas, New Mexico, Colorado, and Arizona than is commonly supposed and states such as New York, New Jersey, and Illinois have traditionally been home to Latinos from many countries, Massachusetts offers a look not only at multiethnic/racial Latino communities but also at *emerging* Latino politics in a diverse state.

The potential to swing national elections may be larger in the "big" Latino states, but as the saying made famous by Speaker "Tip" O'Neill from Massachusetts Goes: "All politics is local." Millions of Latinos live outside of those "big" states and struggle year after year to assert their interests, mobilize their communities, run for office, and gain political power in their local communities. This book is, therefore, an effort to shed light on these struggles, to offer some of the strategies Latino communities have used in this state that might be useful for similar communities in other states, and to examine their prospects for political power.

This book could not have been written without the full participation of Latino activists, candidates, and residents in Latino communities around the state. Their willingness to share their experiences and their passion for politics made writing this book a responsibility as well as a great pleasure. Space is too limited here to recognize all the individuals and groups who deserve acknowledgment. Over the years, the following individuals have consented to be interviewed at length, and, in many cases, repeatedly. Even more important are the contributions to Latino political empowerment made within their communities over the past decades by Latinos and Latinas such as Jaime Rodríguez, Marta Rosa, Felix Arroyo, Carmen Pola, Nelson Merced, Jovita Fontanez, and Diosdado López—pathbreakers all in their own way. They have a passion for politics rooted in their homeland countries and local communities that has translated well to politics in Boston and the other "Latino" cities around the state.

We thank, as well, the countless others who have been tireless in their efforts to mobilize their communities and to achieve political representation and influence, including Maria Aguiar, Yohel Camayd-Freixas, Alan Jay Rom, María Quiroga, Alex Rodriguez, Rita Gonzalez-Levine, Gumersindo Gómez, Isabel Meléndez, Zoila Cueva, Julia Silverio, George "Chico" Muñoz, María Sánchez, Nilka Álvarez, Juan Cruz, José Tosado, José Vincenty, Marcos Devers, Carmen Rosa, Ralph Carrero, Leticia Ortiz, Grace Romero, Juan Vega, Juan Guevara, Betty Medina Lichtenstein, and Diana Lam. Congratulations are in order for our three Latino state representatives: José Santiago, Cheryl Rivera, and Jarrett Barrios. Elected in 1998, together they tripled the Latino representation in the Massachusetts State House. This book draws heavily on the information and experiences shared by all of these individuals and many others. Any errors of fact or interpretation are, of course, ours.

We would particularly like to thank Edwin Meléndez and Andrés Torres, past and current directors of the Mauricio Gastón Institute of Community Development and Public Policy at the University of Massachusetts Boston, for their support of the research needed for this project. This book is based on research funded, in part, by a generous grant from the Inter-University Program for Latino Research; thank you for your support of this and other projects. All the staff at the John W. McCormack Institute deserve recognition for their ongoing support over many years—and for their tolerance of Carol Hardy-Fanta's recent absences to finish this volume. A special thanks from Carol Hardy-Fanta to her colleague and friend Carol Cardozo, for the life stories we share and for your many kindnesses. Thanks to research assistants María Quiñones and Rosalba Bassols-Martínez for the endless hours they spent gathering data, interviewing candidates, and making sense of the massive amount of information from the literature, from news clippings and archives, and on the various civil rights lawsuits. We also would like to thank Carter Irvine for the detailed attention she gave in preparing the city maps that accompany each chapter in

Part I. It was a pleasure working with her. Thank you to our editors at Routledge and to the Race and Politics Series editor, Toni-Michelle Travis. Finally, the contributing authors to this book shared our enthusiasm for documenting Latino politics in Massachusetts. They were willing to extend themselves to produce and edit their respective chapters and we thank them for meeting important deadlines!

On a more personal note, although it may be true that among friends and family *favores no se cobran,* we owe a debt to our families who support us daily: Christopher, Carly, and Allison Hardy-Fanta, and Laura, Gabriel, and Amelia Gerson.

A todos—¡se lo agradecemos muchísimo! ¡P'alante!

> Carol Hardy-Fanta
> Jeffrey Gerson
> Boston, Massachusetts

Introduction
A Statewide Overview

As the Latino population in the continental United States continues to grow, interest in Latino politics has grown as well. Latinos currently make up 12.5 percent of the population (whereas blacks are 12.3 percent and whites 75.1 percent). Census data suggest that Latinos currently constitute approximately 11 percent of the voting-age population.[1]

Because of this population growth, candidates for national and local office are now taking note of the increasing presence—and potential political clout—of Latino communities around the country. Witness the special attention paid to Latinos by both parties during recent elections. During the first presidential and congressional elections of the new millennium, this attention increased considerably. In addition, there are several congressional districts in which the Latino vote is crucial and may very well determine which political party controls Congress in years to come. Due to Latino political independence, neither party can take the Latino vote for granted (Milligan 1999).

Political scientists have begun to devote increased attention to Latino politics during the past decade. If the 1980s was supposed to be, according to the media, the "decade of the Hispanic," then surely the 1990s was the "decade of the Hispanic/Latino" for political science as a discipline. In a recent and comprehensive review of Latino politics in the United States (Affigne, Jackson, and Avalos 1999), for example, there were 10 references from the 1970s, 17 from the 1980s, and over 70 from 1990 to 1999!

LATINO POLITICS IN THE "BIG NINE" STATES: A REASONABLE BUT LIMITED FOCUS

Much of the recent, and earlier, attention deservedly focused on areas of the country with the highest Latino populations and longest historical presence: the states of California, Texas, New Mexico, and Arizona. Latinos in Florida, New York, New Jersey, Colorado, and Illinois also have become a significant political force, and have been the subjects of considerable research, by virtue of their percentage of the population and due to the fact that most Latino elected officials came from these states (Brimhall-Vargas 1994, 12).[2]

Latino political representation continues to be disproportionately low, nevertheless. In January 2000, there were, according to the National Association of Latino Elected and Appointed Officials (NALEO), 5,135 Latino elected officials, but they made up only 1 percent of the nation's elected officials (NALEO 2000).[3]

The politics of Latino communities outside of the "big nine" states have begun to receive some attention in recent years. Examples of recent attention include Jenning's (1984) early research comparing Puerto Ricans in New York with those in Boston; Santillan's (1988) history of Midwestern Latino politics; Jennings and Lusane's (1994) exploration of black/Latino relations in Washington, D.C.; Hardy-Fanta's research on gender and Latino politics in Boston (1993) and on Latino candidates in Massachusetts (1995, 1997); and Cruz's (1998) study of politics in Hartford's Latino community.

WHY EXAMINE LATINO POLITICS IN MASSACHUSETTS?

Roberto Villarreal provides support for the study of Latino politics in states such as Massachusetts in his review of *Ethnic Ironies: Latino Politics in the 1992 Elections*. In this review, Villarreal comments:

> Two major ironies stand out in the election of 1992: first, while the turnout among all voters increased over the previous election (1988), the increase in Latino voters in 1992 "did not match the growth rate achieved between 1980 and 1988 and barely kept pace with the growth in the Latino adult population." Second, *if there was any significant impact, it did not come from the large states with heavy Latino populations; instead it came from the small states.* (Villarreal 1996, 906; emphasis added)

Later, Villarreal discusses the conditions "necessary for the creation of an effective Latino electorate. These conditions fall into two categories: contextual—conditions that fall outside the realm of control of Latinos— and strategic—conditions within the realm of Latino influence" (1996, 906). Villarreal also suggests that "the ethnic and political diversity of the Latino population defies generalization and continually pushes researchers to deconstruct that population at the local level" and urges greater attention to municipal and state elections. Massachusetts offers an opportunity to examine Latino politics precisely in these local settings—cities with varying degrees of Latino diversity, different contextual conditions (e.g., at-large versus district election systems, Latinos as a large percentage of the population versus a minority), and distinctive community strategies for gaining political power.

Although some Latino scholars, such as Villarreal, are now calling for more research on Latino politics in the states with smaller Latino populations, little is known about the struggle to gain political representation at the municipal and state levels outside of the nine most populous states—or about the specific contextual and strategic conditions Villarreal considers so important.

It is important to document the political struggles of Latino communities outside of the large Latino states and at the community or municipal level for several reasons. First, not doing so will continue the pattern of making Latino politics in those communities invisible, which discourages activists in those states. Second, more attention needs to be paid to comparative state politics. We need to know whether national trends in Latino politics are mirrored in the smaller states. Third, there is a growing interest in the field of political science in the politics of mid-sized cities, which has been ignored for decades by scholars of urban and ethnic politics (Bowers and Rich 2000). Finally, it is important to examine the struggles, strategies, successes, and prospects of Latino communities such as those in Massachusetts that share certain characteristics with many other states: considerable Latino diversity by country of origin, political participation and representation that are *emerging* rather than established, and, in many cases, a Latinos as a relatively small percentage of the city and/or state population.

The studies in this volume reveal that increasing Latino voter registration and voting, as well as the growth in numbers of candidates running for office and winning seats, are not simply a national trend. One of this book's main arguments is that success, wherever it occurs, breeds further success. Rather than a unilinear, cause and effect model where increased political participation leads to increased representation and, presumably, greater Latino political power, we suggest that success at gaining representation or political effectiveness (i.e., power) creates a momentum for greater participation. The experiences described in the chapters that follow examine the different ways Latinos face the variety of contextual factors and devise strategies that simultaneously increase participation as they are increasingly successful in gaining representation.

This book explores some of the following questions: What are the political experiences in Massachusetts communities where Latinos continue to be large in numbers but still a minority? Why is the pace of political change greater in some Massachusetts cities, such as Lawrence, than at the national level whereas, in some, such as Lowell, the pace is slower? The readings in this volume make clear the need for assessments of different success rates through comparative studies in some of the smaller states.

The chapters address questions tied to both contextual and structural factors. Questions related to contextual factors include the following: What barriers to participation and representation exist for multiethnic Latino communities? How important are structural obstacles to political empowerment, such as at-large and/or nonpartisan elections, preregistration requirements, and the decline of the political party, and various industries at the local level, and what strategies have been successful in overcoming them? What is the impact of different social, economic, and political contexts (as well as demographics) on levels of representation? How instrumental are national organizations, such as the National Association of Latino Elected and Appointed Officials (NALEO), that provide leadership and campaign skills training in boosting Latino candidacies and election victories?

Questions related to strategic factors—those that are, to a greater extent, within the control of Latino communities—include the following: What electoral or other strategies are most effective in gaining increased political representation and influence? What is the impact of gender and ethnic diversity within Latino communities on the political efforts and strategies of those communities?[4] Are Latinos joining forces with other minority groups and progressive reformers to achieve power or do they prefer a go-it-alone strategy? What is the relationship between homeland politics and mainland politics after migration to the continental United States?

THE POLITICAL MEANING OF ETHNIC LABELS: LATINO OR HISPANIC?

We would like to acknowledge that by using "Latino" we are choosing one term for what is in reality a complex diversity of national identities. "Latino/a" is not just a neutral term for those individuals or groups who come from a wide variety of Latin American countries. Those whose backgrounds are firmly rooted in an identity that is clearly "Puerto Rican," "Dominican," "Mexican," or "Cuban" may prefer those terms instead. Others prefer the term "Hispanic" to "Latino/a" for a variety of reasons.[5] Some authors in this volume use Latino/a and Hispanic interchangeably because of patterns of use within the communities being described; quotes include the term, Hispanic or Latino/a, that is used by the person being interviewed. For the most part, however, the term "Latino" generally will be used throughout this book to refer to individuals who can trace their ancestries to Latin America. It is offered as an alternative to "Hispanic," which emphasizes (some would say overemphasizes) the Spanish colonial experience in the Americas. We needed to use a commonly accepted term rather than listing all the alternatives and have chosen "Latino/a."

LATINO POPULATION IN MASSACHUSETTS

Latinos currently make up 6.8 percent of the 6.3 million Massachusetts residents. The 2000 census counted 428,729 Hispanics/Latinos in the state, an increase of 25 percent since 1990. Whereas in 1980 the U.S. Census counted 141,043 "persons of Hispanic origin" (2.5 percent of the population), that number more than doubled by 1990 to 287,549 (4.8 percent of the state's population). The Latino population's rate of growth between 1980 and 1990 in Massachusetts, 104 percent, was almost twice that for Latinos nationwide—53 percent (Rivera 1991, 3). By 1990, Latinos had become the state's largest ethnic minority, outnumbering African Americans.[6] The projected figure for Latinos in 2010 is 566,731 or 8.4 percent of the state's 6.7 projected million residents (Torres and Chavez 1998, 2). State Representative Jarrett Barrios of Cambridge speaks for many when he said that these figures mean Latinos have "reached a point of demographic inevitability" in Massachusetts (Finucane 1999).

Although the state's Latino population is still small, especially when compared to states like California, Texas, and New York, the Commonwealth of Massachusetts ranks as the thirteenth state with the largest number of Latinos in the country.

Compared to African Americans, who tend to be concentrated in the city of Boston, Latinos make up large portions of several cities. The Latino population in Massachusetts is dispersed in cities throughout the state, with the greatest concentrations located in the seven cities we focus on in this book: Lawrence, Chelsea, Holyoke, Lowell, Springfield, Boston, and Worcester.[7] Map I.1 shows the percentage Latino and geographic location of these cities in the state; we provide the map to orient readers unfamiliar with the state of Massachusetts. The chapters on each city included in Part I of this book describe the Latino communities in greater detail.

As can be seen from the map, Lawrence is located in the northeastern part of the state. It is in the center of the Merrimack Valley; Lawrence is also the seat of Essex Country. It is home to the largest Latino community of any city in the state and is one of the largest on the East Coast. Ten percent of the Commonwealth's Latino population lives in Lawrence. The 2000 census (see Table I.1) indicates that 59.7 percent of the city's population is Latino. In 1990 Lawrence ranked as the poorest city in the state and the twenty-third poorest in the country. It has very high rates of poverty, crime, and arson on a per capita basis (Office of Planning 1994, 2). In Lawrence, Puerto Ricans officially amounted to 51 percent of all Latinos in 1990, down from 59 percent of Hispanics counted in the 1980 Census. Dominicans are now estimated to outnumber Puerto Ricans in Lawrence. From the middle 1960s until today the fastest growing

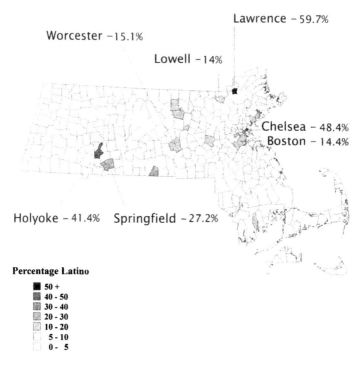

Lawrence – 59.7%

Worcester – 15.1%

Lowell – 14%

Chelsea – 48.4%
Boston – 14.4%

Holyoke – 41.4%   Springfield – 27.2%

Percentage Latino

- 50 +
- 40 - 50
- 30 - 40
- 20 - 30
- 10 - 20
- 5 - 10
- 0 - 5

Data Source: 2000 Census, P.L. 94-171

population is from the Dominican Republic. During the past decade over 66,000 Dominicans have gone through naturalization (over 10,000 a year in the mid-1990s).

Chelsea is a very small industrial city across the Mystic River from Boston (see map I.1). It has traditionally been a place of first settlement for many European immigrants in the nineteenth and twentieth century and for Latinos in recent decades. According to the 2000 census data, Latinos officially make up 48.4 percent of the city's population. Juan Vega, director of the multiservice agency and the city's lone Latino city councilor, *Centro Latino,* believes Latinos make up at least half of Chelsea'a population. Puerto Ricans constitute about one-half of the Latino population, with the remainder consisting of a large number of Central Americans (primarily from El Salvador, Guatemala, Honduras, and Costa Rica), Colombians, and Dominicans.

Holyoke is located in the southern part of Western Massachusetts on the Connecticut River. Latinos make up 41.4 percent of the city's population. The Latino population in Holyoke has the highest percentage of Puerto Ricans of the seven cities studied. In 1990 Puerto Ricans in Holyoke constitute 93.5 percent of the population. Springfield is also located in the western portion of the state, just five miles south of Holyoke (see Map I.1). Over one-quarter (27.2 percent) of Springfield's population of 172,648 were Latinos. Best estimates suggest that Puerto Ricans are currently approximately 89 percent of Latinos in the city. Mexicans and Cubans comprise the remaining 11 percent.

Worcester is located in central Massachusetts on the Blackstone River and is known for its once mighty tool machinery industry. It is the second most populous city after Boston: Worcester's population is currently 172,648. As seen in Table I.1 the official count of the Latino population is 26,155 or 15.1 percent. Eighty percent of Latinos in Worcester are Puerto Rican.

Boston, the capital of Massachusetts, is located in the Eastern part of the state at the mouth of the Charles and Mystic Rivers on Massachusetts Bay. Boston is the seat of Suffolk County and is the largest city in all of New England. Boston is a center for the finance, education and health care industries, and has one of the largest Roman Catholic Archdiocese in the United States. The "minority population" in Boston now makes up the majority: 50.5 percent of city residents are from communities of color and 14.4 percent are Latino. After experiencing a rapid rise in the Latino population in the 1970s and 1980s, and despite the high cost of living and shortage of affordable housing, the Latino population in Boston grew by 50 percent between 1990 and 2000.

Table I.1   Latino Population in the State and Selected Cities,
                 2000 Census

	Total Population	Latino Population	Percent Latino
Statewide	6,349,097	428,729	6.8
Lawrence	72,043	43,019	59.7
Chelsea	35,080	16,984	48.4
Holyoke	39,838	16,485	41.4
Springfield	152,082	41,343	27.2
Worcester	172,648	26,155	15.1
Boston	589,141	85,089	14.4
Lowell	105,167	14,734	14.0

Source: Mauricio Gastón Institute for Latino Community Development and Public Policy, University for Massachusetts Boston, 4 April 2001.

Lowell is a city of about 100,000 located 10 miles west of Lawrence and known, like Lawrence, for its once-dominant textile mills. Today, the Latino population of Lowell is 14.0 percent of the city. The Latino population in Lowell is approximately 70 percent Puerto Rican, 20 percent Colombian, with the other 10 percent Dominicans, Cubans, and Mexicans.

Latinos face numerous social and economic problems in Massachusetts reinforcing the importance of achieving increased political influence and positions of power in government, which has many tools to address, ease, and possibly solve them.

Latinos in Massachusetts trail all racial/ethnic groups in all socioeconomic indicators—and the pattern holds true in all cities. They have the fewest years of schooling completed, the lowest proportion of adults with a college degree (10.7 percent); the highest percentage of nonenrollment (21.9 percent), and the lowest proportion of high school completion (44.8 percent).[8] Latinos are overrepresented in the lower-paying occupations and have the highest proportion of those not in the labor force. Nearly half of Latino families (46.6 percent) live in poverty, the highest incidence of household poverty for any group in Massachusetts. Latino average income per capita, $7,510 in 1995, was the lowest for any racial/ethnic group.

LATINO REPRESENTATION IN MASSACHUSETTS: THE STATE OF THE STATE

Latinos in many communities in Massachusetts have often expressed discouragement about their low levels of political representation and influence. The relative isolation of the various Latino communities in cities around the state, a lack of attention both in the mainstream and Spanish language media to Latino political organizing and candidates, and the fact that most organizing takes place locally limit the visibility of Latino campaigns.

A recent study by Hardy-Fanta (1997) suggests, however, that, even though Latinos certainly have not achieved parity in terms of political representation in the cities and state of Massachusetts, Latinos are running for office in increasing numbers and they win election at a respectably high rate. Sixty Latino candidates ran for office between 1968 and 1994. In addition, there was a considerable surge in the number of Latinos running for office during the 1990s. From 1968 to 1980, for example, there were only nine Latino campaigns in the state. The number increased slowly during the next decade: between 1980 and 1989 there were 31 campaigns. There were, therefore, 42 Latino campaigns in the 21 years between 1968 and 1989.[9]

In just four years between 1990 and 1994 there were, however, a total of 48 campaigns by 33 Latinos running for elected office in Massachusetts (Hardy-Fanta 1997, 6–10). And, despite the sense of discouragement within Latino communities here and elsewhere, Latino candidates in Massachusetts have a very respectable track record in winning election. Of the 60 Latino candidates who were identified as having run for office between 1968 and 1994, 14 (24 percent) were elected. Twenty-four of the 87 campaigns during these years (28 percent) resulted in victories (Hardy-Fanta 1997, 9).

Although a comparable study has not yet been done for the years since 1994, it seems clear that the surge in the number of Latinos running for office has not abated. Figure I.1 shows the exponential growth in the number of Latino campaigns in Massachusetts since the first campaign by a Latino in 1968 through 1999.[10]

The chapters in Part I of this volume provide a history of many of the campaigns and other organizing efforts that are reflected in this figure. Here it will suffice to note that the surge that began in 1990 coincided with the election of Nelson Merced, the first Latino state representative, an event described at length in Chapter 2. Merced's election energized Latinos around the state and opened up a sense that winning was, indeed, possible. Marta Rosa won election to the Chelsea City Council the next year—the first Latino city councilor in the state, thanks to a number of strategic and contextual conditions discussed at length in Chapter 1. Latinos continued to gain seats in municipal level offices around the state. By 1999, an unprecedented 11 Latino candidates ran in the City of Lawrence alone, which was the total number of campaigns in all the years from 1968 to 1994. In 1999, Latino support, at the voting booth and in the campaign organization, was crucial to the election of the first in the nation Cambodian-American city councilman, Rithy Uong, in Lowell. Latinos have also continued to press for representation in Holyoke, where they continue their effort to "run a Latino in every election" (see Chapter 4).

Number of Campaigns

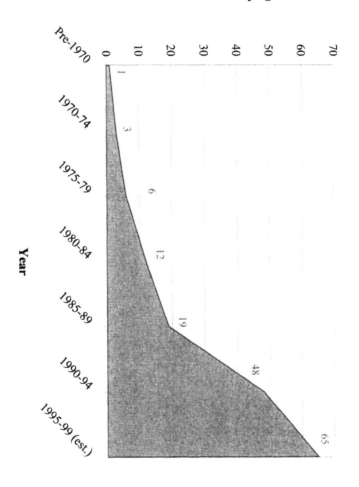

Year

The efforts to gain representation have paid off. Whereas there had been rarely more than a few Latinos in office at any given time in Massachusetts during the early decades, this number rose to 7 in 1994 and 12 in 2000. And although until 1998 there had been only one Latino ever elected to the State Legislature, there are currently three Latino representatives: José Santiago from Lawrence, Jarrett Barrios from Cambridge, and Cheryl Rivera from Springfield. As can be seen in Table I.2, there are, in addition to the state representatives, six Latinos on City Councils, and three Latino School Committee members.

Table I.2   Latino Elected Officials in Massachusetts in Office May 2000

Name	Office	City
Nilka Álvarez	City Council	Lawrence
Jarrett Barrios	State Representative	Cambridge
Ralph Carrero	School Committee	Lawrence
Juan Cruz	City Council	Holyoke
Marcos Devers	City Council	Lawrence
Diosdado López	City Council	Holyoke
Cheryl Rivera	State Representative	Springfield
José Santiago	State Representative	Lawrence
Julia Silverio	City Council	Lawrence
José Tosado	School Committee	Springfield
Juan Vega	City Council	Chelsea

The demographic characteristics of Latino candidates in Massachusetts suggest that they reflect—and thereby are likely to represent—the diversity of the Latino groups that live in this state. In 1994, 71 percent of candidates were Puerto Rican, 13 percent Dominican, and 16 percent South or Central American or Mexican. According to Torres and Chávez (1998, 2), in 1990, Puerto Ricans accounted for 53 percent of the Latino population in the state, with Dominicans 11 percent and other groups 7 percent.

The fact that a larger percentage of Puerto Ricans have run for office reflects the history of migration in a state where non-Puerto Rican groups are more recent arrivals and are less likely to be citizens. Contrary to the attribution that Latinos are less likely to invest in U.S. politics due to a presumed lack of attachment to the continental United States, Hardy-Fanta (1998, 14) found that less than half (45 percent) of the Latino candidates were born in the continental United States; 32 percent were born on the island of Puerto Rico and 23 percent were born outside the United States. Attachment to their local communities is strong: on average, the Latino candidates in Massachusetts resided an average of 15.2 years in the cities from which they ran for office. Latino politics in Massachusetts has also made it onto the national "radar screen." As can be seen in Chapter 10,

Latino political organizations such as the National Association of Latino Elected and Appointed Officials (NALEO) and others have begun investing training and other resources to the Latino election campaigns in this state in part due to the recent election successes.

LATINO POLITICAL MOBILIZATION IN MASSACHUSETTS: THEORETICAL PERSPECTIVES

Examining Latino political representation and mobilization at the statewide and local level in Massachusetts requires a dynamic theoretical perspective that contains elements from pluralism, political incorporation, resource mobilization, and gender analysis. The experiences of Latinos in Lawrence and Chelsea in the early 1990s seem to "prove" the inevitability of ethnic political succession in cities where the Latino population has become (or is about to become) a majority. Though conflict is part of the succession process, political change typically involves a relatively orderly, irreversible sequence. As Latinos replaced earlier immigrants in the various neighborhoods in these cities, conflict did occur but—even as they challenged the barriers and structural obstacles put in their place by the old power structure—Latinos also responded to grievances by forming interest groups and running for office.

The rate of replacement and the amount of resistance offered by the older, established groups varies, of course, with circumstances—the contextual factors to which Villarreal (1996) refers. Glazer and Moynihan (1970), for example, argue that ethnic political change is a "central dynamic of the city's organizational life" and Latinos in the cities described in Part I of this book confirm that Latinos do indeed both challenge and emulate the norms of previously dominant groups. Challenging the city census to ensure that Latino voters are not dropped from the voting lists, using lawsuits under the Voting Rights Act, and undertaking voter registration drives all involve conflict, but they are also part of an orderly process of political change.

The supposed inevitability of succession, within a pluralistic view of American politics, depends on contextual factors such as the rate of demographic change within a political jurisdiction, the size and distribution of the group, the intensity of political party competition for the ethnic vote, the degree of independence of the new ethnic voters, the quality of ethnic group leadership, and legislative redistricting (Gerson 1990).

Latino communities in Massachusetts with high Latino populations, especially as seen in Chapters 1, 3, and 4 on Chelsea, Lawrence, and Holyoke, show evidence of the three stages of succession Fuchs (1990) identifies: the forming of associations for religious and fraternal solidarity, organizing for economic success, and achieving political power. The formation of the Latin American Cultural Association in Chelsea and the various Dominican social clubs in Lawrence, for example, might appear, at least to those Anglos who view politics through an electoral lens alone, to reflect an "interest in homeland politics" that diverts Latinos from "real" political action. They are, in fact, an important part of the process of ethnic succession. As majority Latino communities begin to approach the third stage of succession, the call for greater ethnic power is usually threatening to established groups—a situation evident in Lawrence today and in Chelsea when Latinos were close to gaining parity in municipal-level offices.

Ethnic succession theory has limits, of course, under conditions where Latinos are not a majority of the population, live in residentially segregated neighborhoods, or struggle with internal divisions. Browning, Marshall, and Tabb's (1990, 9) political incorporation model provides another useful approach for analyzing Latino politics, especially under such conditions. The goal of "political incorporation" in order to achieve desired changes in policy is at the center of their analysis. They use the term to cover a range of possibilities: no minority representation, some representation against a dominant opposition, and the strongest form—"an equal or leading role in a dominant coalition . . . committed to minority interests." The highest form is likely to exercise substantial and sustained influence over spending, revenue, programs, governmental structure, and personnel. And even limited representation, when combined with alliances within a dominant coalition, may offer a modicum of political power to nonmajority Latino communities such as those in Lowell, Springfield, Boston, and Worcester.

Browning, Marshall, and Tabb caution, however, that given the fragmented American political system and the global capitalist political economy, even incorporation may not be enough. Real power may not only be beyond the ballot box, it may be completely beyond the community. In addition, achieving political incorporation may be difficult, if not impossible, in cities where the Latino population is a relatively small percentage of the total. In Massachusetts, the Latino experiences in Boston, as well as Lowell, Worcester, and Springfield—and even Lawrence, Chelsea, and Holyoke where Latinos have achieved or are close to majorities—suggest that ethnic succession and political incorporation are never inevitable.

The struggles for Latino representation and power described in this book also demonstrate the importance of external and internal resources. Resource mobilization theory and the Latino political experiences discussed here demonstrate that, without a doubt, external resources are critical to the success of local community efforts. Chelsea's remarkable achievements in the early 1990s—including achieving near parity in Latino representation—would not have been possible without the infusion of funds, support, and technical assistance from such varied sources as the Teachers' Union, the AFL-CIO, and, of course, the Justice Department. The chapter on voter registration efforts (Chapter 10) also demonstrates that the recent election of three Latino state representatives in one year coincided with an infusion of resources from the National Association of Latino Elected Officials (NALEO) and many other groups. The chapters on Holyoke, Chelsea, and Springfield illustrate that success in gaining representation depends to a great extent on internal resources such as group solidarity, organizational networks, collective action, and coalitions with other groups.

Finally, recent research demonstrates that gender analysis needs to be considered when exploring Latino politics in Massachusetts and elsewhere. The cities in Massachusetts where Latinos have had the greatest success in challenging the dominant power structure and electing Latinos to office are those that have benefited from having—and recognized the importance of—Latina women as organizers and candidates. The key components of a gender analysis are explored at length in Chapter 8 in this volume.

SCOPE OF THE BOOK: STRUGGLES, STRATEGIES, AND PROSPECTS FOR LATINO POLITICS IN MASSACHUSETTS

This book is organized in two parts. Part I is a series of chapters on the seven cities under study: Chelsea, Boston, Lawrence, Lowell, Holyoke, Springfield, and Worcester. Each of these chapters provides a detailed history of the Latino struggles for political participation and representation; as such, they document the emergence of Latino politics in a northeastern state that, heretofore, has received scant attention in the field of Latino politics. Each chapter also demonstrates specific themes related to the contextual and strategic factors that block or support Latino political representation.

In Chapter 1, Glenn Jacobs argues that Boston University's takeover of the city of Chelsea's schools in 1989 was a watershed moment for Latinos in that city and resulted in a remarkable political transformation of the political structure of that city—virtually overnight. The Latino community, for all its presumed apathy, led the struggle against privatization in the educational arena and successfully projected that struggle into the electoral arena. Furthermore, the school conflict served as a lever for political socialization so that the next generation of Latinos has learned the skills of political conflict and strategies from its current leaders. Jacobs also highlights the importance of Latina women as organizers and candidates, the power of external grievance ("the issues") in political mobilization and the critical role of outside resources.

In Chapter 2, Ramón Olivencia argues that multiracial coalitions played the critical role in the election of Nelson Merced as the first Latino elected to the Massachusetts state legislature. Olivencia believes such coalitions are essential for Latinos to gain access to electoral politics in Massachusetts, particularly in cities where they are far from constituting a voting majority, such as in Boston. In cities like Boston and Worcester where Latinos make up only about 14 percent of the population, such coalitions are often necessary for more Latinos to achieve elected office. This chapter is illustrative of the strategies required "behind the scenes"—away from the ballot box—that preceded the election of a Latino candidate in a city and district without a clear Latino majority.

In Chapter 3, William Lindeke argues that the Latino community of Lawrence has now broken through the barriers to political incorporation. A bifurcated population of Dominicans and Puerto Ricans has come together to achieve remarkable success in just the past 5 years. A high Latino population, district as well as at-large elections, strategies developed within the more social organizations applied to the election arena, and a noteworthy surge in the number of Latino candidates have overcome many of the traditional barriers. These barriers include the fact that the community is young, poor, relatively uneducated, and organizationally fragmented; it also has had to confront an extremely resistant Anglo-dominant power structure.

In Chapter 4, Carol Hardy-Fanta, with Rosalba Bassols-Martínez, provide a detailed history of efforts to organize and mobilize the Latino community in Holyoke. Strategic planning in the community includes a commitment dating back to the early 1970s to "run a Latino in every election" and develop local Latino organizations. Strategic planning in the courts has resulted in an infusion of external resources (e.g., the Rainbow Coalition, legal assistance, and a lawsuit under the Voting Rights Act). With these strategies, Latinos finally have achieved their goal of having two Latinos on the city council as well as a Latino supporter (Yvonne García) on the school committee.

In Chapter 5, Jeffrey Gerson examines a subject that has been largely unexplored in the field of Latino politics: the response of the Catholic Church to the migration of Latinos to American cities. He seeks to answer the question: Can the apparent ineffectiveness of Latino political organizations and leadership in Lowell, and the consequent underrepresentation of Latinos in the halls of local government, be explained by examining Church–Latino relations, including the Church's policy, leadership, and organizational response to the newcomers? It is the author's contention that Latino unity and political mobilization were hindered by different pastoral and political approaches to empowerment among the Catholic Church's leading priests in Lowell.

In Chapter 6, José Cruz explores the reasons for Latino underrepresentation in the city of Springfield. Many Latinos in that city believe that the at-large electoral structure is the most important barrier to representation. Cruz finds that, in fact, it may be the least intractable. Latinos have succeeded in being elected in at-large elections. Cruz argues that other contextual realities (e.g., low income and educational attainment) also block

Latino political empowerment in Springfield. Strategic conditions in the city's Latino communities are, according to Cruz, the greatest barriers, however. These include weak Latino organizations, considerable in-fighting and jealousy among Latino leaders, and failure of Latino organizations to endorse Latino candidates.

In Chapter 7, Juan Gómez, a current member for the Worcester City Council and a long-time resident and activist in the city's Latino community, offers an insider's perspective on Latino powerlessness in Worcester. Latinos in Worcester, according to Gómez's perspective, have tended to be reactive to a series of crises rather than proactive and strategic. Gómez believes that despite rising Latino voter registration rates and candidacies for local office, Latinos will remain underrepresented until the community overcomes a history of divisions among Latinos (primarily Puerto Ricans and Dominicans) and between Latinos and African Americans.

Part II shifts the focus of the book to topics of more general concern, especially to those interested in understanding the various strategies and prospects for increasing Latino political participation and representation. The research that informs these chapters was conducted in Massachusetts, but the themes contained therein serve to inform the broader debates about Latino political participation and representation. These include gender and political leadership within Latino communities, civil rights strategies, voter registration efforts, ethnic relations, and multiracial coalitions. We are pleased to include a chapter on Dominicans in Massachusetts politics as well as an assessment of the Latin-American Legislative Caucus after its first year.

Carol Hardy-Fanta begins Part II with a chapter on Latinas and political leadership in Latino communities. She presents evidence from several of her studies of Latino politics in Massachusetts indicating that, contrary to the stereotypes of Latina women in the literature and, not infrequently, in their own communities, Latinas play important leadership roles in both the electoral arena and at the community level. She demonstrates that although their candidacies and electoral successes receive little recognition in the media and the social science literature, Latina women run for office in numbers essentially equivalent to Latino men and, when they run, they are elected at comparable or higher rates. By examining their motivations for running for office, their campaign style and strategies, and the way they interact with Latino community residents, we may gain insights needed for successful Latino candidacies—male as well as female.

In Chapter 9, Seth Racusen examines the demographic constraints on the potential for Latino representation in states like Massachusetts, where they are—and will probably remain—a small overall percentage of the total population. He reviews the critiques of the 1970s and 1980s civil rights redistricting strategies and explores the electoral prospects for Latino communities of alternative representational systems. He explores the prospects

that modified at-large electoral systems would provide for increased political representation of the Latino communities in Massachusetts and suggests that gains could be anticipated in most legislative bodies, with the
greatest increase projected for the state legislature.

One of the topics referred to most in the literature on Latino politics is
voter registration and turnout. Chapter 10, written by Carol Hardy-Fanta
with activist and organizer, Jaime Rodríguez, begins with a critique of this
literature for failing to explore this topic with the depth of detail it
deserves. They then provide an overview of the literature on Latino voting
rates nationally (a topic that has received exhaustive attention), and "best
estimates" of the Latino vote in Massachusetts. The chapter goes beyond
voting rates, however, and provides the first in-depth account of voter registration efforts statewide and in the local communities.

In Chapter 11, James Jennings raises several important questions about
interethnic coalition politics: How do structural changes in the economy
contribute to racial and ethnic conflict among communities of color? How
do cultural patterns, values, and information (or lack thereof) contribute to
racial and ethnic conflict? How does U.S. foreign policy contribute to the
quality and nature of political relationships between communities of color?
Jennings believes that Boston offers an important case study of the political possibilities that emerge from political relationships between black and
Latino interests.

Ramona Hernández and Glenn Jacobs offer a cutting-edge chapter on
Dominicans and Latino politics in Massachusetts. Chapter 12 is appropri-
ately titled *Beyond Homeland Politics* because, in it, Hernández and Jacobs
carefully explore one of the most important debates in Latino politics
today: whether an interest in "homeland politics" is a constraint on Latino
political participation in this country—locally or nationally—or whether
homeland politics offers important resources to Latinos in their local U.S.
communities. This chapter is rich in historical context and interweaves
homeland political experiences with those of a number of Latino candidates in two Massachusetts cities: Lawrence and Lynn.

Jeffrey Gerson, in Chapter 13, offers an assessment of the first year of
the Latin-American Legislative Caucus—formed after the record-breaking
election in 1998 of three Latino legislators. Prior to their election, only one
Latino was ever elected to the legislature—and there had been no Latino
representation in that body since 1992. Having three Latinos elected was a
watershed for Latino politics in this state. Gerson examines the stiff challenges these three, Cheryl Rivera, José Santiago, and Jarrett Barrios, face as
freshmen representatives. These challenges include an authoritarian leadership structure, the need to focus on wining reelection, and issues rooted in
their different backgrounds, electoral districts, and political ideologies.

Finally, the editors conclude with a Postscript suggesting that, based on
the information provided in the preceding chapters, prospects for Latino

representation in cities across Massachusetts are hopeful. At the same time, success in increasing representation and power depends to a great extent on increased communication and collaboration between the various Latino communities about strategies that have been successful. Building on civic and cultural traditions (including those rooted in homeland politics); strengthening coalitions with other groups; recognizing the importance of gender in political organizing; and supporting recent political action initiatives are also essential for developing both a unifying Latino political agenda and effective Latino/a leadership.

NOTES

1.   Source: U.S. Bureau of the Census (2000b, 2). Please note, because up to 40 percent of Latinos are not citizens, the actual size of the potential electorate is estimated to be closer to 5 or 6 percent. See Garcia (1997, 31–43).

2.   As of 1992, 96 percent of all Latino elected officials were elected in these states (half from Texas alone).

3.   At the time this book was going to press there were no Latinos in the U.S. Senate, 19 House members, 52 state senators, and 138 state representatives or assembly persons. There were also 1,466 municipal level office holders (NALEO 2000).

4.   In 1992, Pachon and DeSipio wrote: "Nationally, women hold 17.5% of elected offices (Census, 1988). In the Hispanic community, women currently hold 20% of the offices" (1992, 215). By 1994, NALEO reports that 31 percent of offices held by Hispanics were held by Hispanic women.

5.   Please note: In addition to the question of which term to use is the issue of accents. The use of accents is an important feature of the Spanish language. In this volume, we have endeavored to be correct in our use of accents, including in proper names. In cases where we know that an individual customarily does not include an accent in his or her name, we have omitted the accent. In cases where we were unsure, we erred on the side of correct accent usage. We apologize for any mistakes.

6.   All Latino population data are from sources based on the U.S. Census. For 1980, see Rivera (1991) for 1990–2000, see Torres and Chávez (1998). The data from the 2000 census are from the *Boston Globe* (2001).

7.   Other cities in Massachusetts with over 10 percent Latino population include Lynn, Southbridge, Fitchburg, and Framingham. Space does not allow chapters for these cities but they should be included in future studies of Latino politics in Massachusetts.

8.   Unfortunately all socioeconomic data are not yet available for the 2000 census. All socioeconomic data provided here are from Torres and Chávez (1998).

9. For a detailed analysis of the study and results, see Hardy-Fanta (1997); this study also produced a *Directory of Latino Candidates in Massachusetts, 1968–1994* and *Speaking from Experience: A Handbook of Successful Strategies by and for Latino Candidates in Massachusetts*. Both are available by contacting the Gastón Institute at the University of Massachusetts Boston.

10. The data for 1968 to 1994 are from the study by Hardy-Fanta (1997). The number of campaigns from 1995 to 1999 were estimated from telephone interviews with key informants conducted by Jeffrey Gerson in the Spring of 2000. The analysis and chart were prepared by Carol Hardy-Fanta.

REFERENCES

Affigne, Anthony, M. Njeri Jackson, and Manuel Avalos. (1999). "Latino Politics in the United States: Building a Race-Conscious, Gendered, and Historical Analysis." Paper presented at the annual meeting of the American Political Science Association, Atlanta, GA, 2–5 September.

Arches, et al. (1997). "New Voices in University-Community Transformation, by Joan Arches, Marian Darlington-Hope, Jeffrey Gerson, Joyce Gibson, Sally Habana-Hafner and Peter Kiang. *Change*, (29)1: 36–41.

Boston Globe. (2001). 18 March –30 March.

Bowers, James R. and Wilbur Rich., eds. (2000). *Governing Middle-Sized Cities: Studies in Mayoral Leadership*. Boulder, CO: Lynne Rienner.

Brimhall-Vargas, Mark. (1994). "Hispanic Elected Officials 1994." National Association of Latino Elected and Appointed Officials. Washington, DC: NALEO Educational Fund, December 1994.

Browning, Rufus, Dale Rogers Marshall, and David H. Tabb. (1990). *Racial Politics in American Cities*. White Plains, NY: Longman.

Cruz, José. (1998). *Identity and Power*. Philadelphia: Temple University Press.

Finucane, Martin. (1999). "Hispanic Caucus to Focus on Jobs, Child Care, Housing." *The Quincy Patriot Ledger*, 9 February, 6.

Fuchs, Lawrence H. (1990). *The American Kaleidoscope: Race, Ethnicity, and the Civic Culture*. Hanover, NH: University Press of New England.

Garcia, F. Chris. (1997). "Input to the Political System: Participation." Part II in *Pursuing Power: Latinos and the Political System*, 31–43. Notre Dame, IN: University of Notre Dame Press.

Gerson, Jeffrey. (1990). "Building the Brooklyn Machine: Irish, Jews and Blacks in Central Brooklyn, 1919–1964." Ph.D. dissertation, City University of New York Graduate School.

Glazer, Nathan, and Daniel Patrick Moynihan. (1970). *Beyond the Melting Pot: The Negroes, Puerto Ricans, Jews, Italians and Irish of New York City*. Cambridge, MA: Massachusetts Institute of Technology Press.

Hardy-Fanta, Carol. (1993). *Latina Politics, Latino Politics: Gender, Culture, and Political Participation in Boston*. Philadelphia: Temple University Press.

_____. (1995). "Latina Women in Political Leadership: Implications for Latino Community Development." *New England Journal of Public Policy* 11: 220–235. (Reprinted in this volume, Chapter 8.)

_____. (1997). *Latino Electoral Campaigns in Massachusetts: The Impact of Gender.* A research report, with María Quiñones, Lynn Stephen, Nelson Merced, and Anthony Affigne. Boston: Center for Women in Politics and Public Policy and the Mauricio Gastón Institute for Latino Community Development and Public Policy, University of Massachusetts Boston.

Jennings, James. (1984). "Puerto Rican Politics in Two Cities: New York and Boston." Chapter 4 in *Puerto Rican Politics in Urban America*, edited by James Jennings and Monte Rivera, 75–98. Westport, CT: Greenwood Press.

Jennings, Keith, and Clarence Lusane. (1994). "The State and Future of Black/Latino Relations in Washington, D.C.: A Bridge in Need of Repair." In *Blacks, Latinos and Asians in Urban America: Status and Prospects for Politics and Activism*, edited by James Jennings, 57–77. Westport, CT: Praeger.

Milligan, Susan. (1999). "Hispanic Vote Gains Influence for 2000 Vote." *New York Times*, 13 September, A3.

NALEO. (2000). Interview by Jeffrey Gerson with Rosalind Gold, 6 June.

Office of Planning and Community Development. (1994). "Application for Lawrence/Methuen Enterprise Zone." City of Lawrence.

Pachon, Harry, and Louis DeSipio. (1992). "Latino Elected Officials in the 1990s," *PS: Political Science and Politics* 25(2)(June), 212.

Rivera, Ralph. (1991). *Latinos in Massachusetts and the 1990 U.S. Census: Growth and Geographical Distribution.* Boston: Mauricio Gastón Institute for Latino Community Development and Public Policy, University of Massachusetts Boston.

Santillan, Richard. (1982). "Latino Politics in the Midwestern United States: 1915–1986." Chapter 5 in *Latinos in the Political Systems*, edited by F. Chris Garcia, 99–118. Notre Dame, IN: University of Notre Dame Press.

Torres, Andrés, and Lisa Chavez. (1998). *Latinos in Massachusetts: An Update.* Boston: Mauricio Gastón Institute for Latino Community Development and Public Policy, University of Massachusetts Boston.

U.S. Bureau of the Census. (2000a). Projections downloaded from the internet, 1 May from www.census.gov/population/projectionextract/nation/ nprh9600.asc; www.census.gov/ population/projection-extract/nation/nprh1530.asc.

_____. (2000b). "Projections of the Voting-Age Population for States: November 1998." *Current Population Reports, Population Characteristics*, P25-1132, by Jennifer C. Day.

———. (2001). "Overview of Race and Hispanic Origin. *Census 2000 Brief*, C2KBR/01-1, March.

Villarreal, Roberto. (1996). "Review of Ethnic Ironies." *American Political Science Review* (December): 906.

Part I

History and Lessons
from Massachusetts Cities

CHAPTER 1

Educational Grievance and Latino Mobilization
Chelsea

GLENN JACOBS

During the early 1990s the premier case of privatization of a complete pub-lic school system, in a worn-out industrial city on the northern border of Boston, catapulted Chelsea and its Latino community into metropolitan and national headlines. Prior to the Boston University takeover of the pub-lic schools in 1989, Chelsea's Latino community, if not having slept through Chelsea's civic affairs, found itself more a hapless supplicant to the powerful than a respected player in city politics. The coming of Boston University provided an opportunity to observe systemic educational priva-tization in a "natural" setting, and to recognize the critical role of *griev-ance* in stimulating Latino political mobilization.[1]

In 1990 the city of Chelsea had the third highest percentage of house-holds in Massachusetts with an annual income below $10,000, and the highest percentage of residents living below the poverty line. Within this context, Latinos fared worst, as we learn from the Foreword of a survey sponsored by Chelsea's Commission on Hispanic Affairs:

> By almost every economic and social indicator, Chelsea Hispanics[2] fare poorly—not only in relation to non-Hispanics, but also in comparison with Hispanics in Boston. On average, Chelsea Hispanics are poorer, are more likely to be employed in declining sectors of the economy, have high-er rates of unemployment, are more likely to be employed part-time or only part of the year, have lower levels of formal education and have lower levels of facility in English. (Kennedy et al. 1990, ii)

In addition to their depressed economic conditions, Chelsea's Latinos were, and continue to be, a diverse population. According to the 1990 cen-sus, approximately 9,000 Latinos, or 31.4 percent of a total population of 28,700 lived in Chelsea; by 2000 the official number had risen to 16,984 or 48.4 percent. As can be seen by Map 1.1, Latinos live in all areas of this small city, but are concentrated primarily in the Shurtleff–Bellingham and

Map 1.1   Population in Chelsea (2000), by Census Block Group, with
Neighborhoods

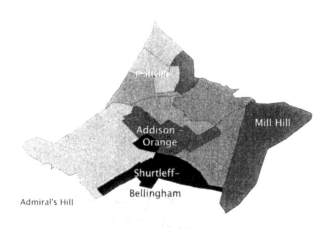

Lower Broadway/Waterfront

0   0.5 Mile

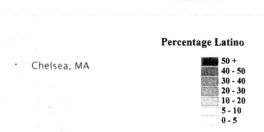

Percentage Latino

Chelsea, MA

50 +
40 - 50
30 - 40
20 - 30
10 - 20
5 - 10
0 - 5

Source: 2000 Census, P.L. 94-171

Addison–Orange neighborhoods where they make up well over half of the population. In contrast, their numbers are much smaller in the upper-class Admiral's Hill, the upscale "Waterfront," the middle-class Prattville, and the older working-class Mill Hill neighborhoods.

At the time of the 1990 census, Puerto Ricans constituted about one half (49.6 percent) of the Latino population, with the remainder consisting of a large percentage (35.6 percent) of Central Americans (El Salvadoreans, Guatemalans, Hondurans, and Costa Ricans), 4.5 percent South Americans (especially Colombians), 3.2 percent Dominicans, and 7.1 percent other Latinos (Torres and Chávez 1998, 3; Kennedy et al., 1990, 1, 5–8).

Despite their poverty, their educational underpreparedness, their diversity, and, in many respects, their political inactivity, segments of this population, were aroused to fight for their children's educational rights and to engage in other community issues. The awakening of Chelsea's Latinos into political activism is of historic significance due to both its stimulus—systemic educational privatization—and its apparent suddenness. Its advent offers object lessons for Latino empowerment. Coming on the heels of severe recession and the Reagan and Bush administration assaults on government services and welfare, privatization initiatives in education, social services, and prisons appeared plausible.[3]

In this respect, the erosion of welfare institutions in the wake of the recession of the 1980s, as both a cause and effect of economic instability for the poor, had, with the allied conservative assault on public education, displaced frustrations over social tensions onto public schooling. Education in our society was, and to an extent continues to be, an imputed cause of social instability and the failure of minorities to achieve upward mobility (Shapiro 1990). Just as schools bore the thrust as proxies for residential desegregation in the 1960s and 1970s, so did they bear the brunt of being both identified causes and effects of poverty and of societal deterioration (Weisman 1992). Education became a prominent target for the discrediting of public service at the receiving end of a self-fulfilling prophesy of inefficiency, inadequate standards, assessment and curriculum, and the faulty professionalism of teachers. Currently, schools occupy center stage for the enactment of scenarios of violence, mass murder, and their amelioration. As a result, it becomes difficult to separate real educational crises from reified ones—in this case, the schools as causes or effects of social problems and their student populations as villains or victims.[4]

THE PERILS OF PRIVATIZATION: EDUCATIONAL STRUGGLE, THE REDEFINITION OF CITIZENSHIP, AND THE POLITICS OF REFORM

Notwithstanding the pronouncements of societal surrogates that the resistance put up to educational reforms such as privatization is obstructive, the efforts on the part of dissenting groups to seek participation in the reform process itself may be viewed as attempts to implement *democratic* processes. These struggles actually represent loyal opposition to the status quo because they remain within the orbits of civil society, but they do transcend the narrow boundaries of education and go to the heart of the constitutional arrangements of our society, that is, into the sovereign relations among citizens and those who govern. In the words of the rap group *Public Enemy*, minority educational activists "Confront the power!" Educational struggles in particular speak to the wider problems and struggles encountered by people of color in our society. Historically speaking, as Katznelson and Weir (1985, 178–179) remind us, for minority groups united on the basis of color "[i]n contrast to the fragmented character of white working-class participation, [they] engaged in school politics with a single identity forged in response to policies that denied them access to public education or relegated them to a separate and inferior position within that policy domain." The continuing struggle for schooling is central to bringing minorities together "as a group with particular political demands and a distinct history of political practice centered around education issues" (Katznelson and Weir 1985, 191). In this respect, educational struggles waged by people of color more broadly impinge upon and reflect the larger issue of their status and roles as citizens of our society (Turner 1986).

The Chelsea case thus offers a profound example of the manner in which school reform and policymaking reflect wider social and political issues for Latinos. Chelsea had been ravaged by the economic turnaround begun in the mid-1970s and its population underwent transformation from a predominantly white European one to a diversified mix of Latinos, Southeast Asians, blacks and whites. Privatization of the schools leavened this mix into a conflict of wider significance than the schools themselves.

With respect to the effect of privatization of public services on citizenship, one author notes that, "Privatization leads to a loss of control and a decline of citizen participation in government" and *generically* identified the Chelsea Project as an example of the danger privatization schemes hold for democratic accountability:

> When Boston University was negotiating to run the Chelsea School District in Massachusetts, the University, a private institution, demanded exemption from state laws requiring open meetings and public records. The university also insisted that it could not be held liable for any lawsuits brought against the district. (Bilik 1990, 7–8)

The author insists that public administration is "integral to our system of checks and balances" and that privatization, relying on the motives of private gain, compromises democracy.

Thus when the Chelsea Project was announced, the reservations of eminent educators gravitated toward issues around educational rights. Harold

Howe, former Commissioner of Education under President Johnson, and later a member of the governor's appointed State Oversight Panel for the Chelsea Project, opined that the city's contracting away of their authority obviated the rights of citizens to inquire into the operations of their school system (Fulham 1988, 34). Similarly, Charles V. Willie of Harvard University noted that the undertaking had serious implications for self-determination and accountability since Boston University's "self-perpetuating board of trustees is simply not accountable to the citizens of Chelsea as a school board would be" (Daniels 1988).

Lawsuits filed by Chelsea's Commission on Hispanic Affairs and the Chelsea Teachers' Union in the Spring of 1989 would address in detail the issues of accountability, openness of meetings, legal susceptibility, and University recordkeeping in connection with the Chelsea project. The Commission on Hispanic Affairs suit challenged the basic structure of the contractual agreement between the city and Boston University, contending that "important constitutional safeguards of public accountability and public control over public education had been abrogated." The Chelsea Teachers' Union suit contended that violation of the state constitution had occurred, to wit, that public money should not be used to subsidize any primary or secondary school not publicly owned or exclusively controlled by officers or public agents authorized by the Commonwealth or federal government.

When "enabling" legislation, exempting the new arrangement from the strictures of state law, was introduced under a cloud of cautionary criticism by the Massachusetts Department of Education, the governor created a blue ribbon panel to oversee the university's mandated consultation with community representatives for the 10 year duration of the contract. The event was duly reported in the Boston press and its preparatory phases had made news for several years in educational journals and newspapers. The *Boston Globe* editorialized the *social implications* of privatization of public services:

> [T]he success of the BU approach depends on the trust, and ultimately the participation, of the students and the parents. It is inconceivable that BU did not make an effort to include them in the process from the beginning. It is not too late for BU to consider Hispanic leaders' concerns about bilingual education and their request for the formation of an advisory board that reflects the racial and ethnic makeup of the students. (*Boston Globe*, 1989b)

HISTORY REPEATS ITSELF: KEEPING CITY GOVERNMENT OUT OF THE HANDS OF THE "DANGEROUS CLASSES"

Chelsea has had a predilection for entrusting its municipal management to private overseers at crisis points in its history. Significantly this occurred when city government seemed most threatened by the prospect of broad scale immigrant participation. Chelsea's history represents a trajectory from old-style urban machine politics through a period of receivership of the city government by a Control Commission following a devastating fire in 1908, through a subsequent return to its patronage and graft prone system in 1911, to, most recently, a "leveraged" takeover of its schools by a private ("nonprofit") corporation (1989) and a full circle return to receivership of the city government in 1991.

Following the 1908 fire, testimony at public hearings called to discuss petitioning the state for suspension of the regular city government and formation of the Control Commission was prescient for the Boston University question 80 years later. Securing the confidence of the business community was considered the most valuable asset in rebuilding the city. The graft-fraught and patronage-ridden local government, which was open to immigrant participation, was derided as corrupt and inefficient. As William E. McClintock, Chairman of the Chelsea Board of Control put it in a retrospective (1910, 16) article, "After the fire there was a widespread feeling that the city could not be quickly and economically rebuilt and remodeled by the Mayor and the Aldermen."

Then, as in the late 1980s, well-established white Northern European caretakers of the city saw crisis as an opportunity to solve problems that representative (i.e., immigrant-saturated) government had allowed to get out of hand. Popularly based (i.e., ethnic working-class) opinion, then, as it would later, stressed local self-reliance and the importance of safeguarding the franchise of voters. In a city hearing on the Commission question a Mr. Doherty, who, true to the prejudices of the day was portrayed as an Irish rustic, foreshadowed later popular views on privatization in Chelsea:

> What we want to know about this commission is, what good is it going to be for the city of Chelsea? What authority will it have? Will we have any guarantee that they will govern our city any better than our present government has? Will the city of Chelsea have to pay the bills? I guess so. If the city of Chelsea is going to pay the bills they ought to have the right to say who is going to spend the money. If the money lenders won't lend the money, what guarantee will you have that they will lend it to the commission? (Anonymous 1908)

Will "they" benefit the city and its citizens? How much authority will they have? Will they hold our interests to heart? Will they be able to make good on their promises of funding and if we share the costs, shouldn't we also have input into the way it is spent? As Kopf (1974, 68) points out, "To the immigrants, commission government was not reform; it was disenfranchisement."[5]

Eighty years later, Mr. Doherty's questions were succeeded by those of Latinos coming from quarters also patronizingly cast as naive, and, alternately, as obstructive and nonrepresentative of the community. Until 1989, the year of Marta Rosa's accession to the School Committee, no Latino had been elected to public office in Chelsea. As Hardy-Fanta suggests, Rosa's reasons for running for office both typified a common theme characterizing other Latino candidates—the need for Latino representation—and were unique, considering the community crisis and Latino politicization precipitated by "the proposed 'takeover' of the Chelsea school system by Boston University" (Hardy-Fanta 1997, 30). This event became a watershed for Latino politics in Chelsea.

ENTER THE LEVIATHAN: BOSTON UNIVERSITY TAKES OVER CHELSEA'S SCHOOLS

The Boston University/Chelsea project grew out of School Committee member (also former mayor, state representative, and senator) and publisher of the *Chelsea Record*, Andrew Quigley's request (1985) to John Silber for Boston University to manage the Chelsea schools after Silber's offer to do the same for the Boston schools had been refused. The Management School rather than the Education School ran the project according to its dean, George McGurn, because U.S. business was worried about "our global competitiveness and schools of education were part of the problem" (McGurn 1990).

Boston University's report on the Chelsea public schools, "A Model for Excellence in Urban Education," underscored the Latino community's isolation and alienation. The Report noted that parents felt excluded from their children's education by dint of strained communications between the families and their schools and the parents' "inability to feel in control" (Boston University 1988, VI–11), and concluded that

> Lack of community support and parental involvement in the schools is a widespread problem, but is particularly noticeable in Chelsea's Hispanic and Asian communities. Most teachers, administrators, and other white elites ascribe the problem to apathy, disinterest, and cultural barriers. The minority leaders we have talked with, however, place the problem along class and racial lines. With anecdotal evidence, they argue that their constituents have been denied access to government, schools, jobs, housing, health care and other community institutions. (Boston University, 1988: VI–18)

It added that efforts to mobilize support for minority candidates failed "due to fractured alliances, lack of money, and the inability to overcome competing interests with common concerns, but wrongly predicted that "It is unlikely that these minority groups could effectuate change through the political process, even if they could coalesce" (Boston University 1988, VI–18).

The acuity with which Boston University assayed Latino isolation and alienation was not matched by a foretelling of the politicization of Latinos, nor by empathy with the needs and aspirations of the Latino community leadership in its stewardship of the public schools. The city government and Boston University (BU) miscalculated the Latino community's desire and capacity for social action as it did its own insensitivity and resistance to negotiating the latter's demands. In turn, this posture aroused Latinos to elect their first public official, School Committee member Marta Rosa.

The approach taken by BU was totalistic and top-down, that is, it emphasized complete control of the school system's finances and personnel. McGurn (1990), taken with the small size of Chelsea, exclaimed, "It was so small you could wrap your arms around it. It was microcosmic. Frankly, if you were to take over the Boston system, who would ever know?" Elsewhere, such paternalism waxed unfettered, when McGurn stated, "We have to remember that Boston University is larger than the population of Chelsea. We can't be like Lenny in John Steinbeck's *Of Mice and Men* who breaks the neck of the puppy" (Bering-Jensen 1988, 17). Such delicacy also presupposed full control. As Education School Dean Greer put it in an interview, "We were going to take all the risks. Why shouldn't we have full control?" (Greer 1990c). That educational and civic virtue might be conceived differently by Latinos and other dissenters was anathema to Boston University.[6]

For John Silber the project was the actualization of a paternalistic vision of wider social reform conceived in the 1960s when his "Proposal for a Measure Attacking Poverty at Its Source" was entered in the *Congressional Record* (U.S. Congress 1965, 7352–7353). A program for preschool education, it contained the premise that "Children born into Negro families and families whose native language is other than English are not sufficiently stimulated verbally or are insufficiently trained in English to compete successfully in the public school whose programs are designed for English-speaking children." Among other things, the proposal provided for education "of mothers of slum children," schools in "renovated slum houses [sic]," tutoring, remedial summer schools and, presciently, "a massive crash program in one or two communities of a moderate size" (U.S. Congress 1965, 7352).

A SLUMBERING GIANT AWAKENS: LATINOS STRUGGLE TO BE HEARD

Predictably, when they entered the fray the Latinos found the legitimacy of their participation questioned. In the School Committee's deliberations over the impending contract in 1988, Latinos were largely absent from public hearings, but in early 1989 they turned out in force, contending that virtually no information had been disseminated to the Latino community in English or Spanish and that the Latino leadership was ignored by the

School Committee, Aldermen, Mayor, and PTA.[7] In February the Hispanic Commission wrote to the Boston University Management Team chair, Peter Greer, that "we, the Hispanic population, have been neglected. Considering that over 50% of the school population is Hispanic we should have direct input into the proposed plans."

Although the topic was aired in *The Chelsea Record* for some length of time, this newspaper's long-exhibited antipathy to Latinos, whom it depicted in a stereotyped manner, excluded their readership, inured them to its contents, and helped maintain civic apathy in their community.[8] No outreach had been done by the city government because there was no felt need to do so. Thus, the uproar that began in March 1989, after the placid hearings of July through November 1988, came as a shock to Chelsea's Anglos. It was, indeed, as if it had come out of nowhere.

The apparent belated activism on the part of the Latinos was actually the end of their social exclusion, but it was construed by proponents of the contract as a forfeiture of the Hispanics' prerogative to participate in the negotiations and to shape the final product. What appeared as obstructionism were the stirrings of a minority community for self-determination. Mayor Brennan, Andrew Quigley, Alderwoman Marilyn Portnoy, and Rosemarie Carlisle, President of the Parent Teacher Organization (PTO), among others I interviewed, felt that "they [Latinos] had their chance" and flubbed it by not taking enough interest and participating actively early in the debate when the time came for community input. On the Boston University side, as we shall see, the Latino activists were characterized as obstructive impostors.

A typical response was that of Rosemary Carlisle when she, the former President of the PTO and Andrew Quigley's replacement on the School Committee, was reelected. When asked if she thought that Hispanics had been excluded from the process of installing the contract, she briskly replied, "Hispanics were never excluded—and I don't know where you got that information. They had all the rights as I did as a citizen of Chelsea to be active in the BU partnership." When I asked, "So why do you think they were so upset at the time?" she answered,

> Because they came in too late in the process. If they had come out when Boston University first came here a year and a half ago and kept on track on top [sic] of everything, they would have been able to voice their opinion like all of the other citizens. I have no idea why it took them so long to voice their opinions. They should have voiced them earlier like we [i.e., the rest of the community] did. (Carlisle 1989)

Accusing Hispanic activists of being Johnny-come-latelies is a rhetoric of exclusion, as if to say, "better never than late!" It reflects the continuing resistance to Latino participation in civic life and surprise at the apparent suddenness of their entry into it when the Latinos overcome their own political apathy. Hence the urgency on the parts of the (largely white) supporters to implement the new arrangement.

The school system, originally designed to prepare a white ethnic working class for local industrial employment, in tandem with the other municipal institutions, could be said to have been in crisis, but this "crisis" had been going on for more than a decade, when in 1985, Boston University president John Silber was asked to intervene.

The real crisis was that of the European-dominated political machine and its voter base that was threatened by a burgeoning Latino and Southeast Asian population. Hence, the crisis may more usefully be seen as a social panic reaction of elements and representatives of Chelsea's shrinking European population, whereupon a cry for help was issued to Chelsea's new Great White Hope for gentrification and the dilution of its minority population. As Mayor John J. Brennan Jr. explained:

> All of your middle-class middle-aged people are going. . . . There's no more children of the white middle-class. That's what I honestly see. I think with BU here and a new school that we hope to build, I believe then that we'll draw people in a financial bracket that can pay for a good home and not be able to pay for private schools. (Brennan 1990)

Thus the halcyon dream of Chelsea's earlier white *working-class* for middle-class respectability would now hopefully be fulfilled in the postindustrial age. As for the growing minority populations, their invisibility had become transmogrified into the blur of an advancing wave of color and culture that could be stemmed only by forceful intervention, in this case, in the school system. Thus the traditional white-dominated power centers tried to reinforce and defend the old structures of domination or control, first by inviting Boston University to run the schools and afterward by succeeding in aiding the city to get the state to finance an extensive school building and renovation program. With renewed vigor, a larger population and a new crop of young leaders, Chelsea Latinos would find in the school question all of the material they needed to launch a revitalized organization and an electoral campaign destined to change the contours of Latino politics.

Latinos in Chelsea had attempted for more than a decade to secure a foothold in the city's civil service and political affairs. A variety of organizations, represented by moderate figures, emphasized accommodation to the white Democratic leadership of the city. Confrontational groups such as LUCHA (*Latinos Unidos en Chelsea para Acción*) found themselves beleaguered and neutralized by hostility and harassment from City Hall (Jacobs 1991). The Hispanic Commission, initially chartered under Mayor Nolan in 1987, was an accommodative group, but as noted, the events of 1989, including the hiring of a Puerto Rican community organizer by the teachers' union to stimulate Latinos to support an opposition school committee slate to Boston University, succeeded in transforming the organization into an autonomous-activist one.

As the conflict over the impending contract intensified, the Commission found itself casting an eye toward elective office. To accomplish this the arousal of the Latino electorate was necessary. Chelsea's Commission on Hispanic Affairs mulled the topic over and decided to launch a voter registration campaign.

Voter registration became and continues to be an important agent of politicization in the community. Resistance was high within and outside the Hispanic orbit, but provided a current for change agents to work with. Ángel (Tito) Rosa (Marta Rosa's husband) organized the voter registration drive. According to him (Rosa 1990), Chelsea contained only 650 registered Hispanics: "We had to figure out why these people did not want to register and why they didn't want to vote." Apathy, ignorance, and timidity greeted him in the trenches. "I had to develop a strategy," Tito confesses. Tito found that he could persuade many to listen and even to register to vote. He had no prior political experience and found himself thrown back upon his own personal and cultural resources. He would knock on a door, for example, and ask,

"Would you like to register?," and the reply might be, "Why do I have to register; what do I get out of it?" Tito would reply, "It's your right to be a registered voter. How do they know you live here?," and the reply might be, "I pay the rent." "No!" says Ángel, "If your name is not found on that census, you don't live here my friend. You're invisible. How do they know José González lives here?" By now, interest would be aroused and his interlocutor in disbelief would exclaim, "What do you mean?" "That's how it works," he might say, and "It's not only to register for government, it's to show the city that you *occupy* a place in Chelsea!" By now, recovering his or her composure, the person might parry, "So you are a politician and want my vote." Not to be undone, Tito would reply, "How many Hispanics are representing us in City Hall?" and the fellow would think and say, "None." "Do you like that?," Tito would ask. "Don't you think one of us could be up there?" And so it would go (Rosa 1990).

Marta Rosa insists that she had no prior political experience per se that primed her for her political career. However, it was her active involvement and leadership in Pentecostal church activities as a young adult which prepared her for the rigors of campaigning and gave her the opportunity to develop the skills of organizing groups and group activities. In addition, Rosa would have to appeal to a segment of the population, the elderly, that Latino candidates might initially cross off due to the fact that it was mostly white. Although it was customarily thought that the elderly do not vote for schools and their advocates, it was necessary to capture this vote. In an interview with Carol Hardy-Fanta, Rosa ascribed her success in dealing with this population, despite her initial fear of it, as resulting from her tactic of bringing her children with her to campaign events and from the fact that "I'm a caring person." She elaborated on this attribute as follows:

> Everybody says the elderly don't care about the schools but they do. . . . I could be their daughter and the fact that I'm Hispanic, some of them understand the need to have Hispanic representation. Isn't that bizarre? It's really interesting to me when I talk to the elderly: "Oh your people need representation. I'm going to give you a vote." (Rosa 1995)

Lynn Meza, Marta Rosa's campaign manager, corroborated this observation, noting that in addition to being female ("now the elderly are mainly women"), by bringing her children to campaign with her, Rosa cultivated her image as a family-centered candidate and thus succeeded in transcending the ethnic and racial barriers to her election (Meza 1995).

The election of Marta Rosa in 1989, among a slate of School Committee candidates cosponsored by the Chelsea Commission on Hispanic Affairs, the Chelsea Teachers Union, and its parent the American Federation of Teachers, represented a victory for a popular front against the long arm of privatization and white supremacy. The teachers union (AFT) had sent a Puerto Rican community organizer into Chelsea and this aided Rosa's campaign. The emergence of Rosa in particular fits an emergent trend: the appearance of independent grass-roots leaders, that is, leaders whose agendas and candidacies are not dominated by those of the dominant political party leadership (Jennings 1984, 80–81). Lyn Meza, a veteran Chelsea activist and Marta Rosa's campaign manager in the 1989 and 1991 elections, noted that the time was ripe for change (Meza 1990): "This was something that we had been waiting for, working for, hoping for years in this community—for responsible leadership to develop."

THE POLITICS OF THE REVOLVING DOOR

Although election of minority leaders is a source of strength and pride to minority groups, it is a threat to established interests. In an article in *Education Week*, Management Team chair Peter Greer (1990b) complained about citizen groups in Chelsea who "see the university's presence as a grand opportunity to gain power—even at the expense of students" through a "vote counting back door." Marta Rosa had already been elected (in November 1989) and the reference to a "vote counting back door" implied that her election somehow was underhanded—sub rosa, as it were!

An *Education Week* article quoted Greer as saying, "The Hispanic community happened to gear up at an untimely moment—the very moment when the agreement was about to be signed" (Snider 1989). Although Greer thought that it was "really healthy" that Latinos were forming to fight for education, he preferred "to see them expend their energies on implementing the project rather than trying to hold it up." Only one month earlier president Silber accused the discontented Latinos of being manipulated by the Chelsea Teachers Union, implying they lacked the autonomy and judgment to act on their own (Sleeper 1989). The Latino community immediately protested the accusation as demeaning (*Boston Globe* 1989a). Almost a year later the accusation of obstructionism and opportunism would be leveled again, this time in response to Chelsea activist Tito Meza's charge that Silber was making premature and false claims about the project's success in his gubernatorial campaign propaganda and that the project was an exercise in government by secrecy. A diatribe from Greer, in the BU student *Daily Free Press,* asserted that "I don't really take that criticism seriously. . . . The Hispanic leaders are just trying to get more power, and I think it is totally unfair to use John Silber as a means to gain power" (Benson 1990). Claiming color blindness, Greer asserted, "Our view is that students are students, not Hispanics, whites, or blacks." He criticized the Hispanic leaders for wanting a majority of members on the Chelsea Executive Advisory Committee (CEAC) "because the council is supposed to represent all of the groups in Chelsea . . . not just the Hispanics." Therefore, "[i]nstead of fighting, we decided to work with the people through other groups and simply bypass the leaders" (Benson 1990).

I have suggested that Boston University employs a "revolving door" strategy of community relations, typifying the manner in which dominant power holders seek to manipulate minority group organizations (Jacobs 1990). When minority leaders do not fall into line with majority group strategies, the former are discredited as not being truly representative of their constituencies. Majority leaders and caretakers then threaten to work around these "false" leaders, that is, to work with the "true" community.

Boston University, chagrined at the resistance put up by Latino community representatives when it could not keep them in line, strove to discredit them and support other leaders it deemed more worthy. In 1991 the Management Team strove to insinuate themselves into the Latino community by offering blandishments to the service agency, *El Centro Hispano,* and frequently alluded to their harmonious relations with *El Centro* when the issue of the Team's poor record of community relations was publicly raised. *El Centro's* director, José Fernandez, strove to navigate an autonomous course—one charted by Latinos—and assiduously steered *El Centro* away from the shoals of internecine conflict while resisting the seductions of the university to render material aid and other support.

The university's aggrandizement of power and top down implementation of this "partnership" obviated its pretensions to educational reform. Here the literature on educational partnerships is instructive. Those partnerships between universities and school systems that work best eschew corporate models and hierarchical and elitist arrangements and favor participant/egalitarian ones (Goodlad 1987, 1; McGowan and Powell 1990). An appraisal of university–public school partnerships (Harkavy and Puckett 1990, 12) categorizing these arrangements into three models (university control, allied elite and participant), fit the Chelsea Project into the first—university control—and concluded, after examining this conflict-ridden arrangement, that "[w]hile we vigorously applaud Boston University's vision, boldness, and comprehensiveness, we have several concerns about the appropriateness and feasibility of the Chelsea Project—especially as a model for other universities to emulate." Their concerns were "directed primarily toward the style of the reform—the structuring of roles and relationships of the Chelsea Project," which in the context of a "privatized . . . urban school district . . . is expert-driven, unidimensional, and only marginally participatory." Finally,

> There is persuasive documentary evidence . . . that the University has exacerbated the tensions that would normally be expected in the kind of change proposed for Chelsea. Rather than build alliances with teachers, administrators, and parents, Boston University officials have ignored the concerns of these groups at critical junctures, eschewed their participation in significant planning and decision-making, imposed the University's agenda as a set of non-negotiable demands, and reacted indignantly to criticism from these quarters. (Harkavy and Puckett 1990, 13)

For example, BU's hiring of an Hispanic Superintendent of the Chelsea schools, Diana Lam, which was intended to score points with the Latino population, only heightened the Latinos' antipathy to the school takeover, for she was not welcomed with open arms by Chelsea's Latinos.

Claiming to run an open superintendency, Lam acquired a reputation for stubbornness and resistance to unsolicited community input that marked her as a Boston University functionary. At the end of January 1990, intending to forge a consensus, Lam convened a meeting with the Latino leadership. She became evasive and defensive, however, at the leaders' insistence that she respect their grievances with the university, with the result that the boundaries remained drawn as before. A disappointed Lam lamented, "It looks like what we're going to get out of this meeting is another meeting" (Fieldnotes, 1/24/90; 1/25/90). Having already been reprimanded by Boston University Vice President Westling for her admiration of Nelson Mandela, Diana Lam's position, no matter how competent and feisty she seemed, was structurally compromised. She was even willing, when new school budget cuts were announced in winter 1991, to eliminate the directorship of bilingual education. This aroused the ire of the Latino Bilingual Parents Advisory Committee and it threatened suit against the School Committee and the Management Team. Throughout her stay, until the Spring of 1991 when she declared her ill-fated candidacy for the mayoralty of Boston, Lam walked a tightrope (Schattle 1990).

Although the educational process was forced to remain nominally open (i.e., Management Team, School Committee, and CEAC meetings), Boston University had only consented to open meetings as a result of popular pressure surrounding the initial home rule petition, and continued to resist popular demands for inclusion in the policymaking process as affronts to what it conceived were its prerogatives.

FROM PROTEST TO POLITICAL INCORPORATION: CHELSEA'S LATINO POLITICAL WATERSHED

Upon completing the second year of its management of the Chelsea public schools, the university's stance toward the Latino community had not changed. At a talk given at a National Education Association Higher Education Conference (2 March 1991), Marta Rosa characterized Boston University's management of Chelsea's schools as an "arranged marriage." Others, suggesting that "the proper role of a major university would be to offer to direct its resources. . . in an open accountable manner," called it a "leveraged buyout" (Fine 1989). "The residents of Chelsea feel taken over," Rosa asserted: "My greatest criticism of the project is that there is a lack of understanding on the part of BU of the culture of the community." She reported that her constituents felt ignored, frustrated, and apprehensive and were confused over the roles of parents in the project. Criticizing the Management Team's eagerness to score public relations points in the name of hastily conceived programs, she asked, "Is this so-called partnership empowering the community? Is it addressing the causes of the downfall of public education in urban communities?"[9] With the city having experienced receivership and a School Committee whose powers were suspended, the university's hand was even stronger and its stance toward the community more arrogant and paternalistic.

Yet, Rosa had made her mark as a viable Latino politician—a path breaker—who opened the field for others to follow. On the other hand, the Hispanic Commission remained too transparently Rosa's support organization and this alienated some of the more moderate, less confrontational Latino figures who were chagrined by her aggressiveness and unwillingness to couch her positions on issues in more conciliatory terms. In addition, the Commission had difficulty, as it moved into the middle and late 1990s with reconciling the cultural differences between the Caribbean and Central American constituencies it claimed to represent. Moreover, the commission's methods of dealing with internal conflict and other organizational difficulties through a kind of shunning and pressure on those whom the leadership disapproved of to leave the organization, was a weakness that was detrimental to its viability as the nucleus of a Latino political and social base. The result was that the membership contained few Central Americans, especially El Salvadoreans and Guatemalans. These considerations proved to be limitations on Rosa's and the Commission's effectiveness as a supportive basis for Latino politics in the city, as attested to by the recent shrinkage in Latino political representation (see below).

Marta Rosa was reelected to the School Committee in 1991 and 1993. Whereas, in 1989 and 1991, the electoral field in Chelsea contained only three Latino candidates (and only Rosa was elected), it mushroomed to four in 1993 and eight candidates in 1994. In 1993 Leticia Ortiz, Juan Vega, and Carolyn Boumila-Vega ran for city council along with Marta Rosa for school committee. Vega, Ortiz, and Rosa won. In 1994, having run and lost a campaign for an at-large City Council seat; she was finally seated as a lead runner-up when the winner, Harry Gurman, declined to take office.[10] Even that accomplishment was the result of a successful political fight by the Latino community; the city government at first demurred, stating that the replacement had to be someone who had received 20 percent of the vote (in a field of eight). Juan Vega organized a group to lobby the city council to make Rosa be the one to take Gurman's seat. The U.S. Deptartment of Justice Community Relations Department, which had been following the Chelsea elections, moved in when it looked like the council would block her.

In 1999 two candidates ran for city council with Juan Vega reelected again, in this instance holding the distinction of being the first Latino president of a city council. All told, however, Rosa's success, for the reasons mentioned above, proved to be more of an immediate than long-standing stimulus to Latino political representation.

The privatization of the schools precipitated the election of the first Latino/a, Marta Rosa, to public office. These unusual circumstances undoubtedly occasioned unusual political figure-ground (i.e., candidate agenda-party support) relations with respect to candidates' political affiliations and ideologies framed against the background of local party politics. In other words, the unique historical circumstances—the Chelsea school takeover—serving as a context for initial Latino politicization, enabled a candidate with a bold demeanor and openly oppositional agenda to succeed without the support of the extant Democratic political machinery. Marta Rosa views herself as a distinctly autonomous figure, unbeholden to established party connections and entrenched interests. In some respects, this reflects political gender linkages: Latina candidates' motivations for running tend to reflect greater concern over public policy issues than do male candidates (Hardy-Fanta 1997, 30–31). Gender does not, however, by itself explain Marta Rosa's particular policy focus for in 1991, 1993 and 1994, other Latinas ran for office and Rosa's stance was one of distance from many male *and* female Latino candidates. As she put it in response to a question concerning Latinos' unqualified voting exclusively for Latino candidates in an interview with Hardy-Fanta in 1995,

> I think you need a mix. I think there are Latino candidates that don't represent my views and I wouldn't vote for them. _____ [a male] is one of those. [As for] _____ [a female], it is questionable whether I would vote for her if she was in my district, or not, to be real honest, because a lot of

the way she presents the community sometimes isn't the way I would present it or the way I think they should be presented. [Question: Like what?] I'm very adamant about that. I'm very adamant that I don't have to use the white community in Chelsea to speak about the needs of my community. . . . So our philosophies . . . are very different and I think I am more confrontational than she is. So it's a matter of style and philosophy. (Rosa 1995)

Indeed, Rosa's posture alienated her from Latino and non-Latino civic activists and political figures who thought of her as too radical, too confrontational, or too "abrasive." Here again, her stance derived from her experience of the struggle with Boston University and with Chelsea officials who cooperated or sought accommodation with Boston University. The reminiscence of Rosa's campaign manager, Lyn Meza, corroborates this interpretation in outlining her reasons for supporting Rosa:

Well, [in my days as a labor organizer], I supported independent political action [and] the need for a labor party as opposed to the Democratic/ Republican "Tweedle Dum-Tweedle Dee" situation. I was thrilled that there was a young Latino woman who was serious about running for office in Chelsea that seemed to have the interest of the community at heart. (Meza 1995)

Indeed, Rosa's agenda, and her assiduous carrying out of her duties as a School Committee member, indicate that she did, indeed, have the community's interest at heart, although several Latino candidates and civic activists disputed that contention. Countering the privatization agenda was (is) not a strategy designed to placate a constituency with promises; rather it built upon Latinos' sense of exclusion from and deprivation by the extant political machinery and by an institution (Boston University) managed from the top down that countenanced dissent, within and without, with dismissal. Under these circumstances, the community interest could be more broadly and deeply conceived and enunciated. Rosa and the Hispanic Commission did not by themselves initiate the conflict, but when they joined it, the conflict took on added significance and non-Latino splinter groups joined the struggle. Thus, the issue of the loss of accountability, which is perhaps the chief demurral of privatization initiatives, became attached to the issue of ethnic exclusion from the centers of power. On the other hand, perhaps Rosa's success could have occurred only under these conditions. Viewed from this standpoint, Rosa's success did more than project her simplistically as a role model for other Latino/a candidates and would-be political figures; it created a point of reference for them ideologically, whether they shared her views or not. The latter often saw her as a race/ethnic traitor and occasionally took her ideological forthrightness to be *personal* aggressiveness, but as Rosa interprets it, in 1989 she felt it important to challenge racism against the Latino population:

[A]t that point, there was a real need to be real aggressive, to make a stand for the Latino community, to change the perception of who they [white officials] thought we were. The perception was "these poor people who come here on their own welfare lines and they're draining our system and they're ruining our streets," and there's still some of that now, . . . and it's the political climate across the country against immigrants and people of color. (Rosa 1995)[11]

Indeed her aggressiveness was perceived as abrasive by Latinos and Anglos alike. Thus, Rosa relates an anecdote about a conversation she had with James Carlin, Chelsea's receiver: Noting that in her 10 years of political life "I've taken a lot of heat. . . . I've had to be real aggressive," and have been criticized "by the white boys" for it, she recollects:

When Jim Carlin first met me, when he became receiver, he said, "I was told that you're an aggressive bitch and that you're never satisfied with anything that you get for your community. You want it all." I said, "You were informed quite right" [laughs]. That's hard to swallow when you first hear it. On the other hand, if that's what got the community where it is today, fine." (Rosa 1995)

She registers similar responses from Latino males whom she views as alternately arrogant and suspicious of politicians because of their disenchantment with false campaign promises. On the other hand, she characterizes herself as being "more inclusive" and as having "opened the door" for other Latinos wishing to enter politics.

In contrast, other Latino politicians and candidates in Chelsea have been more moderate concerning gender issues, if addressing them at all, and have striven to be more diplomatic, preferring harmony among Latino political figures to argumentation over issues. Thus one candidate who ran for School Committee characterizes himself as a "bridge builder. I'm a peacemaker and I'm sort of a diplomat." Toward the end of Hardy-Fanta's interview with him, he stated that "all I want you to walk away with, is that we are much more united in Chelsea than divided." He felt that a united front would make Chelsea a "role model for Boston and for Springfield and other communities." However, it is apparent that the *appearance* of such unity for this figure, as for many moderates, takes precedence over substantive unity. Much of the interview contained discussions of conflicts and rivalries, but he stressed that "I hope I didn't give you an impression I was focusing too much on whatever tensions there are."

CONCLUSION

There is no doubt that Latino politics in Chelsea have been forged and shaped by a conflict with a well-established and powerful institution that has assumed control over the city's schools. The Latino community, for all of its presumed political apathy and powerlessness, paradoxically led the struggle over privatization and successfully projected that struggle into the public arena. On the other hand, the managers of Chelsea's schools enacted an erstwhile scenario of privatization: the tendency to discredit the public sphere (Starr 1989, 43–44) and to substitute, that is, to invert the inviolability of the private for the public realm. In this case, it is not public *service* that is being discredited, but the public forum itself.

It is clear that boundary redefinition was at the heart of the matter in this face-off between segments of a city's population and its caretakers. The Chelsea conflict etched the skirmish line for the conflict between popular and private interests as the first recent historical occasion of community struggle against urban educational privatization in the United States. The democratic prerogatives of the citizenry—of its rights to know, to participate, and to have those who serve it be accountable to it—were contested in Chelsea. This became the crucible in which the city's Latino leadership was forged and in that the first elected Latino/a to public office won credibility by direct confrontation of a public issue which played the major role in shaping the city's future. The more secure pathways of accommodation, compromise, and patient consensus building were eschewed. Rather than simple risk-taking, the process is more aptly a politically passionate one, for the community found itself able to rally around an issue viewed as a threat to Latino family life, its children's futures, its own identity, and its definition of citizenship.

If Boston University claimed to uphold an agenda concerned with simply educating effectively, the opposition stressed its *manipulation* of the community. The conflict over the schools, shaped by Boston University's preoccupation with control over public discourse, was highlighted by the university's preference for molding the minds of the very young, their admitted emphasis on primary over secondary education, and, therefore, the sacrificing, in the eyes of Latinos, of those youth on the threshold of adulthood now deemed "ruined" by schooling prior to the advent of Boston University (Jacobs 1992). Insofar as "the privatization of the schools would symbolize a final retreat from the already faded ideal of bringing the disparate children of a community under a common roof," privatization marks a diminished commitment to "include the poor in the national household" (Starr 1989, 135).

On the national scene Latinos "have not been passive recipients in the educational process" (Rodríguez 1989, 139). Boston University's perception of *La Comisión* as obstructionist, with its attempts to discredit the organization, its leadership, and Marta Rosa, bespeak the tendency of political and social establishments to perceive Latino struggles as a "disinclination to assimilate" (Rodríguez 1989, 139). This is a half truth contingent upon our evaluation of assimilation with its loss of cultural identity and social and political autonomy. If we see it as desirable, paternalistic, nonparticipatory reforms will hold sway.

If school reform or reform in general proceeds top-down, then assimilation will be its goal. Contrariwise, if we conceive of reform preferably as a bottom-up affair, or certainly a negotiable one, then we may view the Latino struggle in Chelsea as a search for a solution instead of a problem (Rodríguez 1989, 139). The remedy is not concentrated authority, as it already exists, but more shared power. In all public school systems, "more participatory forms of management could do much to diffuse the authoritarianism that pervades all too many school boards and educational administrative structures" (Thayer 1987, 169).

Just as proponents of privatization view this contrivance "more as learning . . . than as imitation or imposition" (Starr 1989, 39), so the lessons of resistance to it are educational in themselves. The struggle over the schools, then, was an ordeal by fire for Chelsea's Latino leaders and would-be leaders and gelled the base for the political socialization of the city's Latino population. The voter registration drives of Chelsea's Commission on Hispanic Affairs, the political versatility of Marta Rosa, and the Commission's influence on the creation of a Latino public formed an important part of that base.

On the other hand, it is clear that the fervor of the struggle over the schools already has subsided. With that struggle having evoked Latino political representation, one might speculate on how Chelsea's Latino political leadership will evolve and which stimuli will shape its development. It is possible that the leadership will be centrist and accommodative, preferring unity, respectability, and civic peace over strife and confrontation; it is also possible that the school conflict served as a lever for political socialization so that emergent leadership will have the advantage of having learned the arts of social and political conflict from its elders, and thus the techniques necessary for waging conflict should the need arise. On the other hand, the force of assimilation might blunt the ardor for social justice in the second generation of Latino leaders.

One thing is certain: Latino politics have become an institutional reality in this city. The forms that it will take, however, will be shaped by the economy and Chelsea's evolving demographics, particularly with respect to its growing Asian and diversified Latino populations and their competition for a substantially increased resource pie occasioned by the priming of the city's economic development (and, hence, employment) by state-level officials and business investors. Should that pie decrease with an economic downturn, by increased costs and decreased supply of housing for the poor, or with increased demands from its in-flowing poorer populations, the

Latino political configuration might find itself adapting to new circumstances either in familiar ways or with new untried tactics and strategies as it found itself doing in 1989.

The infusion of economic prosperity into the city might also bring with it increased *gentrification*, especially in the housing sector, and, of course, that might be construed as progress by those who welcomed Boston University into Chelsea in the first place. It is questionable that Chelsea's immigrant populace would benefit from this. Should gentrification evoke opposition, more aggressive candidates conceivably could again galvanize a response in the community and among the extant Latino leadership. On the other hand, the panoply of business and state investment in the city, including the established legitimacy of Boston University (it was asked to continue its stewardship of the schools beyond the 10-year contract period), represents a much stronger establishment. In the face of this, Latino political figures will be required to unify with and draw support by building bridges to varied Latino and non-Latino constituencies, e.g., Asian (Cambodian and Vietnamese) and Haitian, in order to wage any struggle for inclusion. Here, the experiences of the late 1980s and 1990s could prove to be beneficial, but these would have to be tempered by analysis of the failure to galvanize the broad spectrum of Latino groups. Now the movement would need to progress toward an institution-building phase (King 1986). Although Rosa's ideological platform was cosmopolitan, her organizational one failed to be. Consequently, the organizational support base would have to evince the vitality of the Hispanic Commission but also would have to transcend that organization's parochialism. In short, increased Latino political success could proceed incrementally in tandem with Chelsea's changing demographic profile as Latinos continue to migrate into the city, but much broader scale and speedier incursion into office might require greater cosmopolitan organization building. The danger here, of course, lies in the dilution of Latinos' felt concerns within a broader multiethnic agenda. In view of these considerations, it will be interesting to see what developments lie in store for Chelsea's Latinos in a city that has traditionally been a gateway for newcomers but that now is experiencing the pressures of globalism.

NOTES

1.   This chapter and its analysis are based upon the author's field research on Chelsea, Massachusetts, commencing in January 1990, using participant observation, interviewing, and content analysis of documentary materials. The analysis of Latino election efforts in Chelsea after 1994 is based, in part, on data from interviews conducted by Carol Hardy-Fanta as part of a study on gender and Latino politics in Massachusetts (Hardy-Fanta 1997).

2.   Although recognizing the preferences for one term or another, the author generally uses the term "Latino" in this chapter, except when the cited document or interviewee uses another term such as Hispanic, etc.

3.   The intertwining of the school issue with ethnic politics continues to be with us today. Thus, in Massachusetts we find that just about every city in the state had a battle in the mid- to late 1980s over bilingual education and busing. The city of Lawrence, for example, has chronically faced state receivership with a high school remaining unaccredited, a second school superintendent search within 3 years underway, and bilingual education assaulted by bad staffing decisions and a consequent reduction in staff as the numbers of bilingual students surge.

4.   As Larry Cuban adroitly perceives, "economic instability, shifts in population, and social change uncover tensions." Frustration over the persistence of social problems overflows during times of economic and social crisis into the most vulnerable and plausible institutions thought to be capable of eliciting change— schooling. No matter that educational institutions cannot by themselves solve or resolve social, political, and economic problems. Schooling becomes the arena for societal reform and media and other groups "translate the unrest into recommended policies for schools to enact" (Cuban 1990, 6). As one discussion of the "education smokescreen" suggests, "it is extremely dangerous to saddle the schools with the nation's economic malaise," for it succumbs to the supply-side ruse of attributing the demand for talent—jobs—to such talent's availability (Weisman 1992, 721).

5.   Kopf says that, "by 1915 the numbers of aliens and their offspring had increased to 140 percent of their 1905 levels. Immigrants and their children constituted two-thirds of Chelsea's people in 1905; this proportion had increased to 84 percent in 1915, just seven years after the Fire" (Kopf 1973, 65).

6.   This speaks to the question of why there has been an absence of outside evaluation of the project. During the controversial preliminary period of approval for the contract, Peter Greer said that the need to hire an outside evaluator of the project was critical, but the university has never sponsored evaluation from within or outside of the Chelsea Project (Cohen 1989). The State Oversight Panel underscored the need for evaluation. For example, at the panel meeting/hearing in Chelsea on December 12, 1990, after the BU Management Team made its presentation (which included a turnout of members of the Chelsea High School Rowing Team) panel member John T. Dunlop dryly commented, "Someday down the road, somebody in the state or federal government is going to write this story. Was it good, or how good, and I regret to say, whether you like it or not, putting together a set of numbers is going to be a large part of the story. There ought to be one or two people developing *indices* on a time series basis. . . . One of these days somebody's going to want to look back and measure the change. I would feel more comfortable if somebody was devoting some time to do that. I know one or two people in your establishment is competent to do that" (Fieldnotes, 12/10/90). In response to this statement, Superintendent Lam said, "I think you're absolutely right that we need a database and, with the limited resources we have, I can't promise you that" (Fieldnotes, 12/10/90).

7.   Noteworthy are the public forums at St. Rose's Church on March 22, 1989, the school committee meeting and vote on the contract and hearing on March 29, and the aldermanic meeting to vote on the enabling legislation for the contract on April 24.

8.   For an excellent analysis of the prejudicial treatment of Latinos by The *Chelsea Record* and other print media, see Neidhardt (1990).

9.   Similar ground is covered by the evaluation of the State Oversight Panel in its report on the project's first year, which underscored the need for the university to improve its community relations, abjured the Management Team's "arrogant" manner in dealing with minority parents and the Team's advisory committee, and emphasized the need to "create an atmosphere of inclusion for community groups and others in school policy decision-making" (Boston University 1990, 2). Boston University's reply (November 20, 1990) to the report contends that the panel's criticisms overstep the boundaries of the legal contract, i.e., "the Panel has no mandate to re-do the agreement between the School Committee and the University."

10.   Harry Gurman resigned because he was on the Conservation Commission and the new city charter said that if a person is in elected office he can not also serve on an appointed board and, according to Marta Rosa, Gurman had an issue he was concerned about so he wanted to be on the Conservation Commission.

11.   See Note 1.

REFERENCES

Anonymous. (1908). "Enthusiastic meeting." *Chelsea Gazette*, 9 May.

Benson, Alan. (1990). "Chelsea Committee Blasts BU's Treatment of Hispanics." *Daily Free Press*, 19 January, 1.

Bering-Jensen, Helle. (1988). "A Last-Ditch School Remedy Gets a Go-ahead Near Boston." *Insight*, 15 August, 14–17.

Bilik, Al. (1990). "Privatization: Selling America to the Lowest Bidder." *Labor Research Review* IX (Spring): 1–13.

Boston Globe. (1998a). "Hispanics Rebut Silber Manipulation Charge," 2 April, 44.

———. (1998b). "BU's Chelsea Oversight," Editorial, 6 April, 14.

Boston University. (1988). *A Model for Boston University. Boston University's Report on the Chelsea Public School Excellence in Urban Education*. Boston: Boston University.

_____. The Chelsea School Chelsea Oversight Panel. (1990). *Report on the First Year of Implementation of Committee—Boston University Agreement 1989–1990*, 20 November.

Brennan, John J. (1990). Interview with the author, 22 January.

Carlisle, Rosemary. (1989). Interview with author, 10 April.

Cohen, Muriel. (1989). "While Pupils Play, BU Plays for Chelsea Schools." *Boston Globe*, 13 August, Metro/Region.

Cuban, Larry. (1990). "Reforming Again, Again, and Again." *Educational Researcher* 19 (January), 30.

Daniels, Lee A. (1988). "Doubts Abound on Boston U. Plan to Run Schools." *New York Times,* 10 August, Education.

Fine, Bernard J. (1989). "BU 'Takeover' of Chelsea Schools." *Science* 24(6 November), 984.

Fulham, Dana. (1988). "BU–Chelsea School Plan Criticized: Specialists Cite Loss of Local Control as One Potential Problem for City." *Boston Globe,* 31 July, section 2.

Goodlad, John I. (1987). "Linking Schools and Universities: Symbiotic Partnerships." Occasional Paper No. 1, Center for Education Renewal, College of Education, University of Washington, Seattle.

Greer, Peter R. (1990a). "Boston University/Chelsea project." *Science* 247, 9 March.

———. (1990b). "Boston University and Chelsea: First Lessons." *Education Week,* 16 May, 24, 32.

———. (1990c). Interview with the author, 16 February.

Hardy-Fanta, Carol. (1997). *Latino Electoral Campaigns in Massachusetts: The Impact of Gender.* Boston: Center for Women in Politics and Public Policy and the Mauricio Gastón Institute for Latino Community Development and Public Policy, University of Massachusetts Boston.

Jacobs, Glenn. (1990). "Education or Manipulation? What Boston University Needs to Learn about Community Relations." *El Faro,* November, 4–7.

———. (1991). "Latinos Confront Leviathan: The Paradox of Isolation and Activism in a Small Eastern City." Unpublished manuscript.

———. (1992). "Joint Meeting of School Committee and BU Team Discusses School Shortcomings." *El Faro,* May.

Jennings, James. (1984b). "Puerto Rican Politics in Two Cities: New York and Boston." Chapter 4 in *Puerto Rican Politics in Urban America* edited by James Jennings and Monte Rivera, 75–98. Westport, CT: Greenwood Press.

Katznelson, Ira, and Margaret Weir. (1985). *Schooling for All: Class, Race, and the Decline of the Democratic Ideal.* New York: Basic Books.

Kennedy, Marie, Michael Stone, et al. (1990). *The Hispanics of Chelsea: Who Are They?* Boston: Center for Community Planning, CPCS, University of Massachusetts Boston.

King, Mel. (1986). "Three Stages of Black Politics in Boston, 1950–1980." In *From Access to Power,* edited by James Jennings and Mel King. Cambridge, MA: Schenkman.

Kopf, Edward J. (1974). "The Intimate City. A Study of Urban Order: Chelsea, Massachusetts, 1906–1915." Ph.D. diss., Brandeis University.

Meza, Lyn. (1990). Interview with author, 24 April.

———. (1995). Interview with Carol Hardy-Fanta, 9 May.

McClintock, William E. (1910). "The New Chelsea." *New England Magazine* 42, 15–25.

McGowan, Tom, and Jim Powell. (1990). "Understanding School-University Collaboration through New Educational Metaphors." Contemporary Education 61(3), 112–118.

McGurn, George. (1990). Interview with author, 3 May.

Neidhart, Frank S. (1990). *Chelsea's Hispanic Community: How is it Served by the Local Print Media?* Boston: Center for Community Planning, College of Public and Community Services, University of Massachusetts Boston.

Rodríguez, Clara. (1989). *Puerto Ricans: Born in the U.S.A.* Boston: Unwin Hyman.

Rosa, Ángel (Tito). (1990). Interview with author, 18 January.

Rosa, Marta. (1995). Interview with Carol Hardy-Fanta, 9 May.

Schattle, Hans. (1990). "Acting BU President Backs Away from His Remarks about Mandela." *Boston Globe*, 1 March.

Shapiro, Svi. (1990). *Between Capitalism and Democracy: Educational Policy and the Crisis of the Welfare State.* New York: Bergin and Garvey.

Sleeper, Peter B. (1989). "Silber Hits Union Foes of Chelsea School Takeover." *Boston Globe*, 31 March.

Snider, William. (1989). "Management Plan for Chelsea Schools is Approved." *Education Week*, 5 April, 5.

Starr, Paul. (1989). "The Meaning of Privatization." In *Privatization and the Welfare State*, edited by Sheila B. Kamerman and Alfred J. Kahn, 15–48. Princeton, NJ: Princeton University Press.

Thayer, Frederick C. (1987). "Privatization: Carnage, Chaos, and Corruption." In *Private Means–Public Ends: Private Business in Social Service Delivery*, edited by Barry I. Carroll, Ralph W. Conant, and Thomas A. Easton, pp. 146–170. New York: Praeger.

Torres, Andrés, and Lisa Chavez. (1998). *Latinos in Massachusetts: An Update.* Boston: Mauricio Gastón Institute for Latino Community Development and Public Policy, University of Massachusetts Boston.

Turner, Bryan S. (1986). *Citizenship and Capitalism—The Debate over Reformism.* London: Allen and Unwin.

U.S. Congress. (1965). "Senator Ralph Yarborough Entering John Silber's Proposal for a Measure Attacking Poverty at its Source into the Congressional Record." *Congressional Record*, 9 April, 7352–7353.

Weisman, Jonathan. (1992). "The Education Smokescreen." *Phi Delta Kappa* 73 (May):721.

CHAPTER 2

Multiracial Coalitions in the Election of the First Latino Legislator
Boston

RAMÓN OLIVENCIA

The election of Nelson Merced to the Massachusetts State Legislature in November 1988 represented a milestone in state politics. He became the first Latino[1] ever elected to state-level office in Massachusetts. Merced was elected to the State Legislature after winning the Democratic primaries in the Fifth Suffolk District in Boston; he received 43 percent of the vote among a field of six candidates, three of them African American. In this chapter, I argue that Merced's election was the result of a strategy framed within a multiracial coalition. Such coalitions are crucial for Latinos to gain electoral representation in Massachusetts, particularly in cities such as in Boston where they are far from constituting a voting majority due to a realtively small Latino population and low levels of voter participation. Latinos currently make up 14.4 percent of the population in Boston (U.S. Census 2001) and have one of the lowest voting rates in the city (Chapters 9 and 10 in this volume).

Three characteristics of Latinos in Massachusetts limit their levels of voter participation: they are relatively young, have a low rate of U.S. citizenship (except Puerto Ricans, who are U.S. citizens by birth), and face a high poverty rate.[2] A relatively small population and lower levels of voting make it imperative for Latinos to work with other racial and ethnic groups. Browning, Marshall, and Tabb (1984) found, for example, that the major factor leading to the election of minorities in a group of northern California cities with small minority populations was the emergence of liberal coalitions. These coalitions generally included racial–ethnic minorities, the poor, and white liberals, particularly Democrats. Borrero, Cuadrado, and Rodríguez (1974, 95), in a discussion of the role of Puerto Ricans in interest-group politics, also argue that political and economic power lies in building coalitions of Latinos with other minorities and with the poor. They state that, furthermore, noncoalition political models keep these constituencies divided and weak.

An example of a successful multiracial coalition was the election of Federico Peña as mayor of Denver, Colorado.[3] In 1983 he became the first Latino elected mayor of a large city. At that time, Denver had a voting-age Latino population of just 10 percent, while voting-age African Americans made up 9 percent of the total population. In Boston, where minorities now make up a majority of the population (50.5 percent according to the 2000 U.S. Census), multiracial coalitions often require a delicate balance among whites, African Americans, Latinos, and Asians.

De la Garza et al. (1974) found that Anglos were reluctant to vote for Mexican-American candidates in state and local elections in El Paso, Texas, especially when the candidates made "ethnic appeals." Moreover, Baird (1977), in a study of Texas cities, noted that Chicano candidates had to receive a "dual validation" from, or be acceptable to, both the minority (Chicano) and majority (Anglo) communities. Certain characteristics of a Chicano candidate might make the office seeker more acceptable to Anglo voters than would otherwise be the case. Age was important: Chicano candidates between 35 and 45 years of age were most successful at the polls. Involvement in civic activities, being of higher socioeconomic status, and having a moderate political ideology and a relatively minor "ethnic" emphasis in campaigns and activities seemed more attractive to Anglo voters than were militant political stands.

LATINO CANDIDATES IN BOSTON: 1968–1988

The first Latino to run for office in Boston was Alex Rodriguez. He ran for state representative from the South End (see Map 2.1) in 1968 but was defeated (Hardy-Fanta 1993, 105). At the time of his campaign, the total population of the South End consisted of about 20 percent Latinos, the vast majority of them Puerto Ricans (Uriarte-Gastón 1988). Rodriguez, a Puerto Rican born in New York City, later led efforts in establishing the Latino Political Action Committee (Latino PAC) in Massachusetts.[4]

The first Latina to run for state-level office in Massachusetts was Carmen Pola. In 1980, Pola, who 27 years earlier had moved to the United States from her native Puerto Rico, ran for State Representative from the district including Jamaica Plain and Mission Hill (Hardy-Fanta 1993, 105). At that time, Latinos accounted for about 25 percent of the neighborhood (Camayd-Freixas and López 1983). Pola lost by less than 80 votes, but her candidacy pushed the area's representative, Kevin Fitzgerald, to be more responsive to his Latino constituents, according to Felix Arroyo; Arroyo later ran for the Boston School Committee in 1981 and 1983. Arroyo, who was born and raised in Puerto Rico, won in the 1981 primaries but finished eighth in the final election with some 27,000 votes. He reported that his campaign increased the number of Latino registered voters by about 7,000 (Hardy-Fanta 1993, 106). (Arroyo is currently running at large for Boston City Coucil.)

Map 2.1   Latino Population in Boston (2000), by Census Tract,
with Neighborhoods and Fifth Suffolk District

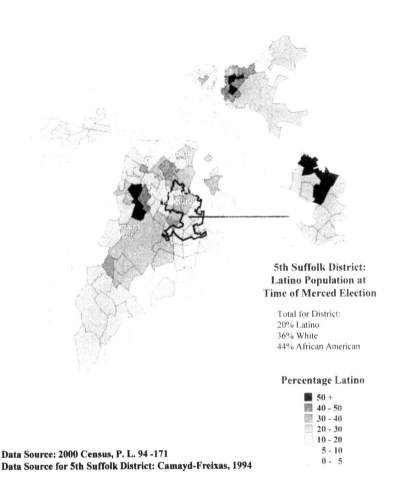

5th Suffolk District:
Latino Population at
Time of Merced Election

Total for District:
20% Latino
36% White
44% African American

Percentage Latino

■ 50 +
░ 40 - 50
░ 30 - 40
░ 20 - 30
░ 10 - 20
  5 - 10
  0 - 5

Data Source: 2000 Census, P. L. 94 -171
Data Source for 5th Suffolk District: Camayd-Freixas, 1994

The first Latino/a elected to public office in Massachusetts was Grace Romero. She was elected to the Boston School Committee in 1983. Romero, a black Panamanian, got most of her support from African-American voters, who made up more than 22 percent of the city's adult population (Hardy-Fanta 1993, 106). According to one observer, her campaign did not gather much support or enthusiasm in the Latino community for she emphasized her African-American, rather than Latino heritage.

In 1988 Nelson Merced, the third Latino from Boston to run for state-level office, made history by becoming the first Latino state representative in Massachusetts. Merced also disproved some of the aforementioned characteristics that are supposed to make minority candidates more "acceptable" to nonminority voters. Although he was 40 years old when first elected, he was not of a high socioeconomic status and had a very progressive, not moderate, political ideology. As I will explain later, he did underplay his ethnic heritage to whites and, to a lesser extent, to African Americans. More important to his success were the steps taken to create conditions favorable to his candidacy, namely, redistricting and coalition building.

THE FIFTH SUFFOLK DISTRICT: OPPORTUNITIES FOR A LATINO CANDIDATE

The Fifth Suffolk district was redrawn after a coalition of primarily minority groups sued in Federal Court to challenge the Legislature's 1987 plan to redraw the state's electoral districts. The plaintiffs were alleging a violation of the Equal Protection Clause of the Fourteenth Amendment to the U.S. Constitution, the one-person, one-vote principle, because the state, using data from the 1985 Decennial Census for the Commonwealth of Massachusetts, had created districts where the difference in the number of voters between the largest and the smallest districts was as much as 25 percent. They argued that because of different-sized districts one person's vote did not have the same power in all districts.

On February 2, 1988, the three-judge U.S. District Court ruled in *Black Political Task Force et al. v. Connolly*[5] that the 1987 plan was unconstitutional based on the one-person, one-vote principle because it did not equitably reflect the population distribution as reported in the 1985 Massachusetts Decennial Census.[6] The court said that "the 1987 reapportioning [of] the Massachusetts House of Representatives, is violative [sic] of the Equal Protection Clause of the Fourteenth Amendment to the US Constitution" (Black Political Task Force et al. 1988, 131).

To settle the case, Alan Jay Rom, one of the plaintiffs' attorneys, said that "the Legislature agreed to form a Boston district where a minority candidate could be elected" (Rom 1994). The Black Political Task Force (BPTF), the Latino Political Action Committee (PAC), the Asian-American Political Action Committee, and the Boston Rainbow Coalition were all involved in these new efforts. In a case of "politics makes strange bedfellows," the Massachusetts Republican State Committee also became a plaintiff because it was eager for the benefits redistricting would have in the suburbs. By creating "minority districts" where nonwhites could be elected, whites would be shifted to "white" districts; Republican candidates would then face fewer challenges from (presumably more Democratic) minority voters.

Yohel Camayd-Freixas, a Cuban American, organized a new group, the Latino Democratic Committee (LDC) with an explicit purpose of electing the first Latino elected official. According to Camayd-Freixas, during negotiations with the other coalition members, the BPTF was eager to have another African-American seat in the Legislature but accepted a "coalition district" where no minority would be a majority. "An agreement was made to let the best candidate, whether African-American, white or Latino, win the post" (Camayd-Freixas 1994).

The main problem confronted by the LDC was that there was no viable district with a Latino majority. Camayd-Freixas said that "the district was marketed as a Latino one, although it was known that Latinos were not a majority" (Camayd-Freixas 1994). As can be seen on Map 2.1 of the Latino population in Boston showing the borders and location of the Fifth Suffolk District, the district was 20 percent Latino, 44 percent African American, and 36 percent white at the time of Merced's election in 1988.

THE CANDIDACY OF NELSON MERCED: AGAINST THE ODDS

Camayd-Freixas and the Latino PAC already had their sights on Nelson Merced as a potential candidate for the Fifth Suffolk District. They made sure that Merced's house in the Dorchester neighborhood of Boston was in the newly created district. There were, of course, no guarantees of endorsements from the other coalition members. Merced first consulted with several friends and advisers. He called former state representative Mel King, an African American who in 1983 had run for mayor of the City of Boston and was Merced's friend and adviser, as well as Miren Uriarte, a Cuban-American community activist, and others. At a meeting among African-American, Latino, and white activists at Uriarte's house, they all urged Merced to run; and he agreed (Merced 1994).

PERSONAL AND PROFESSIONAL QUALIFICATIONS

Nelson Merced was born in 1948 in Queens, New York, but shortly thereafter his family moved to the South Bronx, where he grew up.[7] His father worked for the city's public housing authority and his mother was a hospital laundry worker. In 1964, he and his family moved back to Puerto Rico, where he lived in a poor section of San Juan called *Caño Martín Peña*. After graduating from the high school at age 17 he joined the U.S. Navy because "to a youth who wasn't sure what he wanted to do, it seemed as good a place as any to go" (Ribadeneira 1988, 29). He served for 3 years.

It was while in the Navy, he said, that he became "politically aware." The antiwar movement, civil rights activism, and other ongoing struggles gave him a broader outlook on life. After his return to Puerto Rico from the Navy in 1971, Merced and his wife became involved with a group of 400 families who refused to leave land they were occupying in a section of the town Trujillo Alto called *Villa Margarita*. It was one of the first major squatters' occupations in Puerto Rico.[8] Merced explained the impact of this involvement on his political consciousness: "I learned that people can work collaboratively to accomplish some striking goals. . . . At that time, taking the housing issue into our own hands was a strong statement" (Ribadeneira 1988, 29).

Merced enrolled at a small 2-year community college in San Juan, where he became involved with the *Federación de Universitarios Pro-Independencia* (FUPI or Federation of University Students for Independence), an active proindependence group of university students in Puerto Rico. He also became a member of the Young Lords Party in Puerto Rico, an organization of young Puerto Rican activists in the 1960s and 1970s. The Young Lords had its main chapter in New York City.[9]

Merced moved back to the United States in the early 1970s settling in Hartford, Connecticut. There he worked as a paralegal for the Farm Worker Division of Neighborhood Legal Services, Inc.[10] While in Hartford, Merced enrolled at the University of Connecticut, where he earned his undergraduate degree in anthropology in 1975. A year later he moved to Dorchester, a neighborhood in Boston, where, temporarily unable to find work, he volunteered as the director of the local office of the League of United Latin American Citizens (LULAC), a national Latino organization. He then became director of the Hispanic and Portuguese program at the state's Department of Public Welfare.

In 1981 Merced was named the Director of *La Alianza Hispana*—the largest social service agency serving Latinos in Boston (and New England). During his tenure *La Alianza* went from being an agency in serious fiscal trouble to one whose budget tripled from $400,000 in 1981 to $1.2 million in 1986 (Ribadeneira 1988, 29).

Merced's position at *La Alianza* gave him many opportunities to get to know the community (Merced 1994).[11] Merced also played an important role in establishing the Dudley Street Neighborhood Initiative (DSNI), a grassroots community organizing agency just a few blocks faway.[12] When the new Fifth Suffolk District was drawn, it gave certain advantages to Merced as a candidate. From *La Alianza* and DSNI, Merced not only reached out to Latinos but also to African Americans—a factor instrumental in him being chosen as "the perfect candidate" to run in the Fifth Suffolk district (Camayd-Freixas 1994). "It was a great district," Merced said. "It covered all of the *La Alianza* neighborhoods where I had worked and was known" (Ribadeneira 1988, 29). His tenure at *La Alianza* and his role at DSNI also gave Merced "political capital" in the form of name recognition and the stature to become a potentially powerful candidate in a district that was primarily composed of minorities.

STAVING OFF CHALLENGERS

When Merced became an official candidate in April 1988, rumors started circulating that a progressive white woman, Kristen McCormack, was seriously thinking about running. Her potential candidacy would have diverted the progressive white vote away from Merced. Faced with that uncertainty, Merced and Camayd-Freixas went to talk to her. They urged her not to run so that another progressive candidate (i.e., Merced) could become the first Latino state representative. They also asked her to chair Merced's campaign, a volunteer position. She agreed to both requests.

Although members of the multiracial redistricting coalition were aware of Camayd-Freixas's intention to push for Merced's candidacy, they could not formally endorse him because they first needed to consult with their own respective groups. Lloyd King, president of the Black Political Task Force (BPTF), played a neutral role so as not to be seen as biased toward or against Merced (Merced 1994). Some in the BPTF were actually leaning to endorse one of the African-American candidates, Barry Lawton. Lawton, a liberal who had been a legislative aide for the Black Legislative Caucus, was a member of the BPTF. It was Merced, however, who ultimately received the BPTF endorsement.

GATHERING SUPPORT: THE PROGRESSIVE WHITE ROLE

Many of the district's whites, mostly Irish and a few Italians, threw their support behind William Farrell, a white conservative. Although relatively unknown among the district's African Americans and Latinos, Farrell had some strong ties in the white community (Cunha 1994). He had the support of Dan Pokaski, a former state representative from one of Merced's wards (Ward 15), who was well known among the Dorchester neighborhood political establishment.

Although some whites supported Farrell, others contributed significantly to Merced's campaign. Progressive whites played an important role in working on the campaign. Joyce Cunha, for example, is a woman of Portuguese and Italian descent who at the time was working with Mass Choice, a prochoice group. She learned about Merced from Ken Wade, an African-American activist from Roxbury, at a 1987 regional coalition-building retreat at the United Auto Workers (UAW) Retreat Center in Black Lake, Michigan. Having just moved to Dorchester, Cunha volunteered to work in Merced's campaign and became a key strategist (Cunha 1994).

Wade and Cunha participated in the UAW retreat as members of the Commonwealth Coalition, a group of about 30 organizations and labor unions throughout the state that supports and helps elect progressive legislators. The Commonwealth Coalition later worked to elect Merced and, once at the State House, to assist him in his legislative work. David Barry, a white member of the campaign staff, also worked hard to gain support for Merced in the white community (Merced 1994). The tactic of Merced's advisers was, as he bluntly put it, "to divide the white vote . . . that way they would not have a single candidate that would gather all their support" (Merced 1994).

GATHERING SUPPORT: THE IMPORTANCE OF THE "MINORITY" VOTE

At the time of Merced's 1988 campaign, minorities in the Fifth Suffolk District accounted for 64 percent of the voting-age population. They were composed mostly of African-Americans, Cape Verdeans, West Indians, and Puerto Ricans, but also some Haitians, Asians and Dominicans. Seventeen of the 19 precincts, nevertheless, had never had a minority representative before. Although Merced was the only Latino candidate, there were three African-Americans, including Barry Lawton and Roy Owens—the principal African-American candidates (Cunha 1994). Lawton would later receive 9.8 percent of the votes in the 1988 primaries, to tie with Roy Owens, another African-American candidate. Merced still had to gain the support of the voters themselves, creating a multiracial campaign was both a political necessity as well as one of his major achievements.

THE CAMPAIGN

By all accounts, Merced had the most racially diverse campaign of all candidates for the Fifth Suffolk seat. He recalled: "When I called the first meeting, the cross section was there: African Americans, Hispanics, Cape Verdeans, gays, women, progressive activists, politicians and [labor] unions. I was enthused" (Diesenhouse 1988, 48). Joyce Cunha added that

> Merced had the best organized campaign. It published [Spanish-English] bilingual materials, sometimes even in Cape Verdean Creole. We were the only ones to publish bilingual campaign materials. . . . Adalberto Texeira, who later became Mayor Flynn's liaison to the Cape Verdean community, was precinct coordinator in one of the heavily Cape Verdean precincts. (Cunha 1994)

Latinos were important to the Merced campaign, although they were a small part of his voting base. When Merced was asked whether Latinos participated in proportion to their percentage of the district's population, his answer was emphatically "No" (Merced 1994). Until his election, Latinos had, for the most part, shied away from the political arena. Latinos who played an important role in the campaign included Túbal Padilla, Maria Aguiar, Elmo Ortiz, Estela Carrión (Merced's wife), Carlos Cruz, and Jaime Rodríguez. Many of these had focused much of their earlier efforts on grassroots community organizing and some were skeptical of using the electoral process for political empowerment; this changed with Merced's campaign. Merced's candidacy raised the enthusiasm and level of political participation among Latinos.

Deciding on the campaign manager was an important matter. On the one hand, choosing a Latino would have emphasized the fact that Merced was Latino. On the other hand, because a white woman was already the campaign chairperson, Merced was pressed to look for somebody who would attract African-American voters; he thus sought an African-American campaign manager.

Mel King recommended an African-American activist, Peter Hardie, for the position of campaign manager—the only paid staff position. Hardie had been working for Local 285 of the Service Employees International Union (SEIU). Before deciding whether to take the job, Hardie, who lived in the Fifth Suffolk District, attended one of the campaign meetings at *Nuestra Comunidad,* a Community Development Corporation on Dudley Street in Roxbury. Hardie, who said he "had never before been convinced of using the electoral arena for community empowerment," came out of the meeting thinking that this would be a great opportunity for coalition building, especially between Latinos and African Americans. A past president of the BPTF, Hardie was "excited about having a Latino candidate" (Hardie 1994). The campaign's office was located above the Dublin House Pub in the Uphams Corner section of Dorchester, in the heart of one of the district's major African-American neighborhoods.

At first, said Hardie,

> The focus was to build on [racial] diversity. The campaign emphasized building bridges between communities that had been relatively isolated politically from each other, particularly African Americans and Latinos. The campaign also stressed that people in the neighborhood can make a difference. (Hardie 1994)

Building a multiracial coalition included convincing whites to vote for Merced. In Hardie's opinion "the most difficult task of the campaign was gaining the trust and support of the traditional white conservative precincts and gaining the vote in the predominantly African-American precincts" (Hardie 1994).

Hardie and a young, dynamic African-American woman named Charlene Gilbert became Merced's campaign managers. The campaign's main issues were education, youth development, community development, and housing. Asked whether public safety was also an issue, Merced's answer was different from the traditional sound-bite much of the public has become used to. He replied: "Yes, but to the extent that you deal with the above issues, the public safety issue would be taken care of" (Merced 1994).

Table 2.1   Nelson Merced's Progress to the State House

1981–1986	Nelson Merced named director of La Alianza Hispana; the agency's budget increases from $400,000 to $1.2 million in 5 years.
1985	Massachusetts Decennial Census.
1987	Redistricting performed by the Massachusetts House of Representatives.
February 1988	U.S. District Court declares 1987 redistricting by the House of Representatives illegal based on the one-person, one-vote principle (*Black Political Task Force, et al.* v. *Michael Joseph Connolly*).
March 1988	Alternate redistricting plan proposed by a predominantly minority coalition is accepted by the State Legislature.
April 1988	Merced decides to run for state representative.
September 1988	Merced wins Democratic Party's State Primary with 43 percent of the vote among a field of six candidates.
November 1988	Merced receives 64 percent of the vote on his Fifth Suffolk District, becoming Massachusetts' first Latino Legislator.
September 1990	Merced wins Democratic Party primaries among a field of three candidates with 64 percent of the vote.
November 1990	Merced is reelected with 49% of the votes among a field of three candidates.
August 1992	Merced's required voter signature papers are declared invalid because of a technicality. He thus fails to gather enough valid signatures to be placed on the ballot again and decides to run a "sticker" campaign for the state primaries.
September 1992	Merced loses the primaries with 31% of the vote.

Merced and his campaign staff carefully averted possible tensions between representing the Latino community and the broader interests of his district. He made sure that his campaign was racially integrated and, although his name conveyed that he was Latino, he did not stress his Latino heritage to white and African-American voters. Instead, the campaign emphasized his role in the community in collaboration with the Latino and African-American communities, as well as with whites. For Latinos, however, emphasis was placed on the fact that Merced had a good chance of becoming the first Latino representative in the state. Merced said that he personally knocked on about 80 percent of houses in the district. The emphasis was on getting the people out to vote in the primaries (Table 2.1).

THE ROLE OF THE MEDIA

Local community newspapers, most of them with strong ethnic and racial constituencies, played an important role in covering Merced's campaign before both the primaries and the final elections. According to Merced, the city's most influential African-American weekly newspaper, *The Bay State Banner*, actively followed his campaign before the primaries (Merced 1994).

The *Dorchester Community News*, whose readership is composed of ethnic whites, African Americans, and some Latinos, did some "routine" coverage, according to Merced, although they endorsed him during his second election in 1990. Though Merced's candidacy represented the first time a Latino was elected to state-level office, the region's largest and most influential newspaper, *The Boston Globe*, failed to acknowledge his achievement until 1 month *after* the election. That was 10 days after an article had appeared in *The New York Times* (Merced 1994).

The Spanish-language media played an important role in the election. Circulation and readership of the Spanish-language newspapers in and around Boston traditionally have been small, primarily due to the relatively small size of the community. Nevertheless, these papers do have some influence. During the candidacy of Mel King for mayor of Boston in 1983, for example, both *El Mundo* and *La Semana*, weekly newspapers owned by Cuban Americans, endorsed the well-financed favorite David Finnegan over African-American Mel King, the Latino favorite. *El Mundo* was ardently pro-Reagan (Bruno and Gastón 1984, 71) and tried to turn the election into a referendum on President Reagan's hard-line position on Cuba. Nevertheless, in 1988 *El Mundo* did endorse Merced.

Ironically, Nelson Merced, a progressive who was in favor of normalizing relations with Cuba, got positive coverage in the Spanish-language media, at least in part because he was Latino. It would have been difficult for the Spanish-language newspapers to oppose Merced who was well liked and had a good record in the Latino community. Moreover, Merced already had good relations with the Spanish-language media, and the rest of the media in general. "They [the Spanish-language newspapers] knew of my progressive views, they just never really questioned me on some of them," said Merced (1994).

La Semana also endorsed Merced's candidacy. Peter Cuenca, who owned not only *La Semana* but also Boston's Spanish-language television channel, *Cuencavisión*, agreed to run a (free) public service announcement featuring Merced on the need to register to vote. The Spanish-language segments on Boston's English-language TV stations played a more limited role.

Perhaps the most influential Spanish-language media in Boston is the radio which reaches virtually all city households. The two existing Spanish-language radio stations at the time, *Radio Continental* and *La Fabulosa,* also gave Merced strong support. The former, owned by Antonio Molina, a Puerto Rican businessperson, played a key role. He repeatedly spoke in favor of the Merced campaign throughout his daily talk shows.

The "Latino press was pretty good in making sure that the community was informed and [the press] realized the election's importance," stated Merced (1994). He was able to utilize the different ethnic and minority media outlets in Boston to his advantage throughout his initial campaign, although this would later change in the 1992 election as we will see.

THE STATE PRIMARY

There were a total of six Democratic candidates running for the Fifth Suffolk District in the September 1988 state primary. Winning the primary essentially guaranteed Merced's win in the final election in November since the district and, indeed, the entire city, are overwhelmingly Democratic. Moreover, the Republicans did not have a candidate for the November elections; instead, there was an independent African-American candidate, Althea Garrison.

As Table 2.2 shows, in the five precincts with the largest white voting-age populations (Ward 13, prec. 5; Ward 15, prec. 4; and Ward 15, prec. 7-9; with 29 percent to 61 percent white), Merced received an average of 35 percent of the vote. Voters in those precincts supported Merced in a 2:1 ratio compared to the other five candidates.[13] The five precincts with the heaviest African-American voting-age populations (Ward 12, prec. 4 and 6; Ward 13, prec. 1 and 4; Ward 15, prec. 5; with 64 percent to 88 percent African American) gave Merced an average of 75 percent of their votes during the primary, or 4.5 times the threshold. The five precincts with the heaviest Latino adult populations (Ward 7, prec. 10; Ward 8, prec. 6 and 7; Ward 13, prec. 2; and Ward 15, prec. 8; with 28 percent to 40 percent Latino) gave Merced an average of 52 percent of their votes, or three times the threshold. As the percentage of Latinos in these last precincts was low relative to voters of other races, especially whites, the support for Merced was likely to have been diluted with the white vote, which consisted of 6 percent to 32 percent of those precincts' populations. Still, the precinct with the largest percentage of Latinos (40 percent)[14] gave Merced his strongest support, with 71 percent voting for him.

Merced won the primary with 42.9 percent of the vote. Although the breakdown of votes by race discussed here is not definitive, it does suggest that African-American and white voters in Boston were willing to vote for a Latino when he spoke to their issues. On the night of the primary, candidate Farrell went over to Merced campaign's office to congratulate and support him in the November elections. He then introduced Merced around his neighborhood.

Table 2.2   Votes Cast for Merced in Democratic State Primaries, 1988

Ward	Precinct	Votes Cast			District's Voting Age Population*		
		Total Votes	Merced Votes	Merced (%)	White* (%)	Black* (%)	Latino (%)
7	10	199	99	49.7	24.3	18.4	32.2
8	5	142	72	50.7	10.2	26.3	27.3
8	6	53	26	49.1	25.4	11.9	31.0
8	7	111	66	59.5	6.3	59.6	30.6
12	4	138	62	44.9	1.7	86.6	10.4
12	6	128	55	43.0	4.7	87.7	6.2
13	1	108	48	44.4	6.8	73.0	13.8
13	2	55	39	70.9	6.3	46.7	40.3
13	4	110	63	57.3	9.7	64.3	23.2
13	5	152	101	66.4	30.7	34.9	20.5
15	1	166	66	39.8	11.9	54.5	21.1
15	2	108	36	33.3	11.3	58.4	18.5
15	3	125	32	25.6	26.9	43.8	23.7
15	4	264	56	21.2	31.6	30.8	19.9
15	5	99	66	66.7	6.4	65.1	20.6
15	7	169	52	30.8	29	38.5	21.4
15	8	90	29	32.2	32.4	30.3	28.1
15	9	261	67	25.7	61.2	20.8	8.4
17	2	113	76	67.3	17.4	61.6	17.9
	Total	2,591	1,111	42.9	18.64	48.06	21.85

*Non-Latino. Source: Doc. No. 10; Boston Election Department (1990).

THE NOVEMBER ELECTION

On November 8, 1988, Merced won the final election with 64 percent of the vote against his opponent, independent candidate Garrison.[15] State Senator Royal L. Bolling, an African American who served 18 years in the Massachusetts Legislature, hailed Merced's election: " Merced's election is significant for future minority participation in state politics. There wasn't a battle between African Americans and [Latinos] because their agendas coincide almost 100 percent: housing, jobs, socioeconomic integration. It's a perfect marriage" (Diesenhouse 1988, 48).

Hubie Jones, an African-American political analyst, also greeted Merced's election with enthusiam: "It's an incredible boost to the Latino community in their move toward political empowerment" (Ribadeneira 1988, 29). Merced took office as the first Latino elected to statewide office in January 1989.

NELSON MERCED ON BEACON HILL: AGENDA AND CHALLENGES

LEGISLATIVE AGENDA

Once at the State House, the main issues that Merced worked on were bilingual education, housing, language rights, education, immigrant program rights, and welfare rights. During his first 2-year term, Merced served on the Committee on Housing and Urban Development. (During his second term, he served on and became vice-chair of the Commerce and Labor Committee and again on the Housing Committee.)

In 1989 Merced and fellow representative Kevin Fitzgerald (D-Mission Hill), both lobbied forcefully for a $225,000 legislative appropriation to fund New England's first institute dedicated solely to research on Latino issues, the Mauricio Gastón Institute for Latino Community Development and Public Policy at the University of Massachusetts Boston. Other legislative efforts included House Bill 1626, which made Massachusetts a multilingual state at a time when other states were voting to make English the "official language" of the state. In addition, Merced joined with other African-American leaders to oppose Mayor Ray Flynn's decision to replace the elected Boston School Committee with an appointed one; Mayor Flynn (who had also opposed school desegregation during the 1970s) prevailed and, although the minority representation on the Boston School Committee increased dramatically, minority voters lost an important arena for exercising their political power.

Merced enlisted the support of union workers and leaders by participating at a United Auto Worker retreat in New Hampshire, along with other progressive elected officials and political activists (*Boston Globe* 1991a). He did not hesitate to support the campaign of progressive African-American candidate Reverend Graylan Ellis-Hagler for mayor of Boston in 1992, even though Ellis-Hagler's chances for winning over incumbent Ray Flynn were considered slim. Nevertheless, Merced's support ensured the continued alliance among African Americans, Latinos, and progressive whites.

Merced received praise for his legislative efforts from several organizations with diverse memberships: labor unions, women, liberal whites, and minorities in general. In 1992, for example, the AFL-CIO cited Merced, along with only four other state representatives, as having a "perfect" labor record. The National Organization for Women (NOW) also endorsed Merced, along with 14 other state representatives, during the 1992 elections. In addition, the Citizens for Participation in Political Action, a progressive nonprofit group, endorsed Merced and seven other state representatives. The Human Services Coalition gave Merced, and 16 other state representatives, a perfect score of 100 for his voting record.

Merced was also well respected among his colleagues on Beacon Hill. "He was very keen on issues affecting Latinos. He made me look at things from a perspective that I would not have thought about otherwise," said former state representative Patricia Fiero, a white Democrat from Gloucester who served from 1984 to 1991 (Fiero 1994). "I liked Nelson, he treated women with respect, unlike many other House members," she added. During his tenure as a state legislator, Merced was elected chairperson of the Black Legislative Caucus. His election to this position represented not just a symbolic appointment by his African-American colleagues, who had large Latino constituencies, but rather a reaffirmation of the common agenda between African-Americans and Latinos and the respect African-American legislators had for Merced.

CHALLENGES

Merced identified four major challenges that he faced while at the State House. First, he found that given the depressed state of the economy in the late 1980s, furthering his agenda was difficult. Second, he voiced concern about articulating the voice of his constituents in a productive and energetic way. Third, he sometimes found it difficult to maintain a balance between advocating the interests of his district and those of the Latino community throughout the state. Fourth, he was not able to fulfill his intention to maintain a campaign office in the community.

During his first term, the economy in the Commonwealth was in a recession, the end of the so-called "Massachusetts Miracle."[16] There was also a lame-duck governor, Michael Dukakis, serving his last 2 years after losing the 1988 Presidential election. "It was a tough time to be in state office, as a lot of programs were being cut," said Merced (1994). The depressed state of the economy prevented Merced from enacting many of the programs at the heart of his progressive agenda. During his tenure, he voted to raise the personal income tax from 5 to 6 percent. He also voted to increase cigarette and other "sin" taxes. Merced (1994) said he did not have second thoughts about raising taxes: "It was either that or cutting [social] programs."

Being the first-ever Latino state representative, most of the Latino community still lacked mechanisms to channel their concerns in an organized manner. This made it even more difficult for Merced to articulate the legitimate problems of his district, particularly those of the Latino community. Merced also received many invitations from other Latino communities in the state to speak about issues affecting them. As the only Latino in the State House, he felt compelled to participate in many of these activities. Critics felt that he should have focused on his district, but Merced sought a balance between the needs of his district and those of the state's under-represented Latino communities. Gus Newport, for example, the African-American director of DSNI, advised Merced to learn to say "no" to some invitations he received from *outside* his district (Cunha 1994). Nevertheless, although Merced was the representative of the Fifth Suffolk district, issues he worked on at the State House, such as bilingual educa-tion, had implications for Latinos throughout the state and he felt the need to respond to calls from outside his district. Indeed, his presence on Beacon Hill inspired Latinos to run for office around the state as evidenced by the exponential growth in Latino campaigns discussed in the Introduction.

Finally, Merced acknowledged his failure to maintain a continuous cam-paign office that would keep working in his district. A busy work schedule at the State House, as well as family commitments, prevented him from investing more time into organizing a local campaign office in his district.

Although unable to maintain a campaign office in his district, Merced did participate actively in many grassroots community efforts. These included an important rally in 1992 by the Asian community against dis-criminatory remarks made by City Councilor Albert (Dapper) O'Neill about Vietnamese residents of Dorchester (*Boston Globe* 1992).[17] He also contributed to the founding of the Association of African American and Latino Elected Officials, led by Mel King—a first in Boston politics (*Boston Globe* 1991b, 17). Merced was also a frequent visitor, and sometimes lec-turer, at a highly successful English language and literacy program for Latina women in Dorchester, *Mujeres Unidas en Acción* (Women United in Action) where many participants regarded him as a role model.

Reelected in 1990, Merced's tenure lasted only one more term. Upon fil-ing just above the minimum number of signatures to be placed on the 1992 Democratic Party ballot, one page of valid signatures did not have "Boston" written at the top of the page, so his nomination as a candidate was disqualified. He ran a "sticker" campaign but lost the 1992 election receiving only 31 percent of the vote.

After his loss, several Latino media outlets complained that Merced had not done enough outreach to the Spanish-speaking community. A newspa-per article entitled "*Indiferencia Hacia Prensa Hispana Pudo Haber Sido Uno de los Factores de su Derrota*" (Indifference Towards Hispanic Press Could Have Been One of the Factors in His Defeat) appeared in *El Mundo* (1992). Some Latinos working in the Spanish-language media (although none was based in the city of Boston, it should be clarified) spoke about the lack of communication they had with Merced. Marcos Vázquez, for example, owner of *Radio La Fabulosa*, said that Merced "never had any communication with this station." As well, Isabel Dominiconi, director of

Radio Atlántica, told *El Mundo* that she "did not know [Merced]. Maybe that is why he did not get reelected: his indifference towards the Hispanic press." The article concluded by stating that "the same indifference Merced had with *Radiolandia 1330* and *El Mundo,* both of which, primarily the latter, played an important role in the elections some years before when he first got elected" (*El Mundo* 1992).

Other criticisms included those from supporters at *Mujeres Unidas en Acción:* in the summer of 1992, just before the September primary, despite being one of the main speakers, he failed to attend the organization's graduation ceremony. In addition, just a few nights before the September 1992 primary, during his "sticker" campaign, Merced reportedly did not attend a scheduled meeting with some 20 other supporters at the Dublin House in Dorchester, where he was supposed to hand out his "stickers" for the ballot.

Merced's (and/or his campaign's) negligence in submitting the requisite number of signatures to be placed on the ballot again may not have been simply a sign of lack of organization, but also suggested that he had lost some of his desire to stay in the Legislature. Months before, he was already conveying to some of his closest associates that he did not want to stay in the Legislature for much longer. At that time, state representatives were paid $30,000 a year, considered low when compared to other state legislatures. As a homeowner in a city with one of the highest cost of living in the nation, his personal financial resources were stretched thin. Moreover, family pressures—he has four children—were reportedly also a factor. What is perhaps more clear is that he was often left alone to do the uphill job that the Latino community, and his other constituents, very much needed and wanted. "Burnout" resulting from being the only Latino state representative and one of only a small number of minority legislators may have played a role as well.

Merced (1994) admitted that "in a way, I was somewhat relieved that I would not be officially on the ballot again." Had his name been officially on the ballot again, many in Boston believe that Merced would still be in the Legislature today. On the other hand, since his defeat in 1992, the Fifth Suffolk District has consistently been held by an African American, lending support to the idea that when Latinos are not a majority in a given legislative district, they are more likely to support African American candidates than African Americans are to support Latino candidates (Romero 1996, 14).

CONCLUSION

The use of a multiracial coalition was crucial in the 1988 election of Nelson Merced to the Massachusetts State Legislature. Because Latinos currently represent only 6.8 percent of the state's population, such coalitions are necessary to achieve greater Latino political representation at the level of state legislative races. The composition of such coalitions will vary depending on the constituency of the locality in question. In Merced's case, for example, although African Americans and Latinos together constituted 64 percent of the district's voting-age population, efforts to gain white support were especially important, particularly as whites generally vote more than African-Americans and Latinos.

As noted earlier, the lower level of voter registration by Latinos in Massachusetts are due to several socio-demographic characteristics including the youthfulness of the population (Latinos in the state have the lowest median age compared to whites, African Americans, and Asians); lower citizenship rates among non-Puerto Rican Latinos; and their low socioeconomic status.

Efforts to increase the representation of Latinos should focus, therefore, on voter registration. Such efforts have increased dramatically in recent years. The Massachusetts Hispanic Voter Registration Project, for example, claimed to have registered 6,000 Latinos from 1992 to 1994.[18] At the same time, Merced's experience shows that in order to elect more Latinos, multiracial coalitions may be even more important than registering Latino voters. (For a review of Latino voter registration efforts in Massachusetts, see Chapter 10 in this volume).

Electing Latino candidates in districts where they are not a majority clearly requires strong support from Latino and African-American voters but Latino candidates simultaneously have to make extraordinary efforts to appeal to nonminority voters or at least to lessen electoral opposition from them. Merced accomplished that without stressing that he was a "Latino" candidate, except to his Latino constituents—a tactic open to the criticism of downplaying Latino connections and issues. The Merced experience suggests that Latinos are concerned with many of the same issues as other nonwhite communities and may be able to gain high elected office through a broad appeal, emphasizing multiracial common concerns.

Redistricting obviously played an important role in paving the way to Merced's victory. The campaign in Massachusetts to ensure Latino compliance with the 2000 Census and the subsequent redistricting will have a crucial impact on Latino political representation at the State House in the near future. It is in the smaller cities and towns, such as Holyoke, Chelsea, and Lawrence, where we can expect a continued upsurge in Latino elected officials. Whereas, 44.1 percent of African Americans in Massachusetts live in Boston, 80.2 percent of Latinos are dispersed throughout the state. With only a 14.4 percent share of the population, Latinos in Boston will continue to need to rely heavily on coalitions.[19]

When Nelson Merced was elected to the State House in 1988, he was one of only three Latino elected officials in Massachusetts. By 1994, there were 11 Latinos elected to state and city positions: three state representatives, six city councilors, and two school committee members (see Introduction).

Merced's candidacy mobilized many grassroots activists, particularly African American and Latino, who, to a great extent, had abandoned previously the electoral arena. His legacy included building a multiracial coalition in a city that has long been dominated by the white political establishment. Merced's experience also showed that forming coalitions to campaign for and elect minority public officials is not enough, for such officials, once elected, need to have the continued support and collaboration of the people that brought them to power. In addition, continued contact with the press, particularly minority media, is crucial.

The election of Nelson Merced represented a great triumph not only for Latinos in Massachusetts, but also demostrates the importance of coalition building between Latinos, and working-class and progressive whites, political empowerment.

NOTES

1. As discussed in the Introduction, the term "Latino" will be used throughout this chapter to refer to individuals who can trace their ancestries to Latin America. It contrasts with its counterpart, "Hispanic," which emphasizes, or overemphasizes, the Spanish colonial experience of the New World (see Muñoz 1989; Acuña 1988; Giménez 1989).

2. See Cruz (1997) and Hero (1996) for a further discussion of the limits to Latino electoral participation.

3. For an in-depth analysis of Peña's election, see Hero (1992).

4. In 1988 Rodriguez was appointed by Governor Dukakis to head the Massachusetts Commission Against Discrimination (MCAD) and in the mid-1990s he became Deputy Assistant Secretary for Administration at the U.S. Treasury. He returned to Boston and ran again for State Representative in 1998 but lost the election.

5. *Black Political Task Force et al. v. Michael Joseph Connolly et al.,* and *Massachusetts Republican State Committee et al. v. Michael Joseph Connolly.* 679 F. Supp. 109 (D. Mass. 1988). The plaintiffs had lost an earlier challenge, having argued that the state had undercounted minorities, particularly Latinos.

6. The plaintiffs were also alleging that the 1985 Massachusetts Decennial Census had undercounted minorities. The Court, however, refuted the plaintiffs' arguments by alleging that their method of counting minorities was exaggerative. Nevertheless, the 1990 U.S. Census proved that the estimates of the minority population were correct target, if not conservative, according to attorney Rom(1994). The Massachusetts Decennial Census was abolished during a state referendum in the 1992 elections.

7. Details about Merced's life are from an interview with Merced, 1 April 1994.

8.   The squatters' movement in Puerto Rico is a de facto land redistribution where large tracts of land concentrated in the hands of the government or a few powerful elite families are taken over by squatters. The families often are forced to settle in court battles over the land.

9.   For a discussion of the Young Lords, see Guzmán (1984).

10.   His colleague there was Alan Jay Rom, the lawyer quoted earlier who would later serve as the plaintiffs' attorney in the redistricting fight that led to Merced's election to the Massachusetts State House.

11.   Merced's career path from agency director to candidate supports Jennings's (1984) contention that Boston's Latino leadership could be considered "poverty-crats."

12.   DSNI later became a nationally recognized grassroots community organization (see, for example, Eisen 1994).

13.   The Massachusetts Elections Statistics (1988) book does not provide the number of votes received by the other candidates in each precinct.

14.   Ward 13, Precinct 2.

15.   In November 1992, after Merced failed to qualify for the primary, he lost to Garrison.

16.   The "Massachusetts Miracle," in fact, was not very miraculous for Latinos or African Americans. See, for example, Osterman (1992).

17.   Peter Kiang, the driving force behind the creation of the region's first Asian American Institute, was quoted as saying that this "is the first time that the Vietnamese community of Boston has come together to rally on their behalf" (*Boston Globe* 1992).

18.   Personal communication from the Project's former director, Fernando Milán.

19.   Boston, Brockton, Chelsea, Holyoke, Lawrence, Lowell, Lynn, Somerville, Springfield and Worcester (Torres and Chavez 1998, 3). The three current Latino representatives are not from Boston but rather Lawrence, Springfield, and Cambridge.

REFERENCES

Acuña, Rodolfo. (1988). *Occupied America: A History of Chicanos*, 3rd ed. New York: Harper & Row.

Baird, Frank L. (1977). "The Search for a Constituency: Political Validation of Mexican-American Candidates in the Texas Great Plains." In *Mexican Americans: Political Power, Influence or Resource*, edited by Frank L. Baird. Lubbock: Texas Tech Press.

Black Political Task Force, et al. (1988). *Black Political Task Force v. Michael Joseph Connolly, et al., and Massachusetts Republican State Committee, et al. v. Michael Joseph Connolly.* 679 F. Supp. 109 (D. Mass.)

Borrero, M., L. Cuadrado, and P. Rodríguez. (1974). "The Puerto Rican Role in Interest Group Politics." *Social Casework* 55(2), 94–99.

Boston Election Department. (1990). Public Document 10.

Boston Globe. (1991a). "Progressives Gather in Search of a Common Political Vision," by Royal Ford, 3 October, 3.
———. (1991b). "Blacks, Hispanics Build Ties," by Steve Marantz, 29 March, 17.
———. (1992). "Vietnamese Find Their Voice: After Boston Councilor's Remarks, Community Focuses on Political Power," by Irene Sege, 26 June.
Browning, Rufus, Dale Rogers Marshall, and David H. Tabb. (1984). *Protest Is Not Enough: The Struggle of Blacks and Hispanics for Equality in Urban Politics.* Berkeley, CA: University of California Press.
Bruno, Melania, and Mauricio Gastón. (1984). "Latinos for Mel King: Some Reflections." *Radical America* 17 (6) and 18 (1): 67–79.
Camayd-Freixas, Yohel. (1994). Telephone interview, Miami, Florida, 9 April.
Camayd-Freixas, Yohel, and Russell Paul López. (1983). *Gaps in Representative Democracy: Redistricting, Political Participation and the Hispanic Vote in Boston.* Boston: Hispanic Office of Planning and Evaluation, Inc.
Cruz, José. (1997). "Latinos in the 1996 Connecticut and Massachusetts Presidential Races: Beyond Politics as Usual," 14. Paper presented at the Latino Leadership Conference sponsored by the Commonwealth Coalition, Clark University, Worcester, MA, 21 June.
Cunha, Joyce. (1994). Interview, 3 May.
de la Garza, Rodolfo O. (1974). "Voting Patterns in 'Bi-cultural' El Paso—A Contextual Analysis of Chicano Voting Behavior." In *Dilemmas of Pluralist Democracy* (1982). New Haven: Yale University Press.
Diesenhouse, Susan. (1988). "From 'Migrant' to State House in Massachusetts." *New York Times,* 27 November, 48.
Eisen, Arlene. (1994). "Survey of Neighborhood-Based, Comprehensive Community Empowerment Initiatives." *Health Education Quarterly* 21(2): 235–252.
El Mundo. (1992). "*Indiferencia Hacia Prensa Hispana Pudo Haber Sido Uno de los Factores de su Derrota Electoral*" (Indifference Towards Hispanic Press Could Have Been One of the Factors in His Electoral Defeat), Boston, 23 September, 7.
Fiero, Patricia. (1994). Interview, 20 April.
Giménez, Martha E. (1989). "Latino/Hispanic—Who Needs a Name? The Case Against a Standardized Terminology." *International Journal of Health Services* 19(3): 557–571.
Guzmán, Pablo "Yoruba." (1984). "Puerto Rican Barrio Politics in the United States." In *The Puerto Rican Struggle: Essays on Survival in the United States,* edited by Clara E. Rodriguez, Virginia Sanchez Korrol, and José Oscar Alers, 121–128. Maplewood, NJ: Waterfront Press.
Hardie, Peter. (1994). Interview at Roxbury Youth Works in Boston, 11 May.
Hardy-Fanta, Carol. (1993). *Latina Politics, Latino Politics: Gender, Culture and Participation in Boston.* Philadelphia: Temple University Press.
Hero, Rodney E. (1992). *Latinos and the U.S. Political System: Two-Tiered Pluralism.* Philadelphia: Temple University Press.

————. (1996). "Hispanics in Urban Government and Politics: Some Findings, Comparisons and Implications, in Politics." In *The American States and Communities, A Contemporary Reader*, edited by Jack R. Van Der Slik, 105–115. Boston: Allyn & Bacon.

Jennings, James. (1984). "Introduction: The Emergence of Puerto Rican Electoral Activism." In *Puerto Rican Politics in Urban America*, edited by James Jennings and Monte Rivera, pp. 75–98. Westport, CT: Greenwood Press.

Massachusetts Elections Statistics. (1988). Public Document 10. Boston: City of Boston Election Department.

Merced, Nelson. (1994). Interview, 1 April.

Muñoz, Carlos. (1989). *Youth, Identity, Power: The Chicano Movement*. New York: Verso.

Osterman, Paul. (1992). "Latinos in the Midst of Plenty." In *Latinos in Boston: Confronting Poverty, Building Community*, edited by Miren Uriarte, Paul Osterman, Carol Hardy-Fanta, and Edwin Meléndez, 37–71. A background paper for the Boston Persistent Poverty Project. Boston: The Boston Foundation.

Ribadeneira, Diego. (1988). "Latino Scales Beacon Hill Merced Bears the Hopes of an Ethnic Community." *Boston Globe*, 6 December, 29.

Romero, Angela L. (1996). "Black and Hispanic Representation in State Legislatures: The Case for a '50 Percent Rule'." Paper presented at 1996 Annual Meeting of the American Political Science Association, San Francisco, 29 August–1 September.

Torres, Andrés, and Lisa Chavez. (1998). *Latinos in Massachusetts: An Update.* Boston: Mauricio Gastón Institute for Latino Community Development and Public Policy, University of Massachusetts Boston.

Uriarte-Gastón, Miren. (1988). "Organizing for Survival: The Emergence of a Puerto Rican Community." Ph.D. diss., Boston University.

U.S. Bureau of the Census. (2001). City data provided by the Mauricio Gastón Institute for Latino Community Development and Public Policy, University of Massachusetts Boston, 4 April.

CHAPTER 3

Latino Political Succession and Incorporation
Lawrence

WILLIAM A. LINDEKE

Lawrence, Massachusetts, is home to the largest Hispanic[1] community of any city in the state (at 59.7 percent of total population) and one of the largest on the East Coast. It has 10 percent of the Commonwealth's 428,729 Latinos. At the same time it is the poorest city in the state and the twenty-third poorest in the country. It has very high rates of poverty, crime, and arson on a per capita basis (Office of Planning 1994, 2). What has linked the population size and poverty characteristics has been the powerlessness of the Hispanic community over the public and private institutions that control the policy agendas of the city.

Although the powerlessness of the community has been well known and documented since the "riots" of 1984 and the studies by Duran (1985), Camyd-Freixas et al. (1985), and the Phillips Andover Academy (1986), more recent events and studies show some important new shifts that indicate a long-awaited change in the political incorporation of the Latino community. The weakness of Hispanic leadership often has been singled out as a critical problem in the city. In an *Eagle Tribune* interview for a special series on Latinos in Lawrence, Isabel Meléndez, a long time community activist, emphasized the point: "We're lacking strong leadership. That's the biggest problem we have" (Meléndez, 22 September, 1992). In the 1990s several long time residents began to change the political landscape of the city both by challenging the legal status of the local power structure and making gains at the ballot box.

Lawrence elected its first Hispanic officeholder, Ralph Carrero, in 1991 to an at-large seat on the School Committee. This breakthrough was followed by a district election victory to the City Council by José Santiago (and another by an African American) in the 1993 city elections. By contrast, the city of Boston had only appointed Latino officeholders, who by definition are in office at the will of another and have neither the legitimacy nor the autonomy of elected officials. By the end of the 1990s, Latino candidates in Lawrence were targeting and gaining the highest political offices. Santiago won the seat for State Representative in 1998 followed by three City Council victories in 1999. Latinos were poised for gaining a commanding share of power.

Electing officials to press the interests of the community in the public arena as legitimate representatives of a democratic process marks a significant new stage of community empowerment (Browning, Marshall, and Tabb 1990). The gains at first were more symbolic than practical given their small numbers. However, they were still important in several respects. First, the precedent was established so that future election of leaders will become routine rather than controversial. Second the pressure of being "the" representative or the presumption of trying to become "the" voice of the community has now been replaced with the easier and less contentious task of becoming another voice or another leader. In the fragmented Hispanic community of Lawrence this represents an important step toward empowerment and mobilization.

Nevertheless, the representation remained minimal at first. As will be shown, a sizable difference remains between the total city population, the body politic, and the electorate. The powerful institutions and policies continue to be dominated by the old ethnic power structure. Unrealistic visions of a "restoration" of some previous romanticized past continued to dominate their public discussions.

The problems of leadership for Lawrence Hispanics and the resistance of the existing power structure of Anglo-dominated institutions are the most important barriers to Latino empowerment. Additional barriers come from Latinos themselves, especially the bifurcated population of Dominicans and Puerto Ricans. Furthermore, the population is very young, poor, uneducated, and organizationally fragmented.

Therefore, a fuller transformation and breakthrough in the political process had to emerge during the 1990s. All of these efforts required the education and mobilization of the Hispanic community to register, vote, and challenge or change the established power structure. Once the symbolic breakthrough had been achieved, what were the continuing barriers to the qualitative breakthrough of political incorporation of the Hispanic community in Lawrence and what achievements were made? The answers to these questions will be examined in this chapter.

LAWRENCE IN THE 1980S

A City Charter reform, narrowly approved by the voters in November 1983, was instituted in January 1986. The new charter was developed in response to decades of political inaction and neglect of the economic health of the city. It created a more centralized and potentially responsible governing structure. The key feature was a strong mayor, independently elected for 4 years (rather than 2 years), and a city council elected both by district and at large (Bain 1986). School Committee seats are still at-large, which limits one common entry option for minorities.

Politics, however, did not change. The first mayor's race was won on an openly racist appeal asserted in a widely circulated letter to the editor that advocated "giving the city back to those who built it." Other successful candidates usually followed or benefited from the older tradition of ethnic appeals and voting patterns. Elections in 1985 and after brought all new faces into city offices, but reproduced Irish, Italian, and French-Canadian candidates and victors for the most part (Bain 1986 and city election data).

Hispanic voters could have taken advantage of the district system, as minorities have done elsewhere, but they failed to do so effectively until 1993. On the whole they offered weak candidacies or none at all and exhibited low voter registration and turnouts.

The existing power structure is not monolithic nor is it especially robust. The most important centers of power are public officials who can mobilize public (especially state) revenues for common purposes. State officials who support social service funding have not challenged the old relationships by promoting voter registration or bringing Hispanics into their inner circles. Bain (1986, 20) sees a decline in patronage aspects in the early years of the new Charter and some increased educational levels and gender inclusion for local politicians with women elected to the City Council, School Committee, State Legislature, and Mayor's office. Yet respondents almost universally attribute Hispanic powerlessness to the attitudes and policies of the local power structure.

HISPANIC MIGRATION TO THE UNITED STATES AND LAWRENCE

Unlike Hispanic communities in the Southwest, there is no dominant country of origin for the Lawrence Hispanic community (a trait shared with Lawrence Anglos). The first Latinos were displaced agricultural workers from Puerto Rico who remained to occupy low level jobs in the industrial and service sectors of the local economy in the 1940s and 1950s. These were followed by the first wave of Cuban exiles in the early 1960s and again by a hundred or so "*Marielitos*" in the early 1980s (Zaiter 1983).

From the middle 1960s until today the fastest growing population is from the Dominican Republic. Dominicans left the island of Hispaniola in the mid-1960s due to the violence of their civil war and United States military occupation. Their early migrations were to San Juan, Puerto Rico, (with the fourth largest concentration of Dominicans) and New York (the second largest). Later movements were to escape the overcrowded conditions in these cities and seek quieter areas that offered low-cost housing and employment opportunities. The remaining mills in the Lawrence area provided the jobs, and Lawrence itself became a magnet for Dominicans and Puerto Ricans, first those escaping New York, and then family and friends coming directly from the islands.

Diversity within each nationality group is also great. Although there are no hard data, respondents suggested that migrants include those from urban and rural backgrounds. Many peasants flee the overcropped, worked-out soils of Puerto Rico and the Dominican Republic to seek an urban platform to reach their ultimate destination: the United States mainland (Castillo and Mitchell 1987, 34).

As a consequence, the education levels in Lawrence are lower than in other Massachusetts Hispanic communities, and Dominican educational levels are lower than other Latino immigrants, at least in New York, where two-thirds of U.S.-based Dominicans reside (Youssef 1994, 93). Educational attainment for Lawrence Hispanics in the late 1980s was below grade nine level on average, and 62 percent had less than high school diploma. The school dropout rate was around 60 percent (Camayd-Freixas et al. 1985, 5; Clausen and Alomar 1988, 12–13; *Chronicle* 1990, A37).

Poverty rates also are very high (45 percent in 1980 and 1990 or four times the state average), and the job and language skills to escape poverty are lacking for a substantial number (37 percent) (Camayd-Freixas et al. 1985, 53; U.S. Census 1991, 5/P30). As the critical mass of the Latino population grows, English language skills remain important for economic success (Osterman 1993, 63), but not necessarily to function in the community, where entertainment, shopping, services, friends and family share the Spanish language.[2]

Roughly 80 percent of the immigrant population in Lawrence originates from the Dominican Republic.[3] The serious decay in the Dominican economy, such as the periodic high unemployment and inflation rates, results in a large emigration from the island. Indeed, the government may encourage such departures as part of a development strategy to relieve domestic unemployment pressures and increase essential remittances for balance of payments and capital accumulation. Coupled with the large settled immigrant population ready to bring their relatives to the states, this means that the Dominican population in Lawrence, like that in the United States, will continue its rapid growth (165 percent in New York, the largest center, between 1980 and 1990 and over 103 percent in Massachusetts).

For Puerto Ricans the citizenship status makes it easier to migrate. Less than 5 percent of the Puerto Rican workforce works in agriculture, yet over 14 percent of Puerto Rican emigrants during the 1980s were farm laborers (Rivera-Batiz 1989, 9). However, job growth in the lower skill sector has not kept pace with the number of job seekers. Unemployment rates for Latinos were around 25 percent in the 1990 census data. Labor market participation rates are low in Lawrence (60 percent) with women at about 51 percent, less than the nationwide Latina average. Forty-four percent of the households are headed by women.

In Lawrence, Puerto Ricans officially amounted to 51 percent in 1990, down from 59 percent of Hispanics counted in the 1980 census. Fear, distrust, and lack of effort lead to undercounting of Hispanics in general by 7.4 percent in 1980 and 4 to 7 percent in 1990, according to the Census Bureau (Exter 1985, 29; Rivera 1991, 2). However, other Hispanics in Lawrence were categorized together for census purposes in 1980, making it harder to calculate trends and the multiracial choices in the 2000 census makes comparisons between 1990 and 2000 more difficult. Dominicans are now estimated to outnumber Puerto Ricans in Lawrence, and Hispanics now constitute a majority (59.7) of the population.

Although Latinos are now interspersed throughout the city and adjacent towns, they have historically concentrated north of the Merrimack River in and around the center of the city. The major Latino neighborhoods are Arlington Heights, Tower Hill, Downtown, and the area where the Beacon Courts Housing Project is located (see Map 3.1). The densest concentrations are along Route 28 (or Broadway Street) that runs north/south through the Arlington district. This constitutes election District "C," while the adjoining Districts "B" and "D" have majority or near majority Latino populations. No distinct separation occurs between Dominican and Puerto Rican populations.

HISPANIC LEADERSHIP IN LAWRENCE

A large number of very able, educated, successful Hispanics are running or working in a variety of agencies serving not just the Hispanic community but others as well, providing the strongest leadership base. In health care, employment, housing, and other services a core of very effective, often young, practitioners exists representing diverse country origins. As is common for such practitioners, they are very active in various community services and projects and serve on advisory boards for other agencies. This is a common path for Hispanic political success.

However, the limited number of skilled professionals also leads to burnout and overcommitment. They can and do move to the surrounding suburbs to seek a better school system for their children, better housing, and a bit of relief from the community's demands on their time and energy. This well-known process of middle classes moving elsewhere takes these leaders out of the voting and candidate pools for Lawrence and separates them from the community they try to serve.

At the same time, these service providers are still dominated by Anglo executives and boards, who control policy. Often leaders can be constrained by the risks of losing well-paying jobs. Sometimes the closeness to the power structure also costs one community support. Hardy-Fanta (1993) has shown clearly that in Boston the distance between the "professionals" and the *"gente del pueblo"* or common people weakens the

Map 3.1   Latino Population in Lawrence (2000), by Census Block
Group, with Neighborhoods and Election Districts

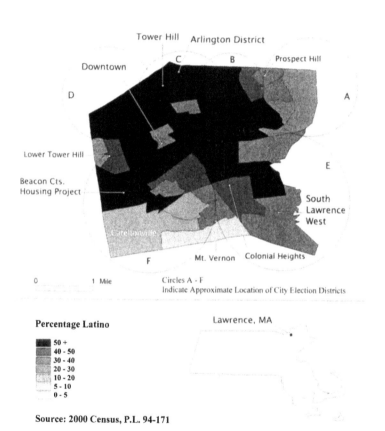

Percentage Latino

- 50 +
- 40 - 50
- 30 - 40
- 20 - 30
- 10 - 20
- 5 - 10
- 0 - 5

Lawrence, MA

Source: 2000 Census, P.L. 94-171

empowerment process in several ways. The same processes are at work in Lawrence, but to a lesser extent.

Some Latino professionals have emerged in government service. Positions like the Human Rights Officer, Affirmative Action Director, Assistant to the Mayor, and Economic Development Director have been held by Latinos. However, for the most part, these visible posts were held by Latinos from smaller, nonthreatening power bases (Chilean, Mexican American, and Venezuelan backgrounds). These "designated leaders" and spokespersons might have a harder time mobilizing the community or developing a power base that would give them greater independence and voice in public affairs. The power structure has been careful to avoid including those who might be able to effectively mobilize Latinos in Lawrence.

In education there are also a few outstanding leaders in responsible positions including principals, teachers, and counselors. The relative number in this group may be smaller than the city's or school system's Hispanic population due to several factors including the recent explosion in Hispanic school population. Tenure systems, civil service rules, and collective bargaining slow the turnover rate for teachers and administrators compared with the rapid changes in the student body experienced by many school systems. The most important limitation seems to be that the educational establishment remains controlled by the local Anglo community (Phillips 1986, 41–43).

The previously small local Hispanic population created a small pool of applicants who have received credentials over the years. Only since the 1980s has Massachusetts' Hispanic population exceeded a few percent of the total population. Hispanics in Lawrence reported only 1.7 percent with college degrees in the 1980 census, up to 2 percent in 1990, versus a U.S. Latino figure of 8.6 percent in 1987 and a Boston rate of 9 percent. Dominican immigrants in New York also have very low college graduation rates (Youssef 1994, 93). This highlights a critical failure in the community and a shortage of qualified, ambitious talent pushing the system to deliver for Latinos. The Lawrence Public Schools also are not producing satisfactory results on statewide testing, which points to a continuing small talent stream (*Boston Globe* 1998). Many teachers and aides in the bilingual programs lack the minimum required training. The number of Hispanics in college has risen 10 percent nationwide, but only two local colleges have any significant percentages or numbers of Hispanic students (*Chronicle* 1990, Al). However, 8 percent of Latino adults are currently enrolled in college (U.S. Census 1991, 10/P29).

The city is widely criticized for milking the state-funded bilingual programs and shortchanging the educational efforts for Hispanic children. Many of the educational disputes, for example over drugs, teenage pregnancy, discipline, or bilingual programs, are very controversial within the Hispanic community and fail to provide a unifying arena to assert the community's strength. Likewise parent–teacher organizations have not been a successful arena for public mobilization. Women might be expected to confront these problems, due to their stronger family responsibilities. However, their lack of education and their traditional cultural and class pressures inhibit greater assertiveness, while the daily struggle for survival takes priority for most poor women in Lawrence. Community activist Marisa Melendez contrasted the turnouts for a welfare reform meeting and a Parent Teacher Organization meeting several days later: "The welfare meeting packed the hall, while only six parents came to the PTO meeting."

In the business community there are also several leading Hispanic figures especially from real estate investors, travel agencies, insurance, and small shop and restaurant owners. Large numbers of small shops, *bodegas*, and other businesses dot the neighborhoods. Especially high growth rates have been experienced in the intercity minivan services (seven) that provide direct connections to New York and the wire transfer businesses (twenty-nine) that send money to the islands (Sennott 1994).

Although a few business leaders led by Eduardo Crespo (an Ecuadoran) have joined the larger Chamber of Commerce, the Hispanic business community, numbering some 200 or so, have formed their own organization— the Minority Business Council. Most of these businesses are small and subject to business difficulties common to small enterprises (long hours and high failure rates). Some representatives of each country group can be found here, though the Dominicans are especially active as small merchants representing 80 percent of the Hispanic businesses (Zaiter 1983). Some of the older, established Latino business leaders serve on advisory boards. Among these are executives with larger Anglo firms such as banks as well as entrepreneurs.

In the religious community the leadership has not ventured as much into the public arena as one might expect.[4] Unlike much of Latin America, where the Church is a uniform Catholic experience, both Puerto Rico and the Dominican Republic have diverse evangelical Protestant traditions as well. People migrating to Lawrence bring those traditions or convert to them, making for a fragmented community experience. More than 40 churches are currently operating in Lawrence in the evangelical and Pentecostal traditions alone.

Some of these churches eschew political or community roles. For example, Reverend Dan O'Neill complained that some Protestant churches refused to cooperate with the 1990 census project to get an accurate count of Hispanics, despite being asked to do so by Hispanic community leaders. Electoral activity for them as individuals and as an organized base in the community is largely out of the question. On the other hand, some of the leading figures in the Latino community are either religious leaders or have strong ties to churches. As with other leadership groups, the religious leaders have a high turnover rate (75 percent in one association of churches over a 5-year period). Many of the smaller churches prefer to avoid politics altogether, and several have forced their ministers to abandon any community leadership positions.

Catholic churches often segregate by ethnicity (Irish, Italian, French-Canadian, and Hispanic). Priests are shared by the different nationalities, and the affairs of the church, such as the Anglo-run schools with 2,900 students and other tasks associated with running the 13 parishes, absorb much of the energy and funds. Hispanics regularly attend three parishes in very large numbers (700–1000), where they mix rather than separate by country of origin. However, the Catholic parishes, which are being consolidated by the church hierarchy, lack the close social bonds of the smaller evangelical churches. They have not become a political mobilization vehicle for Latinos as they were for earlier immigrants. The churches remain potential but conflicted and fragmented mobilizers of the Latino community in Lawrence.

Communication is essential for political mobilization and leadership. The absence of an independent unifying voice for the community continued to hinder its mobilization. After numerous earlier failures a new paper was established in the late 1990s by Cuban-American Dalia Díaz called *Rumbo*. This paper concentrated on local issues and was distributed free in the Merrimack Valley communities. It helped to unify the community and keep attention on public issues.

One of the other potentially effective forces for mobilization of political support and leadership should come from the numerous social clubs. Most ethnic groups in Lawrence and other Massachusetts towns maintain social clubs. Some of the Hispanic ones cater to a specific group, while others are more open. At the moment there are several Dominican clubs, a Cuban, an Ecuadoran, a Guatemalan, and a Puerto Rican club, and several that are mixed. In his study of the 1984 riot, Joseph Duran (1985, 97) cites an informant who claimed that clubs could mobilize a hundred people on an hour's notice. To date these clubs have not provided much political energy or leadership. They stick to cultural events and sports while remaining politically neutral. One reason for this is the power that city officials have to grant licenses and enforce code violations. The most important mass organizations are effectively immobilized out of fear for what the city's power holders might do in terms of police, liquor control, or immigration control.

Because of the large percentage of young Hispanics (median age 20.7 years in 1990), the gangs, students, and other more established youth organizations could be an important source of mobilization politics like the role played by the Brown Berets in Los Angeles. Their role is not visible in Lawrence except as extensions of the adult organizations of social clubs, churches, Boys Clubs, or the YWCA. Young Latinos are more likely to identify as Latinos and as Lawrencians than with their parents' country of origin. They are not yet a dynamic leadership group.

CONFLICT AND COOPERATION AT THE LEADERSHIP LEVEL

Despite the community developments, unified leadership is slow to develop. Although very skilled leaders are found in a variety of settings, something seems to hold them back in the political arena. Latino politics is traditionally very personalized with loyalties attached more to the person than to issues, ideology, or party. Fragmented leadership is not a new phenomenon. The 1990 Dominican elections featured 34 different parties. In Lawrence there are several factors that hinder effective leadership and prevent unity.

One concept that will help clarify the issue is that of "ownership." If an event or organization becomes identified with a particular individual or group, others are not likely to feel incorporated and consequently will either ignore, walk out, or sabotage the effort. Many respondents told of different cases of this process. In addition to nationality, church affiliation, club membership, and other institutional affiliations may elicit similar responses. In the words of Dan O'Neill, "If one church group learns that another will be involved in an event, they will all boycott it." In part, one may attribute this to culture, but there is also a lack of practical skills and experience (Camayd-Freixas et al. 1985, 2). Over the past decade several political organizations have been founded, only to fail soon thereafter. Unity requires cooperation not "ownership."

A second pattern that was widely reported was the claiming of leadership status or the idea of "voice." Self-proclaimed leaders abound and are often adopted by media or officialdom, which frequently guarantees that they lose any chance of having a substantial following. In part this reflects the lack of practical experience in organization building, but also the frustration of being blocked from the influence that the community's numbers should give them. Examples of this process can be seen in the weak political campaigns for offices that far exceed the resource base of unknown candidates, and the repeated failure to mount campaigns for School Committee or Council District. Some candidates were pushed forward by the Republican Party's offer of assistance and campaign funds associated with reapportionment (Barnes 1990, 837). This was particularly true of Alba Castillo's 1990 state senate campaign in 1990. But Lawrence voters, including Hispanics, are overwhelmingly Democrats (six-to-one). Lawrence is not Miami. Voters tend to be conservative, "lunch box" Democrats, not liberal, diversity-oriented ones.

These leadership trends reflect a theme of conflict and jealousy that is repeated by several Hispanic interviewees. Such jealousy is complicated by the differences in status on the islands compared to the status in Lawrence. Differentials such as citizenship or English proficiency can exacerbate jealousy and rivalries. The body politic differs from the electorate, and this creates rival power bases that weaken support for any given political strategy. Two other leadership characteristics are commonly reported. One is the "spent force"—leaders who have already peaked and failed to reach or cannot reach the next plateau at this time. Reverend Dan O'Neill, for example, has been an appointed city official and is a respected, long time Latino activist. Yet he has failed in three attempts to be elected in Lawrence. This could in part be because he is a Republican, but there also must be other factors that limit his ability to mobilize voters. He is not alone in this respect. The other category is the "shooting star." This is someone who arrives in Lawrence, makes a big show, and then quickly burns out or moves on. Again Alba Castillo had a big presence in 1990 and was nowhere to be seen in Lawrence 5 years later.

In looking for political leadership for mobilization or electoral strategies, other factors must also be considered as leadership constraints. First, as mentioned above, many of the so-called leaders work, but do not live, in Lawrence. Instead they have moved to the nearby middle-class suburbs. Other Latinos have also spilled over into bordering towns leaving fewer voters than might appear at first impression. Second, many leaders just burn out or give up and move away, perhaps a dozen in the past 5 years. A number of this study's interviewees contemplated leaving as well. That makes leadership continuity and unity harder to achieve.

Hispanic leaders in Lawrence have been unable to create viable political organizations, despite numerous efforts. They still lack an institutional base for sustained political efforts such as the Democratic Party and political machines provided for earlier ethnic groups. When such a large percentage of the population is in a constant struggle for survival, building or even maintaining a community is a difficult task. Hardy-Fanta (1993) has emphasized the leadership role of women in building community through interpersonal relations as opposed to positional or institutional approaches emphasized by men. Similar activity can be found in Lawrence, though it was not the focus of the present study. Community building in Lawrence is especially difficult given the low income, employment, education, and citizenship levels and the fragmented country origins and high transience levels compared to other Latino communities. Even in Boston one survey showed three-quarters of Latinos were not familiar with any community organization (Osterman 1993, 59).

POLITICS AND THE ELECTORAL OPTION

Nationally, Hispanics who are registered turn out to vote in similar proportion to other groups, but they do not register or become citizens at the same rates as other foreign born. Thus, in Lawrence only 75 percent of Latinos were citizens in the 1980 and 1990 census counts. Lawrence Hispanics also do not vote in competitive numbers compared with other residents. This fact not only weakens Latino candidacies but also causes Anglo candidates to ignore them as a voting bloc. Anglos outnumber Hispanics as registered voters in Lawrence by more than 2 to 1, which explains why they continue to dominate elections. Partly this low turnout is accounted for by the very young average age of Lawrence Hispanics and the young age group's low voting turnout generally. That situation and the citizenship rates will improve as the community matures (Camayd-Freixas et al. 1985, 61).

Another problem is more perverse. The registration system in the United States discourages the poor and non-English speaking from full participation (Hardy-Fanta 1993). The Motor-Voter registration process may help reverse this problem. Lawrence Election Officials reported more than 1100 mail-in registrations in the first 6 months of 1995, with concerted community and candidate efforts still to come. However, the city actively purges the rolls each year based on city census participation. The district boundaries were drawn without the participation and to the disadvantage of Hispanic voters in much the same way that a successfully challenged Boston district plan was (Camayd-Freixas et al. 1985, 61). But protest mobilization and legal challenges were not common features of Latino politics in Lawrence.

In the past decade and a half several Latino candidates have sought public office through the electoral route. Beginning in 1981 more than two dozen candidates have sought various offices. For the most part these early candidacies faltered badly. Many candidates have sought offices at higher levels than they or the community were prepared to contest effectively. Other candidates lacked the seriousness of purpose necessary for success. For example, more than one Hispanic candidate has stated that it was not important to win or that they expected to lose their races. This may help save face or soften the blow to one's ego, but it does not inspire one's supporters. Other candidates have contested office on the Republican Party ticket, which is not the natural constituency for Lawrence's Hispanics. Female candidates have sought public office in numbers only during the late 1990s, despite the significant number of women activists in the community.

By the 1990s however, stronger candidacies were in evidence. Younger, energetic candidates who were raised in Lawrence were able to achieve the breakthrough with effective campaigns. These breakthroughs have encouraged additional candidates (both new and old) to seek office in the latter 1990s.

The first successful candidate, Ralph Carrero, ran in 1991 for the School Committee, which is elected at large. In the primary election, Carrero placed fifth out of seven candidates with 1,871 votes (33.5 percent of voters), enough to qualify for the final election. In the November balloting he placed second with 4,189 votes (46.5 percent of those voting), easily enough to make him the first elected Hispanic in the city's history.[5] A local product, Carrero had worked in the juvenile justice system and as director of the bilingual counseling program at Greater Lawrence Vocational and Technical High School. Although he usually votes with the minority bloc on the committee, he feels that his presence has brought greater attention and respect to Hispanic educational issues in an Anglo-dominated school system that is over 75 percent Hispanic and has 35 percent of its students in Transitional Bilingual Education programs.

Hispanics also have made progress in City Council elections. In 1993 José Santiago, a police officer in a neighboring community, but a long time resident of Lawrence, challenged for an open seat in District C. In a targeted campaign, Santiago defeated four other candidates in each of the five precincts gaining 479 votes (53.5 percent) in the primary. In the November runoff he gained 606 (60 percent) to easily win the seat as the first Hispanic City Councilor. District C has a very low registration and turnout rate compared with the other districts (see Table 3.1). In District D an African-American candidate defeated the incumbent by 1,149 votes to 697. Because the city Council is a larger body, the minority representatives have had less visible impact there. A larger representation was clearly needed to move beyond the powerless minority status.

Table 3.1.   Characteristics of Election Districts in Lawrence, 1993

District	Latino (%)	Voting Age (%)	Puerto Rican Born (%)	Foreign Born (%)	Registered to Vote (%)	5 Years in City (%)
A	33	70	4	5	45	78
B	55	69	6	8	42	75
C	74	62	9	10	27	67
D	42	66	4	5	45	78
E	15	76	1	2	61	87
F	28	69	3	3	51	81

Source: City of Lawrence (1993).

The purposely created Latino majority state legislative district illustrates the problems of extending empowerment to further levels. Although the district has a 53 percent Latino majority, the demographic distribution of age differences and citizenship reduces the figure to about 44 percent among registered adults. Voter turnout patterns could bring the figure to about one-third. Lacking a strong organization, a vital issue, or a dominant personality to mobilize the community, Latinos will have to count on a weak opposition or a candidate who can draw voters from the Anglo community. But will such a candidate be able to deliver to the Latino community? The cross-pressures of trying to represent this broader constituency and be the only Latino elected state representative since Nelson Merced (see chapter 2) would test that candidate's leadership qualities. Was there such a candidate in the district?

MUNICIPAL ELECTIONS IN 1995

The second half of 1995 was marked by the municipal election. The election process elicited some important gains, but came up short of the hoped for advances for the Latino community. In sum, no candidate, issue, or organization emerged that was sufficient to overcome in any dramatic way the shortcomings and problems already identified in the political life of Lawrence Hispanics.

The election season was tranquil. Early enthusiasm for voter registration (augmenting motor-voter procedures) and an unprecedented eight Latino candidates for the primaries led to high expectations. At the last minute the incumbent for the District B council seat (who was also a State Representative) chose not to run. District B is a majority Latino district and a strong candidate emerged in Julia Silverio, a respected businesswoman and long time resident of Lawrence. Despite being a last minute campaign, it was well financed and gained enthusiastic support. Three Latino candidates sought the at-large council seats (two repeat candidates and one newcomer); the two incumbents (Ralph Carrero, At-Large School Committee, and José Santiago, City Councilor from District C) ran again, while one newcomer challenged for the District D seat and another launched a write-in campaign for School Committee. This was the largest field yet with four veteran campaigners and four newcomers.

Unfortunately, the inexperience and previously mentioned difficulties began to take a toll. Voter registration efforts gained several hundred new voters, but were not sustained, and voter education lagged. The most visible early candidate Jeffrey Hernández, challenging the African-American incumbent in District D, learned the hard lesson about filing forms and meeting deadlines and had to run a "write-in" campaign. Jennifer López also ran a write-in campaign for School Committee due to the small field of candidates.

The primary election in early October produced some encouragement. A record six Latino candidates qualified for the final ballot: Carrero and López for the School Committee, newcomer Christopher Clark for an At-Large Council seat, Hernández for District D, Santiago for District C, and Silverio as the leader out of five candidates in District B. Only the two repeat, at-large council candidates (Daniel O'Neill and Marcos Devers) failed to advance. Not only was this a best ever effort, additional winners were a real possibility. The November results would be very disappointing by contrast.

In November Clark received 2,157 votes (from 28.5 percent of the voters) in his election effort. Although he lost by more than a thousand votes, it was a strong first effort. Hernández received one-third of the votes (407) in District D. José Santiago won easy reelection but failed to mount much of a campaign. He received 373 votes (71 percent), but the low turnout did not help at-large candidates, nor did it help mobilize or politicize the most heavily Latino district. Although Ralph Carrero also won reelection to the School Committee with 54.6 percent of the voters giving him one of their three votes, he too received fewer votes than he received in his previous victory. Jennifer López finished last out of four candidates for the three School Committee positions, after a third place finish in the primary signaled a likely seat gain. But she received 3,067 votes (40.5 percent)—a strong showing that saw her win in 5 of the 24 precincts.

In District B the outcome was the most disappointing. The well-financed, enthusiastic campaign of Julia Silverio went down to defeat by a vote of 746 to 600 (42 percent of the votes) (*The Eagle Tribune* November 8, 1995, 1). The major reason for the defeat was the anti-Latino reaction, especially from older voters in part of the district (she carried two of four precincts). The elderly housing projects had voted for the past not the future. It is widely believed that an anti-Latino "whisper campaign" propelled an unknown and poorly financed Anglo candidate to victory. This candidate was politically connected to local interests. But the political weakness of the Latino community had also contributed to the loss. Despite enthusiastic efforts, the mobilization of Latinos was insufficient to overcome the hostility of most Anglo voters in the district.

The rain-dampened turnout was lower than previous elections at 33 percent, even with a casino legalization measure on the ballot. Perhaps it hurt Latino candidates more than others, but turnouts were lower citywide. The hoped-for breakthrough in officeholders did not materialize. Some new and promising candidates did appear and ran credible, if losing races. However, Latinos failed to lay stronger groundwork and momentum to seek higher offices such as mayor or state representative or to achieve the desired breakthrough in political incorporation. Inadequate voter education, registration, and mobilization continued to weaken electoral efforts. Some community leaders hoped that the defeats and bitterness of the continued rejection of Hispanics might provide the needed motivation at long last for sustained and intensified electoral success.

BUILDING MOMENTUM

In 1997 School Committeeman Ralph Carrero launched a determined bid for the city's highest political office. This long anticipated step came at a time when the city had suffered several low points including continuing economic stagnation, the loss of accreditation for the high school, the highly contentious dismissal of the School Superintendent James Scully, continued tensions between the city's older and newer ethnic groups, and constant bickering between elected officials and the community as well as among the officials themselves. Carrero risked a great deal in a serious effort to unseat the incumbent mayor Marie Clare Kennedy, given Massachusetts political culture of "don't get mad, get even."

Carrero led a registration drive that claimed over 2,500 new Hispanic voters. The cumulative impact of easier "motor voter" procedures also meant that Latinos were more likely to register and to remain on the voting rolls than in the past. In this campaign, unlike his past ones, Carrero sought to emphasize ethnicity as a campaign issue and to mobilize what many Latino activists thought was a potential 10,000 Spanish speaking voters.

In part the ethnic identity strategy was viable due to the large field of eight candidates, which indicated that many others also sensed a vulnerable incumbent. The general election in November would include a large number of anti-incumbent voters making a second place strategy in the primary within reach for an ethnic strategy. Five other Latino candidates were also on the ballot contesting local offices, which would help to increase voter turnout across the city for Hispanic candidates.

Unfortunately for Mr. Carrero, who continues to be a strong vote-getter at the School Committee level, his record after several years in office was not sufficient to unify Latino voters. He had not emphasized ethnic positions sufficiently in the past to effectively campaign on that issue. Indeed, there were several candidates who appealed to the same Hispanic voters and the more progressive city voters, dividing the votes among themselves. In the end Carrero gained fewer votes than the number of people he claimed to have newly registered. The final election replayed the old dynamic of one conservative faction of the old guard backing the Republican Mayor and mainstream Democrats supporting eventual winner Patricia Dowling, a lawyer and party activist. For Hispanic voters there were several promising candidates in the primary, so votes were split among this contingent. Many activists gained valuable experience in the campaigns and Hispanic voters were actively sought by many candidates. Although finishing well back in the race, Carrero made a serious run for the office. He eventually supported Mayor Kennedy's unsuccessful reelection bid.

ELECTION 1998

The culmination of the efforts of Silverio and Carrero came in a surprising upset in the 1998 primary campaign for the Sixteenth Essex State Representative contest. The Sixteenth Representative District was widely perceived to have been created to give Latino voters an opportunity to gain representation or at least strongly influence the choice of representative. The redistricting effort was only one of many over the years by outside authorities to try to influence the local power structure. In this race City Councilor from District C, José Santiago, stunned incumbent Paul

Iannuccillo with a narrow victory in a closely contested effort. A recount of ballots left Santiago with a 50 vote victory (Suris 1998, 3, 6). Both the Essex County District Attorney's Office and the Secretary of State's Office monitored voting due to questions raised by the campaigns and city officials. No unusual occurrences were reported (Flemming 1998a, 1,5).

Santiago, who is of Puerto Rican parentage and was raised in Lawrence, was able to maintain the support of the Latino community. Santiago had broken with many others to support the challenge by Patricia Dowling against the former incumbent Mayor. Representing a district with over 70 percent Hispanic voters, he had developed over time a more confrontational posture toward the power structure and on behalf of the Hispanic community than had Carrero. This effort was assisted by the growing strength of Latino media, especially *Rumbo*, to bring attention to community issues that might not be kept in the public eye by outsiders. The community perception in this two-person contest precisely pitted the older power arrangements against the Latino community's hopes to restructure power in the city. Santiago was also perceived to have been targeted by the city's establishment for harassment, so he had some degree of community sympathy for his cause.

Finally, the victory must be credited to the usual hard work by the candidate and the campaign to get voters registered, to get them to the polls, and to provide assistance when necessary. In the case of Latino voters in Lawrence and elsewhere, transport to the polls and information about the complex ballot offices and issues can overcome the confusion and difficulties that hinder participation. Santiago's campaigns have always featured this extra effort. Even so, the outcome was a surprise to all. The defeated candidate attributed the outcome of a 50 vote defeat (after the recount) to demographic changes. Most especially, voting from the housing projects for the elderly was markedly changed for the first time. This was also the traditional stronghold of the incumbent. The change here was far more than the margin of victory. The incumbent did not seek an independent challenge in the general election, where there was no opposition to the Democratic Primary winner. The critical mass of Latino voter participation had finally produced a shift in power.

In the end several factors had contributed to this major statewide victory for Hispanic voters. Latino unity was a crucial factor that had been missing in other contests. The cumulative experiences of prior campaigns and registration and voter education efforts played important roles as well. The candidacies over the decade of the 1990s gained maturity and seriousness of purpose with the real possibility of victory now in nearly every case. The stronger candidates such as Santiago, Carrero, and Silverio were also able to draw non-Hispanic voters.

Santiago's victory was not as dramatic as the outcome might have been, because two other Latino candidates were also victorious in elections to the same chamber of the legislature. This marked the first time since 1991 that there was any elected Latino representation at the Commonwealth level. With three state representatives there was more attention to Hispanic issues in Massachusetts politics (Mooney 1998, B1, 5).

LEGAL CHALLENGES TO VOTING IN LAWRENCE

Just after the election victory by Santiago, the U.S. Justice Department, following citizens' complaints, filed suit against the City of Lawrence for violating the Voting Rights Act. Although the city had been negotiating with the U.S. Attorney's Office in Boston and had taken some steps to address the enumerated problem areas, not enough progress had been made to avoid the suit. Three specific areas were at the heart of the suit: districts and at-large seats may have been created or used to weaken voting power of the Hispanic population, not all election materials were provided in Spanish (required when a city has more than 5 percent of a given language group), and the city had failed to provide sufficient Hispanic poll workers and an environment conducive to voting for Hispanics. In the latter two areas some progress had been made, but there were complaints from the 1997 primary election, when some Spanish-speaking voters were unable to vote due to lack of materials and lack of assistance if not active interference (such as requiring identification and refusing to provide information or voting assistance). Other potential voters, by implication, were too discouraged to try (Dowdy 1998, B1).

As in other areas of city hiring, the progress at the Elections Office was slow and required confrontation to make more than token change. By the 1998 general election 53 out of 250 poll workers were Hispanic, despite the likely majority Hispanic population and an officially claimed one-third of registered voters being Hispanic (Flemming 1998b, 1; Rozemberg 1998, 1). In 1991 only about 12 percent of registered voters were Latino (Hart 1998, B4). The percentage has grown in recent years with the maturing of the population and easier procedures for registration efforts in the community. Still, many Latino voters expressed criticism at the way in which officials conducted business at election time including allowing campaign workers for Representative Iannuccillo to take part in the counting of ballots during the primary election and frequent challenges of Latino voters (*Rumbo* 1998, 2).

By September 1999 a deal had been struck between the city and the Justice Department. There was agreement on the issues of poll workers and new procedures for bilingual information provision, but not on the overhaul of the structure of the districts (*Boston Globe* 1999, B5). The hiring of several dozen new poll workers, according to Councilor Julia Silverio, made a huge difference among the city's Latino community. Latinos have felt intimidated by the political process in Lawrence. "It had a tremendous impact in giving the people the confidence that they could go into the poll and see a familiar face that they might not know but they could relate to" (Armano 2000, 29).

The 2000 census—showing that Latinos now make up 59.5 percent of the population in Lawrence—will provide the demographic basis for another challenge should the city not make adjustments appropriate to the new political reality. The politics of the city may speed up the process and break down the resistance of the older entrenched political forces. The next round of voting certainly marked a major turning point.

THE FINAL BREAKTHROUGH

The 1999 city elections marked the biggest breakthrough for the Hispanic community of Lawrence. A record 11 Latino candidates qualified for the general election. Ralph Carrero won reelection to the School Committee with the largest vote total among the five candidates. After the election he announced that he did not intend to run for another term. José Santiago missed by 19 votes in his bid to move up to Councilman at-large from his District C seat. He took his defeat as a message that he should concentrate on the Beacon Hill job as State Representative. Still he gathered 3,148 votes in a credible showing. Hispanic voters turned out in large numbers to produce a 36 percent turnout for the general election (Vogler 1999a, 1).

The big gains and changes, however, came in the City Council contests. Four incumbents either stepped down or were defeated, leaving the prospect of a more cooperative body that might work more harmoniously with the current mayor (Vogler 1999b, 15). Among the victors were previous candidates Julia Silverio and Marcos Devers. Mrs. Silverio once again challenged for the District B seat. Incumbent Pauline Brown was soundly defeated this time by 873 to 511 votes (Sangermano 1999, 16).

Strong unity behind the candidate and an effective campaign to gain non-Hispanic voter support reversed the result from 4 years earlier. The declining solidarity of the elderly vote also impacted the size of the margin in this contest. Ms. Brown received a hundred fewer votes in Precinct A than did Paul Iannuccillo a year earlier. A strong crossover vote was evident.

Another strong showing was made by Marcos Devers, finally winning in his fifth campaign for the council. Mr. Devers won an at-large seat with the second highest vote total. His victory and that of Mr. Carrero will make the legal arguments against at-large voting harder. Newcomer Nilka Álvarez easily gained the District C seat vacated by Mr. Santiago. Again the turnouts in this heavily Latino district are the smallest in the city—some half to a third as large as most districts. This small voter base hurts the at-large candidates.

Latino office holders in the city are balanced between Dominican and Puerto Rican origins as well as being balanced in terms of gender. This can only help future candidates to find ways to maintain community support and mobilize turnout of Latino voters. Local Latino organizations such as the Council of Dominican-American Voters and Latino Agenda helped register and educate voters and recruit and assist candidates. In addition to Mr. Santiago, six other Hispanic candidates made credible losing efforts. Candidates are continually making themselves available to run for office, and more activists are learning how to campaign effectively in district and citywide contests. The next mayor's race will provide an opportunity to test the political strength of the community.

There was one result of the 1999 election that reveals the old ethnic power structure's continued resistance to Latino political succession. A political novice, Nancy Kennedy, shocked the Latino community by winning the third and final seat on the Lawrence School Committee, largely through a word-of-mouth campaign. Although not officially on the October primary ballot for School Committee, Kennedy was able to run in the November election by running a "sticker" campaign in October. Kennedy persuaded 121 voters to choose her as a "write-in" candidate, fulfilling the 100 signature "write-in" requirement needed to move on to the November general election ballot. Kennedy polled a remarkable 4,376 votes to Edwin Estévez's 3,199 votes and José Balbuena's 2,986 votes (Armano 2000, 44).

CONCLUSION

The empowerment of the Latino community in Lawrence has involved a long and difficult road to achieve the current breakthrough. Despite large numbers in the overall population and 80 percent of the public school student body, several factors have hindered the incorporation of Latinos into the body politic in anything like the degree that the numbers would indicate.

Most important has been the resistance and exclusion by the existing ethnic forces who have dominated Lawrence politics in recent decades. Hispanics in Lawrence have faced avoidance, disrespect, and harassment at the hands of the city power structure. For many years the community failed to respond aggressively to this treatment. The so-called riots of 1986 and an occasional lawsuit constitute exceptions. The last minute "whisper campaign" that defeated Julia Silverio in 1995 may well have been the last straw of exclusion by the old forces. However, the buildup of resentment at this long suffered treatment has contributed to the recent political unity, legal challenges, and success at the polls.

A second factor is the demographic one that follows well-established patterns exclusive of ethnicity. The older population of Lawrence is dominated by the older ethnicities of Irish, Italian, and French-Canadian origin. This group votes in very high percentages and provides a core of local strength for the established factions in Lawrence. By contrast, Hispanics as a population are very young, and like that age group everywhere, its electoral turnout percentage is the lowest of any age group. These trends are slowly changing as the Hispanic population matures and becomes more permanent in the city and the established elderly sectors decline in numbers.

A further factor complicating participation is the division in the community between Puerto Ricans, who have automatic voting rights, and the larger Dominican origin population, many of whom are not citizens and cannot vote. As the Dominican community matures and converts to U.S. citizenship, its strength increases. The Dominican Republic has made it easier in the late 1990s to hold dual citizenship, while fears of the Republican Congress' changes in public assistance programs at the national level also spurs citizenship applications among Dominicans. The high poverty and low average educational attainment of Latinos also are associated with low voting rates in all populations. These population characteristics change slowly over time and continue to erode the status quo.

Additionally, the Latino community had been divided among itself, with divisions between Puerto Ricans and Dominicans as well as intense jealousy within the ranks of potential leaders. Common problems and perceptions have forged better political unity in recent years. Inclusive candidacies and multiple candidates encourage greater participation and cross-over support between the two dominant groups. By the late 1990s there were enough elected Latinos to neutralize much of the jealousy among candidates, but unity cannot automatically be assumed as Ralph Carrero discovered in his mayoral campaign.

Latino organizations and media also contributed to the success of unity, again marking a maturity in the community and stronger commitment by individuals who now see signs of success to keep them at their tasks. The newspaper *Rumbo* has survived for three critical years and candidates such as Ralph Carrero, José Santiago, Marcos Devers, and Julia Silverio became "shining stars" rather than "shooting stars" in bringing success in the electoral arena by also drawing non-Hispanic voters to their cause.

Finally, there have been external influences that have played a part in the changes in Lawrence. One could cite the post-1986 funding from the Commonwealth to support programs in Lawrence, the legislative redistricting, external Hispanic influences at the state and national level, and the U.S. Justice Department's role in hiring requirements and election changes. The last, together with the State Board of Education and accreditation problems at the High School, were major challenges to the way local officials were conducting public business.

In the final analysis the Hispanic community has now broken through the barriers to political incorporation. They have used a combination of the electoral and confrontational strategies with more weight on the electoral side. Lawrence has now entered the phase where the future belongs to the

Latino population (Stevenson 1991). The hard task of governing effectively is now close at hand. Whether the political incorporation of Latinos in Lawrence is a smooth, peaceful one will depend on changes in the attitudes and practices of the existing ethnic establishment and on the ability of the heretofore fragmented Hispanic community to develop the appropriate unity, institutions, and political maturity to capture and wield political power. The alternative is an increasingly resented and untenable domination by the white minority.

NOTES

1.   I have chosen to use Hispanic and Latino interchangeably in this chapter because the census and much of the literature use Hispanic and some members of the Lawrence community prefer it. However, this terminology is more controversial in Boston and other parts of the United States

2.   The United Way survey listed "Difficulty with English" as the fifth most serious barrier to service among Lawrence respondents with 43 percent reporting such difficulty in their household (United Way 1992, "Needs": 74). The census identifies 3,214 Spanish-speaking households as being "linguistically isolated" (Census 1990 p5/P29). English facility causes differential access and opportunities within families and among age and country cohorts. Like citizenship, language can exacerbate rivalries and status differences between those in the country of origin and those in Lawrence. Even in families, authority hierarchies may be undermined when the children must translate for elders. These problems may also weaken confidence and undermine interest and leadership in the community.

3.   For an excellent overview of Dominican migration history see the article by Christopher Mitchell (1992). He summarizes the scholarly estimates of undocumented Dominicans as totaling 70,000–120,000 (121) on the U.S. mainland and 40,400 in Puerto Rico in 1988 (95). See, also, Chapter 12 in this volume.

4.   Compare Lawrence with the active, multiracial church mobilization challenging the power structure in Lynn, Massachusetts examined by *Boston Globe* reporter Don Aucoin (1995) in "Preaching a New Politics: Churches Are at the Forefront of a Grassroots Organizing Campaign in Lynn." For a discussion of the relationship between the Catholic Church and Lowell's latino community, see Chapter 5 in this volume.

5.   In both elections voters were to choose three candidates for three positions. In the final election more than 17 percent of the ballot options were left blank. Carrero received 15.5 percent of all the ballot options, calculated from city election figures (mimeo copies courtesy of the election department).

REFERENCES

Armano, M. J. D., II. (2000). "Hispanic Political Succession in Lawrence, MA."
        Senior Thesis, Spring, Political Science Department, University of
        Massachusetts Lowell.

Aucoin, Don. (1995). "Preaching a New Politics: Churches Are at the Forefront of a Grassroots Organizing Campaign in Lynn." *Boston Globe,* 26 June, 1.

Bain, A. S. (1986). "Lawrence: City in Transition." *Studies in Politics and Government.* Suffolk University, Boston.

Barnes, J. (1990). "Minority Mapmaking." *National Journal,* 14 (April 7): 837–839.

Boston Globe. (1998). "MCAS District Rankings." 10 December, Section B.

———. (1999). "Latino Voting Rights Agreement is Signed." 11 September, B5.

Browning, Rufus, Dale Rogers Marshall, and David Tabb. (1990). *Racial Politics in American Cities.* New York: Longman.

Camayd-Freixas, Yohel, et al. (1985). "Hispanics in Lawrence: A Demographic Report." The Lawrence Area Department of Social Services.

Castillo, José del, and Christopher Mitchel [sic], eds. (1987). *La Inmigración Dominicana en los Estados Unidos.* Santo Domingo: Universidad APEC, Editorial CENAPEC.

Charter and Administrative Code for the City of Lawrence. (1983).

Chronicle of Higher Education. (1990). 11 April, A1.

City of Lawrence. (1993). "Profile of Lawrence." [mimeo].

Clausen, L. B., and J. A. Alomar. (1988). "City of Lawrence Educational Needs Analysis: A Demographic and Socioeconomic Context for Educational Reform." Board of Regents of Higher Education. Commonwealth of Massachusetts.

Dowdy, Zachary. (1998). "Lawrence Hit with U.S. Suit on Voter Rights." *Boston Globe,* 6 November, B1.

Duran, J. D. (1985). "The 1984 Riots: Lawrence, Massachusetts." Masters Thesis in Urban Planning, Massachusetts Institute of Technology.

Exter, T. G. (1985). "Focus on Hispanics." *American Demographics* 7(August), 29–33.

Flemming, Paul, Jr. (1998a). "Santiago Stuns Incumbent, Iannuccillo Mulls Recount." *The Eagle Tribune,* 16 (September), 1, 5.

———. (1998b). "Lawrence Voting under Fire." *The Eagle Tribune,* 6 November, 1.

Hardy-Fanta, Carol. (1993). *Latina Politics, Latino Politics: Gender, Culture, and Political Participation in Boston.* Philadelphia: Temple University Press.

Hart, Jordana. (1998). "Lawrence Vote Process Defended" *Boston Globe,* 7 November, B4.

Melendez, Isabel. (1992). Interview with author, 22 September.

Mitchell, Christopher. (1992). "U.S. Foreign Policy and Dominican Immigration to the United States." In *Western Hemisphere Immigration and United States Foreign Policy,* edited by Christopher Mitchell. University Park, PA: Pennsylvania State University Press.

Mooney, Brian C. (1998). "For Latinos, a Breakthrough," *Boston Globe,* 14 November, B1, 5.

Office of Planning and Community Development. (1994). "Application for Lawrence/Methuen Enterprise Zone." City of Lawrence.

Osterman, Paul. (1993). "Latinos in the Midst of Poverty." In *Latinos in Boston: Confronting Poverty, Building Community,* by Miren Uriarte, Paul Osterman, Carol Hardy-Fanta, and Edwin Melendez. Boston: The Boston Foundation.

Phillips Andover Academy. (1986). "Growing up Hispanic in Lawrence, Massachusetts." The Urban Studies Institute.

Rivera, Ralph. (1991). *Latinos in Massachusetts and the 1990 U.S. Census: Growth and Geographical Distribution.* Boston: Mauricio Gastón Institute for Latino Community Development and Public Policy, University of Massachusetts Boston.

Rivera-Batiz, F. (1989). "The Characteristics of Puerto Rican Migrants." *Migration World* XVII (2).

Rozemberg, Hernán. (1998). "Latinos Praise Federal Suit." *The Eagle Tribune,* 6 November, 1.

Rumbo. (1998). "Editorial." 1 November, 2.

Sangermano, Fran. (1999). "Lawrence Final Election Results—Precinct by Precinct." *The Eagle Tribune,* 3 November, 16.

Sennott, Charles M. (1994). "Dominican Groups Take a Tight Hold of Drug Trade on Streets of N.E. Towns." *Boston Globe,* 14 February, B1.

Stevenson, Kim. (1991). *Hispanic and Minority Owned Businesses in Lawrence: A Market Study of Essex Street and Downtown.* Lawrence, Massachusetts (October).

Suris, Alberto. (1998). "*Gana Elecciones José Santiago*" and "*Resultado del Recuento.*" *Rumbo,* 1 October, 3, 6

United Way of the Merrimack Valley. (1992). "A Report on the Needs Assessment of the 8 Geographic Regions," "Environmental Scan." *Compass* (December).

Uriarte, Miren. (1993). "Contra Viento y Marea (Against all Odds): Latinos Build Community in Boston." In *Latinos in Boston: Confronting Poverty, Building Community,* by Miren Uriarte, Paul Osterman, Carol Hardy-Fanta, and Edwin Meléndez. Boston: The Boston Foundation.

U.S. Census. (1991). "1990 U.S. Census." Mimeograph provided by Lawrence Economic Development Office. Prepared by MISER at University of Massachusetts Amherst.

Vogler, Mark E. (1999a). "Vote at a Glance," "Clean Sweep." *The Eagle Tribune,* 3 November, 1.

———. (1999b). "Four Veteran Councilors Ousted." *The Eagle Tribune,* 3 November, 15.

Youssef, Nadia H. (1994). *The Demographics of Immigration: A Socio-Demographic Profile of the Foreign-Born Population in New York State.* New York: Center for Migration Studies.

Zaiter, J. (1983). "Greater Lawrence Hispanic Community: Past–present–future." Chamber Action. Greater Lawrence Chamber of Commerce (December), 1–4.

Other data sources include Department of Employment and Training. "Monthly Summary of Employment Trends, Northeastern Massachusetts," prepared by Bernard Burns, Boston Commonwealth of Massachusetts and Department of Employment and Training; "Labor Market Information for Affirmative Action Planning: Lawrence-Haverhill MA-NH PMSA"; Lawrence Election Office, detailed election results for various municipal elections 1989–1993 (courtesy of office personnel).

CHAPTER 4

Strategic Planning in the Community and the Courts
Holyoke

CAROL HARDY-FANTA, WITH ROSALBA BASSOLS-MARTÍNEZ

The City of Holyoke is located in the Western part of Massachusetts just north of Springfield between the mountains of Western Massachusetts and the Connecticut River. Holyoke was primarily a farming community until the mid-nineteenth century. Situated on the Hadley Falls, where the river drops almost 60 feet, "Holyoke became a prime location for the textile and paper mills that transformed this rural backwater into a hub of New England's industrial economy."[1]

The mills that rose up along the waterways of Holyoke in the 1850s offered jobs for both skilled and nonskilled laborers. The people who arrived to work in the mills included Irish, French-Canadian, and German immigrants; they were joined by Polish and Italian immigrants later in the century. The immigrants settled, for the most part, in what are now Wards 1 and 2, known as "The Flats," and South Holyoke (see Map 4.1). Although with the passage of time, many immigrants prospered and gave rise to some of today's prominent families of Holyoke, life in the tenements during this period of history was often grim. Crowded and inadequate dwellings, long workdays, unsanitary conditions, and high death rates characterized the immigrant experience.

LATINOS IN HOLYOKE: DEMOGRAPHIC TRENDS

The second wave of immigration for Holyoke began in the 1970s. Western Massachusetts was, at that time, a significant agricultural center and rural Puerto Ricans experienced in tobacco farming were encouraged to migrate to Western Massachusetts to pick tobacco and other crops. Disillusioned with the low pay and harsh conditions of farm labor, these Puerto Ricans began moving to Holyoke to work in the paper and textile industries. The workers brought their families and, given their relative success in the area, other Puerto Ricans moved from New York City and Hartford, Connecticut, to settle in Holyoke.

Unfortunately, by the time the Puerto Ricans arrived, the paper and textile industries in Massachusetts and other parts of New England were in decline. The skilled and unskilled jobs earlier waves of immigrants found began to disappear. Latinos in Holyoke now face a cluster of economic, social, and political barriers to prosperity that, in many ways, resembles the poverty and social dislocation faced by earlier generations of immigrants.

At present time, Latinos make up 41.4 percent of the total population in the city of Holyoke (U.S. Bureau of the Census 2001). Between 1980 and 1990, the population more than doubled (120 percent); the rate of growth has decreased recently, only 21.5 percent between 1990 and 2000. The African-American community is quite small (only 2.6 percent) and Asians make up less than 1 percent of the population.

The Latino population in Holyoke, in contrast to cities in Massachusetts such as Boston, Chelsea, and Lawrence, continues to be heavily Puerto Rican; 93.4 percent of the population in 1990 was Puerto Rican in origin (Cruz 1995, 212). In 1990, the census counted only 84 Mexican-origin people (0.6 percent), 60 Cubans (0.4 percent), and 742 (5.5 percent) "other Latino," generally including individuals from Central and South America.[2]

As discussed in the Introduction, Latinos in the United States are a relatively young population compared to other groups, especially non-Latino whites. Whereas, in 1990, 34 percent of Latinos in Massachusetts were less than 16 years of age, almost half (46 percent) of Latinos in Holyoke were less than 16 years of age (Gastón Institute 1992).

The economic status of Latinos in Holyoke is extremely low on most measures. The Latino poverty rate in Holyoke is higher than that in the state as a whole. In 1990, for example, 59.1 percent of Latinos in Holyoke had income below the poverty level compared to 36.7 percent in the state. In addition, the Latino poverty rate was highest in Holyoke compared to other cities in Massachusetts with large Latino populations. The unemployment rate for Latinos is more than two and a half times that of non-Latino whites. Ninety-five percent of Holyoke's Latino households are renters compared to about one-half of non-Hispanic white families (Vecinos 1995, 14).

Educational attainment is considerably lower for Latinos in Holyoke compared to Latinos in the state as a whole. As of 1990, about a third (33.5 percent) of Latinos attained less than a ninth grade education compared to only 11 percent of the white population (Vecinos 1995, 16). Sixty percent of Latinos in Holyoke (25 years and older) have less than a twelfth-grade education compared to 48 percent of Latinos in the state.

Dramatic shifts in the school population coincided with rising Latino population in the city: whereas in 1980, about 29 percent of the student population was Latino, this percentage had increased to 78 percent by the 1993-1994 school year (Vecinos 1995, 14–15). This dramatic change was not due solely to Latino population increase. The school system in Holyoke responded to the increase in Latino population in a predictably unwelcoming fashion, given the civil rights history in the state (see, for example, Dentler and Scott 1981); the non-Latino white students left the system in droves to attend parochial and other private schools.

Residential housing patterns are quite distinctive in Holyoke. In 1990 there were two neighbirhoods in the city that were over 50 percent Latino—"The Flats" and "Downtown"—and a number of other areas located nearby that were between 20 and 29 percent Latino: South Holyoke, Churchill, and Springdale. As can be seen in the following map using data from the 2000 Census, Latinos have substantially increased their presence in these and other neighborhoods. (Community estimates suggest that all of these areas are at least 50 percent Latino.[3]) On the other hand, there are broad expanses of the city that are virtually free of a Latino presence. In fact, prior research suggests that the majorityof non-Latinos live in precincts that are 90 percent or more composed of whites (Vecinos 1995, 22).

DEMOGRAPHICS AND POLITICAL PARTICIPATION

A multitude of research studies document the negative correlation between certain demographic characteristics and political participation for Latinos: lack of citizenship, youth of the population, poverty, and low educational levels. (For a discussion, see Pachon and DeSipio 1992, and the chapters in this volume.) Because of the high percentage of Puerto Ricans in the Latino population, citizenship rates are quite high in Holyoke compared to other Massachusetts cities such as Lawrence, Boston, and Chelsea; estimates suggest that 95.7 percent of Latinos in Holyoke are citizens (Racusen 1995, 171). Despite the high level of citizenship among Latinos in Holyoke (which would argue for higher levels of political participation), the overall voting-age population is considerably smaller than non-Latino whites due to the younger age of the population. Estimates of the voting-age population in Holyoke range, for example, from 21.9 percent for Latinos (compared to 74.9 percent for non-Latino whites) in 1980 (Vecinos 1995, 18) to only 18.7 percent for Latinos in 1990 (Racusen 1995, 171). The poverty and low levels of education discussed above certainly contribute to the suppression of political participation. Latino voter turnout in Holyoke ranges from percentages indistinguishable from zero in some years to a high of 22.8 percent in 1985.[4]

The electoral system in Holyoke is nonpartisan in municipal elections; candidates can run at-large or from their district. The city holds a preliminary election in October and then a general election in November on odd-numbered years for Alderman (changed to City Council in 1992) and School Committee. Currently, seven City Council seats are voted by wards

Map 4.1   Latino Population in Holyoke (2000), by Census Block Group,
               with Neighborhoods

Percentage Latino

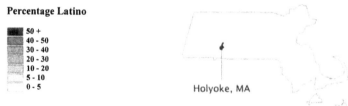

50 +
40 - 50
30 - 40
20 - 30
10 - 20
5 - 10
0 - 5

Holyoke, MA

Source: 2000 Census, P.L. 94-171

and eight at-large (López 2000). The School Committee has seven seats elected by wards and two at-large.

ELECTORAL EFFORTS IN HOLYOKE: 1973–1995

One of the strengths of the Latino community in Holyoke has been its long-standing determination to achieve political representation. Whereas Latinos in other cities such as Chelsea did not begin running for office until the mid- to late-1980s, a Latino has run in Holyoke virtually every year since Carlos Vega ran for School Committee at-large in 1971.[5] At the same time, for several decades, the community's efforts often seemed to be for naught. Until 1995 only three Latino candidates were elected and held office in Holyoke. Furthermore, Latino electoral success has occurred exclusively in district-level elections and, until 1999, in only one of the two "Latino" wards—Ward 2, which encompasses the Flats.[6]

Holyoke, nevertheless, has one of the highest rates of Latino candidates and campaigns as a portion of the Latino population, testimony to a conscious decision by Latino leaders and community organizations to try to have a Latino running in every election. Between 1971 and 1995, a total of 15 candidates ran in 27 campaigns.[7] (A complete list of candidates and campaigns is provided in Table 4.1.) Eighteen (69 percent) of the campaigns were for district-level seats and eight (31 percent) were at-large. Twelve (80 percent) of the candidates were men and three (20 percent) were women. It is noteworthy that Latino candidates have run in Holyoke have run exclusively for municipal seats (City Council and School Committee), in contrast to neighboring Springfield where 5 of the 14 races (36 percent) have been for the State Legislature. (It should be remembered that Springfield, in contrast to Holyoke, has an election system with all at-large races, a fact that discourages running for municipal-level offices in favor of state-level offices.)

Early efforts in the 1970s set the stage for later elections and reflected more of a desire to highlight the presence of Latinos in the city than a belief that election was likely. Carlos Vega ran for School Committee from Ward 2 in 1971 but lost as did Heriberto Flores when he ran for Alderman at large in 1973. Flores's campaign, according to news reports at the time, focused on the need to improve the schools, develop industry and housing within the city, and combat the decay of the central city. He came in eleventh in a field of 13 candidates in the final election with 3,085 votes.[8] Carlos Vega ran again for School Committee from Ward 2 in 1975. Vega, who was born in Ecuador but who had lived in Holyoke for almost 20 years, had been active in Holyoke youth and other community programs. Running against the incumbent, Norman Gladu, in both elections, Vega lost. The write-in campaign of Felix Manarca in 1979 was a response to the feeling "that somebody should run"[9] but there was not an expectation that Manarca would win. Indeed, Manarca lost by 174 to 892 votes. Even

Table 4.1   Latino Candidates and Campaigns in Holyoke, 1971–1995

Year	Candidate	Office	District/At-Large
1971	Carlos Vega	School	District Ward 2
1973	Heriberto Flores	Alderman	At-large
1975	Carlos Vega	School	District Ward 2
1979	Felix Manarca	Alderman	District Ward 1
1981	Alberto Cruz	Alderman	District Ward 2
1983	Juan Cruz	Alderman	At-large
1983	Joe Gómez	Alderman	At-large
1983	Gilberto Sotolongo[a]	Alderman	At-large
1985	Betty Medina Lichtenstein[b]	School	District Ward 2
1985	Albert Cruz	Alderman	District Ward 2
1987	Betty Medina Lichtensteinb	School	District Ward 2
1987	Orlando Isaza	Alderman	At-large
1987	Juan Cruz	Alderman	District Ward 2
1989	Betty Medina Lichenstein[b]	School	District Ward 2
1989	Carlos Vega[a]	School	District Ward 7
1989	Diosdado López[b]	Alderman	District Ward 2
1989	Lilian Santiago García	School	District Ward 1
1991	Harry Rodríguez Ortiz	City	At-large
1991	Diosdado López	City	District Ward 2
1991	Betty Medina Lichtenstein[b]	School	District Ward 2
1993	Ruth Cruzb	School	District Ward 2
1993	Diosdado López[b]	City	District Ward 2
1993	Harry Rodríguez Ortiz	City	At-large
1995	Diosdado Lópezb	City	District Ward 2
1995	Alejandro Sánchez	City	At-large
1995	Harry Rodríguez Ortiz	City	District Ward 4
1995	George Cruz [b,c]	City	District Ward 1

a Ran in preliminary election only
b Elected
c Did not take office.

Vega ran more to assert a Latino presence than with an expectation of winning; speaking about his 1971 and 1975 campaigns, he was quoted in a 1981 news article: "I really didn't think I was going to win."[10] Clearly evident in the history of Latino politics in Holyoke is the strategy of increasing the visibility of Latinos as candidates and as voters. Holyoke stands out as the city in Massachusetts where—from the early days of a Latino presence—there was this sense of an explicitly political strategy:

> I think it was because some of us who ran early and often . . . saw registering and voting and becoming a part of the political system, the process, as an important mechanism for empowerment, not the only one, because simultaneously a whole lot of other stuff was going on too: housing organizing and neighborhood organizing and other kinds of [organizing] but part of that strategy of empowerment was registering people to vote and then getting people out to vote. (Vega 1996)

Part of that "strategy of empowerment" was recruiting a Latino candidate and encouraging Latinos to vote. Vega goes on to discuss how important consistently running candidates and encouraging Latino voters was:

> It's very difficult to be consistent and it's very difficult sometimes to find the resources to do it, but I think that being consistent, either registering people to vote, getting people to run for office, getting people out to vote, propagandizing what the issues are, all that kind of stuff gradually helps, and we're still not in any way, shape or form, really where we should be in terms of representation of the Latino community on the City Council . . . but I think that consistency helps in bringing about legitimacy to what you're doing, and both legitimacy from the community point of view but also from the "powers that be." (Vega 1996)

During the 1980s, there was a surge in election campaigns by Latinos in Holyoke: 9 candidates ran in 13 campaigns. Despite the relatively high number of campaigns during this decade, only one Latino/a candidate— Betty Medina Lichtenstein—was elected; she won a seat on the Holyoke School Committee in 1985 and was reelected in 1987, 1989, and 1991. Two of the candidates were relatively weak: Alberto Cruz (who ran for Alderman from Ward 2 in 1981) and Joe Gómez (who ran for alderman at-large in 1983). Alberto Cruz "suffered a crushing defeat" in 1981 receiving only 56 votes compared to 222 for William M. Sullivan and 187 for incumbent Arthur J. Beaulieu (*Holyoke Transcript-Telegram* 1981). According to Latino community leaders, Cruz had not campaigned vigorously, had not sought endorsements from Latino community groups, and had "skirted such controversial issues" as the dilapidated housing and arson in his own precinct.[11]

In the 1983 elections, both Juan Cruz and Joe Gómez ran for Alderman at-large but Joe Gómez, in particular, was only minimally connected to the Latino community and did not appeal for Latino votes. Running, in essence, against each other was a low point for Latino strategic planning. He and Juan Cruz, "ranked, respectively, first and third among Hispanic voters."

White-bloc voting also hindered the ability of Latinos to be elected outside of Latino majority districts during the 1983 election. There was, for example, a high degree of bullet voting, especially for Cruz and Gómez. By contrast, non-Latino "white voters ranked Juan Cruz fifteenth and José Gómez sixteenth. . . . In this election, Hispanic voters exhibited a clear pattern of cohesion behind minority candidates; whites voted *en masse* against them."[12] Even the news media were open about the difficulty a Latino would have attracting white votes. One "political insider" said: "I don't know how many Caucasians are ready to vote for (minority) candidates" (Werth 1983). Low voter turnout among Latinos was another factor contributing to their loss, however. Turnout was only "301 votes for Cruz and 230 for Gómez out of a total city-wide Hispanic voting age population of 2,835" (Vecinos 1995, 23).

In the 1985 municipal election, there were no at-large Latino candidates. Betty Medina Lichtenstein ran in her district and won election to the school committee against Elaine Pluta. Medina Lichtenstein won in large part because of strong support from Latino voters and the ability to overcome white-bloc voting in the non-Latino precinct in Ward 2. Latino support was not automatically given to any Latino candidate, however, in the 1985 election: Juan Cruz was defeated in his bid for Ward 2 Alderman. "There was no minority cohesion with respect to Cruz's candidacy" (Vecinos 1995, 24). Even though Latinos did not automatically give their support to all Latino candidates, the presence of Medina Lichtenstein and Cruz on the ballot demonstrates the impact of Latinos running on Latino voter participation: the voting rate for that election was 22.8 percent, the highest of any year thus far.

Medina Lichtenstein easily won reelection in 1987. The bigger challenge faced Orlando Isaza's at-large campaign for Alderman. Isaza received the endorsement from two major newspapers and widespread public support from influential non-Latino community leaders as well as the Latino community. When the votes were counted, Isaza came in first among Latino voters. Bullet voting by Latinos was high and he received 48.5 percent of the Latino votes cast. In contrast, he received only 4.7 percent of non-Latino white votes, ranking eleventh in a field of 14 candidates. Election analysis suggests that "despite excellent credentials and serious outreach efforts, Isaza's campaign was unable to translate this support into a sufficient number of votes from non-Hispanic white voters in Holyoke to win the election" (Vecinos 1995, 25–26).

Juan Cruz also ran again for Alderman in 1987 from Ward 2 but he lost to the incumbent 42 percent to 58 percent. Analysis of election results suggests that there was not the same degree of cohesion behind his campaign within the Latino community as there was for Orlando Isaza. Cruz did win in the heavily Latino precincts but by only four votes in Precinct B and 31 votes in Precinct C. White-bloc voting was still evident in Precinct A, however, where he lost by 127 to 315 votes.

Cumulative wisdom among Latino leaders and candidates against the likelihood of winning at large seemed to prevail in the 1989 election: no Latino candidates ran at large that year. Diosdado López ran in Ward 2 for Alderman but was defeated by Elaine Pluta (a non-Latino who had lost to Betty Medina Lichtenstein in the 1985 School Committee race).[13] During a recent study of Latino candidates (Hardy-Fanta 1997), López explained that part of the reason for his loss in 1989 was that he started campaigning late—a situation he was quick to remedy when he ran again (and won) in 1991. Also in 1989, Betty Medina Lichtenstein ran unopposed and data support the conclusion that she received overwhelming support from Latino voters.[14] Lillian Santiago García, a newcomer to Holyoke, was defeated by the non-Latino incumbent in the Ward 1 race for School Committee.

The 1989 election season marks the emergence of the strategic planning evidenced among the Latino leadership in Holyoke. Latino leaders carefully examined the various races and determined that there might be an opportunity for Latinos to expand beyond Wards 1 and 2, especially in Ward 7. An open seat (i.e., no incumbent was running) combined with the potential to appeal to the more liberal voters of Ward 7 seemed to offer an opening for a Latino candidate outside of the Latino strongholds of Wards 1 and 2. Latino community activists had analyzed past voting trends in Ward 7 and found that "when you look at the breakdown, Ward 7 always gave a good number of votes to Latinos. . . . They were more inclined to go with the minority Latino candidate than the other wards, Wards 3, 4, 5, and 6" (Vega 1996).

Carlos Vega agreed to run in Ward 7. Much to their dismay, however, once Vega announced he was running, "Sue Clayton announced *she* was running, and it struck me as somewhat counterproductive." When asked if he felt her announcement was a conscious attempt to block a Latino candidate, Vega answered: "Yes, because I think there were some people who said, 'We'd rather have somebody else that we would feel safer with,' and so I think, in some ways, that may have propelled her response to jump into the race." Vega then lost in the preliminary election, gaining only 165 (16 percent) out of 1,008 votes cast.[15] Susan Clayton won in the general election but stayed in office only one term.

In 1991, Diosdado López won election in Ward 2 to become the first Latino Alderman in Holyoke. Although López did win a slight majority of votes in Precinct A (which was only 41 percent Latino), he won over-whelming support in the Latino-majority precincts: 76 percent in precinct B (75 percent Latino). Medina Lichtenstein again ran unopposed for School Committee. Harry Rodríguez Ortiz ran at-large for City Council against Elaine Pluta; Pluta ranked first among Latinos (53 percent to Ortiz's 34 percent). Analysis of this race suggests that "Pluta would have won even if Hispanics had completely withdrawn their support, simply based on her non-Hispanic votes. . . . Rodríguez Ortiz, though he ranked [relatively] high among the Hispanics who did vote, did not inspire sub-stantial turnout and, apparently because of his conservative political stance, was not favored by many Hispanics" (Vecinos 1995, 29). The con-sensus among Latino leaders in Holyoke is that Ortiz generally runs low-profile campaigns that do not draw people together.[16]

In 1992, in part to stave off a court decision, Holyoke changed the struc-ture of its city elections, including moving from a Board of Aldermen to City Council. Despite his loss in 1993, Harry Ortiz ran again for an at-large City Council seat. He lost again even though he ranked first among the Latino voters; remarkable in this election was the extremely low turnout among Latinos: only 2 percent of the Latino voting-age popula-tion. More encouraging—and perhaps a partial explanation for the low Latino turnout—is that the other two Latino candidates were running unopposed: Diosdado López for the City Council from Ward 2 and Ruth Cruz, who was running for the seat vacated by Betty Medina Lichtenstein when she retired for personal reasons after four terms on the School Committee. With Medina Lichtenstein's clear support, Ruth Cruz won without a contest. Medina Lichtenstein recalls: "She had a good group of people, really an exciting group of people on her campaign. Ruthie ran unopposed. . . . Ruthie was the President of the Bilingual PAC. . . . She already had a following. She already had some recognition with the Latino parents. She was also very creative. Ruthie's mind is incredible. She's a very brilliant woman, and we said, 'It would make sense for Ruthie to take this over.' People up there knew her; everybody loved her, so it would only make sense" (Medina Lichtenstein 1996). For a brief time, it seemed that Latinos finally had a clear path to consistent political representation, at least in Ward 2, and were beginning to make inroads in Ward 1.

Despite all the strategic planning behind Ruth Cruz's election, however, the strengths or weaknesses of the candidate ultimately determine the out-come: within a short period Ruth Cruz had to withdraw from office under a cloud of scandal not long after the election. Medina Lichtenstein moved back into her old spot on the School Committee and held office until Yvonne García was elected to the Ward 2 spot in 1995. (García is not Latina but rather a French Canadian; her husband is Puerto Rican.)

The 1995 elections were, in some ways, a step forward and, in other ways, a step back. A large number of Latinos ran for City Council:

Diosdado López from Ward 2, George Cruz from Ward 1, Harry Ortiz from Ward 4, and Alejandro (Alex) Sánchez at large. Diosdado López again faced no opposition and was elected into office. George Cruz also won his election against James McDermott, 429 to 341 votes. For the first time it looked as though Latinos would have two representatives on the City Council. And although no Latino ran for School Committee, Yvonne García ran unopposed in Ward 2 and received strong Latino support across the ward. As will be discussed below, the sense of progress with George Cruz's election was short lived. Conflict of interest rules prevented him from taking office since he already held a position in city government.

BARRIERS TO LATINO POLITICAL REPRESENTATION IN HOLYOKE

One advantage Latinos face in Holyoke, compared to cities such as Springfield (see next chapter), is that district-level elections with Latino-majority districts do permit a modicum of electoral success within those districts at least. Latinos have been elected to both the School Committee and the City Council in Holyoke from Wards 1 and 2 (The Flats). There seem to be a number of barriers, however, to achieving adequate level of political representation and influence: (1) white-bloc voting, (2) low voting among Latinos due, to at least in part, to the youth of the population, (3) procedures used in the city census, and (4) divisions within the Latino community, and (5) in a few cases relatively weak candidates.

In Holyoke there is ample evidence of white-bloc voting in the at-large elections and no Latino candidate has won an at-large election. White-bloc voting has been visible in Holyoke's ward-level elections as well. In 1985, for example, Latino voter turnout was at an all-time high: 22.8 percent of Latino voting age population (Vecinos 1995, 24). In Ward 2, Betty Medina Lichtenstein was running against Elaine Pluta for School Committee. In Precinct 2A of Ward 2 (with a 10 percent Latino voting age population), Medina Lichtenstein ran second behind Pluta, receiving 30 percent of the votes cast. In the Latino precincts, 2B (80 percent Latino) and 2C (77 percent Latino), Medina Lichtenstein received 80 percent and 66 percent of the vote, respectively. The total number of votes cast for Medina Lichtenstein was 563 compared to 459 for Pluta. It was clear that Latino political cohesion helped elect Medina Lichtenstein—and that there was significant white-bloc voting. Latino candidates are often split between the need to appeal to non-Latino voters. However, when they do, white-bloc voting against them seems to prevail *and* the attention given to the non-Latino wards seems to suppress Latino voting rates.

Low voter turnout in Latino neighborhoods is a problem for Latino candidates in Holyoke, as was discussed earlier. An examination of the voting data shows, however, that *given a reason to vote*, Latinos turn out in higher numbers. Peak Latino voter turnout in Holyoke coincided, for example, with the first 2 campaigns of Medina Lichtenstein for School Committee (22.8 percent and 19.3 percent), the year Massachusetts Governor, Michael Dukakis ran for president (13.3 percent), and the presidential campaign of 1992 (8.1 percent) (Perlmutter 1996). High turnout helped elect the first Latino to office in Holyoke and seemed to stimulate high turnout the following year. As will be discussed below, these years were also marked by vigorous efforts within the community to register Latino voters.

Holyoke is distinguished by more than residential segregation and low Latino voter participation, however. One of the major barriers to Latino voter participation faced by Latinos in Holyoke and across the state is the relationship between the annual city census and voter registration—a barrier mentioned later in Gómez's chapter on Worcester. Theoretically, a city uses data from the annual census to verify that a person listed as a voter continues to reside in the city, and, in the case of district elections, in the same district in which he or she is registered. Chapter 51, Section 4 of the General Laws of the Commonwealth of Massachusetts states, for example, that "In any City or Town which communicates by mail, the communication must state in large boldface type: 'WARNING—FAILURE TO RESPOND TO THIS MAILING MAY RESULT IN REMOVAL FROM THE VOTING LIST.'"[17]

Prior to the late 1980s, the census materials—and the warning—were mailed only in English. In addition, if the forms were not returned, the residents were automatically dropped from the voting list despite the fact that hundreds of census forms were returned as undelivered even though the resident had merely moved to another address within Holyoke. Prior notification that the resident was to be eliminated from the voting list, the so-called "drop notices," were generally not sent, and if they were, these were again sent only in English. Police often were used as census-takers when a door-to-door count was conducted and out of date street lists commonly were used. Finally, bilingual census-takers and poll-watchers were extremely rare or nonexistent and "before April of 1993 the city had no Spanish-speaking clerk to handle voter registration at the City Clerk's office."[18]

The disregard for Latino political participation on the part of the city government is mirrored across the state from Boston and Chelsea to Lawrence and Springfield—and highlights a major barrier for Latinos. In the 1991 Holyoke election, for example, there were a number of important referenda under consideration by the voters. When the community finally took the city to court in 1995, the plaintiffs argued that

> City officials viewed the [referenda] text as too long to print on the ballot in English and Spanish. The ballots and polling place informational postings were therefore printed only in English, with a separate printed handout translating the referenda questions into Spanish. However, only 200 copies of the handout were printed and the city prepared no advance publicity on the use of the handout. In at least two Hispanic precincts, some

of the bi-lingual [sic] poll workers failed to appear. As the crowning indignity, the public postings of the ballot questions, in English only, carried a warning against defacement—in Spanish but not English. (Vecinos 1995, 33)

Not all of the reasons for Latinos failing to win elections are attributable to structural causes such as white-bloc voting, low Latino voting rates, and obstacles structured into the electoral system. Problems within the community itself include prejudice among Latinos and mistakes made by candidates. Prejudice may have played a role in Orlando Isaza's loss in 1987, for example. Referring to his at-large campaign, Betty Medina Lichtenstein states: "Orlando is Colombian and our people, as much as we have been hurt and disenfranchised by racism, we are just as bad; we are just as prejudiced as the next guy. We're prejudiced among our own, if we live in the east or the west or the north or the south, we're just as bad. *Si somos blanco, rubio, negro*, or, you know, we're just like that" (Medina Lichtenstein 1996). And, in reference to an earlier campaign for City Council by Juan Cruz in 1983, she says:

> Juan didn't win because he wasn't a resident. . . . He lived in Amherst. . . he didn't live in Holyoke. . . . There's the firehouse on [Holyoke's] Main Street and then there's a building right next door to it. There's a church in the storefront. The storefront was the church; right upstairs from it. He kept on claiming that that was his apartment. It was empty. It was always empty. . . . So that when he would go campaign and say, 'I want to do things for Holyoke,' people would say, 'You're crazy. You're out of your mind.' That's why I think he didn't win, and when you're not a resident, people know that you're not a resident. (Medina Lichtenstein 1996)

News reports from that year also suggest that Juan Cruz's campaign in 1983 was very divisive within the Latino community as a whole. Whereas, in general, there was a remarkable sense of unified purpose and planning in the community, Cruz's campaign demonstrates that divisions could and did exist. Carlos Vega stated, "Juan Cruz was someone who went off on his own and he was hard to work with. He ran as a Puerto Rican, but he was not the kind of guy that was into collaboration" (Vega 1996). Cruz even set up an alternative Latino political organization—the Political Action Congress of Hispanic Affairs (PACHA)—in direct competition with the Minority Action Coalition headed, in part, by Carlos Vega.

Another example of candidate limitations is the case of George Cruz. George Cruz ran for City Council from Ward 1 in 1995—and won. After so many years of having only one Latino city councilor, Holyoke was on the brink of having two. However, Cruz did not take his seat on the City Council because his position in Holyoke city government precluded his holding office on the council. Although considerable dismay was expressed by Latino leaders since other elected officials held positions in city government and on advisory boards, one might say that questions about potential conflict of interest should have been clarified well before the election. Failure to resolve such issues in advance suggests that the community's lack of coordination seriously interfered with their otherwise successful efforts in strategic planning.

LATINO POLITICAL ORGANIZING: 1970S TO 1995

Concurrent with efforts to elect Latino candidates, Latino community leaders and activists have organized continuously to achieve changes within the community and the political system. Compared to other cities in Massachusetts (such as Chelsea) that have focused on developing community service organizations (with political functions) or Springfield whose political action committee tended to support non-Latino candidates, Holyoke's Latinos have formed many explicitly political organizations in support of Latino political empowerment. In addition to running and supporting Latino candidates, the organizations maintain a strategic focus on (1) registering Latino voters, (2) using the provisions of the Voting Rights Act to challenge Holyoke's election system, especially the discriminatory implementation of the city census, and (3) joining forces in coalition with others to take the city of Holyoke to court in a redistricting battle.

VOTER REGISTRATION EFFORTS

Voter registration has consistently occupied Latino community activists in Holyoke from the early 1970s. Key activists such as Hector Reyes, Carlos Vega, and others met around the time of elections and in between to strategize about how to increase Latino voting power. By 1978, more formalized voter registration drives began to take place and received note in the local press. One early drive resulted in "over 800 Hispanics register[ed] as new voters" (*Holyoke Transcript-Telegram* 1983b). Embedded in the stories of voter registration in Holyoke, however, are two themes: (1) conflict between city regulations and the community agencies trying to register Latino voters; and (2) the need for ongoing voter *education*—not simply *registration*.

In the 1978 case, for example, eight Latino residents were deputized under the direction of community activists Teresa Rosario and Hector Reyes. A news article from that year describes Ms. Rosario as a "volunteer drive organizer"; the article also noted that shortly before the registration effort Ms. Rosario was fired from her position as executive director of *Casa Hispana* by then Mayor Ernest Proulx. Because of a "federal Housing and Urban Development Department rule that excludes workers of a federally funded agency such as *Casa Hispana* from participating in the drive," Ms. Rosario's actions on behalf of Latino voters cost her her job at *Casa Hispana*.[19] This case illustrates one of the major dilemmas facing

Latino political organizers at that time. Many, if not most, of the activists worked in community agencies that received some form of state or federal funding. Prior to the enactment of the so-called "motor-voter" bill, and earlier efforts to register clients at a variety of human service agencies, workers at Latino agencies were virtually prohibited from participating in any political activities, including voter registration. When Piven and Cloward (1988, 1989, 226) wrote *Why American's Don't Vote*, they noted that the "federal statute prohibits antipoverty agencies from using federal money to conduct voter registration." In many cases, workers were prohibited from political activities even in their spare time outside of their normal working hours. For Latinos in Holyoke, as in other cities around the state and country, political organizing was an activity that had potentially costly personal consequences.

Community activists continued to organize politically, nevertheless. One of the first Latino political organizations in Holyoke was the United Citizens Action League (UCAL), which was formed in the early 1970s. This coalition, whose goal was to foster minority political empowerment, sponsored public forums, determined an election platform, and undertook intensive voter registration drives, especially in the Latino neighborhoods of Wards 1 and 2. A major focus of the group was to adopt a platform and educate residents about the candidates' positions on a variety of issues.

Hundreds of new Latino voters were registered during UCAL's 1981 voter registration drive. An African-American candidate was running at large and Alberto Cruz was running in Ward 2 for the Board of Aldermen in that election. A news report from that time (*Morning Union* 1981, n.p.) stated: "If the action league [sic] meets its goal of 500 new registrations by the end of the month [September], the presently all-white complexion of the 15-member Board of Aldermen could be in for a change."

The deliberate effort to link voter registration in Latino wards with Latino candidacies was evident in Holyoke at that time and throughout this period. Protest marches and mass registration were some of the techniques used. Prior to the preliminary election on October 6, Wards 1 and 2 had gained almost a hundred new voters; by the time of the November 3 general election, 422 new voters were added from those two wards. In contrast, each of the other wards had gains of 60 voters or less.

Empowering Latino community members to register voters was an important strategy in Holyoke and Carlos Vega was at the forefront of this strategy; a news report dated October 24, 1981, stated that "Carlos Vega, who is empowered to register residents, had signed up more than 300 in the wards [1 and 2], according to Registrar of Voters Helen A. Griffin" (*Holyoke Transcript-Telegram* 1983b). On election day, the organizers from the United Citizen Action League used bullhorns and door-knocking to "get out the vote." Hispanic voter turnout was said to be the highest ever in the city's history. Unfortunately, voter turnout in Wards 1 and 2 was still the lowest in the city—although considerably higher than in other elections—and only one of the five candidates endorsed by UCAL was elected.

One characteristic of Holyoke's Latino political organizing common to other cities is that many political organizations would form for a specific purpose and then dissolve after a period of time.[20] The United Citizens Action League followed this pattern, although it continued to work together at least through the elections of 1985 and beyond. In 1983, voter registration was carried out by UCAL, the Committee for a Puerto Rican Parade, a coalition group from the New England Farm Workers Council, and the NAACP (National Association for the Advancement of Colored People). UCAL was very active during this election and began publishing a bilingual newsletter informing Latinos about candidates' positions on a variety of issues: The Thorn/*La Espina*. This newsletter includes articles on candidates UCAL was supporting, information about poll hours and locations, the organization's platform, and exhortations to vote. The Thorn/*La Espina* also included UCAL's recommendations on how to vote on the various referenda facing the community.

What is striking about Holyoke's political organizing history is that contrary to a commonly held view that strategic planning requires one large, well-organized, consistent organization, Latino activists in Holyoke formed multiple organizations over the years and yet still pushed forward with an organizing strategy that was relatively effective. For example, in the summer of 1983, many of the same individuals who were active in UCAL founded the Minority Action Coalition. Although the percentage of Holyoke residents who were black was small at that time (2.4 percent in 1980 [Rivera 1991]), the group was made up of blacks from the local chapter of the NAACP and Latino community leaders such as Carlos Vega, Sylvia Robello, and Andrea Cruz. A major focus of this group was to schedule political rallies "to educate the populace on political issues," to endorse candidates, and to launch a voter registration drive. Rallies were held at various locations throughout the city during August 1983.

Over 500 new Latino voters were registered that election season. The Holyoke Registrar of Voters remarked: "We've never had anything like it" (*Holyoke Transcript-Telegram* 1983b). Multiple Latino organizations worked together to register Latinos. Besides UCAL mentioned above, and the Minority Action Coalition, Benjamin Bonilla of *Casa María* and candidate Juan Cruz of the New England Farm Workers were authorized to register new voters. The NAACP was also active.

Of course not all of these groups worked in harmony. A case in point occurred during 1983 election when Juan Cruz organized PACHA, to some extent in competition with the Minority Action Coalition (MAC). Controversy raged about whether MAC was, as Cruz stated in the press, "politically naive," or whether, as spokespersons for MAC countered, Cruz was a "front-man for Ernie Proulx"—the incumbent mayor who was running against MAC-endorsed Terence Murphy (*Morning Union* 1983a, 1983b).

It is clear from reports on this conflict between MAC and PACHA that the lack of unity created by competing organizations certainly contributed to the defeat of the only Latino running for office that year: Juan Cruz. At the same time, it is evident that multiple organizations are not necessarily counterproductive in the goal of increasing Latino voter registration as they increase political debate and interest in the election campaign. Data suggest, on the other hand, that voter turnout among Latinos was quite low in the 1983 election, especially in contrast to the turnout for Betty Medina Lichtenstein in 1985. It can be concluded that high levels of voter registration as a result of intensive voter registration drives do not translate automatically into increased Latino tournout or political representation without a candidate that the community can support.[21]

CHALLENGING THE ELECTION SYSTEM

Major changes occurred in Holyoke's Latino political organizing in 1984. The Holyoke Rainbow Coalition was formed after a visit by presidential candidate Jesse Jackson. Many of the same Latino community activists who were members of UCAL and MAC joined in the efforts of the Holyoke Rainbow Coalition—but with a new strategy. Besides voter registration efforts that emphasized educating Latino voters one-to-one or in groups about the benefits of political participation, the Rainbow Coalition challenged the structural obstacles faced by Latino voters. The Rainbow Coalition carried out this challenge in Holyoke City Hall and in the Attorney General's Office of the Commonwealth of Massachusetts.

As discussed earlier, Holyoke's election system tied voter registration to the city census carried out each year. If residents did not return the city census, they were dropped from the voter registration lists. The census forms were in English only and were mailed using inaccurate lists. The entire procedure clearly disadvantaged Latinos who moved more often and who, in many cases, could not read English. The strongly worded warning that they would be dropped from the polls was, the Coalition claimed, intimidating, as well. Correspondence and news clippings from that period, as well as interviews with key informants, demonstrate that Latino organizers had a clear strategy to use the legal system to increase Latino political representation and not to rely exclusively on increasing the number of Latino voters in Holyoke.

The campaign by members of the Rainbow Coalition (many of whom were members of the United Citizens Action League, as well) began with a letter to Mayor Proulx challenging the procedures of the city census, especially the warning that failure to respond might result in removal from the voting list and the fact that the forms were in English only and used outdated street lists. Written in May 1984, the letter states that "Voting is a basic democratic right. Removal from the voting list would be an arbitrary, anti-democratic violation of that right."²² The initial response from the Mayor and the City of Holyoke was in defense of the procedures: "[M]any of the regulations governing voter registration are mandated by state law and as such, the City has little or no control." The matter was referred to the municipal law department.²³

Following this response, the Coalition released a press statement summarizing their objections to the election procedures and making certain demands: (1) the census forms should be mailed to "occupant" and bilingual census-takers should follow-up door to door; (2) bilingual materials should be used; (3) since hundreds of forms were returned unopened, voters should not be dropped from the voting lists "unless they are dead, have shown to be registered in another town, have received prior notification and have been given the opportunity to defend themselves in a hearing"; and (4) that the current year's census be stopped until the legal issues were resolved.²⁴ The response in the English-language press was less than supportive of the Coalition's goals; the headline for an article written following the press conference was "Census forms in English only, group *gripes*" (*Morning Union* 1984, emphasis added).

Legal wrangling continued through 1984 and 1985 and culminated with a letter to the office of the Attorney General of the Commonwealth of Massachusetts. Correspondence from this period indicates that the Rainbow Coalition was growing increasingly sophisticated in its overall strategy. In a letter dated March 18, 1985, Nina Tepper, spokesperson of the Rainbow Coalition, states that both the lack of materials in Spanish and the warning that voters would be removed from the voting lists "violate the 1964 Voting Rights Act." Holyoke, a city in which more than 5 percent of the population speaks a language other than English, was covered by that act and "all voting materials must be provided in that language." This letter ends with an eloquent plea: "In America, Democracy is our greatest strength and hope for the future. Resolving this issue will further protect those who have traditionally been disenfranchised."²⁵

Response from the Attorney General's office was relatively prompt. By June 11, 1985, the State Census Supervisor was instructed to have the warnings and the "drop notices" printed in both English and Spanish. In addition, instructions placed responsibility on election officials, not only on the voter, for ensuring that previously registered voters be assisted in being able to vote. The office stated, for example, that previously registered voters could present some form of verification and the election official was required to check their registration records *at the polling place.* "If the person was previously registered, the person is allowed to vote."²⁶

Despite this victory of law over custom, problems continued in Holyoke. Just prior to the October 2, 1985, preliminary election, the Coalition determined that 4,742 bilingual "drop notices" had been sent to Holyoke residents, many to those with Spanish surnames. The Coalition demanded that not only the warning that failure to return the city census might result in being dropped from the voting list but *all* materials relating to voting should be in Spanish as well as English, as required by the 1964 Voting Rights Act. In addition, city officials had instituted a supposedly corrective procedure whereby voters whose names did not appear on the voting list when they went to vote would have to go to City Hall for the verification process. After gaining legal advice, the Rainbow Coalition insisted that phone lines and voting lists be provided to all polling places so questions about voter registration could be resolved on the spot.

A formal letter of complaint was lodged by the Rainbow Coalition and, again, the law came down on their side. The Office of the Secretary of State informed the City Clerk's office that not only should the Rainbow Coalition's process for voter reinstatement be implemented, "election officers must receive sufficient training to understand and carry out these requirements." In addition, a clear-cut message was sent about civil rights in Holyoke: "Holyoke is covered by Section 203 of the federal Voting Rights Act of 1965, as amended, 42 U.S.C. §1973aa-1a (1982), which requires the city to provide *all materials or information relating to the electoral process in the Spanish language*. This includes providing *Spanish-speaking election officials at the polls*."[27]

Even with this clear victory, Latino community organizers in Holyoke continued to struggle against structural obstacles to voting. The Holyoke Rainbow Coalition continued to write letters to the City Clerk's office and the Registrar of Voters documenting instances of Latino voters who were dropped from the voting list, who were not reinstated as directed, who were not able to have their past registration verified by phone, or who were denied the assistance of bilingual poll workers. Despite these continued obstacles, Latino voter turnout was at a record high in 1985—22.8 percent of the Latino voting age population.[28]

Voter turnout dropped slightly in the next municipal election, to 19.3 percent; this was followed by a sharp decline in subsequent years. Causes of the decline included cutbacks in the number of special deputy registrars and insufficient bilingual poll workers, the lack of a Spanish-speaking clerk to handle voter registration at the City Clerk's office prior to 1993, and removal of Latinos from the voting lists when they did not complete the city census forms, which, prior to 1984, were not accompanied by Spanish instructions (Vecinos 1995, 32–33). Finally, the training election officials and poll workers were supposed to receive to ensure that Latino voters were not kept from voting due to being dropped from the voting lists was extremely spotty at best or failed to materialize at worst.

By the late 1980s, it was clearly evident to Latino community leaders and political organizations such as the Rainbow Coalition that a higher level challenge was needed. Community activists and leaders began working with the Lawyer's Committee for Civil Rights under the Law of the Boston Bar Association to prepare a legal case against the city of Holyoke.

REDISTRICTING AND THE VOTING RIGHTS ACT: LATINOS TAKE HOLYOKE TO COURT

The third arena for Latino political organizing in Holyoke was the judicial system. Latino leaders including Vega and Medina Lichtenstein sought judicial relief under Section 2 of the Voting Rights Act through a court case, Civil Action No. 92-30052, *Vecinos de Barrio Uno, et al. v. City of Holyoke et al.*, which was filed in 1992. The case began to make headlines outside of the local press. Kevin Cullen of the *Boston Globe* wrote:

> Eight Hispanic plaintiffs, including those who ran citywide but failed to attract white votes, charged the eight at-large seats were used as a permanent majority for the white establishment, and that ward lines were drawn to dilute the voting strength of Hispanics. Hoose and Gleason, who took the case pro bono, said they would have preferred to compromise. But they said city leaders refuse to acknowledge there is a correlation between the city's political structures and the dramatic underrepresentation of Hispanics in local government. (Cullen 1995, 1)

The complaint was two-fold. First, the Holyoke election system violated the one–person-one-vote principle in the way district lines were drawn; the numbers of people within the different wards differed substantially.[29] Second, the plaintiffs claimed that the at-large nature of the Board of Aldermen and School Committee violated the Voting Rights Act. They presented data demonstrating racially polarized voting in Holyoke and the fact that no Latino—or any minority—had ever won an at-large election in the city. In addition, the structure of the newly created City Council (formerly, the Board of Aldermen) would dilute any Latino political representation gained by winning district-level seats on the City Council: eight seats were at-large seats and only seven were elected in the wards. The plaintiffs argued that racially polarized voting ensured that they could not win at large, and because their majority status in only two wards limited their representation on the council to only 2 of the 15 seats (14 percent), their potential representation would consistently fall far short of their population (22 percent of the voting-age population and 31 percent total).

The fact that Holyoke was accepted for such case in Massachusetts was not an arbitrary decision. The above discussion of the limitations or "mistakes" in Holyoke's record of strategic planning might include the persistent attempts of candidates to run at large, despite the apparently dismal prospects of success. Somewhat ironically, the determination to have a Latino run every year—and lose consistently when running at large—provided the opening for the legal case to force redistricting within the city of Holyoke. In fact, when the Lawyer's Committee for Civil Rights under the

Law of the Boston Bar Association first joined the case against the city of Holyoke, it also examined other cities such as Springfield. Although Springfield's election system of all at-large elections poses an even greater barrier to Latino political representation than did the mixed system of Holyoke, the fact that two Latinos had been elected at large would have made any court case against that city extremely weak. The fact that no Latino had ever won at large in Holyoke greatly buttressed the arguments for judicial redress.

Combining these facts with the socioeconomic disparities convinced the court to rule in favor of the plaintiffs on several points. US District Judge Michael A. Ponsor ruled that the composition of Holyoke's 15-seat City Council, with a majority of eight at-large seats and never more than one Hispanic in any of the district seats, "works to dilute the vote of Hispanics and prevent them from participating equally in the political process. . . . It is manifest," Ponsor wrote, "that local historical, social and economic conditions have interacted with the electoral system to substantially undermine Hispanic opportunity to participate in the local political process" (Cullen 1995, 1). Ponsor had agreed that the city had used its at-large system of electing most city councilors to deny Latinos a fair chance at election and ordered a reduction of the number of at-large seats on the 15 member Board of Aldermen from eight to two.

The City quickly transformed the board into a City Council but appealed the case to the First Circuit Court. Appeals court Judge Bruce Selya vacated the judgment not because he disagreed with the conclusions but because he did not see sufficient evidence in the court record to "square the lower court's factual findings with its ultimate conclusion of vote dilution" (*Boston Globe* 1996, 23). Although City Solicitor Edward Mitnick called the ruling a "victory for the city," the lawyers representing the Latino plaintiffs indicated that the court was merely seeking more information.

Divisiveness within the community itself may have contributed to the plaintiffs' loss in the 1995 court case and exemplified one of the "strategic conditions" Villarreal (1996) refers to (i.e., conditions under the control of the Latino community). The city of Holyoke apparently enlisted Alejandro Sánchez who was running for city council to testify against the lawsuit. Diosdado López, a city councilor since 1995, states that Sánchez's decision to support the city was "not good for the Hispanic community and his family. Everywhere he went to speak, Latino candidates didn't want to be near him. We were divided. We were divided. . . . City Hall tried to get me to support the city's position. They did the same with Harry Ortiz. So they got Mr. Sánchez to do it." Although it may be easy to criticize Mr. Sánchez for undercutting the Latinos' case, the city certainly used a "divide and conquer" strategy as is common in such situations. Holyoke, according to

López, is "not an easy city to win. People here know how to do things to get you out" (López 2000).

CONCLUSION: LATINO POLITICS IN HOLYOKE SINCE 1996 AND PROSPECTS FOR THE FUTURE

Vecinos de Barrio Uno ultimately lost their lawsuit against the city—whether due to an inherent lack of unity within the Latino community or in response to the "divide and conquer" strategy by the city of Holyoke. Progress toward Latino political empowerment has begun to be made, nevertheless. Latinos have secured Latino poll watchers, bilingual materials, and other concessions from the Holyoke election system. Latinos in Holyoke also have continued their effort to "run a Latino in every election." In 1997, there were four candidates and, in 1999, 11 Latinos ran for office in Holyoke—the largest slate in any one year. Juan Cruz won election to the City Council from Ward 1 and Diosdado López won reelection from Ward 2. Latinos have finally achieved their goal of having two Latinos on the City Council. They also have a Latino supporter (Yvonne García) on the School Committee. They have not yet achieved victory in an at-large election, but they are undaunted in their continuing efforts to maintain a strategic approach to gaining political power for the Latino community.

The political history of Latinos in Holyoke offers many important lessons for the study of Latino politics in general. First, Holyoke is distinctive in its record number of Latino campaigns; its long-standing commitment to running Latino candidates and history of drawing on internal and external resources are unique in the state.

Second, a strategy of "running a Latino in every election" has strengths as well as certain weaknesses. By running so many losing campaigns in at-large races, the Latino community was able to generate evidence for the lawsuit that challenged the city's election practices and removed some barriers to Latino participation. At the same time, criticisms of this strategy include the following: persistent losses erode the community's confidence that voting serves any purpose; the community would be better served by uniting behind a few strong candidates than diluting its energies on the weaker candidates or those who run divisive campaigns; and the community needs to examine what campaign practices it can change to win at large, as Marta Rosa did in Chelsea (see Chapter 1) and Marcos Devers (see Chapter 3) did in Lawrence.

The third lesson Holyoke offers is that, generally speaking, the successful municipal candidates draw on deep connections within the Latino communities—connections that support their election and make them effective once in office.

We can conclude from the above analysis that prospects for Latino representation in Holyoke—and in other cities across Massachusetts—are hopeful. The prospects may depend, however, on establishing greater communication between Latino communities. Indeed, what may be missing for Latinos in Massachusetts politically is *un intercambio de ideas* (an exchange of ideas), whereby the lessons Latinos have learned in Holyoke can be shared with communities that are also challenging the political system. At the same time, leaders and candidates from Chelsea and Lawrence —and those who won at large in Springfield—might have some useful information for Holyoke's Latinos as they endeavor to expand beyond ward representation. Even Boston, which has seen a decrease in Latino candidacies in recent years, may provide a blueprint from the carefully constructed "behind the scenes" politics that led to Nelson Merced's victory (described at length in Chapter 2), which could lead to a more focused and effective effort in Holyoke. Perhaps it is time to create a "Latino political machine"—*Bring Back Tammany Hall!*—in Holyoke, at the local level, and statewide.

Ethnic succession and resource mobilization theories suggest that Latinos in Holyoke, because of their determination to gain political representation, the sheer size of their population, and their utilization of external resources such as the lawsuit and input from national organizations, may be poised to break through the obstacles posed by internal, strategic barriers as well as the contextual conditions that have limited their success thus far to ward representation. The need to build links between the various Latino communities to learn from each others' experiences may be one of the most important lessons Holyoke's history has to offer.

NOTES

1.   Note: Much of this history is taken from following the legal case: Civil Action No. 92-30052-MAP, *Vecinos de Barrio Uno, et al. v. City of Holyoke, et al.*, filed in the United States District Court for the District of Massachusetts. The order is from March 27, 1995, Judge Michael A. Ponsor, 11–13. We wish to acknowledge Alan Jay Rom, a lawyer who has worked on behalf of the Latino plaintiffs in the case, for his generosity in providing us with many documents as well as his legal and personal knowledge about the case (Rom 1996).

2.   Until more detailed information from the 2000 Census is available, it is difficult to estimate the Latino population by country of origin.

3.   Personal communication from Diosdado López, 12 June 2000.

4.   Latino voting rates have been estimated by various groups. These numbers are courtesy of Steven Perlmutter. The years with Latino voter turnout estimated to be, essentially, zero include off-year general elections in 1983 and 1993, the "on year" [sic] general election in 1990, and the May 14 primary election in 1991 (Perlmutter 1996, 1).

5.   The only exception was 1979. It might be argued that the Latino candidacy of Felix Manarca in 1979 "does not count" because he ran as a write-in candidate. We include it here, nevertheless, because his decision to run as a write-

in candidate came as the result of community pressure to have a Latino run every year (Vega 1996).

6.   They are Betty Medina Lichtenstein in 1985, 1987, 1989, and 1991, Ruth Cruz in 1993, and Diosdado López in every election since 1991. In 1995, another Latino was elected: George Cruz was the first Latino to win election to the City Council from Ward 1. Mr. Cruz did not take office because city officials insisted that since he already held a position in city government, holding a seat on the City Council would be in violation of the city charter. Many Latinos in Holyoke believe that this provision has been applied inconsistently, to the detriment of Latino political advancement (López 2000). Yvonne García was elected to the School Committee from Ward 2 but, despite her name, she is not Latina; she is not included in our count of Latino candidates despite the respect she has gained within the Latino community of Holyoke. Our analysis of election results are based for the most part on data from 1968 through 1995.

7.   See Hardy-Fanta (1997) for a discussion of Latino campaigns in Massachusetts. Several of these campaigns were very minimal or lasted only through the preliminary elections. These include a write-in campaign by Felix Manarca and a short-lived preliminary venture by Gilberto Sotolongo. These names were collected as part of an earlier research project and we apologize for any omissions that inadvertently have occurred.

8.   *Holyoke Transcript-Telegram*, 10/26/73 (n.p.); 11/1/73 (n.p.); 11/14/73 (p. 10). *Valley Advocate*, 11/14/73 (p. 10). Note: We were able to obtain voting results for many of the Latino campaigns in Holyoke, but not for all. Where we do have votes cast, we include those facts.

9.   Carlos Vega interview, 20 May 1996.

10.   *Morning Union* (1981). Note that the years of his campaigns are erroneously given as 1970 and 1974.

11.   Earlier in the election season, the *Transcript-Telegram* indicated that another Latino was running for alderman at large: Gilberto Sotolongo (*Holyoke Transcript-Telegram* 1983a).

12.   Quotes on the 1980s election results were drawn from the civil court case 92-30052-MAP: *Vecinos de Barrio Uno et al. vs. City of Holyoke et al.*, Order March 27, 1995 (Vecinos 1995, 22–30).

13.   Pluta apparently received support from a substantial number of Latino voters, evidenced by López's slim margin of victory in the Latino precincts. Pluta gained a total of 510 votes compared to 471 votes for Diosdado López.

14.   Court case documents report that "the number of blank ballots cast for this seat exceeded the number of votes Lichtenstein received. Apparently, non-Hispanic whites in this ward expressed their dissatisfaction with Lichtenstein [sic] by casting blank ballots" (Vecinos 1995, 28).

15.   Holyoke newsclipping; newspaper unidentified, October 1989. Quotes are from Vega (1990).

16.   Medina Lichtenstein said, for example, "He usually runs them all on his own, traditionally doesn't have key people on his campaign to get the word out and get the vote out" (Medina Lichtenstein 1996.)

17.   Board of Registrars of Voters, City of Holyoke, "Annual City Census & Annual School Census," Letter from the City of Holyoke, no date.

18.   Quote is from Vecinos (1995, 33). Other information is compiled from a collection of letters between the Rainbow Coalition of Holyoke, the City of Holyoke, and the Department of the Attorney General at the Commonwealth of Massachusetts, 1984–1987.

19.   "Over 800 Hispanics register as new voters," unidentified news article, 5/1/78. It is presumed to be either the *Holyoke Transcript Telegram* or the *Morning Union*. Courtesy of Carlos Vega.

20.   In Boston, for example, the Latino Democratic Committee was active during the 1980s but then activity declined when many leaders joined the David Dinkins administration following his election as mayor of New York. The Latino Political Task Force followed during the early 1990s but is now defunct; currently the Latino Agenda and a Latino PAC, and a new organization called ¿Oiste? are increasingly active.

21.   One data source suggests, for example, that less than 1 percent of the Latino voting-age population turned out to vote in the 1983 election, despite the intensive voter registration drive and the presence of a (relatively weak) Latino candidate (Perlmutter 1996).

22.   Letter from the Rainbow Coalition to Mayor Ernest Proulx, May 3, 1984; from the papers of Carlos Vega. The authors would like to acknowledge the generosity of Mr. Vega who shared his extensive collection of documents, election results, and news clippings.

23.   Letter from Mayor Ernest E. Proulx, City of Holyoke, to The Rainbow Coalition, May 15, 1984.

24.   Press Statement from the Rainbow Coalition, May 21, 1984.

25.   Draft of letter from the Rainbow Coalition to Attorney General Francis X. Belloti, March 18, 1985. From the papers of Carlos Vega.

26.   Letter from Allan R. Fierce, Assistant Attorney General, Civil Rights Division, to Nina Tepper, June 11, 1985. From the papers of Carlos Vega.

27.   Letter from David E. Sullivan, Legal Counsel, Elections Division, Office of the Secretary of State, Commonwealth of Massachusetts, to Mr. James J. Shea, City Clerk, City Hall, Holyoke, October 28, 1985 (emphasis added). From the papers of Carlos Vega.

29.   Both plaintiff and defendant concur with this figure: See, for example, Vecinos (1995, 24).

30.   The Voting Rights Act allows only for a 10 percent variation between districts.

REFERENCES

Boston Globe. (1996). "New Twist in Holyoke Vote Case." 4 January, 23.

Cruz, José. (1995). "Puerto Rican Politics in the United States: A Preliminary Assessment." *New England Journal of Public Policy*, Special Issue: Latinos in a Changing Society, Part I. 11(1) (Spring/Summer): 199–219.

Cullen, Kevin. (1995). "Judge's Ruling Divides Holyoke. Hispanics Seek Political Clout to Match Numbers." *Boston Globe,* 24 April, 1.

Dentler, Robert A., and Marvin B. Scott. (1981). *Schools on Trial: An Inside Account of the Boston Desegregation Case.* Cambridge, MA: Abt Books.

Gastón Institute. (1992). "Latinos in Holyoke." Series of Profiles of Latinos in Massachusetts. Boston: Mauricio Gastón Institute for Latino Community Development and Public Policy, University of Massachusetts Boston.

Hardy-Fanta, Carol. (1997). *Latino Electoral Campaigns in Massachusetts: The Impact of Gender.* Boston: Center for Women in Politics and Public Policy and the Mauricio Gastón Institute for Latino Community Development and Public Policy, University of Massachusetts Boston.

Holyoke Transcript-Telegram. (1981). 7 October.

———. (1983a). "Groups Start Campaign to Turn out Hispanic Vote." 9 May.

———. (1983b). "Over 500 New Holyoke Voters Sign Up." 24 October.

López, Diosdado. (2000). Interview with Jeffrey Gerson, 4 January.

Medina Lichtenstein, Betty. (1996). Interview with the author (C.H.F.), 20 May.

Morning Union. (1981). "Complexion of Election May Change in Holyoke." 15 September.

———. (1983a). "Candidate Responds to Criticism." 1 September.

———. (1983b). "Candidate Returns Attack." 2 September, 10.

———. (1984). "Census Forms in English Only, Group Gripes." 19 May.

Pachon, Harry, and Louis DeSipio. 1992. "Latino Elected Officials in the 1990s." *PS: Political Science and Politics* 25(2): 212–217.

Perlmutter, Steven P. (1996). "Holyoke, Massachusetts; Analysis of Turnout by Race." Unpublished paper courtesy of Steven Perlmutter, Law Offices of Robinson & Cole, 7 March.

Piven, Frances Fox, and Richard A. Cloward. (1988, 1989). *Why Americans Don't Vote.* New York: Pantheon Books, 1989 (originally published in hardcover by Pantheon Books, a division of Random House, Inc., in 1988).

Racusen, Seth. (1995). "'New' Civil Rights Strategies for Latino Political Empowerment." *New England Journal of Public Policy,* Special Issue: Latinos in a Changing Society, Part I. Vol. 11(1): 161–182.

Rivera, Ralph. (1991). "Latinos in Massachusetts and the 1990 U.S. Census: Growth and Geographical Distribution." Publication No. 91-01 of the Mauricio Gáston Institute for Latino Community Development and Public Policy. Boston: Mauricio Gáston Institute for Latino Community Development and Public Policy, University of Massachusetts Boston, (September).

Rom, Alan Jay. 1996. Interview with the authors, 15 May.

U.S. Bureau of the Census. (2001). City data provided by the Mauricio Gáston Institute for Latino Community Development and Public Policy, University of Massachusetts Boston, 4 April.

Vecinos de Barrio Uno. (1995). "Civil Action No. 92-30052-MAP. *Vecinos de Barrio Uno, et al. v. City of Holyoke, et al.,*" filed in the United States

District Court for the District of Massachusetts. The order is from March 27, 1995, Judge Michael A. Ponsor.

Vega, Carlos. (1996). Interview with the author (C.H.F.), 20 May.

Villarreal, Roberto. (1996). "Review of Ethnic Ironies." *American Political Science Review* (December): 906.

Werth, Barry. (1983). "City's Minorities Building Ballot Muscle." *Holyoke Transcript-Telegram*, 18 June.

CHAPTER 5

Latino Migration, the Catholic Church, and Political Division
Lowell

Jeffrey N. Gerson

This chapter examines the response of the Catholic Church to the migration of Latinos to the city of Lowell, Massachusetts from the 1960s to the present. It seeks to answer the following question: Can the underrepresentation of Latinos in the halls of local government and the current underdevelopment of Latino political organization and leadership (witness the existence today of only two recently formed community organizations: the Latino Professional Network and *Todos Unidos*, a Spanish-language newspaper.) be explained by examining Church–Latino relations, including the Church's policy, leadership, and organizational response to the newcomers? Historically, the Catholic Church has been a vital institution for organizing Catholic immigrant interests in American city politics (Fitzpatrick 1990; Mitchell 1988; Dinnerstein, Nichols, and Reimers 1996; Fuchs 1990; Schinto 1995).

LATINOS IN LOWELL: AN HISTORICAL AND DEMOGRAPHIC PERSPECTIVE

Ever since Lowell, Massachusetts was founded in 1826 at the confluence of the Concord and Merrimack rivers in Northeast Massachusetts as an industrial city, it has attracted immigrants. The Irish arrived before the Civil War and the French Canadians during and after it; from the late 1800s through the early 1920s, the Greeks, Lithuanians, Portuguese, Swedes, Jews, and Poles came to the city and established ethnic communities. In the decades after World War II, as the once mighty Lowell textile mills fell all but silent, the most recent stream of immigrants and migrants made their way here. First, from the Hispanic Caribbean came Puerto Ricans, Cubans, and Colombians; later, after the Vietnam War, Southeast Asians came, mainly Cambodians, fleeing the horrors of civil war.

The growth of the Latino population in Lowell has been sure and steady since the first migrants came to the city during the middle 1950s. In 1960, there were only 43 Puerto Ricans in Lowell (Borges-Méndez 1990, 115). By 1980, that figure rose to 4.9 percent (or 4,585 out of 92,418). By 1990, the Latino population in Lowell more than doubled to 10.1 percent of the population and results from the 2000 census indicate that there are 14,734 Latinos in the city—14.0 percent of the total.[1] Reports from other sources suggest, however, that the Latino portion of the population is considerably larger; perhaps nearly 17 percent of the city (or 17,877 out of 106,000).[2] Lowell is one of five cities in the state that experienced the fastest growth in Latino student enrollment between 1990 and 1995 (the others are Somerville, Lynn, Chelsea, and Framingham).

The Latino population in Lowell is estimated to be 70 percent Puerto Rican, 20 percent Colombian, and 10 percent comprised of Dominicans, Cubans, and Mexicans. Latinos in Lowell reside mostly within 5 neighborhoods: the Acre, Back Central, Lower Belvedere, Lower Highlands, and South Lowell (see Map 5.1 of Lowell neighborhoods, which is based on the 2000 Census). Demographic information on Lowell's Latino population follows the trend statewide: Latinos have the worst dropout rates and standardized test scores of any minority group, and are the poorest and youngest as well.

LATINOS AND THE CATHOLIC CHURCH IN LOWELL

During the past several decades, the Catholic Church bore a heavy responsibility for ministering to the needs of Latino immigrants, at a time when the city of Lowell, and the Church itself, was experiencing decline. A study of the Church's role in the Latino empowerment movement in Lowell is especially warranted given the absence of strong political parties in Lowell politics during the twentieth century.[3] Claiming to make local government more efficient, reformers in Lowell and elsewhere instituted structural changes, such as nonpartisan elections and at-large elections, which, more than anything, removed local government from the influence of immigrant voters.

The Archdiocese of Boston (which is responsible for the parishes of Lowell) and the local parish priests, some of whom belong to the Archdiocese and some to the religious order Oblates of Mary Immaculate, tried to adapt their practices to meet the religious and political needs of Latino newcomers in Lowell (Carriere 1964; Obin 2000).

It is the author's contention that Latino unity and political mobilization were hindered by different pastoral and political approaches to empowerment among the Catholic Church's leading priests in Lowell, one of whom led his parishioners in the support of a national language parish,[4] a charismatic practice of Catholicism,[5] and an apolitical stance in community affairs. A second priest, an Oblate Father, urged his followers to favor an assimilated cultural identity (the position of the Archdiocese), practice a mainstream Catholicism, and a Saul Alinsky type of community organizing

Map 5.1   Latino Population in Lowell (2000), by Census Block Group, with Neighborhoods

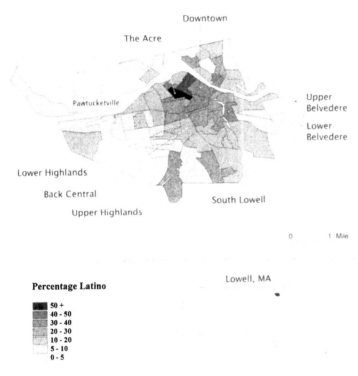

Downtown

The Acre

Pawtucketville

Upper Belvedere

Lower Belvedere

Lower Highlands

Back Central

South Lowell

Upper Highlands

0   1 Mile

Lowell, MA

Percentage Latino

50 +
40 - 50
30 - 40
20 - 30
10 - 20
5 - 10
0 - 5

Source: 2000 Census, P.L. 94-171

for social change.[6] These clashing conceptions and practices were led by equally energetic, youthful (and according to the testimony of Latinos who came to know them), well-intentioned non-Latino priests, who in taking their flocks down separate paths, helped to create a legacy of disunity among Latinos that is still problematic for the Latino political empowerment movement in Lowell.

ORAL HISTORY AND LATINO COMMUNITY ACTIVISM

Oral history is a valuable tool for capturing the human struggle of political life, intimate views of political relationships, and stages in the process of individual and ethnic group political development. As the late historian Herbert Gutman argued, immigrants must be understood in terms of how they dealt with large social forces, making deliberate choices among perceived options (Gutman 1982, 189). Though the immigrants' choice might be limited, the immigrant was never reduced to being merely a passive victim.

Oral history requires researchers to empathize and identify with their subject, but does not imply that researchers accepts their subject's perceptions of the world uncritically. Oral history holds in esteem how people view their life and times, and asks researchers to inject less of their own perception of it.

Other than the articles by Borges-Mendez (1990) and Glaessel-Brown (1991), there is a paucity of written material on the Latino community of Lowell, Massachusetts. To remedy the situation, an oral history project was undertaken, along with a survey of newspaper articles. To prepare for the oral histories, the clippings' files of the *Lowell Sun* were reviewed. Thirty-six community leaders were interviewed over a three-year period, including Latino and non-Latino community activists as well as Catholic priests and nuns. Interviewees were identified from newspaper articles as activists in community organizations that were either self-identified as Latino or purported to serve the Latino community. Once a few activists from the 1970s and 1980s were located by word of mouth or the phone book, the remaining interviewees were selected using a snowball sample, meaning, talking to one person led to talking to others with whom they knew because either they were family members or worked together in community associations.[7] The number of Latino males and females in the sample were roughly equal. Lowellians from Puerto Rico, Colombia, Cuba, the Dominican Republic, and Mexico were interviewed to include a broad sample of the Latino community. Language was not a barrier to oral history interviews with Latinos activists as they are fully bilingual.

THEORETICAL FRAMEWORK

As Kevin Christiano has noted, the literature on the incorporation of Latinos into the Catholic Church in the United States is "thin" (Christiano 1993, 61). Still, there are a number of relatively new studies. Díaz-Stevens (1993), in particular, analyzes the Church's response to Puerto Ricans in the last 100 years and argues that Puerto Rican mountain dwellers, known as *jíbaros*, brought with them to the mainland a type of Catholicism— "oxcart Catholicism"—that was more a way of life than obedience to an institutional Church.[8] The New York Archdiocese failed to treat Puerto Ricans as well as it had previous waves of European Catholic immigrants. The Irish placed Puerto Ricans in a subordinate ecclesiastical world, where their own culture and religiosity were not respected. This study of Lowell's Latino community and the Catholic Church confirms the work of these scholars who found little commitment to the Latino community by the Catholic national church.[9]

ORGANIZATIONAL HISTORY OF LATINOS IN LOWELL: THE FIRST WAVE

Julia Fuce's story is illustrative of the first wave of Latinos, all Puerto Rican, who came to Lowell in the 1950s. Fuce, a former administrator at the University of Massachusetts Lowell and one of the former Executive Directors of Unitas, Inc., a Church-founded community organization that served Latinos in the 1970s and 1980s, was born in Aguada, Puerto Rico, and came to the mainland with her family in 1952 when she was eight years old. Her cousin worked at Ft. Devens in Massachusetts during World War II and after he was discharged from the army he worked there as well. In 1952, she relates, unemployment was high in Puerto Rico. Her father had come to Lowell first, after he had gotten a job at Ft. Devens as a truck driver. The whole family came soon after.

While she was growing up in the middle to late 1950s in Lowell, Julia Fuce remembers there were only six or seven Puerto Rican families who resided in the entire city; they knew each other well, living in the Lower Highlands neighborhood, which was predominately Irish and Jewish. There was no discrimination toward her that she recalls and Puerto Ricans blended into the community largely unnoticed. Other kids thought she was Portuguese because Lowell has had a Portuguese speaking, mostly Azorian community since the turn of the century. Her mother worked in residential homes as a cleaning person and in laundries. "When I graduated Lowell High School in 1963 there were only two Spanish speaking graduates, that's all" (Fuce 1996).

When she returned to Lowell after spending three years in Las Vegas with her family, she remembers the Latino community had grown expo-nentially. The overwhelming numbers were Puerto Ricans, with a handful of Cuban refugees. By 1966 she remembers there were already a few Colombians living in Lowell as well.[10]

THE SECOND WAVE

The first large influx of Latinos to arrive in Lowell came during the middle 1960s when Puerto Ricans were recruited to work in the city's factories. Almost all of these new families moved into "The Acre," a working class Lowell neighborhood that has played host to all of the city's largest immigrant groups. Today, Lowell's newest immigrants and refugees, Southeast Asians, share the Acre with Latinos.

In the 1960s, urban renewal scattered the Puerto Ricans and French Canadians from a section of the Acre and neighboring "Little Canada." This dealt a blow to the establishment of a geographic center to the Latino community, so important for political organization. Around this time, Latinos in Lowell established its first community "home"—the *Centro Latinoamericano* (Spanish American Center), at least partly as a response to their dispersion (see Fig. 5.1).

The building that housed the Center was opened in 1926 as Matthew's Memorial Primitive Methodist Church.[11] The Latino community assumed ownership of the building, with the assistance of the Oblates of Mary Immaculate in October 1966.[12] The Spanish American Center was established inside the former Protestant church building and, under an arrangement with the Archdiocese's Spanish Apostolate, rented the second floor chapel to it for Spanish language services.

During its first decade the Center thrived with Sunday worship services. The congregation or faith community was known as *Nueva Esperanza* or New Hope. Social events were held in the first floor cafeteria hall, which also was used during emergencies, for instance, sheltering the homeless when fires struck Latino residences in Lowell. The Center was financially assisted by the Church's rental fee, small grants from area foundations and government agencies, as well as Center fundraising efforts.

The Center was a traditional immigrant meeting place that created continuity with the homeland and orientation for city life. Its social function was to lessen alienation and to replace town and kinship structures of Puerto Rico. Lowell did not have the cultural support that a city like New York offered Puerto Ricans: radio, cinema, records, television, etc., that could ease the psychological isolation of being newcomers in a hostile, predominantly white ethnic, declining industrial city like Lowell.[13]

What also made the Center special was that the Latinos owned it. It was their home away from home. Father Fred O'Brien was the first priest tapped by Cardinal Cushing to head the unofficially designated "Latino ministry" of the Boston Archdiocese in 1957. Father Fred helped to found the Spanish Center of Boston, later called the Cardinal Cushing Center for

Figure 5.1   Lowell Latino Ministry under the Archdiocese of Boston, 1964–present

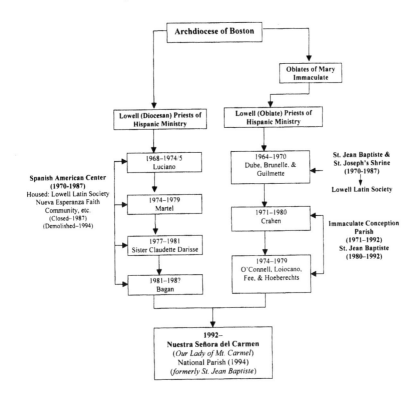

the Spanish Speaking (Boston Archdiocese 1997). He remembered visiting the Center in the late 1960s:

> They really ran things there. I remember them saying to me, "Now wait, Father, for the right moment for the procession"; very detailed. It was theirs. . . . Most of the guys and I would feel they need a place where they can be themselves, so wrapped up with their culture, very much so, more than people realize. To worship you really had to be in their home and do it their way. They're not going to go to a place where everyone has blue eyes, pink skin, tall and high cheek bones. (O'Brien 1998)

Interestingly, the Center was able to thrive during its early years due, at least in part, to the lack of interest and scrutiny exercised by the Boston Archdiocese, which had its attention focused on other tumultuous events of the 1960s: civil rights and school busing to achieve racial integration.

THE VIEW FROM BOSTON'S LATINO APOSTOLATE

Father Fred O'Brien recalls that the Archdiocese really was at a loss as to how to respond to the Puerto Rican migration to the region:

> They left us on our own. Each city had a different experience. Priests working with Latinos were very creative. The Cardinal didn't have a policy. He left it up to what I did. Cushing, he, like a lot of the hierarchy, didn't know what to do. He wanted to do something since these were Catholic people. The Chancery was very cautious. One Chancellor said to me, "Don't trust the Puerto Ricans. You don't know who they are." I said, "Puerto Ricans don't lie to their priests." That's really very insulting. Chancery is the business office of the Diocese. In this country, the hierarchy doesn't know what to make of them, even now. The mentality is quite different than that of Europeans. Puerto Ricans, Caribbeans. Unpredictable. Don't fit the slots. (O'Brien 1998)

Father Fred continued:

> I was told to watch over these places where Latinos settled. I'd go and visit. We had a loving relationship among the priests. They liked to see me, wanted to feel some support. Know that there were connections to other groups. Later we met, twenty-two priests who spoke Spanish. The hierarchy was grateful someone was doing it. They didn't know what to make of the Latinos. (O'Brien 1998)

The financial problems of the Boston Archdiocese no doubt played a significant role in the Church's unwillingness to welcome Latinos in Lowell. Under the Boston Archdiocese, the parish was supposed to raise or borrow money to build its own church, rectory, and school, while the Diocese built seminaries, hospitals, regional high schools, and homes for the elderly. The Archdiocese had little financial incentive to assist the Latino newcomers in Lowell because they represented a class of working poor, uneducated, rural mountain dwellers, with unique spiritual, and obviously great social service needs.

In the early 1970s the Latino Ministry or Apostolate came under the leadership of Father Daniel Sheehan, then serving Latinos in the city of Cambridge. Father Sheehan explains that the Spanish American Center did not receive much financial help from the Archdiocese because it was viewed as a drain on its dwindling resources:

> Father Luciano[14] and the Spanish American Center did not receive much support because of the physical condition of the church. It was becoming difficult for him to maintain it. The roof was in bad shape. Nobody was anxious to maintain churches; no effort was made to do so. Finances were a factor with the numbers in Lowell. Latinos always felt like a minority in the numbers game. They felt we should spend the money but someone in

the Archdiocese would say, "There's only 418 of these people." Few in the Archdiocese were willing to promote Latinos and to be prepared for the future. (Sheehan 1998)

Father Daniel E. Crahen was an Oblate priest who served Latinos in Lowell from 1970 to 1980 and was based at an Irish-French parish, Immaculate Conception. He agrees with Sheehan that the key stumbling block to a national Church for Latinos in Lowell was money:

> The Archdiocese didn't want to take away finances from English-speaking parishes. Those are huge churches in Lowell and to sustain them was getting more difficult. "Don't take money from the parish. Raise money outside the parish." Always the tension; should we have a national parish or incorporate people into the [Irish-French] parish? I think Bishop Medeiros didn't want national parishes, not only in Lowell, but they would have national churches all over the Diocese. Medeiros was concerned over who will sustain the parish if the people are poor. (Crahen 1997)

Father Terry O'Connell, an Oblate priest who has served Latinos in Lowell for a dozen years, believes that it was due to the Archdiocese of Boston's financial difficulties and discrimination that Puerto Ricans found an unfriendly Church when they arrived in Lowell. He remembers that the Latinos who came to Lowell in the 1960s were outcast and unwelcome in the city's Catholic churches. They were bounced around from church to church, later divided among three parishes, and then finally united under one parish only after much protest by the Latino community in the 1990s (O'Connell 1998).

THE IDEA OF A NATIONAL LANGUAGE PARISH

Previous generations of Catholic immigrants were socialized into American life by the Church through a national parish system. Each immigrant group, Irish and German, Italian and Polish, etc., was granted a degree of autonomy in different parishes at the neighborhood level, forming what has been characterized as an "ethnic village." Advantages of a national parish included keeping conflict among Catholic immigrants to a minimum and allowing newcomer groups to assimilate through a position of strength. Life in a national language parish gave ethnic Catholics a group identity that forced the general society to make accommodations itself, even as the newcomers were expected to assimilate.

The national parish fulfilled the religious needs of each specific group, and did not fragment the church by isolating the distinct groups, as was originally feared. What is ironic about the Church's assimilationist policy regarding Latinos is that the Irish-dominated Church hierarchy in the nineteenth century fought Protestant efforts to assimilate them by creating "thousands of parallel social, educational, and athletic groups designed to keep Catholics separated from non-Catholics and free of assimilationist influence." Some groups, such as the "French Canadians, Germans and Poles isolated themselves further on national bases" (Dinnerstein, Nichols, and Reimers 1996, 166). This stance against a national parish for the Spanish speaking in Lowell reversed a century old Church policy that had allowed the establishment of national churches for French, Portuguese, Lithuanian, Polish, and Italian Catholics in the city.

EL CENTRO LATINOAMERICANO: A NATIONAL LANGUAGE PARISH

While the Archdiocese advocated integrated churches for Latinos, the enmity of the white ethnic community toward Puerto Ricans during the 1960s led some Latinos to seek the protection of the next thing closest to a national language parish, the chapel *Nueva Esperanza* at *El Centro Latinoamericano* (Spanish American Center) under the leadership of Father Luciano and Father Leo Martel (see Figure 5.1). Other Latino Catholics sought the protection of a newly arrived non-Latino priest, Father Daniel Crahen, who tried, with mixed results, to integrate Latinos and non-Latinos into an Irish-French parish.

The anti-Latino sentiment in Lowell was painfully remembered by a host of Catholic priests who served the community during that time, and by the Latino parishioners. According to Father Dan, and Oblate Father Jim Loiocano, currently the spiritual leader of Our Lady of Mount Carmel (*Nuestra Señora Del Carmen*), the sole Spanish language church in the city, Lowell's English-speaking community despised the newcomers. Father Dan:

> There were a lot of fires in Lowell during the early 1970s. Pyromaniacs. A lot of suspicious origin. People looking to collect. And our people lived in those fires. . . . I remember a big fire Christmas Eve. Almost 190 Spanish people homeless. And some of the big agencies in the city wouldn't give us blankets. They said they were all at the cleaners. They wouldn't give us blankets because the homeless were Puerto Ricans. I'll never forget that. . . . We had to cut through Culligan's fence to get the people out. A lot of anger and hatred. People didn't like the Spanish in Lowell. (Crahen 1997)

Carlos Malave and his family were victims of the infamous Christmas Eve fire of 1973. He recalled:

> We lived on Watson Avenue, off Westford Street. A building ready to fall down and mostly all Latinos were in there. My brother was living there too. When I first came to Lowell, I lived there. I remember the first night, the train runs underneath the building. I almost had nightmares the house was shaking. The landlord didn't take care of the place, even though he

used to tell me I had a big mouth 'cause I used to tell the people, "If everybody held back the rent, he'd have to fix the place." The place on Watson Avenue was a firetrap. On Christmas Day, 1973 most of us lost everything.

We were outside, a lot of us with no blankets, no shoes. The next day the landlord came around. Father Crahen talked to the emergency helpers and then they finally brought us blankets but not at the beginning. When we went back the next day, the landlord was breaking into the apartments and actually broke down my door. I had some valuable heirlooms, coins my father had left me. I said to him, "Why did you break down my door" and he said "I have the right." I called the Lowell police and they just laughed and left. They didn't do anything. I couldn't go to the police department. The only helpful person was Father Crahen. (Malave 2000)

Father Jim remembered an incident that occurred when he was in Lowell during the late 1970s:

The hostility towards Latinos was horrendous in Lowell. I came from Bolivia in 1978 and spent two to three months here. . . . Anecdotally, there were women working in our [church] kitchen here. They said, "Brother, we want you to know something. We hate the Spanish and we always will. If we burn in hell for all eternity, we'll hate them anyway." It's a good thing they told me after dinner because I would have lost my appetite. I just looked at them and said, "After I die, if ever I pass your way when you're in hell, I will remind you of these words." Something so awful to hear this. That actually is a written invitation to hell. Hatred is a capital sin. Prejudice is a capital sin. (Loiocano 1998)

Although Latino Catholics in Lowell acknowledge the prejudice and discrimination they faced from some non-Latino priests and parishioners, on the whole they are respectful and loyal to the Catholic priests who ministered to their needs, hold little animosity today toward the Church or those who treated them unkindly, and continue to attend Catholic church services (although now at Lowell's Spanish-language parish, *Nuestra Señora del Carmen*).

Carlos Malave is a case in point. He and his family remained as parishioners at Immaculate Conception church for many years, where Mass for Latinos was held in the basement, and where a priest that refused to marry him and his wife, a non-Latina (on the grounds that they were from different cultures and spoke different languages), resided in the upper church. Moreover, Mr. Malave served as a board member of Unitas, Inc., for several years and developed a close pastoral relationship with Father Dan (who is now the pastor of a poor Catholic parish in Tijuana, Mexico), which continues to this day. Father Crahen was instrumental in encouraging Malave to apply to and graduate from the Engineering Program at the University of Massachusetts Amherst. Malave graduated the program in the early 1980s and today works for an engineering firm in central New York State.

Given the ill will Latinos faced in the city in general, and at Immaculate Conception in particular, it is not hard to understand why many chose the Spanish American Center as their communal home. It was to them as the immigrant national parish of the nineteenth century was to the Germans, the Italians, and the Irish: the heart of the immigrant community. Stories are told by those who were active Center participants of how they felt a strong sense of community there and how a communal self-esteem was built, since it was a place of their own in a city of strangers.

Alex Huertas, also a long time Center participant and an unsuccessful candidate for Lowell City Council in 1997, saw an even greater difference between the Center and the Immaculate Conception parish:

> There were two different groups within the Catholic Church in Lowell. A charismatic group and another group, the Oblates [at Immaculate] that doesn't believe in the charismatic movement. This is something we bring from Puerto Rico. Some of us like to pray, with music and dancing. The Oblates said Masses should be quiet and gentle. Somehow they wanted to eliminate the growing charismatic movement. The Center's people were strong believers in this movement. There were so many good things there, not so much the building; it was the effort of a lot of people to get this place and to own it. There was something special in that church there. People's illnesses were healed there by the Holy Spirit. A lot of visitors from different cities and countries came over to the Center. Once they put their first step on the stairs they could feel the Holy Spirit. Since the Oblates saw what was going on in there they told the people, "This place is too big, we can't pay the heating bills, the bills are too high." They were fooling the religious community. The Center people were so full of the Spirit. Oblates believed that contradicting what the priest was saying was committing a sin. They didn't see that the priest was a human being just like anyone else, committing sin like anyone else. (Huertas 1997)

DEBATE WITHIN THE ARCHDIOCESE

The question of whether to establish a national church for Latinos in Lowell and other cities of the Commonwealth of Massachusetts, such as Cambridge, Chelsea, and Boston, was discussed within the Archdiocese of Boston and included the voices of the priests who served in Lowell. Father Fred O'Brien remembers being told from early on, there would be no national parishes, as official church policy. He remembers a meeting in New York City with priests of the Northeast who served Latinos: "We

were told: No national parishes. There was some grumbling because it
would have made life easier" (O'Brien 1998).[15]
Father Sheehan recalls the reason for the Church's policy:

> It was not our plan at the time to build or start a separate church for
> Spanish-speaking. We went through that with other migrations, French,
> Italian, Lithuanian, Polish. We felt that at the time it was not the best
> thing to do. . . . I was head of the church of the Latino Apostolate for two
> years. I went over to New York City for guidance, and it was their policy
> at the time not to start separate churches. The Archdiocese at least went
> along with us; it was more than tacit support. I presumed they paid Father
> Itturalde Luciano of Lowell's salary, they knew why he was there, they
> knew that [*Nueva Esperanza*] was his church. They were happy at the
> Archdiocese to see one place try it, a Spanish language service. The priests
> in general weren't too much interested in Lowell, to be honest with you.
> Funny, Lowell, from the Archdiocese's view, was seen as an Oblate place.
> Lowell was viewed as a place on the fringe [laughing]. They didn't get too
> involved with Lowell. If the same thing Father Luciano had attempted
> [Spanish language service] occurred in Dorchester, or Cambridge or
> Chelsea, we, the priests of the Apostolate, would have been all over it.
> (Sheehan 1998)[16]

LOCAL CATHOLIC PRIESTS SPLIT ON RELIGIOUS AND TEMPORAL IDEAS AND PRACTICES

Father Leo Martel, a diocesan priest and Father Daniel Crahen, an Oblate
priest, led two separate congregations of Lowell Latinos in the early 1970s.
Father Leo was based at the Spanish American Center's chapel, *Nueva
Esperanza*, in a working class area of the city known as South Lowell.
Father Dan was in residence at the Immaculate Conception church, an
affluent Irish and Franco-American parish in downtown Lowell. Father
Leo and Father Dan did not see eye to eye on several of the key questions
before the Archdiocese regarding Latino Catholics in Lowell. Father Leo,
for example, gave his implicit support to the Spanish American Center,
which functioned as a national parish for mostly Puerto Ricans in Lowell.
Father Dan, in contrast, toed the Archdiocese line and discouraged the
notion of a separate Spanish cultural parish.

Father Leo also embraced the Charismatic Renewal movement (also
known as Charismatic Revival) and brought it to *Nueva Esperanza*, whereas Father Dan practiced a conservative, mainstream Catholicism at
Immaculate Conception. Father Leo did not pursue an activist political
agenda, while Father Dan became known as a social activist who sought
social change via community organizing tactics learned from the Saul
Alinsky school in Chicago.

Father Leo backed the idea of a national parish, where Latino immigrants could come to their own church to worship in their own language according to their own customs and to maintain their own language and culture. Father Jim Loiocano, the current pastor of Our Lady of Mt. Carmel and one who shares this view with Father Leo, sums up the arguments favoring it:

> The Catholic Church is made up of every culture in the world. A cultural reality is that each ethnic group worships in its own unique fashion. The Irish worshipped differently from Polish and Franco-Americans. In Washington, D.C., you have black Catholic churches where the gospel thrust is vivid and alive, very different from the normal Anglo Catholic church.

> The parish should promote both culture as well as spirituality. Spirituality is incarnated through the culture of a people. For us, that is why the national church is so important. For us, culture is crucial. It is part of who a person is. Whatever their faith experience is, it is expressed that way. That's why a national church is so important. You can't take a Puerto Rican or Colombian and put them in an Irish Catholic Church. It doesn't work. Nor could you put the Irish here. Sure we've had masses together, everyone may enjoy it for that time but they don't want to come every Sunday for this, nor go there. It also makes people feel more secure within themselves when they have their own national church, to be able to participate with other people because then they no longer feel threatened and have a greater sense of themselves and who they are, a greater cultural ego identity. (Loiocano 1998)

Father Leo respected the wish of the largely Puerto Rican congregation of *Nueva Esperanza* to have a sense of ownership and express their distinctive culture and spirituality:

> You have to realize, "*mi casa is su casa,*" that kind of mentality, a sense of belonging. You have to go to the culture of the people, who are seeking their identity, an island dominated by the United States, seeking statehood or seeking independence, an oppressed people. You have to see it as American foreign businesses, tax free establishing themselves on the island. Where people for a better life work in the factory, where the farmlands and the interior fell apart. People seeking better education and medical treatment, people with the idea of "we do belong to the United States, are American citizens, so therefore we have rights." There was the extended family situation as in so many cultures. Little by little there was this great influx, boom, right into the Northeast, industries, so it is a natural process for people to come, it is a natural process to be among your own. So therefore here is a group of people who owned this particular building,

it was a sense of identity with themselves, that I think is so engrained. We have a tendency to look at it from a *gringo* mentality, but its a place where people gather to celebrate because they are a celebrating people, celebrate their own life, through baptisms, holy days, the weddings, *fiesta*. Feast day is so important to them, innate in their culture.

I appreciated the Latin American and Puerto Rican, because I lived among these people, through earthquakes and liberation theology. I appreciated my Latin American experience, and work not *for them*, but *with them*. Americans tend to see the "poor person," and try to set up something *for them* but not necessarily *with them*.

It's a matter of empowering the people. That's what it comes down to. You can set up a social agency and so therefore your philosophy is you have to get grants to maintain the agency or else it will fall apart. On the other idea, "We'll have our own agency and get it when we can." It's more haphazard but you have more of a sense of ownership. (Martel 1998)

UNITAS, INC.: ACTIVISM AND DIVISION IN THE LATINO COMMUNITY

For Father Daniel Crahen, the only possible policy for the Catholic Church was to assimilate Latinos in an integrated church. Father Dan invited Latinos to worship in the basement of Immaculate Conception, at a separate chapel from the one used by the Irish and French parishioners. Mass, confession, and catechism classes were available to Latinos there. The "basement church" or "lower church," as it is described by some scholars, is a frequent alternative to national parishes. Here, special services in Spanish to Latinos would be held in the form of a Mass in Spanish, in the lower church, and "pastoral services [i.e., baptism, marriage, burial] and devotions in Spanish often by a priest who has learned Spanish and is familiar with the cultural background of the Latino parishioners ... the use of a lower church or chapel or hall sometimes enables the Latinos to have a sense of identity among themselves, a sense of possession" (Fitzpatrick 1990, 163). Father Fred O'Brien believes that the basement church was a great success at the Cathedral in Boston. Latinos actually preferred the basement to the huge Cathedral where one felt small in the presence of the immense space. "It's downstairs but they feel it's theirs. When the Pope was here in 1981, the red carpet that was rolled out for him was picked up by the Puerto Ricans who took it and put it in basement church. . . . Upstairs the place was built for a thousand. It had a feeling of poverty, hard to communicate there" (O'Brien 1998). On the other hand, in Lowell, the basement location of the chapel still rankles Latino community leaders who feel the church basement is a "back-of-the-bus" form of discrimination.

María Cuesta, currently vice principal of the Bailey International School in the Lowell Public School system, a parishioner at *Nuestra Señora del Carmen* and a Center founder, recalls angrily:

> Why did he [Father Crahen] allow masses to be in the basement and not upstairs? Not till Father Jim [Jaime Fee] came over did we start 9 a.m. Mass in the upper church. Never before that. Always in the basement. Why? We paid Immaculate Conception a lot of money to have masses in there [after the Center closed]. Why did they wait until we moved to St. Jean the Baptist [*Nuestra Señora del Carmen*] to put in new rugs to refurbish? Perception. They may say: "We didn't reach our collection goal." My perception is they waited until we left to put the new rugs in. If we were supposed to be equal, then Father Crahen should have said, "I'm bringing the Latino community upstairs; they're supportive of the church. Then we should have 8 a.m. English and 10 o'clock Spanish services in the upstairs church." Not till the 1980s did we celebrate weddings upstairs; before it was downstairs, in the basement. (Cuesta 1997; see also Hernández-Brown 1998, and Huertas 1997)

The Spanish American Center was inward looking—a place of ethnic group solidarity, familiar religious services, a respite from the hostile world of the Irish, French, and Greek ethnic groups and neighborhoods of Lowell. Unitas, Inc., organized by Father Daniel Crahen in 1974, was designed to "work towards the uniting of the English-speaking peoples of the area with the newer arrivals into the community for the purpose of lessening friction, avoiding confrontations and sponsoring progressive community harmony" (Unitas, Inc., n.d.). Unitas was founded to integrate the two communities, in part as a direct challenge to what Father Dan perceived as a lack of a political vision at the Center.

The foundation of Unitas, Inc., was laid in 1971, after Crahen created an after-school tutorial program to help Spanish-speaking youth with school subjects. In the same year Camp Unitas was founded to give both English- and Spanish-speaking kids "a good summer experience for young people from 7 to 13 years of age for the month of July."[17]

According to Father Dan, Unitas grew, originally and officially, out of an effort at the predominately Irish and Franco-American Immaculate Conception parish in Lowell to foster greater cooperation between Lowell's Spanish- and English-speaking communities. Although Father Leo appreciated the desire of Latinos to turn inward, the Oblates, Father Dan and currently, Father Jim, were less sympathetic of this tendency. These priests see the provincialism of the *Nueva Esperanza* church at the Center as harmful to Latino empowerment. Father Jim:

> *Nueva Esperanza* was very insular. They brought that insularity here [Our Lady of Mt. Carmel]. They spiritualize it. Religion is like a drug. I say,

"What about the fact the political system is holding you down; how about the fact that the problems in the economy affects you?" That made no difference. For example, when the Prince pasta factory closed, I went there with the Bishop, too. When I went there, there was only one parishioner present, a Colombian. Nobody from the *Nueva Esperanza* group. I say, where are you? (Loiocano 1998)

Father Dan believed that the Latino community had to address its economic and political powerlessness by organizing social welfare institutions and protesting and demonstrating at City Hall until their cries for quality job training, adequate housing, police protection, etc., were heard. Unitas served the Latino community's social service needs through a number of programs.

As a student of Chicago organizer Saul Alinsky, Crahen created Project ORGANIZE on September 1, 1976. It was funded by the Catholic Church's Campaign for Human Development. Poverty, Crahen understood, could not be addressed without political participation by Latinos in the life of the city. Most immediately, Unitas had to grapple with "poor housing conditions, high rents, tenant abuse by landlords, trash in neighborhoods, infestation and contamination by animals, insects and parasites . . . and dealing with City officials and other agency people." A first time homebuyer fund was established to encourage home ownership by helping with down payments and securing mortgages from local banks. Crahen encouraged voter registration and sent members to an Alinsky leadership-training institute in Providence, Rhode Island. An attempt to form a Puerto Rican Organizer's School was unsuccessful.

Even Crahen's Latino critics say that the early Unitas was very active and had many good ideas. Looking back, however, they do not believe his efforts produced widespread and long lasting results. Unitas suffered from church paternalism and Crahen's imperious rule, intensifying the split among Latinos along ethnic lines, evidenced by competing efforts at the Center and Unitas.

In conclusion, the establishment of Unitas helped to divide the Latino community and fostered an atmosphere of distrust that may have stifled the growth of an indigenous leadership. Moreover, as a result of Crahen's dominance of the agency, when he left Lowell in 1979 to serve in a Florida parish, Unitas lost much of its drive to organize the community from the grass roots. Yet it must be said that under Crahen, a non-Latino leader, Unitas was a dynamic community association that accomplished much for the Latino community.[18]

THE CATHOLIC CHARISMATIC REVIVAL AT NUEVA ESPERANZA

Father Leo Martel started a Charismatic Renewal at *Nueva Esperanza* that was very influential in the lives of the Latino parishioners there. He recalls:

I began while I was at the Spanish American Center what is known as the Charismatic Renewal. It was a spiritual program, movement, that was nonsacramental. Charismatic Renewal in the 1970s was just a powerful movement of prayer within the Catholic Church which had its roots in an ecumenical movement that began in South Bend, Indiana,—the power of prayer, of intercession. The influence it had and still has, one of many movements in all of spiritual life, helped people not just to know *about* *God* but to have a personal experience of God. It's like, Jeff, I know about you but now that we've sat together, I know you. . . . We inherit a whole tradition, but that tradition can be very headish. A lot about our ancestors and what we inherited, and I'm not diminishing that value. It is also complemented by another dimension of the spiritual life which makes the Lord a little bit more personal, less traditional (not in a negative sense) and more relational. A simple, understandable movement, and picked up by the people.

Prior to my coming to the Center, it was a more traditional, sacramental service. The Charismatic Renewal just took off. People from Lawrence came down. It was dynamic, renewing, people loved it, energizing. Consumed a lot of my time. A lot of individual counseling took place.

Remember, too, the evangelical movement by Protestants in the islands is very strong. So many of their families and neighbors belong to extended families and all of sudden they see the Catholic Church has something, wow, similar. Part of an influence in there was they were able to find something, which was simpler, in their understanding of the relation to God. It means much more if it brings them closer to their culture. Its part of their culture to be family- and friends-oriented. Here you are presenting a spirituality, intimacy of small groups, more relational and therefore more cultural and attractive. I think we miss in our traditions, Jewish, Protestant, Catholic, we deal with numbers, we know a lot about God but there is a whole dimension that often times is lacking, for us to gather together to express, "you grow from my faith and I grow from yours." Doesn't matter the tradition. We have so much in common, may we share that together, a bonding takes place. In my mind that is what actually takes places with these people. They found more of a fellowship, call it a Charismatic awareness. It touched home and became very successful. Small groups of people would meet on their own for prayer and it grew. Call me the Charismatic priest. I hate labels. Objectively, Father Leo, he had all these prayer meetings going on. Father Dan tended towards sacramental, traditional Catholicism and a tremendous emphasis on social services. (Martel 1998)[19]

The tremendous growth of Pentecostalism among Latinos in Lowell and elsewhere may indicate that Catholics who favored a more charismatic service, in the wake of Father Leo's departure, may have found it outside the Catholic Church (González Wilson 1996).

Many of Lowell's Puerto Ricans were attracted to Father Leo because, as scholars of religion among Latinos in the United States have noted, there is a distinctive element in the religious style of Latinos. Christiano writes: "Latino Catholicism is rooted in a richly textured folk piety that is conveyed through common people (not priests) and centered in the home (not the church). It is active and celebratory, not decorous and restrained" (Díaz-Stevens 1993, 8–9). Ana María Díaz-Stevens adds that Catholic religiosity in the highlands of Puerto Rico was "lived fully in the absence of the institution" because religion was "a way of life, not a place." She calls the Puerto Rican way of practicing and projecting its own faith, "oxcart Catholicism." Scholars also attribute the dramatic rise in the number of Pentecostal Christians to its emphasis on personal spiritual experience, its democratic principles, and its incorporation of indigenous beliefs (Lattin 1995, 83).[20]

FATHER DAN: CHURCH CONSERVATIVE?

On the other end of the spectrum, Father Dan's pastoral style was considered "conservative" by several priests in the Archdiocese and the Oblate order. By conservative they mean that masses were "the quiet prayers and restrained hymns of a Eurocentric faith" (Wirpsa 1995, 7; Windsor 1993, esp. p. 20). Crahen's brand of mainstream Catholicism is viewed by some scholars of the Latinos in the Church as creating "the outstanding success of Evangelicals and Pentecostals" through its "excessive and coldline rationality" (Windsor 1993, 14). According to the parishioners at *Nueva Esperanza*, Father Dan's pastoral practice was generally presented in a cultural style that a large segment of the Puerto Rican community did not appreciate. On the other hand, Father Dan found support from a growing Colombian immigrant community, more used to his style of leadership.

INTERETHNIC DIVISIONS REINFORCED: COLOMBIANS AND PUERTO RICANS

One of the unintended effects of Father Dan's conservative pastoral approach and radical political practice was to attract the newest Latinos to Lowell, i.e., Colombians, to the Immaculate Conception church, inadvertently aggravating community cleavages along nationality lines. A few thousand Colombians currently live in Lowell; they are widely regarded to be the second largest Latino population in that city.

Professor Jesús Heli Hernández, a long-time community activist in Lowell, a professor of modern languages at the University of Massachusetts

Lowell, and currently a board member of the Coalition for a Better Acre (CBA), who was born in Colombia and came to Lowell in the early 1970s, believes that Colombians gravitated toward Father Dan because his temporal and pastoral style most reminded them of the priests at home.

> For some [at the Center], it was unusual to see a priest so much involved in social issues versus spiritual ones but, on the other hand, this could probably be for those attending who were mostly from Puerto Rico or the Caribbean. In Latin America you have priests that are very much active, politically active, especially in the small towns. The two heads of the town are the priest and the mayor. One doesn't do anything without the approval of the other. Used to be the case. For the Colombians it was not unusual to see Father Crahen do this, and they may have felt more comfortable. The division was created for the two groups, different ways, though Latinos, different views. (Hernández 1998)

In conclusion, the differences in religious and political practices between Father Leo and Father Dan, the Center and Unitas, *Nueva Esperanza* and the Immaculate Conception, created more conflict and competition among Latinos. The effect of their leadership was to make Latino unity for common political cause difficult, though Father Leo's positive influence on leadership development was apparently more long-lasting. After these two dynamic priests left Lowell, however, a vacuum was created in the city's Latino ministry.

A NATIONAL CHURCH FOR LATINOS OF LOWELL—AT LAST

The story of the Latino community's battle within the Church for a Spanish-language parish, with one church in which all Latinos in the city can worship, cannot be told in this short chapter. It is necessary to say, however, that after much struggle, and with the assistance of a few Oblate priests,[21] the community ultimately succeeded in winning a home. In December 1992, the Archdiocese abandoned the policy it held for two and a half decades. Along with the Oblates, the Archdiocese announced the establishment of a Latino national parish for the Spanish-speaking community of Lowell. This was the first Latino parish in the Boston Archdiocese, and the first new parish in Lowell since 1931. The dream of many Latinos had finally come true. The new parish was called *Nuestra Señora del Carmen*, in honor of the thirteenth-century apparition of the Blessed Virgin Mary at Mount Carmel. At its founding in 1992, it had over 1,000 members.

LEGACY OF LATINO CATHOLIC DIVISIONS

As the priests who served both the Spanish American Center's *Nueva Esperanza* and the Immaculate Conception parish after Father Leo and

Father Dan left Lowell will explain, there was a lot of competition and tension between *Esperanza* and Immaculate. Moreover, the legacy of those divisions is felt today. Father Jim states:

> It was hard to integrate Latinos at *Nueva Esperanza* with Latinos at Immaculate Conception. *Nueva Esperanza* parishioners were very closed in. *Encerrados*. They tend to be that way now. I tend to social activism, also Father Terry and Father Dwight, rather than overspiritualize things. Spirituality in that form can be an escape into magic. For us this has been a conflict. Even to this day you see the separation within *Nuestra Señora del Carmen* church. *Nueva Esperanza* folks who came into the Immaculate formed their own group and clique and took over the Mass at 8:00 a.m. Colombians, old timers at Immaculate, kept their Mass at 11:30 a.m. Still a division among them. (Loiacano 1998)

CONCLUSION: IMPLICATION FOR LATINO POLITICS OF THE CATHOLIC CHURCH'S RESPONSE TO LATINO MIGRATION IN LOWELL

The Reverend John R. McNamara, D.D., formerly the Auxiliary Bishop of Boston and Regional Bishop, frankly acknowledges that over the last few decades "the Archdiocese didn't do all it could" to incorporate Latinos. McNamara says that by now, the Archdiocese's less than welcoming treatment of Latinos is a well-known fact (McNamara 1998). In sum, the Catholic Church might have helped to unite Latinos in Lowell; instead it furthered divisions that still stand in the community. One can only imagine what might have been had Father Leo and Father Dan taken the same stance 25 years ago, and had the Archdiocese of Boston seen Latinos as the future of their Church rather than as cultural strangers, too poor to sustain a national church and too willing to maintain their heritage at the expense of assimilation into American culture.

NOTES

1. The 1980 data are from Rivera (1991, 8) and 1990 and 1995 data are from Torres and Chavez (1998, 3), and 2000 census data are courtesy of Mauricio Gastón Institute for Latino Community Development and Public Policy, University of Massachusetts Boston.

2. The author arrived at this estimate using a formula for projecting community population developed by the Massachusetts Office of Refugees and Immigrants. Using this formula, the Lowell school population of 3,438 is multiplied by 5.2 (the estimated average family size) to establish the population figure of 17,877 (Lowell Public Schools 1996, 1).

3. For a discussion of how Progressive Era reformers dismantled the political machine in many American cities, see Hays (1964).

4. According to the late Father Joseph P. Fitzpatrick, S.J., a national language parish or immigrant church allowed newcomers to retain their cultural identity, particularly their language, for religious ceremonies as well as "social affairs, political meetings, and economic assistance groups . . . this was the continuation of the identity of the newcomers; it gave them a sense of security, of solidarity. They knew who they were, and in a foreign world, they had one small space where they were among their own. This was the basis of strength from which they moved with confidence into the mainstream of American society" (Fitzpatrick 1990, 161).

5. The Catholic Charismatic Renewal sought "a return to the type of Christian community and vitality akin to that described in the Bible as characteristic of the first Christians" (Bord and Faulkner 1983, 10).

6. Saul Alinsky, with the help of Cardinal Stritch and the Archdiocese of Chicago, sought to integrate black migrants into the economic and social life of the city. Alinsky's method of organizing was to "look for grievances around which protests could be organized that would galvanize the neighborhood and so create community spirit" (Lemann 1991, 97–102). For more on Alinsky, see Horwitt (1989).

7. Twenty-one Latino activists were interviewed: Pedro Alguila, Ángel Bermúdez, Carmen Hernández Brown, Dalia Calvo, Edi Chico, María Cuesta, Minerva Díaz, Mario Espinosa, Julia Fuce, Jeannette Grullon, Jesús Heli Hernández, Alex Huertas, María López, Carlos Malave, Miguel Malave, David Martínez, Elkin Montoya, Diana Quiñones, Lucy Rivera, María Vejar, and Griselda "Pecki" González Wilson; ten church leaders: Father Arthur Obin, OMI; Father Daniel Crahen, OMI; Father James Loiocano, OMI; Bishop John R. MacNamara, Father Leo Martel, Father John Mendicoa, Father Fred O'Brien, Father Terry O'Connell, OMI; Father Daniel Sheehan, and Sister Claudette Darisse; and five non-Latino community activists: Maria Cunha, Bill Traynor, Charles Garguillo, David Turcotte, and Bruce Akasian.

8. The term, "institutional church" refers to the Catholic Church's choice, at times, to protect the "maintenance of routine in the administration of religious activities, resources and policy" over faith, and, as a result, religious belief suffers (Díaz-Stevens 1993, 24).

9. Dolan and Deck (1994, vii, 58) acknowledge that Latino Catholics are a "people too long neglected by historians of American Catholicism" and aim to give Latino Catholicism the "recognition it rightly deserves." The term, "national church" refers to the institutions of the American Catholic Church based in Washington, D.C., such as the National Council of Bishops and the National Bishops Committee for the Spanish-Speaking.

10. Fuce's recollection is supported by that of Lucy Rivera, whose family belonged to the half dozen "first families" of Lowell's Latino community. All of these pioneering families had one thing in common that distinguishes them from the Puerto Rican tobacco laborers who settled in other Massachusetts cities in the 1950s: they were connected to the region's military bases, Hanscom Air Force Base and Ft. Devens (Rivera 2000).

11. The cavernous Spanish American Center closed its doors in the winter of 1987 and it was demolished over the protest of loyal advocates in August 1994. The *Grupo Pastoral*, a task force of local clergy and members of the Latino community, successfully found one central location to hold Catholic services for Spanish-speaking residents in 1994. St. Jean Baptiste, formerly a Franco-American parish, became the Spanish-speaking parish: *la Nuestra Señora del Carmen*. Adams (1992) reports that the Center's files, photographs, and furniture were lost to the demolition, making the task of recreating the Center's history difficult. One of the contributions of oral history research is the ability to reconstruct historical events in the absence of written documents (Hernández Brown 1998).

12. The destruction of "Little Canada," a working-class Franco-American community, during the early 1960s was instructive to the Oblate priests and community activists in the neighborhood, who realized when it was too late that urban renewal was a grave mistake. One Oblate priest in particular, Father Arthur Obin, along with a young community activist, Charles Garguillo, whose aunt died soon after her forced resettlement from her Little Canada home, vowed to fight the plan to bulldoze the Acre Triangle in 1979 and did so triumphantly. From their resistance arose a community development corporation that still serves the area, the Coalition for a Better Acre (Garguillo 1995).

13. In May 1999, WLLH became Lowell's first all-Spanish-language station (O'Connell 1999).

14. Father Itturalde Luciano was the first diocesan priest to serve the Center. He was on loan to the Boston Archdiocese from the Archdiocese of Quito, Ecuador, from 1968 through 1974. He was replaced by diocesan priest Father Leo Martel upon his return to Quito. Attempts to reach Father Luciano in Quito have been unsuccessful thus far.

15. Father Fred also commented that even with this policy, which Cardinal Medeiros emphasized, exceptions were made, such as a new Portuguese parish in Peabody, Massachusetts.

16. Sadly, Father Sheehan threw out all of his files concerning the Latino Apostolate, including one on Father Luciano, three months before this interview took place. When asked about the files, he said that our conversation was making him feel very guilty that the materials were not deposited in the Archdiocese archive.

17. Unitas, Inc. (n.d.) newsletter. The author wishes to thank Father Daniel Crahen for the Unitas, Inc. documents.

18. The author has only recently been successful in tracking down former Unitas participants of Latino heritage for interviews (see Carlos and Miguel Malave), so their story remains to be told.

19. The Charismatic Renewal broadens Pentecostal influence among both Protestants and Roman Catholics (Bawer 1998). It emphasizes emotion in worship and derives its theology from events that are said to have taken place on Pentecost, fifty days after the Resurrection of Jesus Christ. At that time, Jesus' disciples were filled with the Holy Spirit and began to talk in other languages.

20. There are many reasons for the growth of Pentecostalism among Latinos in the United States and in Latin America. The doors to the small, store front churches are open to newcomers, who are "encouraged to express their personal problems before a responsive community. Participation is not only expected but demanded . . . ordinary people give extraordinary amounts of money . . . in contrast to the Catholic church and historical Protestant churches in Latin America where a paternalistic state or rich patron was expected to provide" (Cleary 1997, 9).

21. Brother Valmond LeClerc and Father Jaime Fee are two Oblate priests mentioned especially deserving of praise. Father LeClerc is now living in Colombia and Father Fee in California.

REFERENCES

Adams, Lisa. (1992). "City Demolishes Former Center for Latinos." *Lowell Sun*, 2 February, B2.

Bawer, Bruce. (1998). "Not Quite Chapter and Verse on Pentecostalism." *New York Times*, 8 February, Arts and Leisure, 15.

Bord, Richard J., and Joseph E. Faulkner. (1983). *The Catholic Charismatics: The Anatomy of a Modern Religious Movement*. University Park, PA: Pennsylvania State University Press.

Borges-Méndez, Ramón. (1990). "Urban and Regional Restructuring and Barrio Formation in Massachusetts: The Cases of Lowell, Lawrence and Holyoke." Ph.D. diss., Massachusetts Institute of Technology.

Boston Archdiocese. (1997). "Celebrating 40 Years, 1957–1997, *El Centro del Cardenal*: A Catholic Charities Community Service Center." Publication of the Boston Archdiocese, 6 June.

Carriere, Gaston, OMI. (1964). "The Man Lowell Remembered: Andre-Marie Garin, OMI 1822–1895." Publication of the Missionary Oblates of Mary Immaculate, translated by Lucien A. Sawyer, OMI, 1998.

Christiano, Kevin J. (1993). "Religion Among Latinos in the United States: Challenges to the Catholic Church." *Archives de Sciences Sociales des Religions* 38(July/September): 53–65.

Cleary, Edward L. (1997). "The Spirit Moves: Why Pentecostals Thrive in Latin America," *Commonweal* 124(17 January), 9–10.

Crahen, Father Daniel E. (1997). Telephone interview with author, 18 March.

Cuesta, Maria. (1997). Interview with author, 19 November.

Díaz-Stevens, Ana María. (1993). *Oxcart Catholicism on Fifth Avenue: The Impact of the Puerto Rican Migration upon the Archdiocese of New York*. Notre Dame, IN: University of Notre Dame Press.

Dinnerstein, Leonard, Roger L. Nichols, and David M. Reimers. (1996). *Natives and Strangers: A Multicultural History of Americans*. New York: Oxford University Press.

Dolan, Jay P., and Allan Figueroa Deck. (1994). *Latino Catholic Culture in the U.S.: Issues and Concerns*. Notre Dame, IN: University of Notre Dame Press.

Fitzpatrick, Joseph P., S.J. (1990). "Catholic Responses to Latino Newcomers." *Sociological Focus* 23(August): 155–165.

Fuce, Julia. (1996). Interview with author, 2 October.

Fuchs, Lawrence. (1990). *The American Kaleidoscope: Race, Ethnicity and the Civic Culture*. Middletown, CT: Wesleyan University Press.

Garguillo, Charles. (1995). Interview with author, 6 May.

Glaessel-Brown, Eleanor E. (1991). "A Time of Transition: Colombian Textile Workers in Lowell in the 1970s." In *The Continuing Revolution: A History of Lowell, Massachusetts*, edited by Robert Weible, 341–369. Lowell, MA: Lowell Historical Society.

González Wilson, Griselda "Pecki." (1996). Interview with author, 10 June.

Gutman, Herbert. (1982). "Labor History and the Sartre Question." *Humanities* 1 (September/October): 187–199.

Hays, Samuel P. (1964). "The Politics of Municipal Reform in the Progressive Era." *Pacific Northwest Quarterly* 55: 157–169.

Hernández, Jesús Heli. (1998). Interview with author, 9 April 9.

Hernández Brown, Carmen. (1998). Interview with author, 26 August.

Horwitt, Sanford D. (1989). *Let Them Call Me Rebel: Saul Alinsky, His Life and Legacy*. New York: Knopf (distributed by Random House, 1989).

Huertas, Alex. (1997). Interview with author, 7 July.

Lattin, Don. (1995). "In Search of the Spirit." *Utne Reader* 72:(November–December): 83–85.

Lemann, Nicholas. (1991). *The Promised Land: The Great Black Migration and How it Changed America*. New York: Knopf.

Loiocano, Father James "Jim." (1998). Interview with author, 13 April.

Lowell Public Schools. (1996). "Table 3. Enrollment By Race, October 1, 1996."

Malave, Carlos. (2000). Interview with author, 22 April.

Martel, Father Leo. (1998). Interview with author, 29 April.

McNamara, Bishop John R. (1998). Interview with author, 23 July.

Mitchell, Brian. (1988). *The Paddy Camps: The Irish of Lowell, 1821–1861*. Urbana, IL: University of Illinois Press.

Obin, Father Arthur. (2000). Interview with author, 19 July.

O'Brien, Father Fred. (1998). Interview with author, 11 August.

O'Connell, Father Terry. (1998). Interview with author, 10 May.

O'Connell, Michael. (1999). *Lowell Sun*, 4 February, 1, 6.

Rivera, Lucy. (2000). Interview with author, 16 October.

Rivera, Ralph. (1991). *Latinos in Massachusetts and the 1990 U.S. Census: Growth and Geographical Distribution*. Boston: Mauricio Gastón Institute for Latino Community Development and Public Policy, University of Massachusetts Boston.

Schinto, Jeanne. (1995). *Huddle Fever: Living in the Immigrant City*. New York: Knopf (distributed by Random House).

Sheehan, Father Daniel. (1998). Telephone interview with author, 7 August.

Torres, Andrés, and Lisa Chávez. (1998). *Latinos in Massachusetts: An Update.* Boston: Mauricio Gastón Institute for Latino Community Development and Public Policy, University of Massachusetts Boston.

Unitas, Inc. (n.d.) Unpublished newsletter.

Windsor, Patricia. (1993). "Does the Church Mishandle its Culture Treasures?" *U.S. Catholic* 58 (February): 14–20.

Wirpsa, Leslie. (1995). "Latinos in the U.S. Church: 'Sleeping Giant' waking." *National Catholic Reporter* 32(17 November): 7–9.

CHAPTER 6

Latino Politics in an At-Large System
Springfield

José E. Cruz

Recent research on Latino political mobilization shows how subgroups have combined the expressive and instrumental aspects of ethnicity to participate in the political process and to achieve political representation (de la Garza et al. 1996; Cruz 1998). There is also evidence that in areas of old settlement some Latino groups have relied on "self-help, institutional development, and entrepreneurship (legal and illegal) to generate political capital, sustain community resources, and promote individual well-being" (Padilla 1993). This notwithstanding, a feature of Latino political development that persists in many localities is a low level of electoral participation and weak political clout. This is true both in established communities and in areas of relatively new but strong settlement (Falcón 1992; Sullivan 1993; Goris and Pedraza 1994).

Not much is known about the constraints and opportunities that local political systems offer Latinos or about the calculus that informs their strategic choices. Furthermore, what little is known is both geographically and demographically selective. With the exception of New York, Northeastern cities are virtually ignored in existing analyses. For example, the only major study that addresses these questions systematically focuses on Mexican Americans and examines their experience in 10 California cities (see Browning, Marshall, and Tabb 1986). A more recent study (Hero 1992) extends the scope of analysis to some Southwestern and East Coast cities but nothing is said about cities in states such as Connecticut and Massachusetts.

This chapter helps fill this gap by exploring the reasons for Latino underrepresentation in Springfield, Massachusetts. In 1990, the city had 156,983 residents. Latinos were 26,528 or 17 percent of the total. Puerto Rican numbers were the highest with 23,728 residents or 89 percent of Latinos. The second largest Latino group in the city was "Other Hispanic" with 2,294 inhabitants counted in that category. According to the 1990 census, Springfield also had 306 Mexican and 199 Cuban residents. Torres and Chavez (1998) estimated Springfield's Latino population to be 30, 681, or 20 percent, in 1995. The 2000 census revealed, however, a more substantial increase. Latinos currently make up 27.2 percent of the population; the increase from 26,528 in 1990 to 41,343 in 2000 means a ten-year change of 58.8 percent.

These numbers would suggest a commensurate Latino presence as candidates for office and in elected positions. This, however, has not been the case—at least not in terms of positions that carry real policymaking power.

Of the 60 Latinos that ran for office in Massachusetts between 1968 and 1994, 11 ran in Springfield (Center for Women in Politics and Public Policy 1995). Three candidates ran for the school committee—which like the city council is elected at-large—five for city council, and three for state representative. One school committee candidate also ran for city council and two city council candidates also ran for state office, bringing the total to 14 candidacies. Prior to 1998, only two were successful, both at the school committee level; neither one, however, ran for reelection. In 1998, a Latina was elected to the state legislature. Presently one Latino, elected in 1999, serves in the School Committee, bringing the proportion of Latinos elected to positions with voting and policymaking power to 8 percent of the total.

Since 1970 the city has channeled citizen input into various issues and concerns such as how it spends Community Development Block Grant monies, zoning changes, and the granting of special permits, through local neighborhoods councils. This is a neocorporatist arrangement whereby neighborhoods elect the Board of Directors of 10 councils under the sponsorship of the city and the supervision of the Community Development Department and the Election Commission. Directors simply "carry residents' messages to officials" (Spencer 2000), and in some cases the councils run social service programs. Latinos elect 5 Directors out of 14 in the heavily Latino North End neighborhoods.

If the 5 Directors of the North End neighborhood council are added to the Latino elected officials in the School Committee and state legislature, the level of Latino representation appears to be robust. In fact, with 7 elected officials out of 24 at the local and state level, Latinos are 29 percent of the total. But this is deceptive as the neighborhood councils have no voting or policymaking power. Thus, in real terms there is a mismatch between Latino representation and Latino power that leaves the community in fact underrepresented.

This chapter addresses the following questions: What is the balance of constraints and opportunities that Latinos face in the city? What factors mediate the strategic choices that Latino elites have made to cope with the city's political reality? What are the prospects for Latino representation and power?

Although it is well known that at-large electoral systems tend to have an adverse impact on the ability of minorities to achieve representation, the literature does not provide consistent findings. This is true of studies that focus on the experience of African Americans and of those analyzing the case of Latinos as well. There is evidence in the Latino experience to support the notion that alternative systems promote electoral success, but the relationship is not always positive or automatic. Such systems might not produce the expected results in part because of the interplay of other factors such as incumbency (see Zimmerman 1995, 302; Racusen 1995, 277). But it may also be the case that the difficulties associated with at-large schemes are overstated, especially in cases where residential segregation is not pronounced and/or where conditions promote coalition-building efforts (see Fraga, Meier, and England 1997, 294; Cruz 1998).

Regarding the calculus of Latino strategic choices, Browning, Marshall, and Tabb (1986) suggest interminority relations as a crucial factor. In their view, the forces that drive Latino choices are group competition and modeling. Competition is triggered both by differences and commonalities. Ideological splits (between "moderates" and "progressives") are one source of elite competition as is the mismatch between needs held in common and the number of opportunities available to satisfy them.

As for modeling, they suggest that prior mobilization on the part of blacks stimulates mobilization of the same sort by Hispanics. It is not clear in their analysis what endogenous variables mediate Latino responses, but it is likely that, just as nativity, age, educational attainment, and income affect participation rates (Garcia 1997), specific modeling and competitive responses are shaped by these same factors.

SPRINGFIELD: HISTORY, ECONOMY, AND POLITICS

Springfield was founded in 1636 by William Pynchon and a small group of settlers from Eastern Massachusetts. Originally named Agawam, it became Springfield in 1640 to honor Pynchon's home town in England. Pynchon and his son, Major John, were among the first so-called "river gods" of the Connecticut Valley—men of great wealth and power who shaped the history of the towns along the Connecticut River.

In 1812 Springfield became the seat of the newly formed Hampden County, of which the city remains a part to this day. By 1820 Springfield had transformed into a manufacturing town, housing the U.S. Armory, a paper mill, and a number of small industries. By 1852 the town had grown sufficiently to be incorporated as a city. Between 1855 and 1865 the city's population increased by 65 percent due to the influx of European immigrants. The building of canals and factories during the first decades of the nineteenth century brought the Irish to Springfield. They were followed by African Americans fleeing the South through the Underground Railroad.

Other groups included French Canadian and Polish immigrants, Jews, Germans, and Italians.

Between 1865 and 1930 Springfield experienced uninterrupted economic growth. Arms manufacturing was the city's principal economic activity, but it also had robust publishing and insurance industries. During the Great Depression the city's economy took a turn for the worse and after World War II the downturn continued largely unabated to this day. Between 1945 and 1985, 45 percent of Springfield's manufacturers closed down. In 1968, the Armory ceased operations after performing vital employment and economic functions for the city for over 150 years. The city's center became an empty shell. Suburbanization and the construction of shopping centers and malls virtually drained all business activity from the downtown area.

During the 1960s urban renewal brought a small measure of revitalization to the downtown area but federal dollars were mostly used to build massive structures such as the Civic Center, an ugly, hulking, concrete mammoth in the city's center, and to fund highway construction projects such as I-91 and I-291. In the 1980s neighborhood and small business revitalization were again sidestepped in favor of monumental projects such as Monarch Place, The Bank of Boston Building, the Federal Building, and Center Square (Springfield Museums 2000a, 2000b). No wonder the city's population went from 164,000 in 1970 to 152,000 in 1980 to its present number of close to 152,000. The change was largely due to white flight. By 1990, the proportion of the population that was white had declined from 76 to 69 percent. In contrast, the proportion of blacks in the city went from 17 to 19 percent. Latinos almost doubled their numbers from 9 to 17 percent. Today, Latinos are more than one-quarter (27.2 percent) of the city's residents and whites make up less than one-half (48.8 percent).

From its very beginnings Springfield had a turbulent political history. In 1650 William Pynchon published his book *The Meritorious Price of Mans Redemption*, which was immediately condemned as heretical by the Massachusetts General Court. The book was banned and then burned and Pynchon was forced to return to England in 1652. In 1787 Springfield was the site of Daniel Shays attempt to capture the Federal Arsenal, as part of his failed rebellion against the budding American federation (Springfield Museums 2000a). Conflict has been perennial—from the attacks on the Irish during the 1850s for their allegedly degenerate character (Burns 1976a, 12) to the characterization of the Italian community of the South End as a "filthy haven for criminals" in the early twentieth century (Burns 1976b, 11); from the black challenge against discrimination in the 1960s (Davis-Harris 1976, 29) to the killing of two Latinos by the police in 1975 and the riots that followed (Grabbe 1975, 4; Phaneuf 1975a, 1); and to the recurrent controversy over the city's at-large electoral system since ward-based representation was rejected in November 1959.

On the other hand, major political changes have often occurred peacefully. For example, the shift in the mayoralty from Irish control to Italian incumbency took place in 1977 after 20 years of Irish dominance. Italian candidates vied for the office for a full decade before succeeding. When Theodore DiMauro ran, his competitor was a coethnic. There was no interethnic competition and the succession process was smooth. In fact, ethnicity—which is often associated with conflict—was downplayed during the election. Campaign issues included downtown business revitalization, tax abatements, police protection, removal of parking meters, budget cuts, and ward representation. The newspapers supported the ethnic successor, but this was largely due to the fact that DiMauro was the candidate of the status quo. The most controversial campaign issue—ward representation—was defeated by a two-to-one margin even though one consequence of having an at-large electoral system was that the majority of council members were from two predominantly white neighborhoods, Forest Park and East Forest Park, while one neighborhood, Indian Orchard, was not represented at all (Clay 1977, Howard 1977).

In 1997—for the third time since 1961—voters were consulted on this question. At that point the proposal was to switch from an at-large to a combined ward/at-large system with eight ward seats and three at-large positions. A majority of the voters (58 percent) approved the proposal, but this proportion was still short of the required 66 percent of the registered voters needed to make it official. In the same year, a group of proponents of ward representation challenged the at-large arrangement in the courts, alleging that the system violated their civil rights. By April 2000, as the city council prepared to decide whether to approve a ballot question for the November election, the lawsuit had become an excuse for some councilors to backtrack on their commitment to the alternative proposal (Turner 2000).

The 1997 referendum on the electoral system brought to light the fact that the existing arrangement was tantamount to a white incumbent protection plan. According to a *Union News* review of the election, if the 18 candidates participating had run for seats in their home wards, only four incumbents would have been reelected and one Latino candidate—Gumersindo Gómez, who obtained 3,809 votes—would have been elected by a landslide (Kelly 1997, 1). Thus, it was no surprise that in wards with heavy Latino concentrations—such as Ward 1, which comprised sections of Brightwood, Memorial Square, Metro Center, and Liberty Heights (see map 6.1)—voters favored changing the electoral system, while in white wards such as Ward 7, which covered sections of East Forest Park and Sixteen Acres, voters were mostly against the proposed combined system. No candidates ran from Ward 4—which comprises portions of McKnight, Bay, Old Hill, and Upper Hill, four predominantly black neighborhoods; there, support for ward representation was overwhelming (Kelly 1997, 1), a fact that confirms the notion that at-large systems discourage candidates, and particularly minority candidates, from entering electoral contests (Adrian 1952).

THE LATINO COMMUNITY: DEMOGRAPHY, SOCIOECONOMIC STATUS, AND POLITICS

Latinos are the latest in Springfield's succession of ethnic groups. The first Latinos to settle in the city were the Puerto Ricans, who began to arrive during the mid-1940s. During the 1950s they worked mostly in the tobacco fields, picking tomatoes and vegetables, and in a few factories. By 1962, there were an estimated 1,200 Puerto Ricans living in the city. Ten years later they were thought to number 11,000, a nearly ten-fold increase. By then the group was a mix of pioneers from Puerto Rico and newcomers from the island and New York City. During the 1970s and 1980s, just as minor improvements in socioeconomic status began to register, larger numbers of educated, professionally trained migrants started coming into the city scene. In 1990 Colombians, Cubans, Dominicans, Mexicans, and Peruvians in the Springfield metropolitan area were too few to be mentioned in official counts, but their presence in the city was apparent.

POPULATION AND RESIDENTIAL PATTERNS

In 1990, the residential distribution of Latinos in Springfield ranged from a low of 156 residents in East Forest Park, on the southeastern part of the city, to a high of 5,520 in Memorial Square, located on the uppermost western corner of the city, almost bordering the Connecticut River.[1] The majority of Latinos concentrated in four neighborhoods: Memorial Square, Brightwood, located on the riverfront, west of Memorial Square, Liberty Heights, which sits east of Memorial Square, and Six Corners, which is south of the city's downtown. Each one of the 17 city neighborhoods has a Latino presence, but 78 percent of Latinos live in just eight of these, all in and around the city's center.

In 1990 Latinos were a majority of the population in two city neighborhoods: Memorial Square and Brightwood, with 81 and 78 percent of the total residents, respectively. In Old Hill they constituted a quarter of the population while in the Metro Center, South End, and Six Corners neighborhoods they were at least one-third of all residents. The South End, Six Corners, and Old Hill neighborhoods were—and are—majority–minority while the combined black–Latino population of the Metro Center area comprised 49 percent of the total (see Table 6.1).

In the following sections, the neighborhoods of Memorial Square and Brightwood are used as proxies for the Latino population in the city (see Table 6.2). Comparisons are made among Latinos, whites, and African Americans using the neighborhoods with the largest concentrations of

Map 6.1   Latino Population in Springfield (2000), by Census Block Group, with Neighborhoods

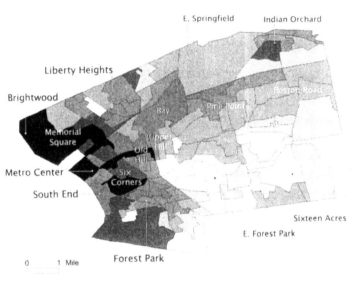

Percentage Latino

- 50 +
- 40 - 50
- 30 - 40
- 20 - 30
- 10 - 20
- 5 - 10
- 0 - 5

Springfield, MA

Source: 2000 Census, P.L. 94-171

Table 6.1   Springfield Population (1990), by Neighborhood

Neighborhood	Whites	Blacks	Latinos	Other	Total
Indian Orchard	6,925	636	830	73	8,464
East Springfield	6,183	242	359	69	6,853
Liberty Heights/ Atwater	12,766	789	2,618	142	16,315
Memorial Square	903	268	5,520	97	6,788
Brightwood	449	422	3,215	25	4,111
Metro Center	3,455	1,358	2,122	96	7,031
South End	2,264	865	1,640	46	4,815
Six Corners	1,955	1,947	2,219	117	6,238
Old Hill	543	3,200	1,301	98	5,142
McKnight	1,189	3,032	963	66	5,250
Bay	687	3,429	920	62	5,098
Upper Hill	2,353	4,549	703	78	7,683
Pine Point	6,069	2,833	878	141	9,921
Boston Road	3,012	475	179	49	3,714
Sixteen Acres	19,143	2,837	797	318	23,095
East Forest Park	10,237	254	156	78	10,725
Forest Park	21,736	1,348	2,108	548	25,740
Total	99,869	28,484	26,528	2,102	156,983

Source: Springfield Planning Department, *Springfield and its Neighborhoods*, May 1993.

whites and blacks in 1990 as representative of the status of these groups in the city at that time. Map 6.1 shows that, while Latino population has increased in many of the other neighborhoods between 1990 and 2000, the greatest concentration continues to be located in these neighborhoods today. These neighborhoods are Sixteen Acres, with a population 83 percent white, and Forest Park, where whites were 84 percent of the residents. Sixteen Acres is located on the southernmost eastern corner of Springfield. Forest Park lies by the river on the southernmost western corner of the city. The black neighborhoods are Bay and Upper Hill, where in 1990 African Americans were 67 and 59 percent of the residents, respectively. Bay and Upper Hill are both located east of the Connecticut River, close to the center of the city.

Although 1990 data on socioeconomic status by race and ethnicity for the city are available (Mauricio Gastón Institute 1994), I chose to use proxies for two reasons: (1) neighborhood-level data are generally consistent with data for the city as a whole; and (2) a neighborhood-level analysis better illustrates the plight of Latinos in the city. Census 2000 data on socioeconomic status at the city and neighborhood level by race and ethnicity could not be incorporated into this analysis before the publication deadline. Between 1990 and 2000 traditional latino enclaves remained demographically strong and Latino numbers grew significantly in predominately white neighborhoods such as Forest Park. Whether this pattern of growth and expansion will result in socioeconomic and political changes remains to be seen.

NATIVITY AND LANGUAGE

In 1980, 13 percent of Springfield's population was either foreign born or born in Puerto Rico or other outlying areas of the United States. Ten years later this proportion had increased to 16 percent. Latino neighborhoods had the highest proportion of those born outside the United States. In Memorial Square, the proportion was 49 percent—the highest in the city— and in Brightwood it was 45 percent. Bay and Upper Hill registered 8 and 5 percent, respectively, while at 2 percent, Sixteen Acres had one of the lowest rates of persons born outside the United States. Forest Park had the second-lowest rate with only 4 percent.

Of the total non-English speakers in the city—a group different from the "linguistically isolated"—almost a quarter lived in Memorial Square and Brightwood in 1990 compared to 19 percent in Sixteen Acres and Forest Park. In Bay and Upper Hill the proportion of non-English speakers was quite low at only 5 percent. In 1990 the largest Latino neighborhood in Springfield was also the most linguistically isolated. The linguistically isolated in Memorial Square were 19 percent of the city's total. Memorial Square and Brightwood had the distinction of housing almost one-third of the city's population in this category, which comprised those that either spoke no English or did not speak it very well. In Sixteen Acres and Forest Park linguistically isolated residents were 15 percent of the citywide total while in Bay and Upper Hill they were only 5 percent.

AGE STRUCTURE

In the selected neighborhoods, differences in terms of age structure between Latinos, blacks, and whites were also apparent. In Memorial Square, 37 percent of the residents were under 18 years old and 9 percent were 65 years old and over. In Brightwood, the proportions were 35 and 6 percent, respectively. In the Bay neighborhood, 35 percent of the residents were under 18 and 8 percent were over 65. The figures for Upper Hill were much lower at 26 and 3 percent, respectively. In Sixteen Acres, only 25 percent of the population was under 18 and 12 percent was over 65. In Forest Park, 27 percent of the inhabitants were under 18 and 13 percent were 65 years old and over. In the Latino neighborhoods, the median age averaged 25 in 1990 while in the white neighborhoods the average was 31. At 22, the average median age in the black neighborhoods was lower, but this could be due to a significant presence of Latinos in these neighborhoods. In Bay, Latinos were 18 percent of the residents and in Upper Hill they comprised 9 percent of the total.

EDUCATION

In 1990, almost three-quarters of Springfield's residents 25 years and older had graduated from high school. Within this cohort, 15 percent received a bachelor's degree or higher. The figures for Memorial Square residents were 37 and 5 percent, respectively. In Brightwood, the high school graduation rate was just one percentage point higher than in Memorial Square, but the college graduation rate was three percentage points lower. Thus, compared to the city as whole, the rate of educational attainment in these predominantly Latino neighborhoods was dismal. In the black neighborhoods educational attainment was considerably higher, although still below the rate for whites. In Bay, 62 percent of residents 25 years and older had a high school diploma and 7 percent had a college degree. In Upper Hill the figures were 70 and 12 percent, respectively. Whites, however, were above the city rate. In Sixteen Acres, 82 percent completed high school and 17 percent completed 4 years of college or more. In Forest Park 76 and 21 percent did so, respectively.

EMPLOYMENT

In 1990, the largest employment sector in Springfield was professional services. This segment accounted for 27 percent of all city jobs compared to 21 percent of jobs in wholesale and retail and 18 percent in manufacturing. Coincidentally, the proportion of residents in the selected whites neighborhoods that worked in managerial/professional, technical/sales/clerical, and service occupations was considerably higher than the proportion of residents from the selected Latino neighborhoods that had similar jobs. In Sixteen Acres, 38 percent of residents were in this sector. In Forest Park 35 percent were similarly employed. In Memorial Square and Brightwood the proportions were 13 and 17 percent, respectively. The proportion for the residents of Bay was 25 percent and for the Upper Hill neighborhood it was 30 percent, rates that were much closer to the white than the Latino situation.

The proportion of Memorial Square residents that was in the production/craft/repair, operators/fabricators/laborers, and farming/forestry/fishing categories was 9 percent in 1990. In Brightwood, 12 percent of residents worked in this sector. Interestingly, 12 percent of the residents of Sixteen Acres were also employed in these occupations and the proportion for Forest Park was 11 percent. In Bay 11 percent of residents worked these types of jobs while in Upper Hill 10 percent did so. But these similarities are very likely a consequence of a higher proportion of families with no workers and a higher unemployment rate in the Latino neighborhoods. In 1990, 43 percent of Memorial Square families had no workers compared to 10 percent in Sixteen Acres; the neighborhood unemployment rates were 17 percent in Memorial Square and six percent in Sixteen Acres. In

Brightwood, 25 percent of families had no workers and the neighborhood unemployment rate was 20 percent. In Forest Park only 17 percent of families had no workers and the unemployment rate was 9 percent. In Bay the proportion of families with no workers was the same as Brightwood's, but the unemployment rate was only 15 percent. Upper Hill had both a lower proportion of families with no workers than the Latino neighborhoods, 21 percent, and a lower unemployment rate, 13 percent.

POVERTY AND INCOME

During the past 30 years the number of Springfield families with income below the poverty level has increased both in absolute and relative terms. In 1969, only 10 percent of all families in the city were poor. In 1979 the proportion was 16 percent and by 1989 it was 18 percent. Between 1969 and 1979 the number of poor families increased by more than half from 3,901 to 5,997; by 1989 the numbers had climbed to 6,884 for a staggering 76 percent increase in two decades.

In 1989, the mean household income for Latinos was the lowest in the city, below the income for blacks and Native Americans. In that year, the figure for Latino households was $17,683 compared to $33,112 for whites, $27,332 for blacks, $21,784 for Asians, and $18,214 for Native Americans. More Latinos were poor in 1989 than any other group: half of Latinos in the city had income below the poverty level compared to 27 percent for blacks and 13 percent for whites.

At the neighborhood level the situation was even worse for Latinos with 58 percent of persons in Memorial Square below the poverty level compared to 21 percent in the black neighborhood of Upper Hill and only 5 percent in the white neighborhood of Sixteen Acres. In Memorial Square and Brightwood the proportion of families below the poverty level in 1989 was 51 and 36 percent, respectively. In contrast, 31 percent of families in Bay and 23 percent in Upper Hill were poor while only 17 percent in Forest Park and 6 percent in Sixteen Acres were in a similar situation (see Table 6.2). For every dollar earned by a Springfield resident in 1979, the residents of the two selected Latino neighborhoods earned $0.41; by 1989 the ratio was 0.50 for an increase of $0.09 in a decade.

LATINO POLITICS IN SPRINGFIELD: 1959 TO 1999

The earliest record of Latino organizational activity dates from 1959 when the Puerto Rican Social Club was established, presided over by one Dr. García Reyes. When Latinos organized the San Juan Fiesta in 1961, the Spanish American Union in 1967, and *Boricuas en Acción* in 1969, they were concerned with both cultural and social issues ("Mayor's Aides" 1962; "Fiesta Begins" 1962; "New Social Action Group" 1969). The *Casa Hispanoamericana*, established in 1963, was social in nature while eco-

Table 6.2   Comparative Demographic and Socioeconomic Indicators in Selected Springfield Neighborhoods, 1990

	Population %	Nativity[a]	Lang-uage+	Median Age	High School Diploma (%)	BA or Higher (%)	Families with no workers (%)	Unem-ployed (%)	Mean Household Income	Families below Poverty (%)
Latinos										
Brightwood	78	45	78	26	38	2	25	20	$18,927	36
Memorial Sq.	81	49	79	25	37	5	43	17	$14,731	51
Blacks										
Bay	67	8	21	23	62	25	25	15	$15,870	31
Upper Hill	59	5	12	22	70	12	21	13	$12,138	23
Whites										
Forest Park	84	4	20	30	76	21	17	9	$20,306	17
Sixteen Acres	83	2	8	32	82	17	10	6	$39,764	6

Source: Springfield Planning Department, Springfield and Its Neighborhoods, May 1993.
a Indicates percent in neighborhood that is foreign born or born in Puerto Rico or other outlying area of the United States.
b Indicates percent of non-English speakers among those 5 years of age and older.

nomic, labor, and educational issues were addressed by the Casa Credit Union, created in 1964, and by the New England Farm Workers Council and the Puerto Rican Student-Parent Union, respectively, both established around 1971 (Buitrago Hermenet 1973).

In 1969, of the estimated 5,000 Puerto Ricans living in the city only 3 percent were registered to vote. This was due to a combination of apathy, language difficulties, lack of encouragement from the political parties, and indifference from electoral officials. Most of those registered had done so encouraged and assisted by the Spanish American Union (*Springfield Republican* 1969).

During the 1970s the dire socioeconomic situation of Latinos was attributed to their weak structural position within the city. They were "younger than other ethnic groups, newer to the city, lower on the economic ladder, and crowded into a densely populated area with less recreational space per capita than residents in other parts of the city" (Schultz 1970). Local lore had it that in the 28 block area where Puerto Ricans concentrated there were as many rats and roaches as people (Briere 1970). Even though some residents and officials were willing to "establish goodwill toward some of Springfield's newer arrivals" (Looking Backward 1966) and to provide them with assistance ("San Juan Fiesta" 1971), prejudice, hostility, and even violence against them were present ("Feedback" 1977; Filosi 1975; Gerena 1996; Hardman 1975a). Elected officials largely ignored them and, to meet their needs, many Latinos relied on the Latino organizations and, according to Quiñones (1977), the welfare system and various social service agencies.

The Puerto Rican Cultural Center, founded in 1976, emphasized culture and identity but other groups such as the Spanish American Union, the Memorial Square Citizens Council (1973), and the Hispanic Citizens Coalition for Justice (circa 1975) paid some attention to policy, electoral, and civil rights issues ("Minority Groups" 1972; "SAU out to Register" 1973a; Briere 1975).

A faint echo of radicalism was also heard in the community during this period when the Puerto Rican Action Youth Defense Committee—a group that hoped to become a branch of the Young Lords Party—railed against urban renewal, the media, and the community service agencies. "The Puerto Rican community will not stand by and be exploited," declared the group's organizer José La Luz, "we are seeking a legitimate solution, but if it does not come we will have to resort to more drastic action" ("Hispanos Demand" 1970).

When riots broke out in the city's North End in August 1975, following the shooting of two Puerto Ricans by the police, community leaders took the opportunity to raise issues of concern before Mayor William Sullivan. Latinos charged the administration with doing "nothing positive, nothing affirmative—nothing to show good faith with the community" (Hardman

1975b). When they marched peacefully, the police chief suggested that their protest was instigated by Communists and bystanders taunted them with comments such as "why don't you go back to Puerto Rico?" (Phaneuf 1975b). The mayor responded by proposing the establishment of a civilian review board and a study of police department rules governing the use of firearms. Seven months later the Hispanic Citizens Coalition for Justice presented him with a list of demands, noting City Hall's inaction and poor record on minority employment and police–community relations. This time the mayor disregarded the group's demands causing disappointment and anger among community leaders (Grabbe 1976).

In 1976 the local public television station broadcast a documentary about Puerto Ricans in Springfield. Titled *These Faces I Have Seen*, the program included profiles of a father, a woman, a youth counselor, and a welfare mother. Following a path previously treaded by the local newspapers (Hardman 1975a), the producers sought to increase the visibility of Puerto Ricans and to put a positive spin on their situation in the city. Copies of the program were sent to City Hall, local hospitals, and the police department.

Two years later in May, the Puerto Rican Cultural Center organized the first Puerto Rican Cultural Festival of Springfield in an attempt at transforming the community's ethnic awareness into an awareness of politics and power. Even though the organizers felt that getting jobs for Puerto Ricans was more important than holding festivals, they saw the celebration as a way of getting the community to think of itself as a political entity. They hoped that ethnic pride would provide the energy required by political involvement (Frail 1978). This was a tempered hope since many realized that Latinos were a "large mass of people with little or no education. There is no system to serve this mass and no push for forums to create such a system" (Andreoni 1978).

During the 1980s, their fifth decade in Springfield, Latinos were poised to leave behind a reputation for electoral apathy. In the 1973 election, Ward 1 had the largest concentration of Latino voters but turnout there was below the 35 percent rate for the city ("Apathy of Voters" 1973). This situation changed dramatically in 1979. Two features of this election made Latinos turn out in droves for the first time in years: a Latino candidate for city council, César Ruiz, and (hard to believe today) a ballot question asking voters whether cable television should be allowed in the city. Another key factor was a vigorous voter registration drive and get-out-the-vote effort—including volunteers to help non-English speakers—sponsored by North End agencies (Filosi and Moriarty 1979). Ruiz finished 12 out of 17 candidates, but the following year he became the first Latino elected official in the city, after winning a special election for a seat in the School Committee. In 1981 he was reelected to a 4-year term with almost three times the number of votes he received in 1979.

Latinos ran and lost in every single Council election between 1981 and 1997. In 1995 they achieved a symbolic victory after Luis García obtained a majority of the vote in Ward 1. In a ward-based electoral system, García would have gained a council seat. But in Springfield's at-large system he had to endure a bitter defeat, despite receiving close to 10,000 votes. This victory-without-representation syndrome repeated itself in 1997 when Gumersindo Gómez also failed to win a city council position despite being the top vote getter in Ward 1.

After Ruiz decided not to run for reelection in 1985, no Latino served on the School Committee until 1993. In that year Carmen Rosa was elected after receiving a massive endorsement from voters citywide. Not only was she the top vote getter, receiving over 15,000 votes—almost as many as the top vote getter in the city council race—but, also, she won in every single electoral district. The day after her victory Rosa expressed optimism about racial and ethnic relations in Springfield. "I think the voters are accepting our differences and celebrating our differences," she said (Pugh 1993). Little did Rosa know that her tenure would end amidst ethnic conflict due to her refusal to support the naming of a middle school after a local Latino (O=Shea 1997). In 1997 she decided not to seek reelection and Luis García ran for the position only to come in last among six candidates. Adding insult to injury was the fact that García's defeat occurred at a time when the composition of the city's school system was 40 percent Latino, 30 percent black, 27 percent white, and 2 percent Asian.

Latinos entered the 1980s being close to 10 percent of the city's population but only a shocking 2 percent of the local workforce ("Minority Jobs" 1981). During the first half of the decade they struggled on multiple fronts—picketing federally funded construction projects that did not hire minorities (Donovan 1981), protesting proposed cuts in bilingual education (Spencer 1981a), or simply trying to show Springfield's residents that their families were in the city to stay (Image Building 1982). Reports about the growing political awareness of the Latino community, of coalition building between Latinos and blacks, of voter registration efforts and growing numbers of voters, and of greater attention toward Latinos on the part of politicians, projected an image of surging organization and growing influence (Spencer 1979, 1981b, 1982; 2nd Hispanic 1983; Nieves 1984a).

At the same time, political representation remained elusive. Recognition was long on symbolism and short on substance, and local leaders feared that if the problems of Latino youth were not addressed, a whole generation would be lost to poverty, crime, mental illness, and substance abuse (Spencer, 1981c; Nieves, 1984b; Tilove, 1984). Carmen Rosa's election in 1993, the election of Cheryl Rivera to the state legislature in 1998, and José Tosado's successful bid for a seat on the School Committee in 1999 suggest that Latinos have no problem winning in at-large races in Springfield. In many ways, however, the at-large system has blocked attempts by well-qualified Latinos to push open the door of political representation.

Non-Latino candidates have sometimes perceived the Latino community as a "swing vote." Thus, they have courted Latinos, typically offering services, contracts, and other forms of support in exchange for their votes. The New North Political Action Committee (NNPAC), an important but erratic organization based in the North End, was often lured into this type of transaction. In 1997 a group of Latinos that included both old timers and Young Turks organized the Western Massachusetts Hispanic Political Action Committee, in part to go beyond the traditional exchange. This new group was also interested in raising the political awareness of the community and in nurturing a new generation of political leaders. Yet, in a city that was highly segregated, most Latinos remained on the margins of electoral participation and political power.

This situation was compounded by chronic internecine conflicts within the community that weakened its electoral muscle, kept its leadership divided, and discouraged potential leaders from stepping up to the political plate. Latino candidates were also discouraged by the unwillingness of Latino organizations to endorse them. The pattern in this regard was to favor "powerful" non-Latino candidates as opposed to Latino "newcomers." The calculus behind such choices was pragmatic rather than solidarity. As Benjamin Ramos, a Puerto Rican activist affiliated with the NNPAC, put it: "We don't support candidates because they are Hispanic or they are Irish or they are Jews or whatever. We support a candidate because they will be able to perform the job for the public" (Hardy-Fanta 1995, 72).

Interestingly, even though it was fairly easy for Latino candidates to rally the support of Latino voters, it was very difficult for Latino leaders to deliver the Latino vote for non-Latino candidates. According to Ramos (1995), "citywide, the majority of the Hispanic community all look at which candidate we (the NNPAC) are supporting in the North End so they can follow us." Yet there is no evidence that Latino leaders could consistently deliver the Latino vote. NNPAC, for example, was not always able to do it. As a result, Latino elites were often poorly positioned to negotiate rewards and benefits for the community with non-Latino powerbrokers in the city. The case of Michael Albano is an exception to this pattern.

When Albano was elected mayor in 1995 he did very well in the Latino community. This was in part due to his support for the establishment of a casino in Springfield, which was sold to Latinos in terms of jobs. As mayor-elect Albano declared: "We must recognize that we can only truly come together as a community by acknowledging that the real strength of our city lies in the pride of our people in the ethnic, religious, and racial diversity of our community" (Johnson 1995).

Although his record was consonant with his rhetoric—as a School Committee member he helped recruit a Latino for the position of Schools

Superintendent, and as Mayor he named a number of Latinos to city commissions and appointed the first mayoral aide of Latino background—by
the end of his first term many were questioning Albano's commitment to
Springfield's minorities. In the words of Richard Mundo, a local leader
associated with the Latino Breakfast Club, "The Latino community has
gotten more from Michael Albano than [from] any of the other recent mayors, [but] with the expectations we had, I can understand disappointment"
(Silberman 1997). In 1999, shortly before the election, Albano improved
his score with Latinos after announcing the appointment of Jorge
Castellano as Director of the newly created Department of Elder Affairs.

WHITHER LATINO POLITICS?

This analysis began by suggesting that Springfield's at-large electoral system and group competition and modeling between African Americans and
Latinos played a critical role in the explanation of Latino underrepresentation in the city. This is true. There is no question that, with a ward-based
system, Latinos could have achieved representation within the city council
as early as 1979. In that year, when César Ruiz ran for city council and
Latinos turned out in higher numbers than ever before, that opportunity
was lost. The 1981 and 1993 elections showed that it was not altogether
impossible for Latinos to get elected in an at-large system. But in 1997, it
was again evident that at-large elections were a more powerful obstacle to
representation than apathy or socioeconomic status.

In terms of black–Latino relations in the city, there is no strong evidence
that competition has been fierce, but it is clear that modeling has hardly
happened. This is largely due to the fact that African Americans are just as
underrepresented as Latinos. In such a context, it would be reasonable to
assume that Latinos and blacks would join forces to achieve representation.
Yet the record shows that attempts at collaboration have been feeble at
best. This is in part due to the fact that aside from a lack of adequate representation, there is little else that Latinos have in common with
Springfield's blacks: African Americans were there earlier, their struggle
was qualitatively different, and today they fare better than Latinos in key
areas. Without a doubt, Latino–black collaboration could be profitable
politically, but the history of black–Latino segregation is perhaps too
strong an obstacle. Furthermore, it is not clear how significant the rewards
of coalition building might be. As long as Latinos and blacks agree that
they can accomplish their goals by relying on separate brokerage strategies,
the incentive to collaborate will be considerably less. Although there are
ongoing efforts to reduce the political distance that exists between Latino
and African-American elites, their history is short.

In any event, these hurdles are compounded by the marginalized, nearly
destitute position Latinos occupy in the city's political economy. In 1990,
more among them than among whites and blacks were born outside the

United States, spoke no English, dropped out of school, and had no jobs or were poor. This notwithstanding, it is clear that the one-two punch of at-large elections and socioeconomic disadvantage does not inevitably lead to electoral apathy and exclusion if Latinos are encouraged by voter registration and education campaigns. If they have the choice of supporting a Latino candidate, participation is also more likely.

Still, their participation record is mixed and this is true not just at the mass level. Compared to the Italian and Irish of Springfield, the level of stamina and persistence of Latino elites vying for political office has been inconsistent at best. In general, the quality of Springfield's Latino elites does not seem to be great. Historically, Latino leaders were unenthusiastic about promoting successors they could not control, but they have not been very good at developing a cadre of loyal replacements either. Yet, in this regard Latino leaders have faced a "catch-22" situation since designated successors have never been to everyone's liking. As of this writing, the big story within the community was whether Barbara Rivera, Director of the New North Citizens Council, would be able to put her son-in-law—Michael Denny—in her place after retiring. A prominent objection was that, like Rivera, Denny was of Irish background; to some this was a disqualifying factor because it suggested the perpetuation of Rivera's leadership style. In many ways, however, this type of succession would be preferable to the situation currently facing the community in which no one seems to be poised to replace the likes of Heriberto Flores, Director of the Springfield-based New England Farm Workers Council, who has been a long standing and key political player within the city's Latino elite.

Due to limited resources, the constraints of the electoral system, and the social distance among elites that chronic infighting and the exodus of Latino community agencies from the North End has created, even well-qualified, competent leaders have not been successful in either gaining or keeping local elected office. Of these factors, the least intractable, ironically, has been at-large elections, although proof of this (provided by the elections of César Ruiz in 1981, Carmen Rosa in 1993, and José Tosado in 1999) was long in coming, infrequent, and inconclusive. For reasons of space it is not possible here to provide a full account of Carmen Rosa's rise and fall; yet it is at least necessary to say that her decision not to run for reelection in 1997 was related to the problems of leadership succession, social distance, and infighting.

The 1998 election of Cheryl Rivera to the state legislature is encouraging even if her nomination was the result of brokerage rather than community standing and despite the fact that it did very little, if anything, to change the state of relations among Latino elites. What more evidence of this could be provided than the fact that her primary contender was none other than Carmen Rosa? The election of José Tosado in 1999—who came in third among five candidates and was able to gather support from Latinos

and non-Latinos as well—is also a sign of positive change. How meaningful that change is remains to be seen.

The case of the past president of the Puerto Rican Cultural Center, Jorge
Castellano, suggests that at the elite level cultural organizations can serve
as springboards for political advancement. Unfortunately, this is not equally apparent at the mass level where a great deal of energy and resources is
spent on the celebration of heritage and culture rather than on the political
process. The problem in this case is not that Latino elites are ignorant of
the political potential of ethnic pride—after all, the Puerto Rican Cultural
Festival was created in 1978 to bridge the gap between ethnic awareness
and power awareness. Instead, what has happened is that conflict among
them has been so fierce that the leaders of cultural organizations have shied
away from politics in order to avoid it.

In 1999 I had the opportunity to verify the disconnect between culture
and politics through participant-observation of the city's Puerto Rican
Cultural Festival. As far as I could see there was no attempt to use this
activity to raise the political consciousness of Latinos in Springfield. Instead
of exhortations to register and vote or encouragement of civic involvement
or community service, participants were offered fun and games and crude
jokes. The music was fabulous; the performance of Tommy Olivencia and
his Orchestra and the singers Marvin Santiago and Ismael Miranda were
the high point of the Festival; unfortunately, the sounds of Salsa were also
a backdrop for a bacchanalia of collective consumption.

According to Juan Gerena, a long standing resident and community
leader, "identity politics is entrenched in this city. To elect someone that
looks and speaks different and has a different last name from the majority
is really hard. The Irish support the Irish, the Italians support the Italians,
senior citizens vote only for people they know, and blacks and Hispanics
do not support each other" (Gerena 1996). In addition, Latinos remain
woefully divided; even ward representation is controversial among elites.
Intragroup competition is significant; the primary between Carmen Rosa
and Cheryl Rivera is a case in point. In addition, in the 2000 neighborhood
council election 11 Latinos fought for five seats in the North End's council. Most important, no Latino leader or group of leaders appears to be
capable of consistently unifying the Latino vote.

This pattern was altered in 1993 with the election of Carmen Rosa, to
some extent in 1998 with the election of Cheryl Rivera, and once again in
1999 with the election of José Tosado. The key question facing Latinos in
Springfield is whether these exceptions can become the rule. An ancillary
question is whether such small victories can yield bigger results in terms of
policy responsiveness. Without denying that structural constraints weigh
heavily against a positive forecast, one feature of Latino politics must be
highlighted: the fact that once the electoral dust settles successful campaigns do very little to secure unity and peace among Latino factions sig-

nificantly reduces the degree to which political achievements have lasting effects.

To break the cycle of Latino underrepresentation in Springfield, a different type of identity politics is necessary, one that pushes hard for ward-based elections, pursues multiracial alliances, builds more aggressively on existing community resources, and demands more accountability and responsiveness from elected officials and their administrators. Exactly how Latinos will make these things happen is hard to say, but it is clear that a focus on structural variables alone is not the answer.

NOTES

1. The data in this section are from the 1990 U.S. Census, as compiled by the Springfield Planning Department in *Springfield and Its Neighborhoods* (May 1993). By 2000, Census Bureau estimates at the national and county level suggested a significant increase in the number of Latinos throughout the Northeast. Unfortunately, the county-level data did not account for differences by subgroup.

REFERENCES

Adrian, Charles R. (1952). "Some General Characteristics of Nonpartisan Elections." *American Political Science Review* 47(September): 766–776.

Andreoni, Phyllis. (1978). "City Must Tackle Problems of Hispanics." *Springfield Sunday Republican,* 17 December, A26.

Briere, Glenn A. (1970). "Is Springfield Doing All It Can?" *Springfield Union.* January 2.

———. (1975). "Puerto Rican Coalition to Press Its Demands." *Springfield Union.*

Browning, Rufus P., Dale Rogers Marshall, and David H. Tabb. (1986). *Protest Is Not Enough, The Struggle of Blacks and Hispanics for Equality in Urban Politics.* Berkeley, CA: University of California Press.

Buitrago Hermenet, Argelia M. (1973). *The Puerto Rican Situation of Springfield, Massachusetts, A Report to Mayor William Sullivan, with Historical Perspectives and a Proposal.* Springfield: Springfield Technical Community College: 23 April .

Burns, Kathryne A. (1976a). *Springfield's Ethnic Heritage: The Irish Community.* Springfield: Bicentennial Commission.

———. (1976b). *Springfield's Ethnic Heritage: The Italian Community.* Springfield: Bicentennial Commission.

Center for Women in Politics and Public Policy. (1995). *Directory of Latino Candidates in Massachusetts 1968–1994.*

Clay, Cash. (1977). "DiMauro Shatters Irish Name Monopoly." *The Morning Union,* 9 November, 2.

Cruz, José E. (1998). *Identity and Power: Puerto Rican Politics and the Challenge of Ethnicity.* Philadelphia, PA: Temple University Press.

Davis-Harris, Jeanette G. (1976). *Springfield's Ethnic Heritage: The Black Community.* Springfield: Bicentennial Commission.

de la Garza, Rodolfo O., and Louis DeSipio, eds. (1996). *Ethnic Ironies, Latino Politics in the 1992 Elections*. Boulder, CO: Westview Press.

Donovan, Karen. (1981). "Minority Commitments." *Valley Advocate,* 18 November, 5.

Falcón, Angelo. (1992). "Puerto Ricans and the 1988 Election in New York City." In *From Rhetoric to Reality, Latino Politics in the 1988 Elections*, edited by Rodolfo O. de la Garza and Louis DeSipio, 147–167. Boulder, CO: Westview Press.

Filosi, Penny. (1975). "North End Group Seeks Probe." *Springfield Union,* 5 September.

Filosi, Penny and Jo-Ann Moriarty. (1979). "Turnout Heavy Among Springfield's Hispanics." *The Morning Union,* 7 November, 6.

Frail, F.S. (1978). "The Culture of Puerto Rico." *Valley Advocate,* 3 May, 20.

Fraga, Luis Ricardo, Kenneth J. Meier, and Robert E. England. (1997). "Hispanic Americans and Educational Policy: Limits to Equal Access." In *Pursuing Power: Latinos and the Political System*, edited by F. Chris Garcia, 286–313. Notre Dame, IN: University of Notre Dame Press.

Garcia, John. (1997). "Political Participation: Resources and Involvement Among Latinos in the Political System." In *Pursuing Power: Latinos and the Political System*, edited by F. Chris Garcia, 44–71. Notre Dame, IN: University of Notre Dame Press.

Gerena, Juan. (1996). Taped Interview, 2 May.

Goris, Anneris, and Pedro Pedraza. (1994). "Puerto Rican Politics in East Harlem's 'El Barrio'." In *Barrio Ballots, Latino Politics in the 1990 Elections*, edited by Rodolfo O. de la Garza et al., 65–81. Boulder, CO: Westview Press.

Grabbe, Nick. (1976). "Damper on a Hot Summer?" *Valley Advocate,* 28 April, 4.

Hardman, Robert. (1975a). "Puerto Rican Community—Don't Generalize About It!" *Springfield Daily News,* 26 September, 1.

———. (1975b). "North End Streets Quiet as Rain Quells Violence." *Springfield Daily News,* 30 August, 1.

Hardy-Fanta, Carol. (1995). "Latino Electoral Campaigns in Massachusetts: The Impact of Gender." An Occasional Paper from the McCormack Institute of Public Affairs, 15 November. Boston: Center for Women in Politics and Public Policy, University of Massachusetts Boston.

Hero, Rodney. (1992). *Latinos and The U.S. Political System: Two-Tiered Pluralism*. Philadelphia, PA: Temple University Press.

Howard, William K. (1977). "Ward Representation Defeated." *The Morning Union,* 9 November, 5.

Johnson, Rhonda Swan. (1995). "'Chilled' Albano Marks Victory with a Hearty 'How Sweet It Is!'" *Union News,* 8 November, B1.

Kelly, Ray. (1997). "Councilors Back Ward Proposal." *Union News,* 6 November, 1.

Mauricio Gastón Institute. (1994). *Latinos in Springfield, Poverty Income, Education, Employment, and Housing*. Boston: Mauricio Gastón Institute, University of Massachusetts.

Nieves, Felipe. (1984a). "Political Coming of Age." *Springfield Daily News*, 13 September, 25.

———. (1984b). "Club Celebrates Its Domino Ability." *Springfield Daily News* March 3.

O'Shea, Mary Ellen. (1997). "Vandals Attack Home After Official's Vote." *Union News*, 1 November, 1.

Padilla, Félix. (1993). "The Quest for Community: Puerto Ricans in Chicago." In *In the Barrios, Latinos and the Underclass Debate*, edited by Joan Moore and Raquel Pinderhughes, 129–148. New York: Russell Sage.

Phaneuf, Wayne. (1975a). "Mayor Under Pressure to Impose Curfew Tonight." *Springfield Daily News*, 29 August, 1.

———. (1975b). "300 Hispanics March to Protest Police Shooting." *Springfield Daily News*, 3 May, 1.

Pugh, Susannah. (1993). "Markel Wins Easily Over Walsh." *Union News* November 3, 1.

Quiñones, Raúl. (1977). "An Inside View of Puerto Rican Life." *Valley Advocate*, 19 January, 8.

Racusen, Seth. (1995). "'New' Civil Rights Strategies for Latino Political Empowerment." *New England Journal of Public Policy*, II (1): 161–182.

Ramos, Benjamín. (1995). Interview with Carol Hardy-Fanta, 5 June.

Schultz, Carol. (1970). "Spanish-Speaking Folk Youngest Ethnic Group." *Springfield Daily News*, 30 January.

Silberman, Ellen J. (1997). "Minorities Say Diversity Promises Need Review." *Union News*, 2 November, 13.

Spencer, Buffy. (1979). "City Minorities Flex Burgeoning Muscles." *Springfield Daily News*, 2 November, p. 14.

———. (1981a). "Hispanic Mothers in Boston to Protest." *Springfield Daily News*, 27 May, 14.

———. (1981b). "Puerto Ricans Considered for Proposed Commission." *Springfield Daily News*, 6 January.

———. (1981c). "Hispanics Want Say on South End." *Springfield Daily News*, 10 August, 17.

———. (1982). "Jordan Calls for Hispanic on Council." *Springfield Daily News*, 23 July, 13.

———. (2000). "Neighborhoods to Elect Councils." *Union News/Sunday Republican*. May 4. Online. Downloaded from http://www.masslive.com/ newsindex/springfield/index.ssf?/news/pstories/se54elec.html.

Springfield Daily News. (1962). "Fiesta Begins on Serious Note, Establishment of Permanent P.R. Affairs Committee Urged." 23 June.

———. (1966). "Looking Backward 10 Years Ago." 13 July.

———. (1969). "New Social Action Group Formed." 15 May.

Springfield Museums. (2000a). "Springfield History." Online. Downloaded from http://www.quadrangle.org/springfield_history/springfield-timeline.htm.

———. (2000b). "Springfield History." Online. Downloaded from http://www. quadrangle. org/springfield-history.htm.

Springfield Republican. (1969). "140 of 5000 Puerto Ricans register to Vote." 2 November.

Springfield Union. (1962). "Mayor's Aides Told Language Barrier Main Problem for Puerto Ricans Here." 10 January.

———. (1970). "Hispanos Demand Recognition of 'Legitimate Needs.'" 13 August.

———. (1971). "San Juan Fiesta to Honor Former Mayor O'Connor." 1 May.

———. (1972)."Minority Groups Picket City Hall." 11 July.

———. (1973). "SAU Out to Register Voters." October.

———. (1973). "Apathy of Voters Citywide Problem." 7 November, 19.

Sullivan, Mercer L. (1993). "Puerto Ricans in Sunset Park, Brooklyn: Poverty Amidst Ethnic and Economic Diversity." In *In the Barrios, Latinos and the Underclass Debate*, edited by Joan Moore and Raquel Pinderhughes, 1–25. New York: Russell Sage.

Tilove, Jonathan. (1984). "Commission Warned of 'Lost Generation' of Hispanics." *Union News*, 18 May, 11.

Torres, Andrés, and Lisa Chavez. (1998). "Latinos in Massachusetts: An Update." *The Gastón Institute Report* (Fall): 4–5.

Turner, Maureen. (2000). "Waffling on Ward Representation." *Valley Advocate*, 6 April. Online. Available: http://www.newmassmedia.com/nac.phtml?code=wma&db=nac_fea&ref =10205.

Union News. (1981). "Minority Jobs Picture Glum." 17 December, 18.

———. (1983). "2nd Hispanic Joins Race for City Council." 23 June, 10.

Valley Advocate. (1977). "Feedback on Puerto Ricans." 2 February, 5.

———. "Image Building." (1982). 9 June, 2.

Zimmerman, Joseph F. (1995). "Election Systems and Representative Democracy." *National Civic Review*, 84(4): 287–308.

CHAPTER 7

An Insider's History of Latino Politics Worcester

Juan A. Gómez[1]

Worcester, once the capital of Massachusetts and currently the seat of Worcester County, is the second most populous city in the Commonwealth. Located in central Massachusetts on the Blackstone River (see Map 7.1), Worcester was famous for its once-mighty tool machinery industry. Worcester's population in 1995 was 171,226 and the official count of the Latino population was 20,955 or 12.2 percent (Torres and Chavez 1998). The 2000 census indicates that the Latino population is currently 26,155 or 15.1 percent of the city (U.S. Bureau of the Census 2001). Approximately 80 percent of Latinos in Worcester are Puerto Rican.

Political activism within the Latino community in Worcester has developed primarily in reaction to a series of crises. This fact, coupled with the short amount of time that Latinos have made Worcester their home, makes gaining political representation difficult for this small, but fast growing, Latino community. Its current at-large form of government and a history of division among Latinos and between Latinos and African Americans are added difficulties.

LATINOS IN WORCESTER: A FAST GROWING COMMUNITY

Unlike New York City, Boston, or Springfield, Worcester was not an original destination point in the continental United States for Puerto Ricans and other Latinos leaving their homelands. The garment factories and other fast growing manufacturers in New York City also had been attracting Puerto Ricans leaving the island since the end of World War II. A large number of Puerto Ricans had settled throughout the Connecticut River Valley, having arrived as migrant workers to labor in the region's tobacco fields and other farms. Hartford, Connecticut, and Springfield, Massachusetts, became popular centers of attraction for this new wave of immigrants. They, like many Latinos after them, moved to Worcester from other cities such as Hartford or New York City (Ojeda 2000).[2]

Map 7.1   Latino Population in Worcester (2000), by Census Block Group, with Neighnorhoods

Burncoat

Great Brook Valley
("The Valley") &
Curtis Apts.

Shrewsbury

Main South

West Side   Grafton Hill

Downtown

0   1 Mile   Plumbley Village

Percentage Latino

50 +
40 - 50
30 - 40
20 - 30
10 - 20
5 - 10
0 - 5

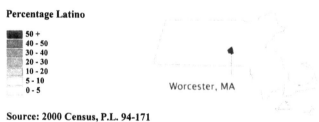

Worcester, MA

Source: 2000 Census, P.L. 94-171

By 1970 there were, according to the City of Worcester's Office of Planning and Community Development, approximately 3,000 Hispanics in Worcester. The first civic and political leaders of the Puerto Rican community naturally rose from among these families. Worcester saw the first major waves of Latino families arrive soon after 1975, when Puerto Ricans lost their jobs in New York, as textile firms headed south to avoid union labor and wages. My own family arrived in Worcester in August 1974.

Most of the Latino families in Worcester in the 1970s lived in a downtown neighborhood known as a "hotbed" for drugs and crime. The Main South neighborhood is part of the Fourth City Council district. Other families settled in the Great Brook Valley and Curtis Apartment projects, the city's first public housing projects. Great Brook Valley, like many public housing developments of the late 1940s, had been built to house veterans returning from World War II. Eventually, it would become the greatest center of concentration for Latinos in the City of Worcester.

LATINO COMMUNITY ORGANIZATIONS RESPOND

A number of organizations began to provide services to this fast growing segment of the community and a number of Latino organizations were established for the purpose of supporting the cultural, educational or socioeconomic needs of Worcester's Latinos. Ángel Camilo Navedo established a chapter of the Happy Friends Club in the Worcester area in 1969. After a stint in the United States Army, Mr. Navedo had made central Massachusetts his home; he is a very well respected member of the Puerto Rican community in Worcester and has worked in the Worcester Vocational School system for over 20 years. The objectives of the Happy Friends Club, a Latino fraternal organization, were to help maintain Latino culture, foster fraternity, and provide support for Latino families (*Clinton Daily News* 1978).

Perhaps most importantly, the Worcester Diocese of the Catholic Church became a strong support system for this community. The Diocese approved holding Mass in Spanish in the basement of the Cathedral. A Latino priest was assigned to provide pastoral services to the Latino community. As was the case in many Massachusetts cities, Catholic Charities (of Worcester) began providing social service advocacy for the newly arrived Puerto Rican families. Catholic Charities started *Centro Hispano* (also known as CH) in 1973 (Ojeda 2000). CH later developed into *Casa de la Comunidad*, which itself evolved into the Latin Association for Progress in Action (ALPA). ALPA was one of the first nonprofit community-based Latino-run organizations in Worcester. It served to support the growing social service needs of Latinos in the city; by using federal and state dollars, for example, ALPA was able to establish *Primera Parada*, a drug prevention and education program. Also in the 1970s, Latinos created *Centro Las Américas* as a Latino run community organization to assist the Latinos in the city; its primary focus was Latino culture and the arts. Finally, WCUW, a local access radio station in Worcester, began the first Spanish-language radio show in 1973.

LATINOS ORGANIZE IN WORCESTER: FROM JUSTICE IN THE SCHOOLS TO THE BALLOT BOX

In recognition of the growing Latino community by the middle 1970s, the Worcester public schools introduced bilingual education. A number of Latino parents then organized the Hispanic Parents Advisory Council. This group included parents of Latino children in the bilingual program in accordance with Chapter 766 of the Massachusetts General Laws (Montánez 2000),[3] and some parents of Latino students in the regular program of the Worcester public school system. These parents felt the city was providing a substandard education for their children.

On 3 June 1978, an unassuming, soft-spoken, small-framed woman named Idalía Vázquez became the voice for the members—mostly women—of the Advisory Council and, together, they built an army to battle the Worcester public schools. Vázquez held a press conference in front of the Spanish Center, located at 831 Main Street, to discuss bringing a class action lawsuit against the school system. The plaintiffs in this lawsuit were the *Centro Las Américas* and eight elementary school children. The defendants included the Worcester public schools, School Superintendent John J. O'Connor, and the Worcester School Committee; the plaintiffs declared that the constitutional rights of Latino children were being violated (*Worcester Telegram* 1978a). Attorney Charles Vanderlinden of the Central Massachusetts Legal Services, as the attorney of record, took on the class action suit.

According to Mrs. Conchita Cruz (2000), a mother of two daughters in regular classes, and one of the most vocal members of the Advisory Council, bilingual students were being taught in janitorial closets, basement hallways and trailers. Some classrooms were very large open rooms with 30 or more students and two teachers who were teaching two separate classes at the same time. Julie Vargas, one of the parents in the group, recounts how, in one of the classes, the children had no desks. She recalls how she demanded that surplus desks in an unessential area of the school be given to these children. To her surprise, the Principal complied.

Arthur Chase is a former State Senator and Republican candidate for Secretary of State of the Commonwealth, who at that time was a member of the Worcester School Committee. He recalls that the school was so crowded that the parents put pressure on the School Committee to come up with a solution. As a result, the School Committee decided to allow students from "the Valley" (i.e., the Great Brook Valley housing project) to attend any other school in the city (*Worcester Telegram* 1978c).

In addition to the deplorable circumstances inside the classrooms, students from the project were forced to walk to the High School through a dangerous shortcut because no buses were provided. Mr. Chase recalled how he walked the route used by the children to prove that it was dangerous not to provide transportation to these students. Ultimately the City provided buses for students from the projects. As in many other cases dealing with Latino issues, Mr. Chase counted on the support of Elizabeth Price, the only African American and the only minority on the School Committee at the time. Mrs. Price served on the Worcester School Committee from 1974 through 1979. (See Table 7.1 for a list of minority office holders in Worcester.)

Table 7.1   Minority Elected Officials in Worcester Politics

• An African American man named Buxby served on the Common Council of Worcester at the turn of the century.
• In the 1940s, Mr. Charles Scott, an African American served on the City Council for six years.
• In 1973, Ms. Elizabeth (Betty) Price was elected to the Worcester School Committee, and was re-elected in 1975, and again, in 1977.
• In 1995, Dr. Shirley Wright, an African-American woman, and the wife of a popular Baptist preacher, was elected to the School Committee, and served one term.
• In 1997, Stacey Deboise, an African-American woman was elected as an at-large member to the Worcester City Council. Ms. Deboise was re-elected in the 1999 election.
• Duboise Luster resigned on 19 July 2000 and Juan A. Gómez became Worcester's first Latino to hold elected office on July 26.

Chase, a Worcester resident of Jewish descent, concentrated his energies and became the staunchest advocate of the bilingual education program in the city. His support within the growing Jewish community afforded him a certain level of political independence. Jewish Americans felt a certain kinship with this struggling community. This insulated Mr. Chase from any backlash he might have felt from the community at large as a result of supporting Latinos in their quest to gain a stronghold in Worcester. Mr. Chase was also very well known for studying issues thoroughly, and for his fierce advocacy for justice and equality.

In 1979, Arthur Chase's support for the bilingual program and Latino causes in general was rewarded by the vote of a loyal Latino community. And, after having placed sixth in School Committee balloting in 1977, Chase became the number one vote getter in 1979. Latinos were credited

with improving his standing in that election cycle. "The Latino community organized and voted like they had never done it before," stated Mr.
Chase. Many of the Latinos who lived in the city at the time still recall
fondly the passion with which Mr. Chase fought "on our behalf" (Ventura
2000).[4]

Statistics for Latino voter participation in the 1970s and 1980s have yet
to be collected in Worcester. The statistics for the 1990s, however, show a
steady growth of both registered voters as well as Latinos who turned out
to vote. In 1993 there were 2,768 Latinos registered to vote, which suggests
a Latino voter registration rate of approximately 17 percent for the City of
Worcester. [5] That year approximately 700 Latinos went to vote citywide, a
Latino turnout rate of 25.3 percent.

Following extensive voter registration efforts by the Latino community,
the number of Latinos registered to vote rose to over 3,300 in 1995.[6] In
1996, Marilyn Reyes took over the leadership of the Worcester Latino
Voter Registration and Education Project; under her leadership, the number of Latinos registered to vote swelled to approximately 5,000. During
the 1997 election cycle, which saw Maritza Cruz run for City Council in
the Fourth District, the Worcester Latino Voter Registration Project and
Maritza Cruz's campaign (in separate efforts) registered a combined total
of over 4,500 voters. Many of these voters were from the Fourth district,
and most were Latinos.

Voter turnout in this district hit a record high in the 1997 election. Close
to 900 Latinos turned out for this election (Santiago 2000).[7] Although the
number of Latinos registered to vote is now estimated at close to 10,000,
voter turnout was very low in 1999. In the precinct that covers the Valley,
only 195 Latino voters actually went out to vote (*Worcester Telegram*
1999). It is clear that despite the large numbers of Puerto Ricans in
Worcester—which means they are automatically citizens and eligible to
vote once they reach 18—there are still many obstacles to overcome before
Latino voter turnout reaches its full potential in this city. Furthermore, as
in other cities discussed in this volume, Worcester residents have to contend
with the annual city census (see also Chapter 10). When they fail to
respond to the census, they are automatically dropped from the roster of
registered voters. Latinos in Worcester constantly complain about being
dropped.

MORE GAINS AND MORE CHALLENGES

While the mothers of the Advisory Council were achieving real and significant measures aimed at improving the education provided to bilingual students and Latino students throughout the city, *Centro Las Américas* and
ALPA were embroiled in a power struggle for leadership within the city
(*Worcester Telegram* 1978b). Latino activists in Worcester see the city government as having contributed to this conflict by denying a funding request

made by ALPA for programs previously funded by the city, and instead granting the money to *Centro Las Américas*. A key Latino community activist believes that power brokers in the city use this type of "divide and conquer" strategy to ensure the stagnation of the Latino community.[8]

On 17 July 1978, the Spanish Apostolate of the Roman Catholic Diocese organized a Latino Festival held at Institute Park to honor the Virgin of Mt. Carmel. Maritza Cruz, daughter of Mrs. Conchita Cruz, and future candidate for Worcester City Council, helped organize a group called *Unión Latina*. This group's two objectives were to organize the *Encuentro Latino*, a friendly cookout, and a major Latino Festival. The celebrations, independent of those organized by the Catholic Diocese, began in the summer of 1977. *Centro Las Américas* later took over the Festival. It is currently one of central Massachusetts's largest events of this kind.

Late in the summer of 1978, another major event would take place in Worcester that would shake Latinos into action once again. Throughout the early months of that year, residents of the Valley had been complaining of the treatment they received from some of the special police officers assigned to the projects (*Worcester Telegram* 1978d). A special police officer (of Latino descent), whose job had been funded with public dollars in an effort to provide opportunities for Latinos in the city, shot and killed a Puerto Rican youngster in the Valley. This created further distrust of "the system" by the Latino community. The incident sent shock waves throughout the city. The outrage of a growing Latino community was unleashed in the form of riots and civil unrest in the projects. The National Guard was called in and police presence was stepped up to prevent any further unrest in the community. A husband and his wife who resided in the Valley would later be charged with throwing a fire-bomb, resisting arrest, and disorderly conduct (*Worcester Telegram* 1979).

Although the streets of the Latino community remained calm for several years, another tragedy sparked Latinos into political action in 1989. During the spring of that year, a fatal event took the life of a young African-American student on the grounds of Worcester's South High School. He and a young Puerto Rican student had been at odds for several weeks over a young lady. Their dislike became hate. Their hate gave way to several fights. One morning while in school, the two young men resumed their conflict. One student lunged at the other, only to be met by a knife. By the end of the day, the young African-American man had died and the Latino youth was in police custody charged with murder. Local politicians were quick to claim that this was the fruit of racial tensions between Latino and African-American children throughout the system. One by one, dozens of students, parents, and professionals took turns at the microphone during an emergency meeting at the *Centro Las Américas* to challenge the assessment that this was a racially charged event.

That autumn a coalition of parents, community activists, and clergy gathered to help the young people at South High School cope with the tragedy. In the aftermath, the coalition came to a decision: the time had come for minorities to gain representation on the School Committee. Two minority candidates entered the race for the Worcester School Committee in 1989. An African-American woman, Shirley Wright, decided to run. As a community activist and long time resident of the city, I saw the opportunity to help influence policy within the school system, and decided to run as well. Neither of us won. (Wright would ultimately win a seat in a second attempt in 1995.)

Although our decision to run could have marked the beginning of a cordial working relationship between Latinos and African Americans in Worcester, it proved to be a missed opportunity for our communities. Latinos worked to support their candidate, while Worcester's African-American community, with a much longer history in the city, were better able to organize a working coalition to propel their candidate more successfully into the political process. And although no animosity developed between us, the two groups remained relatively isolated from each other in the years that followed.

The U.S. Census estimated that in 1995 the Latino population in Worcester had grown to 20,955 or 12.2 percent of the population (Torres and Chavez 1998). Along with the growth of the population, Latino businesses increased and began to be more visible. Today, Latino-owned businesses occupy much of the Main South neighborhood in Worcester (see Map 7.1). Around this same time, an opportunity to create a long lasting working relationship between Latinos and African Americans in our community was lost. The development of a private $215 million construction project by a local hospital brought a coalition of business people together to ensure significant minority participation during the project. This coalition formed the Worcester Minority Business Council (WMBC), of which I was a member. WMBC negotiated a contract for services with hospital owners that was valued at over $1 million. Soon after signing the contract, conflict broke out.

Each racial/ethnic group wanted to control a fair share of the contract. Ultimately, the majority of the money went to black-owned enterprises, and the path breaking organization (WMBC) we formed in partnership and cooperation just 3 years before was abandoned by all but one Latino entrepreneur. The organization's name has since been changed to the Business Inclusion Council. Recently, a Latino was hired as its new Chief Operating Officer. I am still hopeful that trust can be rebuilt, and that Latinos and African Americans can join together again.

STRUCTURE OF GOVERNMENT IN WORCESTER

Latino political representation in Worcester is hindered by the newness of the Latino community, its relatively small size, and conflicts both within the Latino community and between the community and other minority groups. Another impediment to political power for Latinos is the structure of government in this city.

Prior to a charter reform voted by the residents of the city in 1987 (Worcester's Home Rule Charter 1987), the citizens of Worcester elected nine City Councilors who ran at-large. The council elected the Mayor, resulting in a weak mayoral system of government. Since the change, six councilors are elected at-large and five are elected as district councilors. The Mayor is now elected by the voters from among at-large candidates for City Council who declare intentions of running for Mayor as well. A City Manager is appointed by the council to run the day-to-day operations of the municipality. The fact that the district with the greatest concentration of Latinos currently includes some white blue-collar neighborhoods, as well as a very affluent section of the city, makes it an even greater challenge for Latinos to overcome. In addition, the six members of the School Committee, which the Mayor chairs, are elected at large. No Latino has been elected to the School Committee to date.

Appointed positions, such as the Airport Commission, the Worcester Redevelopment Authority, and Human Rights Commission, are confirmed by the city council. The City Manager chooses his candidate from a pool of three people presented to him by the Citizen's Advisory Council. Members to the Advisory Council are appointed in the same fashion as the members of other boards or commissions. Historically, minorities—especially Latinos—have had a difficult time being appointed to serve on the most important boards of the city.

LATINO ELECTION CAMPAIGNS IN WORCESTER: RISING NUMBERS AND A PERSONAL RESPONSE

In 1983, José Pérez, the son of a Protestant pastor and now a pastor himself, ran for the Worcester Charter Commission. He worked very hard but, due to his lack of name recognition, the small number of Latinos registered to vote, and his inability to raise the necessary amount of money to mount a credible campaign in this city, his efforts proved unsuccessful.

In 1993, an outspoken Jewish community activist brought a coalition together to view a home video of an incident involving the arrest of a Latino man by two Worcester Police officers. After viewing the episode, the group was outraged and formed the Worcester Peace Coalition. This group pressed the city to make some immediate changes in the police department's training protocol and arrest procedures, as well as to increase the number of minorities in the police force. This incident—clearly a case of excessive force—once again sparked outrage within Worcester's Latino Community. Latinos filled the halls of the City Council chamber, numbed by reports of how violent the incident had been and by the fact that the victim had died 10 days after the incident (having never recovered from a coma).

Although a few people were calling for violence in the streets and retaliation against the police, the Peace Coalition attempted to calm the public, at the same time as it was working with the city on a proper response to this incident. The days went by, then the months, with little result from the efforts of the Peace Coalition. As one of the frustrated members of the Coalition, I decided to run for a seat on the Worcester City Council in the 1993 election. In what became a very exciting and heavily talked about candidacy, I placed seventh out of 12 candidates, following an Irish man who had run unsuccessfully in 1991. I received over 9,000 votes, but was almost 2,000 votes short. Elections often serve to stimulate change, however, even if the minority candidate loses: since this election, the police department has made attempts to increase minority representation on the force. Sensitivity training was also instituted for the new class of recruits going through the academy.

These measures would later prove insufficient and minorities throughout the city continued to lodge many reports of police brutality against the department and its officers. In 1999 the Human Rights Commission held hearings and determined that many problems were in fact plaguing the Worcester Police Department. A report with specific recommendations would follow.

Following the 1993 elections I was able to establish myself as the front-runner in the 1995 City Council race, at least within the Latino community. In the end, I was unsuccessful. Several factors contributed to my defeat. First, many people knew that I was a registered Republican, Latinos had been asked by Democrats not to vote for me. Second, although I never kept it a secret, most people in the Latino community did not know that although I was born in Puerto Rico, my father is Dominican. Unfortunately, the relationship between these two groups is quite strained in Worcester. The level of mutual distrust is high. Several people approached me during this election season to ask me about my Latino nationality. I could not believe that this issue would affect Latino voters in that election. Although there are fewer Dominicans than Puerto Ricans in Worcester, Dominicans seem to show more interest in politics and are politically active locally. I was fortunate to benefit from the support of a growing Dominican community in Worcester, but that support may have cost me the backing of Puerto Ricans in the city. Finally, personal reasons made me withdraw from the race; in October of that year I was afflicted by what would later be diagnosed as bone cancer.

In 1997, José Pérez ran again for a seat on the School Committee and received over 8,000 votes. Despite evidence that more Latinos were registered to vote and having raised over $2,000, he was unable to win a seat. He cites his lack of funds and failure on the part the Democratic Party to support his candidacy, as the greatest factors in not being able to win.

In 1997 Maritza Cruz, daughter of Mrs. Conchita Cruz, ran for City Council in her district, which has the second highest concentration of Latinos in the city. (The Great Brook Valley has the highest.) She organized the best campaign I (or any Latino activist) ever have witnessed. She is Puerto Rican, but she is married to a very well-known Dominican merchant. In addition, a well-known local political gadfly of Irish decent chaired her campaign. Several things went wrong during that campaign season, however, including apparent vote fraud: her campaign registered over 2,000 people but many of the registration cards were found in the one of the bathrooms of City Hall days after the deadline for registration. Maritza Cruz lost the election and chose not to run in 1999; she indicated that she wanted to spend more time with her children.

In 1999, Sam Rosario ran for the Worcester School Committee. In a race for six seats with five incumbents, and eight candidates in total, one incumbent lost and two new candidates were elected. Rosario was not one of the two who won a seat. The two candidates who won were both of Irish decent. The Democratic political machine heavily supported one, while the other was well financed and heavily coached by the West-Siders, a group that Latinos know as the well-to-do in Worcester. In 1999, after much contemplation, I decided to run one more time for Worcester City Council. I raised 50 percent more money than in the 1995 race. I walked more and knocked on many more doors than I had in past elections. Despite these efforts, I did not win the one open seat vacated by a city councilor.

Although many allude to the decline of party politics in urban America, local politics is dominated by the Democratic Party. Party Politics likely contributed to my loss. Despite having been endorsed by the National Association of Government Employees for my last two City Council bids, the Teachers Union in 1993, and the Police Union during the 1999 election, I have never been endorsed by the Central Labor Council, Trade Unions, the Teamsters, or the Fire Fighters. The Teachers Union, the Teamsters, and the Trade Union are staunchly Democratic (I would go further and say they are controlled by the Democratic Party in the city). Accordingly, it is very difficult for a Republican candidate like myself to get their endorsement in Worcester or other cities in Massachusetts—a virtual one-party state. My perserverance paid off, nevertheless: I became a Worcester City Councilor on 26 July 2000 when Councilor-at-large Stacey Deboise Luster resigned. Having placed seventh in the race for six at-large seats, I took her place due to my standing in the polls.

LATINAS AND THE FUTURE OF OUR COMMUNITY

Although not candidates for office, there are two women who merit mention because of their contributions to the community. Gladys Rodríguez, the daughter of one of the mothers on the Hispanic Parents Advisory Council, is currently the director of Congressman Jim McGovern's district office. If she uses her visibility and power in the community to support a worthy Latino candidate (like Maritza Cruz), she could help make history.

Maritza Cruz, her husband, Ediberto Santiago, and I founded the Worcester Latino Voter Registration and Education Project. After we became disengaged from the program to pursue other projects, Marilyn Reyes, the daughter of one of the first leaders of the Puerto Rican community in our city, took it over. She has been able to register many new Latino voters. In addition, she has been able to gather a wealth of statistics with respect to Latinos and their participation in Worcester politics. She was also able to identify and successfully solicited funding to continue the project. This project is supposed to be nonpartisan and not endorse candidates or issues. Unfortunately, she recently used her visibility in the community to campaign in favor of a non-Latino candidate. Hopefully, she will steer the project away from partisanship and endorsements. However, if she does change the mission of the project to endorse candidates, she will see the merits of supporting a Latino candidate in future elections.

Just as in other Massachusetts communities, there is a segment of Worcester's chief decision makers—"progressives"—that see the merits of helping elect minorities and specifically Latinos. Coalitions between progressives, other minorities, and Latinos, according to Browning, Marshall, and Tabb (1984) may be essential to change the balance of power in Worcester and to increase Latino political influence. Such a group began meeting several years ago under the leadership of Bari Boyer, a local lawyer and political operative, to discuss what they perceived as a leadership vacuum in many different aspects of our civic, cultural, and political life. After several retreats, and years of meetings, some of its participants ran for office. Others embarked upon major projects in our community. This group invited Shirley Wright, Ediberto Santiago, and Maritza Cruz to participate in their initiative. A commitment to help seek funds for the Voter Registration Project came out of the group, as well as the organization that supported Shirley Wright's successful candidacy in 1995 (see Table 7.1). I believe that if this group became involved in the candidacy of a viable Latino candidate, they could very well help elect him or her.

The most important element in a Latina/o's candidacy from this group's perspective is that individual's ability to unify the Latino community behind his/her candidacy. Unfortunately, the Latino community in our city is still very fragmented. We have not learned the lessons of the school struggles in the 1970s when parents working together fought so hard for what has been gained in our community to date. Unity will be the greatest challenge for this community going into the twenty-first century. Hopefully, it will not take another tragic event for our people to come together to demand political representation and respect.

ACKNOWLEDGMENTS

Much of the information in this chapter was gained through interviews conducted by the author in 2000. Interviewees included Francisco Ojeda, 5 April; Ángel Camilo Navedo, 19 April; María Montánez, 6 May; Conchita Cruz, 6 May; Arthur Chase, 7 May; Sonya Ventura, 8 May; Ediberto Santiago, 4 May; Maritza Cruz, 6 May; July Vargas, 25 April; Sam Rosario, 9 May; José Pérez, 11 May; Bari Boyer, 11 May; and John Rodríguez, 25 April. The author would like to acknowledge their invaluable contribution to the history of Latino politics in Worcester.

NOTES

1. Juan A. Gómez is the first Latino to hold elected office in Worcester; he became a member of the Worcester City Council on 26 July 2000. Born in Santurce, Puerto Rico, in 1964, Gómez has been a Worcester resident for the past 21 years. He ran for City Council in 1993, 1995, and 1999 and was eager to document the political history of Latinos in the City of Worcester—from the perspective of his own experiences as an activist, a candidate, and a lay historian. We are appreciative of his contribution and pleased to include his work in this volume.

2. Mr. Ojeda has been a resident of the city since 1967 and a long-time activist as well.

3. María Montánez is a former parent liaison for the Worcester Public School Bilingual program and 27-year veteran of the public school system.

4. Sonya Ventura is a former resident and community activist in Great Brook Valley.

5. As the first coordinator of the Worcester Latino Voter Registration and Education project, I worked with a volunteer and actually went through the entire voter roster in 1994 for the purpose of counting Latinos registered. The Latino voter registration rate was calculated by the editors of this volume based on the Latino 1990 Census population of 16,258.

6. Despite this rise in the number of Latinos registered, the Latino voter registration rate remained unchanged due to the increase in the size of the Latino population.

7. Ediberto Santiago, Maritza's husband, was in charge of the turn out the vote effort for her campaign.

8. Those were the words of an interviewee who chose to remain anonymous.

REFERENCES

Browning, Rufus P., Dale Rogers Marshall, and David Tabb. (1984). *Protest is Not Enough: The Struggle of Blacks and Hispanics for Equality in Urban Politics*. Berkeley: University of California Press.

Clinton Daily News. (1978). "Puerto Ricans Visit Clinton." 1 July.

Cruz, Conchita. (2000). Interview with author, 6 May.

Montánez, María. (2000). Interview with author, 6 May.

Ojeda, Francisco. (2000). Interview with author, 5 April.

Santiago, Ediberto. (2000). Interview with author, 4 May.

Torres, Andrés, and Lisa Chavez. (1998). "Latinos in Massachusetts: An Update." Boston: Mauricio Gastón Institute for Latino Community Development and Public Policy, University of Massachusetts Boston.

U.S. Bureau of the Census. (2001). City data provided by the Mauricio Gastón Institute for Latino Community Development and Public Policy, University of Massachusetts Boston.

Ventura, Sonya. (2000). Interview with author, 8 May.

Worcester's Home Rule Charter, 1987.

Worcester Telegram. (1978a). "Hispanics Air School Changes," 3 June.

———. (1978b). "Two Groups Compete for Latino Leadership Role in City," 11 June.

———. (1978c). "Clark St. Pupils May Get 'Open Enrollment' Offer," 15 June.

———. (1978d). "Tenants at GBV Fight Image," 23 July.

———. (1979). "Husband, Wife Granted Continuances in Assault," 25 February.

———. (1999). Election Report, 4 November.

Part II

Issues in Latino Politics

CHAPTER 8

Latina Women and Political Leadership
Implications for Latino Community Empowerment*

CAROL HARDY-FANTA

Like "power," "leadership" is one of the most complex and elusive of concepts in social science. Leadership has meaning for, and has been studied extensively across, all social science disciplines: politics, business (especially management), psychology, philosophy, sociology, and military studies.[1] Most studies of political leadership reflect certain assumptions about how leadership is conceptualized, who is counted as a leader, and how leadership should be studied. Some of these assumptions seem to tie leadership to holding office or positions in organizations; others focus on the personal traits of the people who are leaders. Still others seem to conceive of leadership as the ability to contribute to a cause, organization, or process and focus on the effectiveness of different leadership strategies or styles. Finally, there are assumptions that lead to an examination of the relationship between leaders and his or her followers. All of these assumptions inform both the research design and the conclusions reached about political leadership. However, it is not untypical for a study built on one type of assumption about leadership to ignore the other dimensions that form the totality of leadership in urban politics today. Although it is not without value to select a narrow aspect of a field to study, what seems to be occurring in the area of political leadership is a certain blindness as to how the implicit or at least unstated assumptions reflect biases about culture and gender.

In a related vein, studies about Latino politics generally ignore the role of Latina women as political leaders or view women as constrained from

* A slightly different version of this chapter appeared in the *New England Journal of Public Policy*, Special Issue: Latinos in a Changing Society Part I, 11(1) (Spring/Summer 1995), 220–235. This chapter is based on a paper presented at the Annual Meeting of the New England Political Science Association, Northampton, Massachusetts, 2–3 April, 1993. Reprinted with permission from the *New England Journal of Public Policy*.

political participation by cultural or gender-based oppression. Cultural values of *machismo* and its female correlate, *marianismo*,[2] appear to create a submissive and passive role for Latina women that suppresses the likelihood that Latina women will become political leaders. These cultural values supposedly exacerbate gender-based attributes that "leave politics to the men."[3] Structural obstacles and gender-based power relations, according to traditional social science analysis, also stifle the political aspirations of Latina women. And yet, Latino activists and researchers alike are extremely concerned about low levels of Latino political participation in the United States and are eager to discover strategies that can serve to mobilize Latino communities in this country—strategies that, in fact, may depend on the political leadership of Latina women.

In this chapter I will show how an examination of the political leadership of Latina women can provide a broader set of answers to three key questions: (1) What is political leadership? (2) How does the definition of leadership depend on gender? and (3) In what ways does the empowerment of Latino communities depend on the political leadership of Latina women? Contrary to their invisibility in the political leadership *literature,* Latina women play important leadership roles in both the electoral arena and at the community level. As political leaders, Latina women make significant contributions to Latino community empowerment.

THE MEANING OF POLITICAL LEADERSHIP

One of the major flaws in much of the literature on political leadership stems from the assumption that leadership is somehow derived from or equivalent to official positions, whether elected office, appointed office, or as head of a formal organization.[4] The assumptions embedded in a Weberian view of the superiority of the bureaucratic leader who is vested with rational/legal authority and legitimacy seem to lead researchers studying leadership to first look to people in positions and then identify the qualities exhibited by those individuals. Those qualities then become associated with definitions of leadership.

The extent to which political leadership is identified with official position is rarely noticed and its implications rarely acknowledged. In a recent analysis of publications on political leadership conducted for this chapter, over 50 percent of the books and articles listed between 1977 and 1994 focus on specific official positions within a government or institutional authority.[5] Thus, the majority of research and writing on political leadership focuses on leadership derived from official positions.

Of course, literature exists that focuses on other aspects of leadership. Numerous books and articles have examined leadership values (e.g., Bealey 1988; Bershady 1989), personal qualities (e.g., Tucker 1977), and the interaction between leadership and democratic processes.[6] In addition, researchers, especially in the fields of psychology and management, have studied leadership style; researchers from these fields also have given the most attention to gender differences in leadership.[7] Nevertheless, it is not uncommon for literature that purports to examine the interpersonal aspects of leadership, i.e., the relationships between leaders and their followers, subsequently to highlight men who are leaders by virtue of institutionally derived "authority" or force of will. William Litzinger and Thomas Schaefer (1984), for example, describe how certain leaders began as "good followers"; unfortunately they provide as illustrations individuals such as Churchill, Bismarck, Caesar, Stalin, Hitler, Idi Amin, Mussolini, and Genghis Khan. Most of this literature assumes, as well, that leaders are embedded in formal organizations, be they in business or politics. Jeffrey Pfeffer (1984), for example, suggests that individuals are selected to leadership positions, and Warren Bennis (1993) states in various ways that "effective" leaders serve the purposes of their *organizations*.

GENDER BIAS AND THE STUDY OF POLITICAL LEADERSHIP

Inherent in the conceptualization of political leadership as position and institution derived, is a specific gender bias. When the focus is on position-derived leadership, the political leadership of women is often overlooked or rendered invisible. Susan Bourque and Jean Grossholtz (1974) suggest that male authors in political science often restrict their attention to male political actors and that researchers today follow the pattern established by men such as Floyd Hunter and Robert Dahl "that . . . the people you study are men."[8] Bennis (1993), for example, in his otherwise compelling discussion of the dynamics and traits of leadership, studied only six women in his sample of ninety. And others (i.e., Porter, Geis, and Jennings [Walstedt]1983), find that when situational cues associated with leadership (such as being at the head of a table) are applied to men, men are identified as leaders; however, women are not identified as leaders even when the situational cues should convey leadership status upon them.

In addition, women are often rendered invisible as leaders in community studies simply by the process of ignoring the fact that they are women. This trend is especially true for minority women. For example, Matthew Crenson's (1983) study of neighborhood politics in Baltimore never comments on the fact that many if not most of the black leaders he writes about are women (identifiable by their names). In Boston, Miren Uriarte-Gastón (1988) fails to comment on the fact that the activists who had the biggest impact on Latino mass mobilization in the 1970s were Latina women.[9] Even works by women such as Jane Bayes's (1982) *Minority Politics and Ideologies in the United States* overlook the unique aspects of the politics of minority women when they focus on women as a minority rather than minority women as political actors and political leaders.[10]

Another way the political leadership of women is overlooked is by defining the *domain* of politics in a way that reflects a male bias: The domain of political leadership is essentially public and formally organized and structured (see, for example, Barber 1984). Hierarchically structured organizations with position-derived leaders may in fact reflect a male preference for hierarchy, authority, legitimacy, and control rather than embody an inherent quality of leadership per se.[11] Women's activism in arenas that reflect their concern for their children, their families, and their neighborhoods is identified as "community activism," at best, or "disorderly," at worst, but rarely is it identified as political leadership to the same degree as male-focused activities. [12]

This rather lengthy discussion of the failures of current thinking on political leadership has been provided because what is left out of such conceptualizations is the role of community leadership—leadership of *the community*. By focusing so heavily on the leaders in high positions, mainstream studies of leadership fail to address the interaction between leaders and followers at the community level.[13] And yet it is precisely community-level political activism that is often the first step toward political participation taken by Latinos in the mainland United States. The political process, especially for those who have previously not participated in politics, typically begins at the community level. The crucial task identified by most analysts of Latino politics is to engage those Latinos who are disaffected or alienated from the political process or who are ineligible to participate due to a lack of citizenship. It is at this community level that Latina women are the most successful at promoting political participation among the disaffected or alienated Latino community members.

LATINA WOMEN AND LEADERSHIP: RESEARCH METHODS

This chapter is based on findings from three research studies. The first was a qualitative study of Latino political participation in Boston, Massachusetts.[14] I conducted in-depth, semi-structured interviews with 31 influential Latinos and 22 "common folk" individuals (*la gente del pueblo*) between 1988 and 1990. The interviews were conducted in English or in Spanish and each lasted between 2 and 3 hours. The influential Latinos were selected using a combination of reputational, purposive, and snowball sampling; the common folk were volunteers from Latino community centers located in the three main Latino neighborhoods of Boston. I interviewed a total of 29 women and 24 men; the ethnic breakdown reflected the current demographic diversity of the Latino population in Boston. In addition, over 100 hours of participant observation of community organizing and other political events added context and richness to the interview data.

The second source of data provides some preliminary findings on Latina women's leadership from a national project on Latina leadership development in relation to the AIDS crisis.[15] This research includes a series of interviews with 18 Latina women from six sites across the United States and

Puerto Rico who were participating in a national project called Latina HIV/AIDS Partnership Plan. The women who were selected randomly from those participating in the project were being interviewed over a 3-year period to track their development as leaders in the area of HIV/AIDS within a national network of Latina women. Included in their interviews were their views on and experiences related to leadership development as Latina women. Data from this study are included here because they provide in-depth information on leadership from a Latina woman's perspective over time and include women from across the United States, including Puerto Rico.

The third source of data is a study that examined the impact of gender on Latino electoral campaigns in Massachusetts. This study gathered information on all Latino candidates who had ever run for office in the state and gathered information on the impact of gender on motivation to run for office and campaign strategies.[16]

LEADERSHIP AS POSITIONS: LATINA WOMEN AND LATINO MEN

Before addressing the ways a focus on leadership as positions prevents us from gaining a complete picture of political leadership, I would like to address the issue of the invisibility of women's leadership even when they hold positions. The literature on Latino politics virtually ignores the political participation of Latina women in general and a common response to comments about Latina women as political leaders is skepticism and doubt. The assumption that Latina women are passive, submissive, and uninvolved in politics is belied by reality, however.[17] Nationally, Latina women make up a larger portion of Latino elected officials than women in general as a percentage of all elected officials.

Although the literature on women in politics stresses the difficulty in recruiting women to run for office[18] (and during the 1990 primary campaign only 15 percent of Massachusetts candidates were women), Latina women in Boston and Massachusetts run for office in high numbers. In Boston, *a full one-half of all Latino candidates have been Latina women.* In addition, the first Latino to run for mayor was a Latina woman, Diana Lam in 1991, not a man. Her candidacy was extremely short-lived due to certain IRS irregularities, but the lack of attention her candidacy received may be attributed to the fact that she was a woman: her announcement that she was a candidate received little press and was placed "below the fold" in the *Boston Globe.* It was only after she withdrew that the *Globe* declared that she would have presented the most serious challenge to the incumbent.

In Massachusetts, almost one-third (32.6 percent) of the Latinos to have run for office have been Latina women. More than half (57 percent) of the candidates who have been elected (i.e., were "successful") have been Latina women. Of the two Latinos to run for mayor, one was a Latina woman. In addition, four of the seven candidates for state level offices or higher (57 percent) have also been Latina women.[19]

The political leadership of Latina women is less visible, therefore, by a tendency to ignore them even when they are candidates or elected officials—i.e., in roles commonly accepted as political leadership within mainstream literature. The assumption that it is males who are leaders, despite the sheer numbers of Latina women who run for office and who are elected, is illustrated as well by what Andrea del Valle,[20] a Latina woman I interviewed, ilustrates the assumption that it is males who are leaders, despite the sheer numbers of Latina women who run for office and who are elected, when she said, "You can have ten women, but, if there's one man, 'Oh! He must be the president!'" In other words, there seems to be a need to see men as being "in charge."

Del Valle attributes the invisibility of Latina women in politics, specifically as leaders, to a particular mindset: leaders must be men. In addition, the assumption of position-derived leadership creates a bias against recognition that political leadership is not located only in those who hold official titles. She herself holds no lofty position and is not acclaimed in the Anglo press as a "leader"; she works to organize others politically. Her politics is not the politics of positions and public speeches; who is president is less important than achieving change. Her work, and the work of other women like her, is rendered invisible by the mindset of researchers who look at public, official, and titular politics.

Mary Pardo (1990, 3) discovered a similar process when she examined the political organizing of Mexican-American women in Los Angeles. She found that the Latina women mobilized Latino men "by giving them a position they could manage. The men may have held the title of 'president,' but they were not making day-to-day decisions about work, nor were they dictating the direction of the group. . . . *This should alert researchers against measuring power and influence by looking solely at who holds titles*" (emphasis added).

Even more important than the fact that Latina women hold *positions* of leadership as candidates or elected officials is the way Latina women and Latino men differ in whether holding a position is an essential feature of leadership. One man, when asked to describe what he did politically, turned to his computer and printed a list of his positions, titles, and memberships in organizations. Latina women, in contrast, talked about politics as making connections between people to take collective action on social problems and to achieve social change.

The gender difference in how politics was defined by men and women was striking. In the Boston study I found that Latino men were *five* times as likely to define politics as positions and status as were Latina women. The men were more concerned about holding positions, defined political participation as gaining access to positions, and identified leadership as serving as role models. Until relatively recently, Latino men in Boston were also more likely to move into positions in government from positions as directors of community-based agencies. As one man said: "If you look at the leadership, every single person has been a director of agencies. I don't think there are any exceptions around. Why? Because those were the only institutional bases available to Latinos ten, fifteen years ago here, so the leadership . . . today . . . came through that bottleneck." And although there are certainly exceptions where women in Boston have been directors of agencies, male dominance of these positions was confirmed by men as well as women. One man said, for example: "It's men making decisions on who gets hired. . . . The men's club."

A preliminary list of influential Latinos in Boston generated using the reputational method, not untypically, yielded names of people in positions—and the list was 60 percent male. When the question was asked: "Who is good at getting others to participate in politics (in other words, to lead others)?" the gender ratio shifted to 60 percent female. In addition, when the individuals not holding positions was scrutinized, it became evident that a full 75 percent of those identified as "being able to lead others into politics" were Latina women.

The idea of "being in charge," of holding a position in an organization, office, or institution, relies heavily on the assumption that leadership stemming from institution-derived authority is superior to charismatic or traditional leadership. The problem with such an assumption is that the concern for legitimacy associated with positions in institutions or organizations may be a male concern or preference more than an inherent feature of leadership. (I would go so far as to suggest, in fact, that the concern for institutional legitimacy—implicit in bureaucratic leadership—goes back even farther to male concerns about legitimate progeny for the purposes of inheritance.)

LEADERSHIP AND PERSONAL TRAITS

Studies of political leadership (and studies of leadership in such fields as management as well) have often focused on personal traits associated with presumed "leaders" (see Hollander 1964 and Homans 1950). One of the most prominent personal traits assumed to be associated with leadership is that of dominance (which of course is linked to power).[21] The assumption that leadership is associated both with having a position and with personal traits such as dominance implies a concern for "being in charge." Being able to convince others that one is right, that one's ideas are "the way to go," seems indelibly linked to our ideas about leadership—and are features of charismatic leaders as much as, if not more so, bureaucratic leaders. However, theories of leadership that stress personal traits often overlook the fact that certain traits are more likely to reflect male styles of leadership than universal or female styles of leadership. In addition, much of the emphasis on dominance as a key trait of leaders derives from early studies conducted almost exclusively on males (usually white males).

Robert Lane (1969, 31), for example, connects politics to the need for power and the need to express or control aggression, but he downplays social relations and affiliative needs. Lane's conclusion that politics is more about power and control than affiliation and social connectedness may result from the fact that the subjects of his research were male and not from an accurate analysis that reflects both male and female perspectives. Implicit in the conception of leadership as positions and a concern for power over social relations is the ability to "command action" and for the followers of leaders to be able to "take orders." William Litzinger and Thomas Schaefer (1984, 140; emphasis in original), for example, state that "many fine leaders *have* been excellent followers. The young Churchill distinguished himself as a faithful taker of orders." My findings suggest that the concern for power over affiliation is not a political trait but a male trait—one that does not capture a complete picture of political leadership.

Catalina Torres, a Mexican-American woman in Boston, tells of her efforts to develop an economic project for the Latino community in Boston. When she contacted agency directors for letters of support, they resisted and complained that she should have come to them first on any project development. She recalled "people saying, 'Who does she think she is? We were here first. Why is she doing it, why didn't you call on us.'" The concern about who is going to be first—competition over turf—the desire to retain power—got in the way of an economic development project. When asked: "Who were these people resisting support for the project?" Catalina Torres replied: "These are the guys." Although it might be pointed out that competition over turf is a mainstay of all political life, it was the women in both studies who pointed specifically to men obstructing the community projects they, Latina women, initiated. It was not the other Latina women who were putting obstacles in their paths.

There is some evidence in the Latino social science literature that men are more concerned about power and turf than women. Gloria Bonilla-Santiago (1990), for example, described her efforts to pass legislation establishing Hispanic women's centers in New Jersey. She indicated that one stumbling block was the opposition by the directors of Hispanic agencies and later stated that the directors who opposed her were virtually all men. Antonia Pantoja and Esperanza Martell (1989–1990) found a similar pattern in New York.

Results from the Latina women's leadership development project discussed above suggest that Latina women see men as being overly concerned with "having the right answer" and dominating the discourse at meetings. A woman I interviewed from California stated that men were likely to get up at a meeting and say "something like, 'There are *three* things you can say about this [problem]' and everybody else is saying, 'Yeah, yeah, there are three things.' And I'm sitting there saying, '*Three* things? Maybe there are more, I don't know.' I just don't like it when people are *so* sure of themselves." She echoed other women interviewed as part of this project when, in discussing what makes a "good leader," she deemphasized the need to be recognized or to control the agenda. Another woman stated that a good leader is successful when "no one know you're leading"; the group members feel empowered to take collective action on their own behalf.

Aracelis Guzmán, in Boston, also identified male concerns for dominance as a source of divisiveness in the Latino community:

> [W]hen they [men] become leaders, they go off on their own and you *cannot* get them down from there. And this is very divisive, very harmful . . . because everyone is there, like this, saying, "*Sí, sí* [nods several times] when, in reality, they do not agree with him. And it's the mental set that the man—*el macho*—has all the answers. (Hardy-Fanta 1993, 91; emphasis in original).

If Latino men stressed positions and status five times as much as Latina women did, what did Latina women talk about? Politics for Latina women stressed making connections at the community level—for them, leadership involves not positions and dominance but the relationships between people. The relationship between leaders and followers is the basis for much of the political leadership of Latina women. They express less concern for control and power over others[22] or for being designated the official leader. (For example, men were almost three times as likely to talk about power as women [Hardy-Fanta 1993, 207]). Instead women stress a collective, shared vision of leadership. One woman said there is a pressure to designate a leader and when someone is seen as effective: "They see you like a ray of light and then this person becomes '*The Leader!*' And even though there are clearly people who have a vision, who have a set of skills that enable them to stir people up later on—to say, 'Look, what we have to do is this and this and this.' I believe that it should be more collective—that there should be more than one head."

This emphasis on multiple sources of leadership and on being able to "stir people up," to *atraer a otros*, is heavily invested in assumptions that leadership has to do with the leader–follower relationship. Political science sometimes seems a little uncomfortable in shifting a focus to the relational side of politics. For example, H.G. Peter Wallach (1988, 1093) criticizes Barbara Kellerman (1986) for "further[ing] the assumption that leadership is largely understood through the leader–follower relationship." Feminist political theory, however, suggests that the emphasis on power, position, and hierarchy reflects male concerns more than a universal set of beliefs and certainly does not reflect women's concerns about leadership. Nancy Chodorow (1974) and Deborah Tannen (1991) find that women's strivings for intimacy, interdependence, and relationship "dovetail with connection" and that men "are working hard to preserve their independence in a hierarchical world."

Leadership for Latina women stresses affiliation—personal relationships—and is located in a domain that is both public and private. María Ramírez, for example, told a story of connecting neighbor to neighbor to fight drugs in her neighborhood. Her concern was not for her own status—in fact, she downplayed her own role in the effort. Her leadership was not derived from a position she held—although she worked in the state legislature. Her leadership is illustrated by and derives from the relationship she has with community members—with the people who follow her lead. María Ramírez works with Latinos in her neighborhood—Latinos who cannot vote, who are not citizens, and who often are in the United States illegally—to solve community problems. She first focuses on the need to connect neighbor to neighbor, whether the people involved are citizens from Puerto Rico or legal or illegal residents from Santo Domingo and Central America:

> I've called a couple of people and said, "Look, these are our kids, we either see them get their heads beat in, put away for life, get shot up or we go out there and we help them." They're not my children *personally,* but they are *our* kids and we all get labeled the same and they [the police] don't care if they [the kids] are Puerto Rican, if they're from Santo Domingo, if they're from El Salvador, they don't care, they speak Spanish, they're Hispanic, that's all they know. So we either *do* something about it or we don't. We're trying to talk to the parents and I have neighbors talking to neighbors, talking saying "Look, let's not have a riot this weekend, let's try to talk—What's the problem?" (emphasis in original)

María Ramírez then described how she succeeded in mobilizing undocumented immigrants in a Latino neighborhood to tackle the problems of drugs:

> We had this drug house and I told the people on Boylston Street—they could not vote, *the majority of those people could not vote. And they weren't Puerto Ricans either.* I said, "You live on this street, you want it to be good, you take responsibility." . . . They first thought I was *crazy*! They said, "What do you mean?"! I mean—*Some of these people were even—illegal,* and I said "I don't care, if you're legal or not, you want responsibility, you do something about it." We have to decide what we want and go after it. . . . They did. We put this march together, we had the New England Telephone Company donate the BAD shirts—Boston Against Drugs—we had buttons, we made banners, they cooked, we rallied in front of the drug houses with the cops and everything. We pointed the people out. *They* did that—I mean, I was there, but they did it. And

every time there was an incident, they came out to the streets and they said "No *more*," and it took us a year, but they [the drug dealers] aren't there anymore. The elected official was there, the police were there and these are people who do not vote! (Hardy-Fanta 1993, 122–123; emphasis in original).

She stresses what "they" did, not what she did. Like Anne Statham, who found that women were less inclined than men to be what she called "image-engrossed,"[23] María Ramírez is less concerned with making an impression or achieving status for herself or controlling the actions of the group. She is more concerned with accomplishing the goals of the group. Her goal, at the most basic level, was to get rid of drug houses; at a deeper level, her leadership empowered groups who are among the most marginalized of all urban groups: the undocumented immigrants—"illegal aliens." Providing leadership for her neighbors empowered them to overcome both the disinclination to get involved associated with poverty, the inability to speak English, and the inhibitions imposed by illegal status. Here, in this example, are Latinos who are *illegal* residents working *side by side* with the police in the city of Boston. They are also being led by Latina women.

POLITICAL LEADERSHIP, CULTURE, AND GENDER

The nature of leadership shifts from a focus on positions and dominance to a focus on interpersonal relationships when one includes the experiences of Latina women. The Latina women who were interviewed for these studies emphasize the relational rather than positional aspects of leadership, are less concerned with power or control of turf, and lead others into political participation through the use of personal relationships. Politics becomes an interactive process oriented toward achieving collectively determined goals. It seems clear that the way leadership gets defined depends on the gender of the researcher and of the leaders themselves.

But is what Latina women do any different from what other women—white women, black women—do? A feminist debate continues to rage about whether there are essential differences between women's politics and men's politics in general. Feminist politics—which typically focuses on white women—emphasizes grass roots, personal politics, a politics tied to individual, family, friendship networks, and community relationships. Martha A. Ackelsberg (1984) and Diane L. Fowlkes (1983), for example, discuss how women's views of politics are connected to home, family, friends, and community, much like the views Latina women in this research exemplified. Virginia Sapiro (1983) and Janet Flammang (1984) also find that women, in general, link private experiences to public politics and that women do differ from men in how they perceive politics and political participation.

Research on black women in politics leads to similar conclusions. In general, private actions and informal personal networks have provided support for lower-class black women to achieve major social changes. Black women seem to provide evidence, therefore, that gender differences in the nature of politics do exist—that politics for women is more personal, stresses interpersonal relationships, and is an interactive process. Everyday concerns and relationships based on day-to-day networks form the basis of political mobilization for black women, according to this literature (see, for example, Dill 1988; Garland 1988; Sacks 1988).

In this chapter I do not claim, then, that Latina women are unique in their ability to generate political participation via their emphasis on connectedness. What is important is not whether Latina women differ from other women in how they perceive the nature of politics and how they work within the Latino community, but rather that (1) Latina women run for office more than their non-Latina counterparts; (2) contrary to prevailing myths, Latina women take on political leadership roles; and (3) by virtue of their connectedness to the community, Latina political leadership may well be the key to Latino community empowerment.

IMPLICATIONS FOR LATINO POLITICS AND COMMUNITY EMPOWERMENT

The study of Latina women in Boston, Massachusetts, and nationally serves to dispel myths about Latina women and leadership and provides insight into issues of political leadership. When leadership is defined as positions in government and elected or appointed office, then males dominate the discourse about the nature of leadership. In addition, by ignoring the extent to which Latina women run for, and are elected to office, the media, social science literature, and community are able to continue to see politics as a male phenomenon. However, by acknowledging the contribution of Latina women as candidates *and* as community leaders, we can begin to examine and recognize the value of what Latina women do to empower Latino communities.

And what is it that they do that is different from Latino men? Latina women seem to work with community members on collectively generated goals that derive from the community members themselves. Political leadership that is based on the community members seeing themselves "in charge" empowers the community in ways that leadership based on dominance may not. The benefits of this leadership style are that it gives voice to Latinos who have not previously participated in politics; it empowers them to speak out at meetings and decide a course of action.

In addition, by focusing on improvements in everyday life in the neighborhoods, i.e., education, street safety, housing quality, and jobs, Latina women are able to mobilize the community around felt needs. It is possible, therefore, to bring into the political process those Latinos who are too often marginalized by a politics based on more traditional, position-derived leadership that emphasizes voting and electoral representation.

Indeed, the picture of Latina women's political leadership that emerges from the three studies that form the basis of the current chapter has several important implications for Latino community development. First, Latina women, compared to men, are less concerned with titles and positions, and more concerned with community connectedness. Because of this, they focus on how to achieve change at the neighborhood, community level. It is at this level that Latinos who see the need for jobs, safety, financial security, health care, and access to high-quality education can become mobilized to participate in electoral or community politics. As a male political activist in Boston said: "Women have been a major force at the grass roots in the Hispanic community—from the day we came here, from the day we came to the United States. At the grass roots, the community level, women have been the major force for change."

Second, the Latino community in Boston makes up only 14 percent of the population and is characterized by considerable diversity. Creating a unified community is a first step toward community empowerment. Building bridges—making connections—between Latinos of all nationalities at the community level is critical at this stage. In addition, generating a sense of empowerment in a community increasingly made up of undocumented immigrants requires a political leadership not constrained by the requirements of an official position or organizational role. Latina women, as illustrated in the efforts of María Ramírez above, generate political participation in ways that transcend legal status. They lead by connecting neighbor to neighbor, by generating a sense of efficacy, and they do this by *not* dominating the process or the people they are trying to lead. Their focus is on social change undertaken in action with others. As Rosa López said, "Politics is promoting change, . . . That's political. That's what I mean by politics. That's what politics means to me."

To achieve Latino community empowerment, it is necessary to begin to acknowledge Latina women as political leaders, to recognize their contribution to Latino political participation, and to learn from their experiences as candidates, community activists, and political mobilizers.

Third, it is important to examine why Latina women run for office essentially in numbers equivalent to Latino men and why, when they run, they are elected at comparable rates, as well. Although their candidacies and electoral successes receive little recognition in the media and the social science literature, they seem to be connecting to the Latino communities they strive to represent. By examining their motivations for running for office, their campaign style and strategies, and the way they interact with Latino community residents, we may gain insights needed for successful Latino candidacies—male as well as female.

A final implication of this research is that it challenges researchers to examine our own work for questions of gender and gender bias in how we define our terms, how we study the elements of politics, who we choose to interview or study, and what assumptions frame our research.

NOTES

1.   For a discussion of both the elusiveness of the topic and the interdisciplinary nature of research on leadership, see, for example, Rosenbach and Taylor (1984) and Bennis (1993).

2.   *Marianismo*, as a cultural value, creates role expectations that derive from qualities attributed to the Virgin Mary.

3.   For a discussion of the impact of restrictive, oppressive, and subservient life conditions on the politics of Mexican American women, see, for example, Guzmán (1976, 231–234), Melville (1980), Mirandé and Enríquez (1979), and Barragán (1980).

4.   In conducting a computer search of literature on political leadership from 1977 to 1994, I have found that the majority of publications on political leadership focus on people in positions, or on the positions themselves, as somehow denoting leadership (see Note 5). Research on Latino politics that follows the same path is exemplified by Martin (1977) and Padilla (1985, 1987).

5.   The computer search was conducted in November 1994 using Multiplatter and the keywords "leadership" and "politic*" (which included not only "political" but also "politics.") This search listed the titles, authors, sources, and abstracts for almost 500 books and articles published between 1977 and 1994. In addition to books and monographs, the data base included all major political science journals. Each search result was categorized based on its title and abstract as to the primary and secondary focus. Percentages of each category were calculated to produce the data cited here. The categories generated included "one head of state/ruler"; "one or more heads of states/conflict over succession"; "conflict between leaders of groups within specific countries (e.g., Arafat as a leader of the PLO; includes leaders of coups and revolutions)"; "leadership offices/positions such as 'state legislators,' 'mayors,' 'appointed officials' (including competition over turf/office)"; "policy/government decisions made by leaders of countries"; "party politics/leadership and 'elite' leaders"; "leadership development"; "types leadership related to government structure (i.e., authoritarianism vs. democracy, particularly in the Middle East, the Soviet Union, Africa, and other foreign countries)"; and "management, especially around 'effective government'"; "leadership and elections"; "gender differences"; "personality and characteristics"; and "community participation/leaders." The categories were not necessarily mutually exclusive but most articles/books, in fact, could be assigned into one major category and in the analysis I calculated percentages based on exclusive categories. The analysis showed that 16.3 percent were about a specific "ruler" of a given country (e.g., Presidents Clinton, Reagan, F.D. Roosevelt; Prime Ministers Trudeau and Thatcher; and other heads of state such as Sukarno of Indonesia and DeGaulle). When publications

about conflicts between more than one head of state/ruler (and issues of succession) were added, 25 percent of the works cited focused on these two aspects of leadership. Finally, when literature about leaders of groups in a given country who were in conflict to become the head of state and discussions about elected/appointed official positions (such as legislators, mayors, etc.) were added, I found that a full 53.2 percent of published works on political leadership were about specific official positions within a government or institutional authority.

6.   This is one of the largest categories in my search of the literature on leadership that is not specifically about official positions. The concern in political science for stability and foreign relations has yielded an extensive literature on the relationship between types of leadership (authoritarian, bureaucratic, charismatic) and forms of government. Many of the publications in this area focus on countries in the Middle East, Asia, and Eastern Europe, especially Russia in the post-Communist era. See, for example, Laleye and Ayeni (1993), Bisku (1992), and Chernyaev (1993).

7.   Hollander and Yoder (1980) examine gender and leadership style, situational influences, and leadership effectiveness. See also, for example, Statham (1987), and Kellerman (1986).

8.   Quote is from Bourque and Grossholtz (1974); see also Hunter (1953) and Dahl (1961).

9.   Uriarte-Gastón corrects this omission in a later publication; see Uriarte-Gastón (1992, 22).

10.   Since this chapter was first written there has been increased attention to Latina politics and leadership. For a recent review, see Montoya, Hardy-Fanta, and Garcia (2000).

11.   For a discussion of the way hierarchy and formal organizations reflect a male bias, see, for example, Ackelsberg (1984, 242–259; (1991) and Warren and Bourque (1985). Rosenbach and Taylor (1984, 135) illustrate the concern for legitimacy when they state that "followers give legitimacy to the leadership role." See also my discussion of this topic in Hardy-Fanta (1993, 83–87 and 90–94).

12.   For a discussion of the way women's political activism gets labeled as "disorderly," see, for example, Carole Pateman (1989) and Ackelsberg (1991).

13.   See Part 3 in Rosenbach and Taylor (1984, 135–230) for a discussion of the concept and implications of "followership" for the study of leadership.

14.   See Hardy-Fanta (1992; 1993–94, 5–25). For a complete discussion of the research methodology of this study, see Hardy-Fanta (1991). Interviews and observations were transcribed into a text-based computer analysis program, The *Ethnograph* (Qualis Research, Amherst, MA).

15.   At the time this article was originally written, I had been analyzing data from the evaluation of the Latina HIV/AIDS Partnership Plan, a CDC-funded project developed by Hispanic Designers International. Hortensia Amaro, Ph.D., at the Social and Behavioral Sciences Department of Boston University School of Public Health was principal investigator for the evaluation; I thank Dr. Amaro for her permission to share findings from this study.

16.   A Grant for Interdisciplinary Collaboration on Latino Policy Research from the Inter-University Program (IUPLR) for Latino Research, provided funding for this study. I wish to thank the IUPLR, which is a national consortium sponsoring Latino research, for their support as well as my co-investigators: Nelson Merced, former Massachusetts State Representative; Prof. Lynn Stephen, Northeastern University; and Prof. Anthony Affigne, Providence College. I would also like to thank our research assistant, María Quiñones, of the University of Massachusetts Boston for her invaluable assistance and the Center for Women in Politics and Public Policy at the University of Massachusetts Boston for sponsoring this research.

17.   For discussions of this view of Latina women see, for example, Mirandé and Enríquez (1979).

18.   Most of the mainstream literature on the recruitment of women candidates clearly states that women do not run for office as often as men. MacManus (1992), for example, refers to the "paucity of female candidates." A recent report from the National Women's Political Caucus also states: "Women have made up a very small percentage of candidates in general elections, particularly at the higher levels" (Newman 1994, 6).

19.   For a discussion of the percentages of Latina women who have run for office from Boston, see Hardy-Fanta (1993, 16). Carmen Pola (1981), Crucita Rivera (1992), and Dorca Arriaga-Gómez (1992) have run for State Representative; Alba Castillo ran against Patricia McGovern for the State Senate (1990). Alex Rodriguez (1968) ran for State Representative; Nelson Merced ran and was elected as State Representative (1988, 1990). He ran again in 1992 but was defeated in a sticker campaign. Juan Soto ran first for State Representative in 1988 and for U.S. Congress in 1990. (Note: As discussed in note 1 above, an earlier version of this chapter was published in 1995. In 1999, three Latinos (one a woman) were elected to the Massachusetts State Legislature.

20.   The names of people I interviewed are pseudonyms; names of public officials are true names.

21.   For a discussion of how dominance is associated with presumptions of leadership, see Porter, Geis, and Jennings (1983).

22.   See Miller (1983, 3–6) and Hardy-Fanta (1993, 30–31).

23.   Statham (1987, 409) finds that "respondents perceived that women were both task and people oriented while men appeared image engrossed and autonomy invested."

REFERENCES

Ackelsberg, Martha A. (1984). "Women's Collaborative Activities and City Life: Politics and Policy," in *Political Women: Current Roles in State and Local Government*, edited by Janet A. Flammang, 242–259. Beverly Hills, CA: Sage Publications.

———. (1991). *Free Women of Spain: Anarchism and the Struggle for the Emancipation of Women*. Bloomington and Indianapolis: Indiana University Press.

Barber, Benjamin. (1984). *Strong Democracy: Participatory Politics for a New Age*. Berkeley: University of California Press.

Barragán, Polly Baca. (1980). "The Lack of Political Involvement as it Relates to their Educational Background and Occupational Opportunities." In *Conference on the Educational and Occupational Needs of Hispanic Women*, by the National Institute of Education. (September), 39–46. Washington, DC: National Institute of Education.

Bayes, Jane. (1982). *Minority Politics and Ideologies in the United States*. Novato, CA: Chandler and Sharp.

Bealey, Frank. (1988). *Democracy in the Contemporary State*. Oxford: Oxford University Press.

Bennis, Warren. (1993). *An Invented Life: Reflections on Leadership and Change*. New York: Addison-Wesley.

Bershady, Harold J., ed. (1989). *Social Class and Democratic Leadership*. Philadelphia: University of Pennsylvania Press.

Bisku, Michael B. (1992). "Sukarno, Charismatic Leadership and Islam in Indonesia," *Journal of Third World Studies* 9 (Fall): 100–117.

Bonilla-Santiago, Gloria. (1990). Speech given at the National Association of Social Workers Conference. Boston, Massachusetts, 15 November.

Bourque, Susan C., and Jean Grossholtz. (1974). "Politics—an Unnatural Practice: Political Science Looks at Female Participation." *Politics and Society* (Winter): 225–266.

Chernyaev, Anatoly. (1993). "The Phenomenon of Gorbachev in the Context of Leadership," *International Affairs* (June): 37–48.

Chodorow, Nancy. (1974). "Family Structure and Feminine Personality." In *Woman, Culture and Society*, edited by M. Z. Rosaldo and L. Lamphere. Stanford: Stanford University Press. Quoted in Carol Gilligan, *In a Different Voice*. Cambridge, MA: Harvard University Press, 1982, 16.

Crenson, Matthew. (1983). *Neighborhood Politics*. Cambridge, MA: Harvard University Press.

Dahl, Robert. (1961). *Who Governs?* New Haven, CT: Yale University Press.

Dill, Bonnie Thorton. (1988). "'Making Your Job Good Yourself': Domestic Service and the Construction of Personal Dignity," in *Women and the Politics of Empowerment*, edited by Ann Bookman and Sandra Morgen, 33–52. Philadelphia: Temple University Press.

Flammang, Janet A. (1984). *Political Women: Current Roles in State and Local Government*. Beverly Hills, CA: Sage Publications.

Fowlkes, Diane L. (1983). "Conceptions of the 'Political': White Activists in Atlanta," in *Political Women*, edited by Janet A. Flammang, 66–86. Beverly Hills, CA: Sage Publications.

Garland, Anne Witte. (1988). *Women Activists: Challenging the Abuse of Power*. New York: Feminist Press.

Gilligan, Carol. (1982). *In a Different Voice*. Cambridge, MA: Harvard University Press.

Guzmán, Ralph. (1976). *The Political Socialization of the Mexican American People*. New York: Arno Press.

Hardy-Fanta, Carol. (1991). "Latina Women, Latino Men and Political Participation in Boston: *La Chispa Que Prende*" Ph.D. diss., Brandeis University.

———. (1993–94). "Discovering Latina Women in Boston Politics" *Harvard Journal of Hispanic Policy* 7: 5–25.

———. (1992). "Latina Women and Politics in Boston: *Somos La Vida, La Fuerza, La Mujer*" *Latino Studies Journal* 3(2): 38–54.

———. (1993). *Latina Politics, Latino Politics: Gender, Culture and Political Participation in Boston*. Philadelphia: Temple University Press.

Hollander, Edwin P. (1964). *Leadership, Innovation and Influence*. New York: Oxford University Press.

Hollander, Edwin P., and Jan Yoder. (1980). "Some Issues in Comparing Women and Men as Leaders." *Basic and Applied Social Psychology* 1(3): 267–280.

Homans, G.C. (1950). *The Human Group*. New York: Harcourt.

Hunter, Floyd. (1953). *Community Power Structure*. Chapel Hill: University of North Carolina Press.

Kellerman, Barbara, ed. (1986). *Political Leadership: A Sourcebook*. Pittsburgh: University of Pittsburgh Press.

Laleye, O.M., and Victor Ayeni. (1993). "On the Politics of Traditional Leadership." *International Journal of Politics, Culture, and Society* 6 (Summer): 555–571.

Lane, Robert. (1969). *Political Thinking and Consciousness: The Private Life of the Political Mind*. Chicago: Markham Publishing Co.

Litzinger, William, and Thomas Schaefer. (1984). "Leadership Through Followership." In *Contemporary Issues in Leadership*, edited by William E. Rosenbach and Robert L. Taylor, 138–143. Boulder, CO: Westview Press.

MacManus, Susan. (1992). "How to Get More Women in Office: The Perspectives of Local Elected Officials (Mayors and City Councilors)." *Urban Affairs Quarterly* 28(1): 159–170.

Martin, George Edward. (1977). *Ethnic Political Leadership: The Case of the Puerto Ricans*. Ph.D. diss., Fordham University.

Melville, Margarita B., ed. (1980). *Twice a Minority: Mexican-American Women*. St. Louis: C.V. Mosby.

Miller, Jean Baker. (1983). "Women and Power," *Social Policy* 13(4) (Spring): 3–6.

Mirandé, Alfredo, and Evangelina Enríquez. (1979). *La Chicana: The Mexican-American Woman*. Chicago: University of Chicago Press.

Montoya, Lisa, J. Carol Hardy-Fanta, and Sonia Garcia. (2000). Latina Politics: Gender, Participation, and Leadership. *PS: Political Science and Politics* 33(3): 555–561.

Newman, Jody. (1994). "Perception and Reality: A Study Comparing the Success of Men and Women Candidates." Executive Summary of the National Women's Political Caucus. Washington, DC: National Women's Political Caucus (September).

Padilla, Felix M. (1985). *Latino Ethnic Consciousness: The Case of Mexican Americans and Puerto Ricans in Chicago.* Notre Dame, IN: University of Notre Dame Press.

———. (1987). *Puerto Rican Chicago.* Notre Dame, IN: University of Notre Dame Press.

Pantoja, Antonia, and Esperanza Martell. (1989–1990). "Mi gente." *Centro de Estudios Puertorriqueños Bulletin* 2(7): 48–55.

Pardo, Mary. (1990). "Mexican-American Women Grassroots Community Activists: Mothers of East Los Angeles," *Frontiers* 11(1): 3.

Pateman, Carole. (1989). *The Disorder of Women.* Stanford, CA: Stanford University Press.

Pfeffer, Jeffrey. (1984). "The Ambiguity of Leadership." In *Contemporary Issues in Leadership,* edited by William E. Rosenbach and Robert L. Taylor. Boulder, CO: Westview Press.

Porter, Natalie, Florence Lindauer Geis, and Joyce Jennings (Walstedt). (1983). "Are Women Invisible as Leaders?" *Sex Roles* 9(10): 1035–1049.

Rosenbach, William E. and Robert L. Taylor, eds. (1984). *Contemporary Issues in Leadership.* Boulder, CO: Westview Press.

Sacks, Karen. (1988). "Gender and Grassroots Leadership." In *Women and the Politics of Empowerment,* edited by Ann Bookman and Sandra Morgen, 77–94. Philadelphia: Temple University Press.

Sapiro, Virginia. (1983). *The Political Integration of Women: Roles, Socialization and Politics.* Urbana, IL: University of Illinois Press.

Statham, Anne. (1987). "The Gender Model Revisited: Differences in the Management Styles of Men and Women," *Sex Roles* 16(7/8): 409–429.

Tannen, Deborah. (1991). *You Just Don't Understand: Women and Men in Conversation.* New York: Morrow; Ballantine edition.

Tucker, Robert. (1977). *The Soviet Political Mind; Stalinism and Post-Stalin Change,* rev. ed. New York: Norton.

Uriarte, Miren. (1992). "Contra Viento y Marea (Against All Odds): Latinos Build Community in Boston." In *Latinos in Boston: Confronting Poverty, Building Community,* edited by Miren Uriarte, Paul Osterman, Carol Hardy-Fanta, and Edwin Meléndez. Background paper for *Beyond Poverty: Building Community through New Perspectives, The Boston Persistent Poverty Project.* Boston: The Boston Foundation.

Uriarte-Gaston, Miren. (1988). *Organizing for Survival: the Emergence of a Puerto Rican Community.* Ph.D. diss., Boston University.

Wallach, H.G. Peter. (1988). "Political Leadership." *Journal of Politics* 50(4): 1091–1095.

Warren, Kay Barbara, and Susan C. Bourque. (1985). "Gender, Power, and Communication: Women's Responses to Political Muting in the Andes."

In *Women Living Change*, edited by Susan C. Bourque and Donna Robinson Divine, 255–286. Philadelphia: Temple University Press.

CHAPTER 9

"New" Civil Rights Strategies for Latino Political Empowerment*

SETH RACUSEN

Latinos became the largest political "minority" group and gained a modicum of political representation in Massachusetts during the past decade. In contrast to 1983, when there was only one elected representative (Camayd-Freixas and Lopez 1983, 24), by 1994, Massachusetts had eight Latino elected officials and there are prospects for increased representation in several districts.[1] These gains follow the national pattern in which Latino population growth precedes increased political representation. They have been achieved through the creation of Latino majority districts and "rainbow" districts in which Latinos and other minority groups, usually African Americans, have combined to form political majorities.

Even with these gains, Latino municipal political power is not nearly commensurate with the size of the Latino population in the cities where Latinos are highly concentrated. Their underrepresentation is more marked at the state level, which until 1999 included no Latino elected officials. This also follows national patterns of Latino underrepresentation in all states except New Mexico (Pachon and DeSipio 1992). Thus, one prominent analyst has suggested that the emphasis on litigation and electoral politics may have reached "a point of diminishing returns without the addition of some new conceptualization, strategies, and approaches for Latino politics in the 1990's" (Garcia 1992).

---

* This chapter, included here with minor editing, originally appeared in *New England Journal of Public Policy*, Special Issue: Latinos in a Changing Society Part I, 11(1) (Spring/Summer 1995), 161–182. Reprinted with permission from the *New England Journal of Public Policy*. Please note: the original article is based on data from prior to 1995 and does not reflect the current status of Latino politics in the state (see Note 1); an update and reanalysis of the changes between 1995 and 2000 are included here at the end of the chapter.

This chapter examines one facet of such a new conceptualization for litigation and electoral politics: the potential impact of alternative electoral systems for increased Latino political representation in Massachusetts. Latino political demographics in Massachusetts and many other states have led many analysts to prescribe alternative electoral systems as more fruitful avenues to achieve increased political representation. The key demographic factors that have led to these proposals are the residential dispersion of the Latino community in many municipalities and political districts of an increasingly multiethnic population. However, advocates for the alternative systems have not closely examined the political demographics of the Latino community. Because the Latino community has a high percentage of nonvoters, I ask: what impact might these alternative systems have upon the political representation of the Latino community? I outline the critiques of the 1970s and 1980s civil rights strategies, present Latino political demographics in Massachusetts, and explore the prospective impact of alternative electoral systems on Massachusetts Latinos.

CRITIQUES OF CIVIL RIGHTS STRATEGIES

The Voting Rights Act (VRA) changed the shape of politics by significantly broadening the demographic makeup of the electorate, restructuring the rules of the game, and making possible the vast increases in Latino and African-American elected officials. In the three decades since the passage of the VRA and particularly since the 1974 amendment to include Latinos, the number of African-American and Latino elected representatives has increased dramatically. The Latino community saw a threefold increase to more than 4,000 as of 1991 (de la Garza and DeSipio 1993, 1,494). The act attacked outright barriers to participation and replaced at-large districting in cities and counties with single-member districts in which Latinos, African Americans, or some combination could comprise a majority of a new district.

PARTICIPATION

The participatory focus of civil rights litigation has successfully challenged many barriers to the political participation of African Americans, Latinos, and Asians. This has included efforts to eliminate outright barriers to participation: including registration requirements, literacy tests, the poll tax, English language ballots, and many forms of Election Day intimidation.

Nevertheless, large segments of the Latino community do not vote. More than 5 million Latinos were noncitizens in 1990, the steepest participation obstacle facing the community. To address this obstacle, there have been calls for naturalization campaigns, targeted voter registration and mobilization, and the inclusion of noncitizens in the electorate, particularly for local elections. Rodolfo de la Garza and Louis DeSipio have proposed allowing noncitizens to vote during the 5-year waiting period for naturalization. Those who participate in municipal elections would become citizens based on their voting and be exempted from the citizenship examination. DeSipio favors the inclusion of noncitizens in all elections, while de la Garza favors it only in municipal elections. Their proposals seek to increase Latino citizenship rates by creating an incentive for noncitizens to vote (de la Garza and DeSipio 1993).

STRUCTURES OF REPRESENTATION

The second focus of the civil rights strategies being reevaluated has been the right to cast a meaningful ballot, namely, to enable communities of African-American, Latino, and Asian voters to effectively exercise their own preferences. Many litigation suits have concentrated on moving from at-large to single-member districts and influencing the shape of the resulting district boundaries.

The courts have defined civil rights districts as remedies for specific circumstances. A three-part standard, established in the 1986 case *Thornburgh v. Gingles*, requires that a district be created for a protected group, as established by the Voting Rights Act, that could be shown to be (1) sufficiently large and compact to form the majority of an electoral district, (2) politically cohesive, and (3) whose preferences had been blocked by a cohesive majority (Davidson 1993). The first prong of the Gingles test has effectively denied the rights of noncompact minorities to cast a meaningful ballot.

District representation has not proved to be the best remedy to increase Latino or Asian[2] representation, owing to residential dispersion.[3] It was extremely difficult to create a municipal-level Latino majority district in Boston in 1983 (Camayd-Freixas and Lopez 1983). Where districts can be constructed, they can effectively provide representation.

District remedies are advantageous to the largest minority group in each municipality, which has led to concern that groups would have interests in distinctive electoral districts and structures, creating a structural basis for competing electoral strategies (de la Garza 1992). African Americans in Florida, Latinos and Asians in California, and Asians in New York City have found their electoral interests conflicting with those of other groups.[4] Because many Latinos have been elected from rainbow districts where African Americans comprise the largest group, these coalitions are viewed as highly strategic for the Latino community. For example, former State Representative Nelson Merced was elected from a district estimated to be about one-quarter Latino and almost half African American (Hardy-Fanta 1991, 136). But there is nothing automatic about these coalitions, which are so strategic for Latino empowerment.[5]

Indeed, one group's gain has come at the expense of another, a dynamic that becomes increasingly difficult as each group becomes larger. To illustrate these dynamics, consider Pacific City, California, a small city whose population is 30 percent Asian, 10 percent Latino, and 4 percent African American, and whose school board has nine at-large members and only one minority member, who is African American. A lawsuit by Latinos and African Americans yielded a district plan with two majority–minority districts. Asians, highly dispersed within Pacific City, subsequently entered the process, favoring a modified at-large system using cumulative voting. In such circumstances, what rights do noncompact minorities possess, and how can the rights of compact and noncompact minorities be evaluated simultaneously (Achieta and Imahara 1993)?

Although some attorneys and scholars envision solutions within the context of the Voting Rights Act to the questions about noncompact minorities and competing claims over the shape of districts (Grofman 1993), many view these issues as neither foreseen nor adjudicable by the Act. Boston's history has demonstrated that it is possible to create multiethnic redistricting coalitions. Nonetheless, the complexities arising from multiple voting claims increase in places with larger Latino, African-American, and Asian communities (Achieta and Imahara 1993). The projected growth of Latino and Asian communities suggests that these complications will increase.

Redistricting has produced unintended consequences. The increase of Latino (and African-American) elected officials has not contributed to sustained increased mobilization and participation, part of the original civil rights vision that led to the VRA. Instead, participation follows a cyclical pattern, initially increasing when a civil rights district is first created, then returning to relatively low participation rates, largely as a consequence of incumbency.[6] Second, the racial dynamics existing within many elected bodies further limits minority power.[7] In some instances, new rules have been devised to limit the power of minority officeholders.

> After the first Mexican-American woman was elected to the school board in a small Texas county, the board changed its rules for putting items on the agenda. Whereas prior to her election, any one member could put an item on the agenda, now it would require a second before issues would be considered. (*Rojas v. Vitoria* 1988)

> Berry [an incumbent African-American city councilor] received the largest number of first ballot choices—more than any of the white candidates. It was the tradition in Cincinnati that the council member with the largest vote would be elected by the council to serve as mayor. . . . After much political maneuvering, the white council member with the most seniority was chosen mayor.[8]

Impeding minority officeholders need not be so explicit. Instead, the majoritarian political environment places extreme limits on politics.

Consider that the California Proposition 13 initiative was partially a majoritarian response to the California assembly, presided over by the African-American liberal Speaker Willie Brown. Bruce Cain (1992) argues that such majoritarian "adjustments" will inevitably limit civil rights efforts.

In Guinier's view, such "disproportionate majority power" is fundamentally "unlegitimate" because majority rule has always presumed a "reciprocity claim," which she states as follows: "While pluralist theories of democracy do contemplate minority losses, they do not necessarily envision a minority that never wins" (Guinier 1991a). Thus, Guinier argued that classical democratic theory presumed that the legitimacy of majority rule rested with the hope that today's loser could become tomorrow's winner. The existence of a permanent minority violates this reciprocity tenet within majoritarianism. Thus, Guinier has called for a new tradeoff between majority rule and minority rights.

The emerging critique of the vision of the civil rights movement points to four principal problems with single-member voting: (1) the impact of incumbency, which depresses voter turnout, is particularly strong in districts;(2) dispersed minorities will not be compact enough to compose a district; (3) the difficulties of mediating between the claims of multiple groups may increase tensions between groups; and (4) minority elected officials encounter unresponsive white legislators. This critique extends beyond the original civil rights movement to consider the majoritarian limitations of U.S. political institutions.

As of 1995, Latino analysts had mostly critiqued the limited applicability of the Voting Rights Act to the specific barriers to the political participation of the Latino community. One important analyst viewed single-member districting as the best, although imperfect, alternative because it produces the greatest levels of representation for Latinos and African Americans, given contemporary realities (Falcón 1992a). To reduce the deflating effect of incumbency on participation, some recommended "influence" districts, in which Latinos would represent a sizable minority, at least 20 percent, of a district's adult population. According to this view, Latino participation would increase because multiple candidates would have to compete for their votes, stimulating mobilization. Latinos would also supposedly be more highly motivated to participate in influence districts than in safe districts. But influence districts would not lead to much increased representation (de la Garza and DeSipio 1993).

However, these analysts had not addressed the critique of majoritarianism as of 1995. Ángelo Falcón criticized Guinier for underestimating the significance between "community and group solidarity" in politics, and those "linkages between community and the political system" (Falcón 1992b). But does group solidarity really emanate from residential proximity? Guinier argues that interest groups tend to be more mobilized in alternative systems.

Nonmajoritarian systems offer fairer representational possibilities for dispersed political minorities and eliminate the fractious redistricting fights. Alternative systems offer the potential to provide representation to dispersed groups with sufficient voting power to be competitive in the alternative systems. However, the very groups that would supposedly benefit from the alternative systems participate in electoral politics at lower levels. Lani Guinier notes this problem and argues that nonvoters would still stand to gain from alternative systems because the systems would mobilize groups, in which they could participate, and create a qualitatively different environment that would generate more responsive public policy (Guinier 1993). This chapter explores what impact alternative electoral systems might have upon the representation of a disperse minority group with many nonvoters, i.e. Massachusetts Latinos.

LATINO POLITICAL DEMOGRAPHICS IN MASSACHUSETTS AS OF 1994

Despite its rapid expansion during the 1980s, the Massachusetts Latino electorate as of 1994 appeared less mobilized than that of other large states. From an estimated 19,959 registered voters in 1982, the Latino electorate grew two and a half times in just 8 years to a total of approximately 48,510 voters in 1990. During this period, the Latino electorate expanded from 0.7 percent to 1.6 percent of the total electorate (see Table 9.1).

The Latino electorate would be larger if several methodological problems were corrected. The figures cited above, based on the U.S. Census Current Population Surveys (CPS) of 1982–1990, underestimated the Massachusetts Latino electorate at any moment because of the continual undercounting of the Latino population. The 1990 electoral data projected population miscalculated Latino adults in the state by 26,374, according to the 1990 census.[9] The 1990 census undercounted the Latino population by 7.3 percent.[10] The adjusted figures (see Table 9.2) project nearly 61,000 registered voters with a turnout of 49,000 in 1990.

When compared with Latino electorates in other states with large Latino populations, Massachusetts Latinos have been participating at lower rates. I analyzed the registration rates, the key indicator of participation, for Latinos in the 12 states for which they are given in the 1988–1992 CPS. The national averages of Latino registration for these three election years varied between 32 percent and 36 percent. Most of the larger states were at or above those levels during all three of the election years. Larger, more densely populated communities tend to be more mobilized because of the structure of the U.S. political system. California, with the lowest Latino participation rates, and Massachusetts, with the next lowest rates, do not

Table 9.1   The Growing Massachusetts Latino Electorate, 1982–1992

	All Latino Adults	Latino Registered Voters		Latino Turnout	
Year	Number	Number	Registered Voters (%)	Number	Registered Voters (%)
1982	120,232	19,959	0.69	11,663	0.51
1984	67,000	19,000	0.62	15,000	0.56
1986	109,975	19,466	0.66	15,177	0.71
1988	142,240	40,965	1.30	30,724	1.09
1990	154,000	48,510	1.56	38,654	1.47
1992	124,000	28,000	0.86	18,000	0.61

Sources: U.S. Bureau of the Census, Voting and Registration in the Election of 1982, Current Population Reports Series P-20, No. 383 [Washington, D.C.: U.S. Government Printing Office (hereafter USGPO), 1983]; Voting and Registration in the Election of 1984, Current Population Reports Series P-20, No. 405 (Washington, D.C.: USGPO, 1985); Voting and Registration in the Election of 1986, Current Population Reports Series P-20, No. 414 (Washington, D.C.: USGPO, 1987); Voting and Registration in the Election of 1988, Current Population Reports Series P-20, No. 440 (Washington, D.C.: USGPO), 1989; Voting and Registration in the Election of 1990, Current Population Reports Series P-20, No. 453 (Washington, D.C.: USGPO, 1991); Voting and Registration in the Election of 1992, Current Population Reports Series P-20, No. 466 (Washington, D.C.: USGPO, 1993).

conform to these national trends in large states. Massachusetts Latinos participated at rates comparable with Latinos nationwide only in the 1990 election. The large number of California Latinos compensates for the relatively low rate of their participation; the Massachusetts Latino community is not of that magnitude. I explore some possible reasons for this lower participation but emphasize there is nothing Latino about low electoral participation. In their homelands, Latinos go to the polls at much higher rates (Hardy-Fanta 1993, 176–185).

I use voter registration as a measure of participation because registered voters of whatever race vote in similar proportions. White registered voters participated at a slightly higher rate than their Latino counterparts in the 1992 elections. The percentage of registered voters that did not vote in 1992 is consistent across the electorates, from a low of 4 percent for the Asian community to a high of 7 percent in the white electorate.

What accounts for differences in registration? Within each electorate, an equivalent percentage of adults is not registered for reasons other than citizenship, from a low of 24 percent for Asians to a high of 31 percent for

Table 9.2   Estimating the Massachusetts Latino Electorate in 1990

		Estimate 1: CPS 1990 Corrected with 1990	Estimate 2: CPS 1990 Also Corrected for 1990
	CPS 1990	Census Data[b]	Census Data[a]
Latino Residents, 18+	154,000	180,374	193,541
(percentage of total residents)	(3.43%)	(3.87%)	(4.21%)
Latino Registered Voters	48,510	56,818	60,965
(percentage of all	(1.56%)	(1.77%)	(1.90%)
registered voters)			
Latinos Voting	38,654	45,274	48,579
(percentage of all voters)	(1.47%)	(1.87%)	(2.00%)

aEstimate 1 applies the registration and voting rates reported in the 1990 CPS to the population figures in PL94-171.

bEstimate 2 applies the same registration and voting rates to the population figures in PL94-171, adjusted by the Census Bureau's estimate of the undercount of Latinos and the overall population.

African Americans. The striking differences are in the relative sizes of the noncitizen population—45 percent of Asians and 40 percent Latinos noncitizens in 1992, compared with 5 percent of African Americans and whites. For these reasons, the overall participation profiles of Latinos and Asians are quite similar, as are the participation portraits for the African-American and Puerto Rican communities (U.S. Bureau of the Census 1993).

REGISTRATION RATE DIFFERENCES

If registered voters of all races vote at similar rates, what accounts for the differences in the numbers of registered voters? In particular, what accounts for the differences between the Latino registered voters in Massachusetts and those in the other major states? The four factors that depress the rate are the high level of residential dispersion, the youthfulness of the population, high poverty levels within the community, and the high numbers of immigrants and relatively low rates of citizenship (Uriarte 1991). None of these factors indicates that there is anything "Latino" about nonparticipation, but they do point to the barriers to political participation.

RESIDENTIAL PATTERNS

Massachusetts Latinos are highly dispersed, residing primarily in white majority areas and secondarily in multiethnic or rainbow areas. The 1990 census indicates that fifty-one thousand, or 18 percent, of Massachusetts

Latinos live in three cities with a large Latino population: Chelsea, Holyoke, and Lawrence; 41 percent live in six rainbow cities: Springfield, Boston, Lowell, Lynn, Cambridge, and Brockton, in which there are also significant numbers of African Americans and Asians. The other 41 percent live in the rest of the state, outside these areas of concentration (U.S. Bureau of the Census 1990).

To portray the residential patterns, I placed Massachusetts political precincts into the following categories:

- Safe   65 percent of the adult population is Latino.
- Majority   50 percent of the adult population is Latino.
- Plurality   33 percent of the adult population is Latino, and Latinos make up largest group.
- Influence   20 percent of the adult population is Latino.
- Rainbow   10 percent of the adult population is Latino, and whites are 50 percent.
- Others   All other precincts.

It is important to distinguish between the precinct, the basic unit of politics, and the political district, which is composed of precincts. A Latino could live in a precinct categorized as "other" and vote in an "influence" district in which the Latino population is 20 percent or more.

In 1990, almost two-thirds of Massachusetts Latinos (65 percent) lived in places where Latinos comprised less than 10 percent of the population. Only 12 percent lived in precincts in which Latinos were a majority. Approximately one in five Latinos lived in rainbow or influence precincts. Table 9.3 presents the distribution of the Latino population in six cities: Chelsea, Lawrence, and Holyoke, with large populations of Latinos, and Springfield, Boston, and Lowell, the rainbow cities with the highest concentration of Latinos. Table 9.3 shows substantial concentrations of Latinos in the three cities where the 1990 Latino population exceeded 30 percent. In Chelsea, Lawrence, and Holyoke, districts could be created that could provide meaningful opportunities for Latino political representation. Springfield and Boston showed few precincts of concentration and many rainbow or influence precincts. Lowell had only two precincts with any Latino concentration.

Most U.S. Latino officials reside in safe, majority, plurality, or rainbow districts. In Massachusetts, most Latino elected officials reside in majority districts. Rep. Merced, however, came from a rainbow district. In Lawrence, Chelsea, and Holyoke, Latinos are the single largest minority group. In Boston, Lowell, and Springfield, Latinos are part of a demographic rainbow. Table 9.4 displays Latino population estimates for these cities and for Massachusetts as of 1990.

The Latino voting age population (VAP) is substantially smaller than its share of the overall population, which indicates the relative youth of the

Table 9.3   Distribution of Latino Population by Categorization of Precincts in Selected Massachusetts Cities, 1990

	Safe[a]	Majority[b]	Plurality[c]	Influence[d]	Rainbow[e]	Other[f]	All
Chelsea	0	2	0	4	0	4	10
Lawrence	4	7	0	4	1	14	30
Holyoke	1	2	0	4	0	8	14
Springfield	4	0	1	3	9	47	64
Boston	0	0	7	9	42	194	252
Lowell	0	0		1	1	33	35

Source: U.S. Bureau of the Census Public Law 94-171, Data File, 1990.
[a]Safe   65 % of adult population is Latino.
[b]Majority   50% of adult population is Latino.
[c]Plurality   33% of adult population is Latino, and Latinos are the largest group.
[d]Influence   20% of the adult population is Latino.
[e]Rainbow   10% of the adult population is Latino, and whites are less than 50%.
[f]Others   All other precincts.

Table 9.4.   Latino Political Demographics in Selected Cities and States, 1990

	Latino Population			
	Overall[a] (%)	Voting Age Population[b] (%)	Voting Age Citizens[b] (%)	Electorate[c] (%)
Lawrence	41.6	29.1	21.2	18.3
Chelsea	31.4	23.1	16.8	13.8
Holyoke	31.1	18.7	18.6	13.7
Springfield	16.9	10.9	10.7	7.4
Boston	10.8	8.4	5.8	4.7
Lowell	10.2	6.5	5.4	4.5
Massachusetts House	4.8	3.9	2.9	2.0
Massachusetts Senate	4.8	3.9	2.9	2.0

[a] Public Law 94-171 Data File, 1990.
[b] Estimated for each town and state from 1990 Census of Population, Social and Economic Characteristics, Report 1990, CP-2-23, 1993, Table 192. Latino citizenship for each town was estimated as follows: Holyoke (95.7 percent), Springfield (94.8 percent), Lowell (85.2 percent), Lawrence (70.1 percent), Boston (69.0 percent), and Chelsea (68.9 percent)
[c] Estimated by applying statewide voting data from Voting and Registration in the Election of 1990, CPS Report P-20, 453, 1991, to estimated Voting Age Citizens in previous column.

Latino population compared to other populations. Latinos represent the youngest population of all ethnic groups in the six cities. In Holyoke, Lawrence, Lowell, and Springfield, half or almost half of the Latino communities were below voting age. These figures were between twice and three times the rate for the white community. The youngest Latino communities, with predominantly Puerto Rican populations, are Holyoke, Springfield, and Lowell.

The Latino voting age citizens (VAC) estimates the citizenship rate among Latino adults. Holyoke and Springfield, whose Latino communities are overwhelmingly Puerto Rican, show high citizenship rates. The three cities with large Dominican or Central American populations have much lower citizenship rates. Large numbers of Central Americans reside in Boston and Chelsea. Many Dominicans, who are primarily located in Lawrence and Boston, are noncitizens. Much of the 1980s Latino population growth in Massachusetts resulted from the, migration of Central Americans, whose noncitizenship rate is much higher than that of Mexicans or Cubans.

Latinos generally are less likely than European immigrants to become naturalized after 5 years of U.S. residence: for example, 40 percent of naturalized Mexicans wait 25 years or more before naturalizing. Of those who become citizens, apparently 81 percent register to vote (Hernandez 1991). Noncitizenship is not unique to Mexicans: 70 percent of Colombians, Dominicans, and Salvadorans also do not apply for naturalization once they become eligible (Pachon 1986–1987).

POVERTY AND CITIZENSHIP

Citizenship is highly correlated with social class. Noncitizenship rates are much higher among those with less than a fifth-grade education than for those with some college. Nearly three-quarters of Latinos with advanced degrees are citizens, compared with about one-third of those with only a fifth-grade education (U.S. Bureau of the Census 1991). Massachusetts Latinos are among the poorest of all U.S. Latinos (Uriarte 1991). Poverty, the low Latino citizenship rate, and the vast increase in Central American immigration in the second half of the 1980s explain the relative lower participation of the Massachusetts Latino electorate in comparison with other large states.

Latinos who live outside central cities vote at much higher rates than those who live in central cities (U.S. Bureau of the Census 1991). This creates a paradoxical situation in which Latinos vote at much lower rates in the places where they are most highly concentrated, and at higher rates in the places of less concentration. This also underlines the importance of the question about the potential impact of alternative electoral systems on Massachusetts Latinos.

THE IMPACT OF ALTERNATIVE ELECTORAL SYSTEMS

As previously noted, Massachusetts Latinos are a highly dispersed minority group and face many obstacles to participation. The following discussion examines the general claim of proportionality advocates that dispersed populations would be more highly represented under alternative voting systems, particularly in communities with many nonvoters.

Political representation is generally measured by comparing the percentage of Latino elected officials with the percentage of a Latino population in a given region or state.[11] This definition does not require or even imply virtual representation, namely, that only a Latino can represent Latinos. As communities of Latino voters have been increasingly been able to vote *meaningfully* by choosing their own representatives, the numbers of Latino elected officials have increased. One would have to assume that Latinos are less likely than the overall population to vote for a Latino to expect another result.

Most Latinos are elected from the majority districts generally created in response to, or anticipation of, voting rights suits. According to the National Association of Latino Elected Officials, the typical Latino official's constituency is 55 percent Latino. In Texas, which has more Latino representatives than any other state, the typical official's constituency is 73 percent Latino! Massachusetts Latino officials have been elected from one of two patterns: four at-large school officials in Lawrence, Chelsea, Holyoke, and Springfield, and four district-based city councilors in Lawrence, Chelsea, and Holyoke. These numbers for the cities with the largest Latino concentrations are in keeping with national trends. The gender of the Latino officials, four female school committee members and four male city councilors, is also in keeping with national trends of females disproportionately serving on school boards (Pachon and DeSipio 1992).

The Latino population and council representation for the six cities in the study and the state of Massachusetts are shown in Table 9.5.[12] The expectation that increased population produces increased political representation is generally confirmed by the data. There is council representation in Lawrence, Chelsea, and Holyoke, where the Latino population exceeds 30 percent and constitutes majority precincts (see Table 9.3). However, the fact that representation (in 1990) was higher in Chelsea than Lawrence suggests that the population impact must be considered a tendency, not a law of politics.

Comparisons of the Latino share of the overall population with the Latino share of council representatives indicate that Latinos, underrepresented in Chelsea, are severely underrepresented in the other five cities. Two indexes of proportionality are usually computed in the literature (see Taebel 1978). The additive index subtracts the Latino population percentage from the representation percentage. The resulting figure varies according to the size of the population: 0 percent represents equitable representation, a positive percentage represents overrepresentation, and a negative percentage represents underrepresentation. The additive method shows Latinos were highly underrepresented in Lawrence (minus 30.5 percent) and Holyoke (minus 24.4 percent), where there were Latino elected officials, and less underrepresented in Boston (minus 10.8 percent), Springfield (minus 16.9 percent), or Lowell (minus 10.2 percent), where there were none.

This method is less sensitive to gains in representation in cities with a more concentrated community. The ratio of representation to population divides the percentage of representation by the percentage of the population and varies from 0 percent for no representation to 100 percent for equitable representation and more than 100 percent for overrepresentation. The ratio method shows that (in 1990) Latinos were most highly represented in Chelsea (70.8 percent). However, this method, which does not reflect population differences in cities with no representation, classifies Springfield, Boston, and Lowell as equally underrepresented.[13] Hence, both calculations are given here.

Table 9.5   Latino Population and Legislative Representation for Six City Councils and Massachusetts State Legislature, 1990 and 1994

	Population		Representatives			Indices of Proportionality	
	Total	Of City %	All	Latino	Of Legislative Chamber %	Additive[a] %	Ratio[b]
Lawrence	29,237	41.6	9	1	11.1	30.5	26.7
Chelsea	9,018	31.4	9	2	22.2	9.2	70.8
Holyoke	13,573	31.1	5	1	6.7	24.4	21.4
Springfield	26,528	16.9	9	0	0.0	16.9	0.0
Boston	61,955	10.8	13	0	0.0	10.8	0.0
Lowell	10,499	10.2	9	0	0.0	10.2	0.0
Senate	287,549	4.8	40	0	0.0	4.8	0.0
House-1994			160	0	0.0	4.8	0.0
House-1990			160	1	0.6	4.2	12.5

Source: U.S. Bureau of the Census Public Law 94-171, Data File, 1990.
[a]Additive: the share (percentage) of representation is subtracted from the share of the population. This percentage is bounded by the Latino population of the city, with 0 percent as proportionate representation and a negative number indicating underrepresentation.
[b]Ratio: the share of representation is divided by the share of the population. This figure generally varies between 0 and 100 percent, with the latter indicating representational equity.

In 1994, there were no Latino elected officials above the municipal level.[14] Table 9.5 also presents the indices of representation for the legislature in 1994 (when there were no Latino representatives) and that of 1990, when Nelson Merced held office. Even when Merced was a member, the ratio for the House of Representatives of 12.5 percent indicates that the Latino population was eight times larger than its share of legislators. Restated, proportionate representation for the 1990 Latino population would have been eight statewide representatives.

THRESHOLD OF REPRESENTATION

Political scientists estimate the possible outcomes of electoral systems by calculating the "threshold of representation," or the number of voters necessary to elect a given candidate. Although there are many types of proportional systems, the two most relevant are proportional representation, which is employed in Cambridge, and cumulative voting, which is in force in a few small U.S. locales. This threshold, which is consistent across the systems, is calculated as follows:

$$\text{Threshold} = 1/(\text{Seats} + 1)^{15}$$

The values for this formula are given in Table 9.6. In a single-member district, 50 percent of the voters are necessary to produce an electoral triumph in a final election. In modified at-large systems, such as cumulative voting or proportional representation, the threshold is calculated on the basis of the number of representatives being elected. In an election for three at-large seats under a modified system, 25 percent of the voters could elect a representative. Consider the case of Alamogordo, New Mexico, 21 percent Latino, which elected Inez Moncada, a Latina, to the Board of Alderman in 1987. Cumulative voting was adopted the same year to elect the three at-large aldermen.

Under this system, voters can express the strength of their preferences and cast all three votes for one candidate or split their votes among two or three candidates. According to analysis after Ms. Moncada's election, she received 73 percent of the Latino vote, with Latinos casting on average 2.6 voters for her. She also received about 22 percent of the white vote. The intensity of that Latino vote suggests the potential use of cumulative voting by a minority (Engstrom, Taebel, and Cole 1989).

In Cambridge, another modified at-large system, proportional representation is used to elect the nine members of the City Council, yielding a threshold of representation of 10.1 percent. Under this system, each voter expresses his or her preferences by ranking the candidates. If a voter's first choice is defeated or elected with an excess of votes during the counting, the second preference on that ballot is tallied. The process of redistributing the secondary preferences, which is why the system is also called the single transferable vote, continues until all candidates have been eliminated or elected. Thus, all voters can exercise a preference.

African Americans, who comprised 13.5 percent of the 1990 Cambridge population, have been able to elect a representative under this system even when their share of the population was under the threshold. Proportional representation has also been used since 1970 in the community school board elections in New York City. Latino and African-American represent-

Table 9.6   Threshold of Political Representation

Seats	Voters	Seats	Voters
1	0.500	9	0.100
2	0.333	10	0.091
3	0.250	11	0.083
4	0.200	12	0.077
5	0.167	13	0.071
6	0.143	14	0.067
7	0.125	15	0.063
8	0.111		

Source: Engstrom (1993).

ation on these boards has approximated the Latino and African-American shares of the overall population for the 20-plus years since. In 1983, for example, Latinos were 20 percent of the city's population and held 17 percent of the community school board seats. New York City Latinos were not as well represented on any other municipal or state body (Amy 1993, 138).

The Latino population (see Table 9.4) in each of the six study cities exceeds this threshold of representation for the city councils if modified at-large systems had been used. These councils vary from 9 members in four of the cities to 13 in Boston and 15 in Holyoke. The thresholds of representation are 10 percent for the four cities with a council of nine, 7.1 percent in Holyoke, and 6.3 percent for Boston.

Although the Latino population is larger than the thresholds for representation in these cities, the most important indicators for the outcome of elections held under alternative systems are the numbers of voters. The 1990 Latino electorate (see Table 9.4) exceeded their thresholds of representation only in Lawrence, Chelsea, and Holyoke, the municipalities where Latinos were already elected through district representation. A much closer examination of the possible impact of the alternative systems is needed.

PROPORTIONATE REPRESENTATION

The impact of alternative systems is more thoroughly presented in Table 9.7, which estimates proportionate council representation based on four population factors and current council size if modified at-large systems were used. Because of the participation factors noted above, the estimates based on Latino voting age citizens and the Latino electorate provide the best figures for proportionate representation. Projections based on voting age population would be relevant for circumstances in which the voting rights of noncitizens are under consideration. While politics would play the key role in determining the ultimate size of the Latino electorate, the estimates of the current electorate and citizens are the most accurate indicators for appraising possible outcomes.

Table 9.7   Proportionate Representation for Six City Councils and
Massachusetts State Legislature, 1995

		Proportionate Representation Based on			
	Overall	Voting Age	Voting Age		Repre-
	Population[a]	Population[a]	Citizens[b]	Electorate[c]	sentatives
Lawrence	3.7	2.6	1.9	1.6	1.0
Chelsea	2.8	2.1	1.5	1.2	2.0
Holyoke	4.7	2.8	2.8	1.2	1.0
Springfield	1.5	1.0	1.0	0.7	0.0
Boston	1.4	1.1	0.8	0.4	0.0
Lowell	0.9	0.6	0.5	0.4	0.0
Massachusetts Senate	1.9	1.5	1.2	0.6	0.0
Massachusetts House	7.7	6.2	4.7	2.4	0.0

Note: "Proportionate" legislative representation estimates the amount of representation that would be proportionate to each population factor.
[a]Public Law 94-171 Data File, 1990.
[b]1990 Census of Population, Social and Economic Characteristics, Report 1990, CP-2-23, 1993.
[c]*Voting and Registration* in the Election of 1990, CPS Report P-20, 453, 1991.

Because of the Latino undercount by the 1990 census and continued population growth since that time, the percentage of voting age citizens listed above may be the best indicator of the electoral strength of the Latino communities in the various municipalities. In addition, an increase in participation of approximately 7 percent could be projected by the change in electoral system. One study, which controlled for the many cultural and idiosyncratic differences between European electoral systems, found that the incentives for voting under systems of proportional representation resulted in a 7 percent expansion of the electorates.[16] If applied to Table 9.7, the estimates would slightly exceed the column for voting age citizens. Because such an increase would bring the Latino electorate in Massachusetts to a level commensurate with Latino electorates in other states, such a projection seems warranted.

Table 9.7 suggests that Latinos would gain in virtually all the legislative bodies considered in this chapter. These contexts might be categorized as (1) state legislative bodies, (2) municipal councils with Latinos elected from districts, and (3) municipal councils without elected Latino representation. The greatest gains from moving to modified at-large systems would occur in the state legislature, where between three and six representatives might be elected. This creates a paradoxical situation in which the greatest potential gain could occur at the higher level, which is considerably more difficult to change.

The municipal councils to which Latinos have been elected through districts offer a more modest increase of two additional representatives. More representation would not be expected in Chelsea, where there has been discussion of incorporating noncitizen voting to offset an otherwise anticipated possible decrease. In Lawrence and Holyoke, there could be representational increases, dependent upon the degree of mobilization of the electorate. The wide difference between the voting age citizens and the electorate in Holyoke is indicative of the low voter turnout in that city. The eligible electorate of Holyoke, the voting age citizens, would be large enough to elect three representatives under an alternative system.

Although the projected gains for Springfield, Boston, and Lowell, the three municipalities without Latino elected council members, are nominal, a modified at-large system could be expected to open access to political representation in these locales and produce two additional representatives. These municipalities have smaller concentrations of Latinos and significant numbers of African Americans and Asians. In these three cities, it seems highly unlikely, with the possible exception of Springfield, that there could be a Latino municipal district for quite some time. In Lowell, however, a citywide coalition of Latinos and Asians could elect a city councilor.

The models presented here are based on conservative figures. The Latino communities in Massachusetts, undercounted as of the 1990 census, have surely grown since that time. Increased participation could be expected under alternative systems to levels equivalent to the Latino electorates in other large states. Estimates based on the electorate in 1995 or beyond would provide much stronger arguments for the alternative systems.

IMPLICATIONS FOR INCREASED LATINO POLITICAL REPRESENTATION

This chapter has explored the prospects that modified at-large electoral systems would provide opportunities for increased political representation of the Latino communities of Massachusetts and that gains could be anticipated in most legislative bodies, with the greatest increase projected for the state legislature.

There are two important implications to these findings. The first is that the proportionality advocates generally overstate the gains that linguistic minorities could achieve through alternative systems. Roughly, the Latino share of an electorate is about half the Latino share of the population. This is an important qualification to those claims.

The second implication is that the alternative systems appear incontrovertibly beneficial in cities and states in which political districts cannot be drawn to represent Latinos. Deciding which electoral system is superior in instances in which districts can be drawn deserves a more complex discussion. However, the potential benefits for all minority groups in multiracial cities require further consideration, particularly given the likelihood that one group's gain often comes at the expense of another's in the competition over districts. This aspect warrants further discussion, particularly given the continued growth of Latino and Asian populations and the strategic importance of political alliances among minority groups for the future of our cities.

Innovative approaches to political participation are also needed. Rodolfo de la Garza and Louis DeSipio's proposal for noncitizen voting warrants further attention within the civil rights community and ultimately the U.S. Congress. The reliance of the alternative electoral structures on participating voters underscores the longer term strategic significance of this aspect.

The considerations to evaluate alternative electoral systems fully vastly exceed the analysis of population presented here and must include questions about the shape of politics and the structures of government in each locale. What political alliances or coalitions exist or might be expected to form? How would the alternative structures affect the relationship between representative and constituency, or the relationship between Latino elected representatives, other elected representatives, and the overall structures of power?

Electoral systems are not easily changed. Nonetheless, the history of the civil rights movement has demonstrated that electoral structures can be changed. Proposals to loosen the geographic requirement for civil rights remedies to political underrepresentation are increasingly being heard in court. In her path-breaking analysis of U.S. electoral politics, Lani Guinier has proposed political structures that have been used successfully in other countries with varying degrees of ethnic division. An important analyst of public policy and ethnic disputes in the international context concluded, "What stands out, in spite of the limitations, is just how important a piece of the incentive structure the electoral system is and what a dearth of imagination there has been in most countries in utilizing its potential for ethnic accommodation."[17]

Ultimately, there will be a need to rethink the relationship between majority rule and minority representation, as Guinier has argued. The structure of political communities includes not merely technical decisions, but profound expressions of how a society approaches the inclusion of its members. This chapter seeks to stimulate further discussion of how the United States will address its increasingly diverse electorates in the twenty-first century.

THE STATUS OF LATINO POLITICAL REPRESENTATION IN MASSACHUSETTS, 2000: AN UPDATE

This chapter is, as indicated above, a reprint of an article that first appeared in 1995. The original article (Racusen 1995) was written at a time of a dramatic change in Latino political mobilization in Massachusetts; the changes have continued over the past 5 years. The exponential growth in the number of campaigns and the dramatic increase in Latino political representation, particularly in four cities, require this update.

Despite the increase in representation, which was greater than projected by the 1995 estimates given above, the broader question posed by the chapter about the significance of the structure of politics for Latino political representation continues to be important. Even with the significant increases in representation, the Latino populations in the major cities remain underrepresented by any traditional measure used by political scientists (see Table 9.8). Only in Springfield does Latino representation on two political bodies approximate the Latino population. In the other three cities, Latino representation is not commensurate with either the 2000 census or community estimates of the size of the Latino population.

Even in places where the Latino population is most concentrated, representation remains well below parity. Electoral structure remains a large part of the story. Latinos are particularly underrepresented in at-large council seats, consistent with the historical impact of at-large districts upon the power of a political minority. A group generally needs to be part of a majority to capture at-large seats. In the four cities with the highest concentration of Latinos, more City Councilors are elected through at-large elections than through district elections (see Table 9.9).

Under the current legal climate, addressing the problem of at-large districts will be difficult. Although a Massachusetts district court was initially sympathetic to the lawsuit brought against the at-large districts in the City of Holyoke, the case was remanded upon appeal and the court reversed its prior finding based upon its interpretation of the 1995 election. The Court found that the estimated 42 percent of the vote received by Alejandro Sánchez from non-Latino voters in the at-large election in 1995 indicated the changing nature and fluidity of Holyoke politics. The Court argued that this did not meet the standards required to demonstrate evidence of racial polarization (*Vecinos de Barrio Uno et al., v. City of Holyoke et al.*, 960 F. Supp. 515, 1997 US Dist. Lexis 5419). Indeed, it ele-

Table 9.8 Latino Municipal Representation in Four Massachusetts Cities with Large Latino Population, 2000

	All Repre- sentatives	Latino Repre- sentatives	Latino Repre- sentatives (%)	Latino Census Projection (%)	Latino Community Estimates[a] (%)	2000 Census
Lawrence				**48.4**	**60**	**59.7**
City Council	9	3	33.3			
School Committee	6	1	16.7			
State Representatives	3	1	33.3			
Chelsea				**38.6**	**46**	**48.4**
City Council	11	1	9.1			
Holyoke				**36.8**	**50**	**41.4**
City Council	15	2	13.3			
State Representatives	4	1	25.0			
Springfield				**19.8**	**20**	**27.2**
School Committee	6	1	16.7			
State Representatives	6	1	16.7			

[a] Data gathered from interviews with Latino candidates and community representatives (See Introduction and Hardy-Fanta 1997).

Table 9.9. Structure of City Council Representation in Four Cities with Largest Latino Populations, 2000

	District Representatives	At-Large Representatives	Total Representatives
Lawrence	6	3	9
Chelsea	8	3	11
Holyoke	7	8	15
Springfield	0	9	9
Total	21	23	44

vated those standards in that finding, which effectively holds that under-representation in a fluid political environment does not warrant remedy. The disturbing aspect of that finding is that evidence of coalitional politics between Latinos and whites was used to undermine plaintiff claims of underrepresentation. The Court viewed the existence of a Latino candidate who attracted white votes and a white candidate who sought Latino votes as contrary to the second and third prongs of the Gingles test. This is an extremely simplistic analysis of politics in which coalitional dynamics develop in a context of systemic underrepresentation.

Indeed, the increased reluctance of courts to oversee the drawing of political districts underlines the question I posed in 1994 about alternative structures of representation. Under alternatives sketched earlier, interests can effectively articulate their preferences and form coalitions of their choice independent of geographic considerations. A political "minority" need not be concentrated to gain representation under alternative systems of representation. Nor would some success undermine efforts for further gains in that circumstance. The possibility of independent articulation in certain circumstances and coalitional developments in other circumstances would also be possible. Indeed, these structural alternatives would enable a more fluid and competitive political opportunity system that the Court in the *Vecinos de Barrio Uno* case in Holyoke seemed to prefer.

ACKNOWLEDGMENTS

I wish to thank the Gastón Institute for sponsoring my research and for the assistance of Ramón Olivencia and Mariana Cruz. I have especially benefited from discussions of these ideas over several years with Nelson Merced, Miren Uriarte, Howard Fain, William Fletcher, James Jennings, Alan Rom, Edwin Meléndez, and Gary Orfield, none of whom, of course, is responsible for any of the chapter's limitations. I also appreciate the thoughtful commentary of the many participants at my presentation of an earlier version of this chapter at the University of Massachusetts Boston, April 12, 1994.

NOTES

1. *Eds. note*: This chapter is a reprint of an article published in 1995. The data reported here are, therefore, current up to late 1994. As of May 2000, there were 11 Latino elected officials in the state. These include three state representatives (Cheryl Rivera, Springfield; José Santiago, Lawrence; and Jarrett Barrios, Cambridge); three City Councilors from Lawrence (Nilka Álvarez, Marcos Devers, and Julia Silverio); one City Councilor from Chelsea (Juan Vega); two City Councilors from Holyoke (Juan Cruz and Diosdado López); and two School Committee members (Ralph Carrero, Lawrence; José Tosado, Springfield). Boston continues to have no Latino elected officials, although, for several years, a number

of Latinos have served on the appointed School Committee. For a full discussion, please see the Introduction to this volume.

2.   See Achieta and Imahara (1993), Bao (1991), Bell (1992), Davidson (1993), Engstrom (1993), Gartner (1993), Grofman (1993), Guinier (1993), Karian (1989), Macchiarola and Diaz (1993), Taebel (1978), and Vedlitz and Johnson (1982).

3.   See Davidson (1993), Grofman (1993), Taebel (1978), Vedlitz and Johnson (1982), Welch (1990), and Zax (1990).

4.   See Achieta and Imahara (1993), Bao (1991), Grofman (1993), Karian (1989), and Macchiarola and Diaz (1993).

5.   See de la Garza (1992) on the strategic importance of this coalition, and Grofman and Handley (1989) on the electoral successes; the important discussions of Jennings (1992), and Falcón (1992a) on the significant barriers and possibilities for African American–Latino alliances. Also see Grofman and Handley (1989) on the role of African American–Latino coalitions in electing African American or Latino congressional representatives.

6.   On this point, see Guinier (1991a) and de la Garza and DeSipio (1993).

7.   Guinier (1991a) particularly makes this critique in "The Triumph of Tokenism." See also Karian (1989).

8.   See the discussion in Amy (1993, 135) of the subsequent change of the white majority in Cincinnati changing its electoral system from proportional representation to at-large voting to thwart this incipient African American political power decisively.

9.   This figure is from the Public Law Database, PL94-171, that was created for redistricting purposes (U.S. Bureau of the Census 1990).

10.   Rivera (1991, 2–3) discusses the undercount in depth.

11.   There are certainly limitations to such a definition, by narrowing the scope of political participation (see, for example, Hardy-Fanta 1991, 1993). However, representation does provide one essential barometer of the political empowerment of a community, which is how it is being used here.

12.   *Eds. note*: The tables included here are based on data available in 1994. Please see Note 1 for an explanation and update.

13.   This was Taebel's (1978) view on the matter.

14.   *Eds. note*: This sentence has been modified from the original to ensure that it does not convey an erroneous perception that as of May 2000, there were no Latino state representatives. In fact, as discussed in the introduction to this book and in Note 1, there are currently three.

15.   Engstrom (1993).

16.   See the study by Blais and Carty (1990), cited by Amy (1993, 145); Blais and Carty controlled for all other electoral rules in their study of 509 general European national elections.

17.   See Horowitz (1985). There is an extensive literature on this subject, which was evident in the controversies during the structuring of postapartheid South Africa. Proportionality was proposed to protect the future interests of the

white minority. See, for example, Arend Lijphart (1985), for a comprehensive review of the literature and one view of this discussion.

REFERENCES

Achieta, Angelo, and Kathryn K. Imahara. (1993). "Multi-Ethnic Voting Rights: Redefining Vote Dilution in Communities of Color." *University of San Francisco Law Review* 27(4): 815–872.

Amy, Douglas. (1993). *Real Choices/New Voices: The Case for Proportional Representation Elections in the United States.* New York: Columbia University Press.

Bao, Su Sun. (1991). "Affirmative Pursuit of Political Equality for Asian Pacific Americans: Reclaiming the Voting Rights Act." *University of Pennsylvania Law Review* 139(3): 731–768.

Bell, Derrick. (1992). *Race, Racism, and American Law.* Boston: Little, Brown.

Blais, André, and R. K. Carty. (1990). "Does Proportional Representation Foster Voter Turnout?" *European Journal of Political Research* 18(2): 167–182.

Cain, Bruce E. 1992. "Voting Rights and Democratic Theory: Toward a Color-Blind Society?" In *Controversies in Minority Voting, The Voting Rights Act in Perspective,* edited by Bernard Grofman and Chandler Davidson, 261–275. Washington, DC: Brookings Institution.

Camayd-Freixas, Yohel, and Russell Paul López. (1983). *Gaps in Representative Democracy: Redistricting, Political Participation, and the Hispanic Vote in Boston.* Boston: Hispanic Office of Planning and Evaluation.

Davidson, Chandler. (1993). "The Voting Rights Act: Protecting the Rights of Racial and Language Minorities in the Electoral Process." *Chicano-Latino Law Review* 13(Summer): 1–14.

de la Garza, Rodolfo O. (1992). "Latino Politics: A Futuristic View." In *Ethnic Politics and Civil Liberties,* edited by Lucius Barker, 137–144. *National Political Science Review* 3. New Brunswick, NJ: Transaction Publishers.

de la Garza, Rodolfo O., and Louis DeSipio. (1993). "Save the Baby, Change the Bathwater, and Scrub the Tub: Latino Electoral Participation after Seventeen Years of Voting Rights Act Coverage." *Texas Law Review* 71(7): 1479–1539.

Engstrom, Richard L. (1993). "The Single Transferable Vote: An Alternative Remedy for Minority Vote Dilution." *University of San Francisco Law Review* 27(4): 781–813.

Engstrom, Richard L., Delbert A. Taebel, and Richard L. Cole. (1989). "Cumulative Voting as a Remedy for Minority Vote Dilution: The Case of Alamogordo, New Mexico." *Journal of Law & Politics* 5(3): 469–497.

Falcón, Ángelo. (1992a). "Black and Latino Politics in New York City: Race and Ethnicity in a Changing Urban Context." In *Latinos and the Political System,* edited by F. Chris Garcia, 171–194. Notre Dame, IN: University of Notre Dame Press.

————. (1992b). "Time to Rethink the Voting Rights Act," *Social Policy* 23(2): 17–22.

Garcia, F. Chris. (1992). "Introduction: Symposium on Latino Political Politics in the 1990s." In *Ethnic Politics and Civil Liberties*, edited by Lucius Barker. *National Political Science Review* 3: 127–131.

Gartner, Alan. (1993). "Redistricting in the 1990s: The New York Example. Introduction." *Cardozo Law Review* 14(5): 1119–1126.

Grofman, Bernard. (1993). "Voting Rights in a Multi-Ethnic World." *Chicano-Latino Law Review* 13(Summer): 15–37.

Grofman, Bernard, and Lisa Handley. (1989). "Minority Population Proportion and Black and Hispanic Congressional Success in the 1970s and 1980s." *American Politics Quarterly* 17(4): 436–445.

Guinier, Lani. (1991a). "The Triumph of Tokenism: The Voting Rights Act and the Theory of Black Success." *Michigan Law Review* 89(5): 1077–1154.

————. (1991b). "No Two Seats: The Elusive Quest for Political Equality." *Virginia Law Review* 77(8): 1413–1514.

————. (1993). "Groups, Representation, and Race-conscious Districting: A Case of the Emperor's Clothes." *Texas Law Review* 71(7): 1589–1642.

Hardy-Fanta, Carol. (1991). "Latina Women, Latino Men, and Political Participation in Boston: La Chispa que Prende," Ph.D. dissertation, Brandeis University.

————. (1993). *Latina Politics, Latino Politics: Gender, Culture, and Political Participation in Boston.* Philadelphia: Temple University Press.

————. (1997). *Latino Electoral Campaigns in Massachusetts: The Impact of Gender.* Boston: Center for Women in Politics and Public Policy and the Mauricio Gastón Institute for Latino Community Development and Public Policy, University of Massachusetts Boston.

Hernandez, Antonia. 1991. "Latino Political Participation: Invigorating the Democratic Process." *National Civic Review* 80(3): 266–274.

Horowitz, Donald L. (1985). *Ethnic Groups in Conflict.* Berkeley: University of California Press.

Jennings, James. (1992). "Blacks and Latinos in the American City in the 1990s: Towards Political Alliances or Social Conflict?" In *Ethnic Politics and Civil Liberties*, ed. Lucius Barker, 158–163.

Karian, Pamela S. (1989). "Maps and Misreadings: The Role of Geographic Compactness in Racial Vote Dilution Litigation." *Harvard Civil Rights-Civil Liberties Law Review* 24 (Winter): 173–248.

Lijphart, Arend. (1985). *Power-Sharing in South Africa.* Berkeley: University of California Press.

Macchiarola, Frank J., and Joseph G. Diaz. (1993). "Minority Political Empowerment in New York City: Beyond the Voting Rights Act." *Political Science Quarterly* 108(1): 37–57.

Pachon, Harry. (1986–1987). "Citizenship as an Obstacle to Political Empowerment in the Hispanic Community." *Journal of Hispanic Policy* 2, 77–80.

Pachon, Harry, and Louis DeSipio. (1992). "Latino Elected Officials in the 1990s." *PS: Political Science and Politics* 23(2): 212–219.

Rivera, Ralph. (1991). "Latinos in Massachusetts and the 1990 U.S. Census: Growth and Geographical Distribution." Boston: Mauricio Gastón Institute for Latino Community Development and Public Policy, University of Massachusetts Boston, Publication No. 91-01.

Rojas v. Vitoria Independent School District. (1988). Cited by Lani Guinier (1991b, 1434).

Taebel, Delbert. (1978). "Minority Representation on City Council: The Impact of Structure on Blacks and Hispanics." *Social Science Quarterly* 59(1): 142–161.

U.S. Bureau of the Census. (1990). Public Law 94-171 Data File.

———. (1991). *Voting and Registration in the Election of 1990.* Current Population Report, P20-453.

———. (1993). *Voting and Registration in the Election of 1992.* Current Population Report, P20-466.

Uriarte, Miren. 1991. "Redistricting: Towards Equality in Political Representations, *HOPE* Perspectives." (Fall): 32–37.

Vedlitz, Arnold, and Charles A. Johnson. (1982). "Community Racial Segregation, Electoral Structure, and Minority Representation." *Social Science Quarterly* 63(4): 729–736.

Welch, Susan. (1990). "The Impact of At-Large Elections on the Representation of Blacks and Hispanics." *Journal of Politics* 52(4): 1050–1070.

Zax, Jeffrey S. (1990). "Election Methods and Black and Hispanic City Council Membership." *Social Science Quarterly* 71(2): 339–355.

CHAPTER 10

Latino Voter Registration Efforts in Massachusetts
Un Pasito Más[1]

CAROL HARDY-FANTA, WITH JAIME RODRÍGUEZ

Given the wealth of research and publications on Latino voting in the United States, there is little dispute that voting is a key element in Latino political participation and efforts to gain political power. Wrinkle et al. (1996, 145) affirm that "[t]he mobilization of voters, especially ethnic voters, is one of the most important aspects of electoral success." Lozada (1996) suggests that, through voter registration, Latinos can "alter their political destiny."

Affigne, Jackson, and Avalos (1999), among others, point to the potential of the growing Latino population to determine the outcome of various election campaigns. President Bill Clinton's reelection in 1996, it has been argued, was determined not by the "soccer mom" vote but by Latino and African-American voters (Hardy-Fanta 1997, 2000). Vargas (1998–1999, 4) points to the decisive role of California's Latino voters in Loretta Sánchez's 1996 victory over Rep. Robert Dornan. And Hero (1996, 78) states that in the 1992 Colorado primary, "the Latino vote was key to Clinton's close second-place finish and was thus instrumental in providing momentum to his eventually successful pursuit of the party's nomination."

LATINO VOTER REGISTRATION AND TURNOUT: RECENT ESTIMATES

Virtually all of the literature on Latino politics in the United States highlights the relatively low voter registration and turnout in Latino communities. Numerous researchers have found, for example, that Latinos participate at a lower rate than do Anglos, "typically lagging some 10–30 percent in voter registration and turnout" (Garcia 1997a, 31). De la Garza and DeSipio (1997, 87) state that Latino voter registration and turnout "lag behind those of both the population as a whole and of the African-American population." Casper and Bass (1998) indicate that, nationally, only 26.7 percent of Latinos reported voting in the 1996 election, a decrease from 1992, when 28.9 percent of Latinos reported voting. Affigne, Jackson, and Avalos (1999, 10) present 1996 presidential election data showing that even controlling for citizenship, the Latino registration rate nationally was 14 percentage points lower than that of Anglos and the turnout rate for Latinos was 16.4 percentage points lower.

In state-level elections, Latino voting is also lower than that of Anglos or African Americans. Martínez (1996, 126) found, for example, that, in a 1992 Texas Congressional District election, "even with Latino candidates finishing one, three, and four, this predominantly Hispanic district turned out in extremely low numbers—about 5 percent of registered Democrats actually voted. While exit polls indicated a higher turnout of Latino voters than in previous congressional primaries, this may have been due more to Anglo uninterest [sic] than to Latino activism."

Guerra and Fraga (1996), in their chapter on the 1992 California elections, voice the commonly held view that the Latino potential to influence statewide election outcomes through voting is high but that it is a potential rarely, if ever, realized. De la Garza and DeSipio (1993) also demonstrate that Latinos register and vote at lower rates than Anglos and that although the number of Latino voters continues to increase, their share of the electorate remains far behind their percentage of the population. Garcia (1997a, 32), for example, points to the fact that in 1996, while Latinos made up about 10 percent of the population, they were only 5 percent of the electorate.

REASONS FOR LOW RATES OF LATINO VOTER REGISTRATION

Explanations of lower voter registration rates for Latinos include demographics, psychological/cultural factors, and structural obstacles within the U.S. electoral system. Among the demographic factors are relatively low rates of citizenship, low educational and socioeconomic status, the youthfulness of the population, and ties to homeland that are linked to foreign-born nativity (see, for example, Garcia 1997a, 32–33; Arvizu and Garcia 1996; Calvo and Rosenstone 1989; Hardy-Fanta 1993, 176–187). Psychological and cultural factors typically cited include cynicism, alienation, disinterest, apathy, a history of exclusion, and lack of knowledge (Garcia 1997a, 35). Structural obstacles include decline of the political parties, media and poll driven elections, city census practices, lack of bilingual materials, discrimination and intimidation at the local level, and lack of political outreach (see, for example, Hardy-Fanta 1993, 168–176; de la Garza and DeSipio 1994; de la Garza and DeSipio 1996, 6; Takash-Cruz 1990).

Researchers urge disaggregating the data by national origin and examining closely the effects of age, socioeconomic status and, above all, citizenship. The 1988 Latino National Political Survey (de la Garza et al. 1992, 121–124), for example, reports that voter registration rates among

Latino citizens vary by national origin and that although 78 percent of Cuban and Anglo citizens were registered to vote in 1988, only 65 percent of Mexican-American citizens and 64 percent of Puerto Ricans were registered. National origin is therefore another factor to be considered in searching for the roots of low voter registration.

Others point to the fact that rates of voter turnout, once citizens are registered, are high for all groups—Latinos as well as other racial/ethnic groups—(although like registration rates turnout varies by national origin with Mexican Americans and Puerto Ricans less likely to turn out than Anglos or Cubans). Some studies suggest that "in some circumstances Latinos' rate of participation is greater than previously thought" (Garcia 1997a, 34; referring to conclusions of Hero and Campbell 1996). Structure rather than culture may explain why Puerto Ricans in mainland U.S. elections vote at very low rates when Puerto Ricans in Puerto Rico vote at rates between 80 and 90 percent (Jennings 1988, 72).

EFFORTS TO INCREASE LATINO VOTER REGISTRATION AND TURNOUT: A NEGLECTED TOPIC

Throughout the literature on Latino voting patterns and Latino politics is an implicit if not explicit recognition that voting is not merely an individual act but that efforts are and should be expended to *mobilize* Latinos to register and vote. Guerra and Fraga (1996, 135) state that effective voter registration and naturalization drives are among the most important strategies Latinos can use to influence statewide elections. Voter mobilization usually follows a higher level of civic engagement and activism (Garcia 1997b; Diaz 1996). Diaz (1996) specifically urges increasing Latino membership in nonprofit or other organizations as a way of increasing political participation, including voting. In addition, at the community level, countless community leaders and residents expend considerable energy on voter registration drives. There has been relatively little attention given, however, to a detailed analysis of Latino voter registration efforts per se either locally or generally.

A few authors do discuss the *efforts* to register and mobilize Latinos to vote (see, for example, Guerra and Fraga 1996; de la Garza, Menchaca, and DeSipio 1994; Rey 1996), not just the *results*, i.e., voting rates in a given community or election cycle. They routinely acknowledge the important role of national Latino political organizations in increasing Latino registration by providing technical assistance, funds, as well as legal and other resources to local and statewide groups (Garcia 1997a; de la Garza, Menchaca, and DeSipio 1994).

Considerable attention has been given to voter registration efforts tied to redistricting under the provisions of the Voting Rights Act (VRA) passed in 1965 and extended to include Latinos as a "language minority" in 1970 and extended to the year 2007. According to Garcia,

Provisions of the VRA prohibiting minority vote dilution have provided
the courts with a statutory basis for intervening against acts of intimidation against Latinos, prohibiting English literacy tests and ballots, and
ordering single-member electoral districts and favorable districting patterns. The 1975 amendments were especially useful in empowering the
federal courts to invalidate many state and local statutes and practices
which had served as barriers to electoral participation by "language
minorities." (Garcia 1997a, 37–38)

Community groups across the nation have joined forces with—and/or
responded to overtures from— various national and regional organizations
to coordinate local registration and turnout drives with the resources and
experience they can and do provide. Many communities in Massachusetts
have benefited from such coordinated efforts, as has been discussed in
Chapters 3 and 4 on Lawrence and Holyoke. In the case of Lawrence, for
example, a lawsuit resulted in a settlement agreement between the Justice
Department and the City of Lawrence; the agreement challenged various
city practices, increased the number of Latino poll watchers and bilingual
materials, and provided for an Hispanic Election Coordinator.[2] This legal
action coincided with an intensive voter registration effort and a record
number of Latino candidates running for office. The reinforcing nature of
legal action, Latino candidacies, and voter registration (and high Latino
population) paid off: there are now five Latino elected officials in
Lawrence. (For a full discussion of Latino politics in Lawrence, see Chapter
3 in this volume.)

Much of the literature on voting rates and election outcomes does refer,
albeit relatively briefly, to voter registration and turnout drives (see, for
example, Garcia 1997b; DeSipio 1996; Avalos 1996; de la Garza and
DeSipio 1996; and, for the role of Latinas, Hardy-Fanta 1993, 16-18).
Other than *Barrio Ballots* (de la Garza, Menchaca, amd DeSipio 1994),
however, there has been relatively little detailed analysis of the strategies
Latino communities use to register Latino voters. This paucity of information is even more important since voting takes place at the most local level
—in one's neighborhood, one's community.

LATINO VOTING RATES IN MASSACHUSETTS

Accurate data are lacking on Latino voter registration and voting in
Massachusetts. The U.S. Census reports that in the 1996 election, only
29.7 percent of "Hispanic origin" Massachusetts residents were registered
compared to 68.7 percent of whites and 54.8 percent of blacks. The percentage of those who voted was 22.3 percent for Latinos compared to 58.2
percent for whites and 43.0 percent for blacks (U.S. Census 1998b, 26).
These data represent an almost 40 percentage point difference between
Latinos and Anglos in registration rates and almost as large a difference in

turnout. The available information is limited, however, by the fact that voting rates by Hispanic origin *and* citizenship are not provided for each state. Without knowing the number of Latinos who are *eligible* to vote (i.e., citizens over the age of 18), the official voting rates recorded by the U.S. Census are artificially low.

Regional estimates suggest that, in 1996, 32.7 percent of Latinos in New England (including Massachusetts) who were not registered were also not citizens; controlling for citizenship, the registration rate for New England Latinos in the 1996 election may have been closer to 48.6 percent. However, Latino voting rates in Massachusetts are also very low compared to the rate of Latinos in New England: 38.8 percent of Latinos in New England are reported to have registered in the 1996 election, and 28.5 percent voted (U.S. Census 1998a, 14). Although the data are inadequate and are subject to all of the errors associated with the U.S. Census count of Latino population, these data suggest that Latino registration and voting in Massachusetts are among the lowest recorded in the nation.[3] Massachusetts offers a good opportunity, therefore, to examine Latino voter registration efforts in a state facing some of the greatest challenges to mobilizers.

Estimates of Latino voter registration and voting within the state, i.e., for given cities, may be even more suspect because local conditions that either support or suppress voter participation also affect whether and for what purposes Latino voters are counted. Few of the city or state election offices, for example, gather voter registration and turnout data by race or ethnicity. Recent interviews conducted with election offices and candidates in Holyoke, Chelsea, Springfield, Worcester, Lawrence, and Lowell reveal the sketchy picture of Latino voter participation when data gathering is left up to municipal offices. The Registrar of Voters in Holyoke—a poor city in the western part of the state with Latinos making up 41.4 percent of the population (see Chapter 4)—said that the November 1999 local election was a "good race" with a 59.9 percent turnout. When asked for Latino turnout, however, she replied, "We try to keep track. We're not there yet" (Egan 2000).

Earlier efforts to gather voter registration and turnout data in Holyoke were linked to the Justice Department lawsuit described in Chapter 4; city data from 1983 to 1993 show weighted Latino turnout in Holyoke that ranged from less than 1 percent in 1983 to a high of 19.5 percent in 1985.[4] A study of Latino voting in Holyoke by the Midwest-Northeast Voter Registration Education Project (MNVREP) in 1993 also concluded that "[i]n those voting precincts with large numbers of voting-age Latinos, the registration rates and turnout rates are much lower than in those precincts where whites form the majority" (MNVREP 1993).

Cheryl Rivera, Latina state representative from Springfield, indicates that no information exists on Latino voter registration or turnout in that city (Rivera 2000). Latinos in Chelsea make up about 50 percent of the population. Juan Vega, Chelsea's Latino city councilor, said that about 10,000 of the 30,000 city residents are registered voters and that of these, about 1,800 to 2,000—fewer than 20 percent—are registered Latinos. (It should be remembered that the Chelsea Latino population is very young and made up of many noncitizens.)

The city of Lawrence, in response to the aforementioned threat of a Justice Department lawsuit, hired Manuel Ferreira Jr. to help improve Latino participation in city elections. One result was better data gathering on Latino voting patterns. A recent count of Latino surnames of city residents who were on the active voter list showed that 37 percent of registered voters were Latino—in a city where Latinos now make up 60 percent of the population (Vogler 1999, 9–10).

Measures of Latino voter participation in Boston are generally unreliable. A 1971 survey found that 36.3 percent of Latinos in the South End neighborhood were registered to vote and that 49.4 percent of those registered turned out to vote (Camayd-Freixas and Lopez 1983, 73-74). Camayd-Freixas and Lopez (1983, 74) estimated that in the 1983 Boston city elections, Latino voter registration rates were between 10 and 30 percent lower than those of blacks. More recently, Powers (1993) points to dramatic voter registration differences between a virtually all-white neighborhood in South Boston (93.1 percent in 1992) compared to a precinct in the Roxbury neighborhood that was 56.3 percent Latino (42.3 percent registered). In keeping with the literature, class has a considerable impact on Latino voter registration: of the "influential" Latinos in Boston interviewed by Hardy-Fanta (1993, 32), all indicated that they were registered to vote compared to only 27 percent of the noninfluential sample.

The above discussion clearly demonstrates that, not only is Latino voter participation low, Latino communities in Massachusetts, as well as across the nation as a whole, are underserved by local and statewide election departments. Municipal election divisions routinely do record voter registration and turnout for the general population have no system in place to measure accurately Latino voter registration and turnout. Without such a system, it is impossible to assess Latino voter participation with any degree of certainty and even harder to evaluate the relative impact of any voter registration efforts conducted by local community groups or regional and statewide organizations. To expect Latino organizations to gather and track voting patterns as well as to mobilize communities in the absence of strong political parties dedicated to identifying and mobilizing voters is unrealistic at best—and another institutionalized structural obstacle to Latino political power at worst.

OBSTACLES TO LATINO REGISTRATION AND TURNOUT IN MASSACHUSETTS

Latinos in Massachusetts face many of the demographic and structural barriers to voting described in the literature (see, for example, Piven and Cloward 1989). The most recent U.S. Census data (1995) show, for example, that Latinos have the lowest median age of all racial/ethnic groups in the state: 22 compared to 36 for whites, 26 for blacks and 29 for Asians (Torres and Chavez 1998, 6). In addition, 50 percent of Latinos in Massachusetts are under 25 years of age and almost a third (30.5 percent) are under 15. In contrast, in 1995, only 7.7 percent of Latinos were in the age group that casts the most votes (55 and older), as opposed to 24 percent of whites and 12 percent of African Americans. Latinos also have the highest poverty rates, are overrepresented in the lower paying occupations, and trail all racial/ethnic groups in years of schooling completed (Torres and Chavez 1998). Combined with the well-documented fact that younger age groups participate least in electoral politics, these demographic factors go far in explaining lower Latino registration rates.

Latinos face many obstacles to voter registration that go beyond demographics, however. These include nonbilingual city census forms, election materials and ballots as well as, the requirement to complete the annual city census or be dropped from the voting list. Other obstacles include subtle (or overt) intimidation at registration sites, nonpartisan elections, frequent election dates (e.g., primaries, local, state, national elections), and candidates who fail to reach out to meet Latino voters. Finally, an impersonal and media-driven political culture in the United States alienates many voters, including Latinos who come from countries with a more social, personal, intense, and year-round political culture (see Hardy-Fanta 1993, 153–187).

LATINO VOTER REGISTRATION EFFORTS IN MASSACHUSETTS: HISTORY AND STRATEGIES

Efforts to register and mobilize Latino voters in Massachusetts have been underway for several decades. These efforts, although rarely documented, offer a rich study in the multiplicity of concurrent strategies Latino communities here and in other communities use to increase voter registration and turnout. The lack of campaign and candidate outreach by Anglo political organizations and parties has forced Latino community activists to provide alternative resources (de la Garza and DeSipio 1992, 7). These resources include incorporating voter registration and turnout drives into venues and events that link local and U.S. politics to homeland traditions.

Local, statewide, and national Latino organizations offer additional resources including training, technical assistance, funds, space, and, last but certainly not least, the countless volunteers needed for voter registration efforts. These organizations also supply the legal expertise and con-nections that make it possible to bring—or at least threaten—a lawsuit under the Voting Rights Act. The combination of such a suit together with community registration drives and strong Latino candidates has served in numerous cases to raise voter participation substantially (see the case of Lawrence in Chapter 3). Finally, community registration drives by individ-uals within local organizations cannot be underestimated and deserve a careful analysis of their strategies and effectiveness.

EL FESTIVAL LATINO: CULTURAL ROOTS OF VOTER REGISTRATION AND MOBILIZATION

The literature on Latino politics has generally characterized tying political mobilization to Latino cultural events as "taco" or "fiesta" politics. De la Garza, Menchaca, and DeSipio (1994, 27) point to campaigns that woo Latino voters in the Southwest at "rallies where candidates praise Mexican culture and serve tacos and beer." Piven and Cloward (1989, 31–35) sug-gest that these activities are based in a "tribalistic" political style with roots in nineteenth-century politics. Latino communities throughout the state and elsewhere, nevertheless, routinely take advantage of Latino communi-ty events such as *El Festival Puertorriqueño* (or, in becoming more inclu-sive, *Hispano, Latinoamericano*) to further their goal of political mobiliza-tion.

Every summer, these festivals take place in most cities in Massachusetts. In Boston, *El Festival Puertorriqueño* (currently *Festival Betances*) has been held every year for over 30 years.[5] With days of music, carnival rides, and food, the festival is an event celebrating Latino cultural heritage and pride. Taking advantage of the large numbers of Latinos in one place over a peri-od of days to conduct voter registration and education is also a long-stand-ing tradition in Boston. According to one of the early organizers, Antonio Molina, voter registration booths are a mainstay at the Boston festival. "Every summer we register anywhere from 1,500 to 3,000 people" (Molina 1990).

Gaining the right to conduct voter registration at the festival is itself a Latino political success story. During the early 1970s, community activists had to battle officials at Mayor Kevin White's office to gain permission to put up tables and deputize Latinos to conduct voter registeration at the fes-tival. White based his willingness to smooth the way for easier voter regis-tration procedures in the Latino (and African American) communities, for the most part, on self-interest: after his poor showing among African-American voters in his 1970 run for governor he reduced restrictions on how voters could be registered. Frieda García, a long-time community activist, described "how easy it was to register blacks and Latinos to vote during this period. The mayor made it possible for potential voters to be registered in their homes! Workers were allowed to carry official registration rosters to various sectors in the black [and Latino] communit[ies]" (Jennings 1986, 70–71). In this case, Kevin White's interests coincided with those of Latino activists such as Jaime Rodríguez and Antonio Molina who were pushing for voter registration at *El Festival Puertorriqueño*. Voter registration at the festivals has been tied consistently to voter education about the electoral process and the issues. Festival organizers in Boston, for example, routinely have invited officials and staff from the Mayor's office, and the Elections Division, and any candidates who are running for election to speak at the festival and meet potential Latino voters. Grace Romero was the first Latino candidate to be elected to office in Boston; although she, as a black Panamanian, garnered most of her support from black voters, she also participated in Latino voter registration drives at the Puerto Rican Festival which assisted in her victory (Bruno and Gaston 1984).

Hardy-Fanta (1993, 179–185) suggests that tying political mobilization to events such as *el festival* is not a merely symbolic or cynically manipulative effort by candidates to gain Latino votes but creates much needed links to cultural expectations of how politics is conducted in many Latino countries of origin. Antonio Molina, one organizer of the traditional festival in Boston, decries the stereotype of politically apathetic Puerto Ricans: "We're political animals. We love politics. In Puerto Rico, the election is the fourth of November, for example—the fifth of November they're out campaigning again" (Hardy-Fanta 1993, 179).

The "pageantry, the marching bands, the rallies, the hoarsely shouted slogans" referred to by Piven and Cloward (1989, 31) that were typical in nineteenth-century politics are traditional in Puerto Rico and other Latin American countries today with high voting rates. *El Festival Latino* (or *Hispanoamericano, Latinoamericano)* recaptures and draws on these traditions as described by a woman in Boston: *"Para mí era como una fiesta—porque a mí me gustaba ver a la gente votando, y ¡se pelearon! ... ¡Se mataban por la política!"* (For me, it was like a festival—because I, myself, like to see people voting, and—did they fight! ... They'd *kill* for politics!") (Hardy-Fanta 1993, 181; emphasis in the original).

Isabel Meléndez is a Latina organizer in Lawrence. She founded the Spanish Program at the Greater Lawrence Community Action Council in Lawrence many years ago and currently serves as President of the Council. Isabel Meléndez started the tradition of the Latino festival—*La Semana Hispana* (Hispanic Week)—in that city. She contrasts the political engagement in Puerto Rico with the dull, impersonal political atmosphere in the United States and asserts that she continued the Puerto Rican tradition of voting when she moved to Lawrence:

En Puerto Rico, mis padres y mi familia se criaron en la política. Y a mí siempre me gustaba, tu ves, el sistema político de mi país. Me fascinaba—yo estaba en las fiestas públicas, en toda reunión política, allí yo estaba con mi familia. Yo era la primera que levantaba mi bandera, y hacía lo que había que hacer, tu comprendes. Y siempre me gustó. Y desde que llegué aquí, lo primero que hice—fui y me registré. Aquí el sistema es muy diferente. (Meléndez 1995)

(In Puerto Rico, my parents and my family were raised on politics. And I always liked, you know, the political system in my country. It fascinated me—I was always at the public festivals, at all the political meetings, there I was with my family. I was the first to raise my flag and I did everything that needed to be done, you understand. And I always liked it. And when I first got here, the first thing I did was go and register. Here the system is very different.)

Voter registration efforts at the festivals contribute to ongoing politicization. In Lawrence, Latino activists consider the *Semana Hispana* (Hispanic Week) to have been the first place where all the city's Latinos came together in relative peace; they also may have forged links that were essential for Latino voter unity in the elections of the 1990s. In Chelsea, the Commission on Hispanic Affairs was the more explicitly political of the two Latino organizations. The other organization, the Latin American Cultural Association (LACA), hesitated at first to permit a voter registration booth at their *festival* during late 1989 saying it was a "cultural" festival and the booth would be "too political" (Rosa 1995). The Commission decided to fight for a booth the next year. By 1993, LACA not only welcomed the booth but LACA ran candidates. The Latino slate of candidates included LACA president Leticia Ortiz, the first Latina elected to a City Council (1993–1994) seat in Massachusetts; her time on the City Council marked the zenith of Latino political representation in Chelsea. For a brief period Chelsea had the distinction of approaching parity in terms of Latino representation (see Racusen, Chapter 9 in this volume): three Latinos held municipal-level offices in this city across the river from Boston. The role of political mobilization at Latino cultural events such as festivals and the potentially synergistic relationship between cultural events, voter registration and the emergence and election of Latino candidates would seem to merit deeper examination.

¿VOTAR PARA QUÉ?[6] MOBILIZING DOOR TO DOOR

The struggle to register Latinos requires more than handing out information or telling them to vote. Latino activists around the state have spent countless hours going door to door in efforts to educate Latinos about why they should register and vote. The fight for permission to put up voter registration tables at the festival in Boston during the 1970s also yielded permission to deputize Latinos to register community residents by going door to door.

At that point in time, Boston had a major advantage over other Latino communities: during the 1960s and 1970s, city government officials prevented Latinos in Lawrence, for example, from conducting voter registration (Armano 2000). During the early 1980s, the candidacies of Felix Arroyo for Boston School Committee and Mel King for Mayor galvanized Boston's Latinos into registering by the thousands. Arroyo ran first in 1981 and estimates that about 3,000 of the 27,000 votes he won were Latinos; in 1983, when he ran again, his campaign increased the number of Latinos registered to about 7,000. Running at large in a city-wide election, Arroyo's 55,000 votes were still not enough for his election. Despite these defeats, Felix Arroyo is undaunted in his drive to represent Latinos in Boston. In the early 1990s he was appointed to the Boston School Committee and he is currently running for an at-large seat on the City Council.

Latinos conducted a massive and coordinated series of voter registration drives during the campaign of Marta Rosa in Chelsea (described in Chapter 1). By the end of her first campaign for the Chelsea School Committee in 1989, there were four people working full time going door to door. If a Latino wanted to register, the staff would wait for him or her to "dress up the kids; 'We'll wait for you,' and they actually drove them" (Rosa 1990, 1995). The Latino community was able to have two Latinos deputized and they registered residents in the city's parks and housing projects. She describes setting up a table outside the projects and "the deputies would come. We'd have two people go door-knock and bring the people down to register right in the housing project. It was a *big* effort" (Rosa 1990). (All this effort was frequently frustrated by the structural obstacles discussed above: in 1989, Rosa estimates they registered about 1,200 new Latino voters, but because of the city census procedures that dropped 400 "old" voters, there was a net gain of only 800 new voters.)

One of the main ways Latino citizens are encouraged to register and then vote is to engage them in a discussion of issues. Jaime Rodríguez is a long-time organizer and president of the Massachusetts chapter of the National Congress for Puerto Rican Rights (*El Congreso Nacional Puertorriqueño*). He states that voter registration depends on explaining how voting can improve neighborhood conditions and increase community services. Jovita Fontanez, another long-time activist, has years of experience registering Latinos; she was also the Elections Commissioner for the City of Boston during the late 1980s. Fontanez would explain to prospective voters that officials are more likely to listen to someone who is a registered voter and act on their requests for improved services. And Antonio Molina (1990) echoes Guerra's (1992) contention that "local issues play a fundamental role in mobilizing Latino voters" when he criticizes how mainstream candidates tend to focus on issues of less immediate concern to Latinos—the tax code, for example, instead of Latino high school drop-out rates. Many Latino activists believe that couching voting as something that is "good for you" (i.e., your "civic duty" or a "privilege") is not sufficient motivation. Arroyo (1990) explains that "there is a lot of rhetoric about [voting] but nothing concrete that helps people see how it relates to their housing, to their potential employment, to their day-to-day lives."

In Lawrence, an intensification of voter registration efforts coincided with the simultaneous increase in the number of Latino candidacies over the years (see Chapter 3 in this volume), the redrawing of legislative districts that facilitated the 1998 election of José Santiago, that area's first Latino state representative, and the lawsuit described earlier. Voter education is promoted by annual debates sponsored by the Council of Dominican Voters. Groups such as the Puerto Rican Movement, Hispanic Week *(Semana Hispana)*, the Latin Agenda, the *Club Cultural Latino-Americano*, the *Rumbo* newspaper, as well as individuals such as Carlos Matos (José Santiago's former legislative aide) and Isabel Meléndez of the Greater Lawrence Community Action Council have been active in voter registration and education drives. Isabel Meléndez also illustrates the link between voter registration and education, Latino cultural and political organizations, and electoral office: after decades of community organizing, she has finally decided to run for office. She is currently running for mayor of Lawrence (Gilmanhand and Forman 2000).

"MOTO-VOTO": EFFECT OF THE MOTOR VOTER BILL ON LATINO
REGISTRATION IN MASSACHUSETTS

In contrast to Boston, Chelsea, and Lawrence, Lowell is one of the cities in Massachusetts with a relatively small Latino population: 14 percent. It is also the city where the Asian population (especially Southeast Asians) is larger: 16.5 percent. The potential for conflict as well as minority cooperation is great.[7] Three forces seem to be at work in terms of Latino voter registration in Lowell. First, a strong, local community organization, the Coalition for a Better Acre (see Chapter 5 for a discussion of this group) has taken a strong activist stand for years and conducts regular voter registration drives in the Latino *barrio*. Second, Asians were able to build a coalition between Latinos and Asians around Rithy Uong's successful candidacy for City Councilor at large in 1999. In just a few months prior to the election in November 1999, these efforts succeeded in registering 100 to 200 new Latino voters.

Third, although efforts to link voter registration to voter education on the issues seem to have a greater chance of leading to increased Latino *turnout*, the Election Commission in Lowell clearly states that the single most important factor leading to increased Latino voter *registration* has been the so-called "motor-voter" law. The head of the Commission indicates that the rolls are rising and that "90 percent of new registrants are being enrolled through the motor voter law" (Lowell Election Commission 2000).

A recent count of "Hispanic surnames" on the Lowell list of registered voters verifies a continuing and dramatic increase in Latino registrations in Lowell. When the list was first obtained in July 1997, there were 2,352 Latinos registered out of an official 1995 Latino population of approximately 14,000 (Torres and Chavez 1998, 3). Another 1,751 new Latino names were added by March 1998 (and only 91 were dropped). Thus, the number of registered Latino almost doubled to 4,012 in less than one year. Taking into account that about one-third of Latinos in Massachusetts are not of voting age, and many are not citizens, the best estimate of the Latino voting-age population in Lowell is approximately 9,380, which suggests a current voter registration rate (for those eligible) of approximately 43 percent. The potential impact on local elections is certainly evident: 43 percent is a remarkably high rate for this state and nationally. In addition, a 1997 study of Latino voting in Lowell's 1997 primary and general elections suggests that Latino voter turnout was the same as the turnout for the city as a whole (Gerson 2000). Although, research based on Latino surnames is certainly problematic, these findings suggest a potential positive effect of the motor-voter bill for Latino politics.

Recent research on the impact of the motor-voter bill on minority voter turnout in Boston (Mendez-Morgan 2001) also suggests that expanded voter registration drives have paid off. Minority precincts that were specifically targeted in 2000 by "Boston Vote" showed substantial increases in voter registration and, in some precincts, higher voter turnout as well. In heavily minority Ward 14, precincts 1–7, for example, turnout increased by between 2 to 10.6 percentage points.

The motor-voter legislation also expanded voter registration to a variety of other sites as well, including community organizations and social service agencies. The increase in Latino political power in Lawrence is also likely to be due, in part, to the motor voter legislation. Isabel Meléndez, for example, routinely registers Latinos at the Lawrence Community Action Council's Spanish Program as part of her multiservice work. (During an interview with the author, her work included clearing up problems with someone's driver's license and, as a Justice of the Peace, arranging to marry a couple.) What may be most effective about registering Latinos as part of this broader service delivery (rather than simply as part of applying for a motor vehicle license) is that the Latino community agencies can and do combine voter education with the registration, something that does not occur at the Registry of Motor Vehicles. In the long run, the question whether Latino voters registered under the new, more liberal procedures (as opposed to more connected, interpersonal, or self-motivated process) turn out to vote in Lowell, Lawrence, and other communities still needs considerable research.

THE IMPORTANCE OF OUTSIDE RESOURCES

A central thesis of this volume is that "success breeds success." Political mobilization designed to register Latino voters not only leads to increasing numbers of Latino candidates and representation but increased representation serves, in a reciprocal fashion, to increase voter registration and turnout. Only longitudinal research on "input" (participation), "conversion" (representation), and "outputs" (issues and policies) that accurately tracks which factors increase voter registration and turnout at the local level will demonstrate whether we are correct in asserting a dynamic rather than linear relationship between Latino participation and representation.[8]

Local resources included progressive, religious, and legal associations. In Boston, for example, voter registration in the South End of Boston went hand in hand with community activism against urban renewal during the 1970s and was supported by black–Latino coalitions as well as white seminarians from various churches (see Uriarte-Gaston 1988). During the 1980s, legal resources from groups such as the Lawyers Committee for Civil Rights under the Law of the Boston Bar Association donated time and money to the redistricting case in Boston that ultimately led to the election of Nelson Merced, the first Latino State Representative (described in Chapter 2).

National groups such as the Rainbow Coalition galvanized Latino community organizers in Boston during the early 1980s (Bruno and Gastón 1984). The Holyoke Rainbow Coalition was formed after a visit to that city by presidential candidate Jesse Jackson in 1984. The involvement of national groups such as the Rainbow Coalition and the NAACP as well as the New England Farm Workers led to local efforts such as the Holyoke Rainbow Coalition, the United Citizens Action League (UCAL), and the Minority Action Coalition (MAC)—but with a new strategy. Besides voter registration efforts that emphasized educating Latino voters one to one or in groups about the benefits of political participation, the Rainbow Coalition challenged the structural obstacles faced by Latino voters. The Rainbow Coalition carried out this challenge in Holyoke City Hall and in the Attorney General's Office of the Commonwealth of Massachusetts. The technical assistance and visibility offered by these groups supported the local efforts and led to the legal challenges described earlier (see Chapter 4 of this volume).

Political participation in the United States is often defined in terms of individual activities and input, whether electoral or civic (see, for example, Hero and Campbell 1996; Garcia 1997b). A more expansive view of this input includes, of course, the resources and activities of national and community organizations developed to foster political participation of individual Latinos. National Latino political organizations include LULAC (League of United Latin American Citizens), MALDEF (Mexican American Legal Defense and Education Foundation), SVREP (Southwest Voter Registration and Education Project), NALEO (National Association of

Latino Elected and Appointed Officials), and NCLR (National Council of La Raza).

MALDEF is most active in litigation in the areas of redistricting, minority vote dilution and affirmative action. SVREP runs Latino exit polls and engages in voter registration in the Southwestern states. The National Council of La Raza is a clearinghouse of information on Latinos and a lobbying organization. And NALEO documents the rise and supports the efficacy of Latino elected and appointed officials and, more recently, provides technical assistance and training for candidates.

These national organizations play an important role in mobilizing Latino voter registration and turnout. Garcia (1997a, 34) states: "Such efforts by Latino organizations seem to be particularly important, since core [i.e., Anglo] culture political organizations such as political parties and individuals such as candidates for office seem to ignore disproportionately the Latino potential, depriving them of an important source of voter interest and mobilization and power." After years of paying scant attention to Latino political organizing in Massachusetts, many regional and national Latino political groups have begun to show a presence and have an impact on Latino politics in this state.

The Midwest-Northeast Voter Registration Education Project (MNVREP), for example, is a regional organization that was particularly active in Holyoke during the early 1990s, providing analysis and testimony on Latino voting patterns for the lawsuit against the city (MNVREP 1993). Its Leadership Development Program engages Latino community members in meetings with public officials; the organization's Model for Community Action builds on voter registration drives and educates Latinos to hold elected and appointed officials accountable. Testimony in the Holyoke lawsuit by A. Fredericka Cuenca, MNVREP Northeast Field Director, concluded with a "vision of where we want to be in 10 years—2 city council seats or a mayor—and with strategic planning we can realize our political potential" (MNVREP 1993). Today, 7 years later, Holyoke has reached its goal: two Latinos sit on the Holyoke City Council: Diosdado López (first elected in 1991) and Juan Cruz (elected in 1999).

Another national organization that has contributed resources to Massachusetts Latino political organizing, especially with voter registration, is *Atrévete Con Tu Voto*. This organization began when Nydia Velázquez (the first Puerto Rican woman elected to the U.S. Congress from New York City) was the director of the Office of Puerto Rico in New York. Simultaneous efforts under this initiative in Connecticut, New York, New Jersey, and Chicago led to Latino election victories in those regions. Luis Dávila coordinated the regional office in Hartford; Dorotea Emanuela was the local coordinator in Boston.

Atrévete contributed a budget of funds, workers, technical assistance, and a commitment to the political empowerment of Massachusetts Latinos, especially through voter registration. There were, according to Jaime Rodríguez, 50 volunteers, brochures, flyers, buttons, posters, and—most important—a paid staff person. In addition to providing resources, *Atrévete* challenged the stereotype that a tie to island politics suppresses or blocks political participation in mainland U.S. politics: in this case it was the Office of the Governor of Puerto Rico that was promoting voter participation by Puerto Ricans (and other Latinos) in their local U.S. communities.

Atrévete also provided, for the first time, a truly statewide sense of political organizing that encouraged the sharing of ideas and resources. It was so successful that a group of Latino organizers (including Jaime Rodríguez) developed a grant proposal and received a $25,000 grant from a local foundation for a Latino voter registration project: the *Proyecto Hispano*. Fernando Milán coordinated efforts in Worcester (with Gladys Rodríguez), Lawrence (with Isabel Meléndez), and Lowell. Gumersindo Gómez coordinated efforts in Springfield.

Other efforts have followed. The Hispanic Education and Legal Fund, a New York City nonprofit organization, supported *Voto Latino*, a project of the Massachusetts Hispanic Voter Registration and Education Coalition. The goal of this organization was to register at least 10,000 new Latino voters in Massachusetts in time for the November 1996 general election. Substantial funding was provided by the Hispanic Education and Legal Fund to pay for the organizer and to support the efforts of citizen and noncitizen volunteers.

Voto Latino coordinated its efforts with those of Latino community organizations around the state as well as organizations such as the League of Women Voters to benefit from their past experience in voter registration. The lead organizer was a Latina, Carmen Paniagua. She worked to "coordinate numerous efforts to give our campaign visibility, train volunteers, record our successes and provide community members with information on how and where they can become registered for the vote" (Lozada 1996). Public service announcements on local cable stations on the need to get out to vote was made possible by the Hispanic Education and Legal Fund's connection to the Univisión Television network. *Voto Latino* has determined to make the Latino vote a factor in elections to come.

Most recently, there have been a multiplicity of local and national efforts to coordinate voter registration, political organizing, support from national organizations, and strategies by Latino candidates. The Commonwealth Coalition, a Boston-based organization, provides candidate training and technical assistance. In 1999, NALEO also provided training for Latinos interested in running for elected office—their interest was stimulated by the fact that numerous Latinos were running for the Massachusetts State House. Because only one Latino had ever been elected to the legislature in Massachusetts (Nelson Merced in 1988 and 1999), the unprecedented election of three Latinos to the state legislature has ensured their continued interest and support.[9]

One of these new representatives, Jarrett Barrios from Cambridge, has spearheaded a statewide community political organizing effort called *¿Oiste?* (Have you heard?) to operate as a Latino PAC. The new executive director of *¿Oiste?* is a Latina, Giovanna Negretti.[10] On 24 March of this year, the Mauricio Gastón Institute for Latino Community Development and Public Policy at the University of Massachusetts Boston held the "Statewide Latino Public Policy Conference 2000." Its theme was *¡Un llamado a la acción política!* (A call to political action!). The day's workshops tied action directly to community-level concerns—thus responding to what Latino organizers have said is essential. The Latino Agenda that has developed from these efforts also fulfills Guerra's (1992) admonition that local issues are key in Latino political mobilization and "Tip" O'Neill's now famous aphorism: "All politics is local."

CONCLUSION: WHAT WORKS? HOW CAN WE TELL?

Jaime Rodríguez is a Latino activist in Boston who has devoted decades of his life to Latino voter registration, representation, and empowerment in Massachusetts through his work and leadership in organizations such as the National Congress for Puerto Rican Rights, *Atrévete Con Tu Voto*, and *Voto Latino*, as well as through community political activism. He was also active in building *Voto Latino 2000* in preparation for the 2000 presidential election. When asked which factors contribute most to increasing Latino voter registration, turnout, and influence—the door to door organizing, the booths at the *festival*, the candidate nights at his house, the annual Christmas *jolgorio* he organizes every year, or the outside resources offered by national and regional organizations—he replied, "It all helps in the long run. From the first effort to now, from *Atrévete* to *Voto Latino 2000, es un pasito más*" (Rodríguez 1999).

Although there has been no research on the effects of all of these investments in Latino political mobilization on voter registration rates in Massachusetts, the increased number of Latino campaigns and election victories across the state certainly suggest that outside resources—together with ongoing efforts by grass roots community organizations and at cultural events such as *los festivales* (and perhaps the motor-voter bill)—are beginning to pay off in this state. And electoral success makes it possible, in a reciprocal fashion, to garner interest and resources from national Latino and other political organizations. It is our contention that success in winning elections and receiving these resources serve to increase political mobilization at the community level as well.

NOTES

1.   *Un pasito más* may be translated as "one more step"-one step forward.
2.   The Hispanic Election Coordinator, Manuel Ferreira Jr. and Community Liaison members meet monthly; a Coordinator Report is required by the Justice Department on the "effectiveness of election related activities" (Ferreira and McGravey 2000).
3.   For a thorough discussion of the estimates of and problems in accurately gauging the Latino voting rate in Massachusetts, see Chapter 9 in this volume.
4.   The weighted percents for Latino voting-age population in several years were actually negative numbers—as low as minus 4.9 in the 1991 primary election. These data were provided by Steven P. Perlmutter of the Law Offices of Robinson & Cole (Perlmutter 1996).
5.   Many communities across the state have changed what used to be called a "Puerto Rican Festival" to "Hispanic Week" or "Latino Festival" as the Latino population became more diverse. Not all such efforts at increased inclusiveness have been successful, however: in Lowell, for example, the attempt to create a broader Latin American festival was blocked by the Puerto Rican festival organizers.
6.   "Vote for what?" (Why should I bother voting?)
7.   For a discussion of conflict and convergence in public opinion and political behavior among Latinos, African Americans, and Asians in Massachusetts, see Watanabe and Hardy-Fanta (1998). The 2000 census data are provided courtesy of the Mauricio Gastón Institute for Latino Community Development and Public Policy, University of Massachusetts Boston.
8.   For a discussion of the ways these terms ("input," "conversion," and "outputs") are used, see Garcia (1997c).
9.   See Olivencia (Chapter 2 in this volume) for a discussion of Merced's election, and his defeat, after two terms in office.
10.   For a discussion of *¿Oiste?*, see Miller (2000).

REFERENCES

Affigne, Tony, M. Njeri Jackson, and Manuel Avalos. (1999). "Latino Politics in the United States: Building a Race-Conscious, Gendered, and Historical Analysis." Paper presented at the 1999 Annual Meeting of the American Political Science Association, Atlanta, Georgia, 2–5 September.

Armano, M. J. D., II. (2000). "Hispanic Political Succession in Lawrence, MA." Senior Thesis, Spring, Political Science Department, University of Massachusetts Lowell.

Arroyo, Felix. (1990). Interview with the author, 12 November.

Arvizu, John R., and F. Chris Garcia. (1996). "Latino Voting Participation: Explaining and Differentiating Latino Voting Turnout, " *Harvard Journal of Behavioral Sciences* 18 (2): 104–128.

Avalos, Manuel. (1996). "Promise and Missed Opportunities: The Latino Vote in Arizona." Chapter 4 in *Ethnic Ironies: Latino Politics in the 1992 Elections*, edited by Rodolfo O. de la Garza and Louis De Sipio, 95–100. Boulder, CO: Westview Press.

Bruno, Melania, and Mauricio Gastón. (1984). "Latinos for Mel King." *Radical America* 17(6) and 18(1): 67–79.

Calvo, Maria A., and Steven J. Rosenstone. (1989). "Hispanic Political Participation." *Latino Electorates Series*. San Antonio, TX: Southwest Voter Research Institute.

Casper, Lynne M., and Loretta E. Bass. (1998). *Current Population Reports: Voting and Registration in the Election of November 1996*. P-20-504. U.S. Department of Commerce: Economics and Statistics Administration, Issued July 1998.

Camayd-Freixas, Yohel, and Russell López. (1983). *Gaps in Representative Democracy: Redistricting, Political Participation and the Latino Vote in Boston*. Boston: Hispanic Office of Planning and Evaluation, September.

de la Garza, Rodolfo O., and Louis DeSipio. (1993). "Save the Baby, Change the Bathwater, and Scrub the Tub: Latino Electoral Participation after Twenty Years of Voting Rights Act Coverage." *Texas Law Review* 71 (7): 1479–1539.

———. (1994). "Overview: The Link Between Individuals and Electoral Institutions in Five Latino Neighborhoods." Chapter 1 in *Barrio Ballots: Latino Politics in the 1990 Elections*, edited by Rodolfo O. de la Garza, Martha Menchaca, and Louis DeSipio, 1–41. Boulder, CO: Westview Press.

———. (1996). "Latinos and the 1992 Elections: A National Perspective." Chapter 1 in *Ethnic Ironies: Latino Politics in the 1992 Elections*, edited by Rodolfo la Garza and Louis De Sipio, 3–49. Boulder, CO: Westview Press.

de la Garza, Rodolfo O., Louis DeSipio, F. Chris Garcia, John Garcia, and Angelo Falcon. (1992). *Latino Voices: Mexican, Puerto Rican, and Cuban Perspectives on American Politics*. Boulder, CO: Westview Press.

de la Garza, Martha Menchaca, and Louis DeSipio. (1994). *Barrio Ballots: Latino Politics in the 1990 Elections*. (With a forward by Sidney Verba). Boulder, CO: Westview Press.

DeSipio, Louis. (1996). "Making Citizens or Good Citizens? Maturalization as a Predictor of Organizational and Electoral Behavior." *Hispanic Journal of Behavioral Sciences* 18(2): 194–213.

Diaz, William A. (1996). "Latino Participation in America: Associational and Political Roles." *Hispanic Journal of Behavioral Science* 18(2) (May): 154–174.

Egan, Suzanne. (2000). Telephone interview, Jeffrey Gerson (4 January).

Ferreira, Manuel, Jr., and James McGravey. (2000). "Election Coordinator's Post Election Report, March 7, 2000, Presidential Primary; Election Related Activities and Effectiveness of the Outreach and Publicity Plan." Prepared by Manuel Ferreira, Jr., and James McGravey, City Clerk, City of Lawrence, Massachusetts. Unpublished document.

Garcia, F. Chris. (1997a). "Input to the Political System: Participation." Part II in *Pursuing Power: Latinos and the Political System*, 31–43. Notre Dame, IN: University of Notre Dame Press.

———. (1997b). "Political Participation: Resources and Involvement among Latinos in the American Political System." Chapter 2 in *Pursuing Power: Latinos and the Political System*, 44–71. Notre Dame, IN: University of Notre Dame Press.

———. (1997c). (ed.) *Pursuing Power: Latinos and the Political System.* Notre Dame, IN: University of Notre Dame Press.

Gerson, Jeffrey. (2000). Personal communication, 8 June.

Gilmanheand, Sally, and Ethan Forman. (2000). "Immigrants: We Expect More of U.S." *Lawrence Eagle-Tribune* 21 November, 1.

Guerra, Fernando. (1992). "Conditions Not Met: California Elections and the Latino Community." In *From Rhetoric to Reality: Latino Politics in the 1988 Elections*, edited by Rodolfo O. de la Garza and Louis DeSipio, 99–110. Boulder, CO: Westview Press.

Guerra, Fernando, and Luis Ricardo Fraga. (1996). "Theory, Reality, and Perpetual Potential: Latinos in the 1992 California Elections." Chapter 6 in *Ethnic Ironies*, 131–145, edited by de la Garza and Louis DeSipio, Boulder, CO: Westview Press.

Hardy-Fanta, Carol. (1993). *Latina Politics, Latino Politics: Gender, Culture, and Political Participation in Boston.* Philadelphia: Temple University Press.

———. (1997). *Latino Electoral Campaigns in Massachusetts: The Impact of Gender.* A Research Report, with María Quiñones, Lynn Stephen, Nelson Merced, and Anthony Affigne. Boston: Center for Women in Politics and Public Policy and the Mauricio Gastón Institute for Latino Community Development and Public Policy, University of Massachusetts Boston.

———. (2000). "A Latino Gender Gap? Evidence from the 1996 Election." *Milenio* 2 (February). Notre Dame, IN: Inter-University Program for Latino Research.

Hero, Rodney E. (1996). "An Essential Vote: Latinos and the 1992 Elections in Colorado." Chapter 3 in *Ethnic Ironies*, edited by Rodolfo O. de la Garza and Louis DeSipio, 75–94. Boulder, CO: Westview Press.

Hero, Rodney, and Anne G. Campbell. (1996). "Understanding Latino Political Participation: Exploring the Evidence from the Latino National Political Survey." *Hispanic Journal of Behavioral Sciences* 18 (2): 129–141.

Jennings, James. (1986). "Urban Machinism and the Black Voter: The Kevin White Years." In *From Access to Power: Black Politics in Boston*, edited by James Jennings and Mel King, 57–86. Rochester, VT: Schenkman Books.

———. (1988). "The Puerto Rican Community: Its Political Background." Chapter 3 in *Latinos and the Political System*, edited by F. Chris Garcia, 65–80. Notre Dame, IN: University of Notre Dame Press.

Lozada, John. (1996). "Latino Voter Registration Campaign Launched." Electronic Message from Massachusetts Hispanic Voter Registration and Education Coalition, forwarded by Institute for Puerto Rican Policy (IPR) to IPR Forum Subscribers, 12 August.

Lowell Election Commission. (2000). Interview with election department official.

Martínez, Valerie J. (1996). "Unrealized Expectations: Latinos and the 1992 Elections in Texas." Chapter 5 in *Ethnic Ironies*, edited by Rodolfo O. de la Garza and Louis DeSipio, 113–130. Boulder, CO: Westview Press.

Meléndez, Isabel. (1995). Interview with author, 5 May.

Mendez-Morgan, Lily. (2001). "Impact of the Motor-Voter Bill on Minority Voter Turnout." Master's thesis, Master of Science in Public Affairs, University of Massachusetts Boston.

Miller, Yawu. (2000). "Massachusetts Latinos Launch New Political Action Committee." *Bay State Banner*, 21 December, 2, 19.

Molina, Antonio. (1990). Interview with author, 12 September.

MNVREP (Midwest-Northeast Voter Registration and Education Project). (1993). Testimony presented by A. Fredericka Cuenca, Northeast Field Director, to the Massachusetts Hispanic Advisory Commission, Springfield-Holyoke Public Hearing, 7 August.

Perlmutter, Steven P. (1996). Letter and data on Latino voter turnout in Holyoke, 1983–1993.

Piven, Frances Fox, and Richard A. Cloward. (1989). *Why Americans Don't Vote.* New York: Random House, Pantheon Books, first paperback edition.

Powers, John. (1993). "Invisible Voters." *Boston Sunday Globe,* 1 August.

Rey, Robert. (1996). "Leverage Without Influence: Illinois Latino Politics in 1992." Chapter 7 in *Ethnic Ironies*, edited by Rodolfo O. de la Garza and Louis DeSipio, 149–168. Boulder, CO: Westview Press.

Rivera, Cheryl. (2000). Telephone interview with Jeffrey Gerson.

Rodríguez, Jaime. (1999). Interview with the author, 2 December.

Rosa, Marta. (1990, 1995). Interviews with the author, 12 November, 1990; 9 May, 1995.

Takash-Cruz, Paule. (1990). "A Crisis of Democracy Community: Responses to the Latinoization of a California Town Dependent on Immigrant Labor." Ph.D. diss., University of California Berkeley.

Torres, Andrés, and Lisa Chavez. (1998). *Latinos in Massachusetts: An Update.* Boston: Mauricio Gastón Institute for Latino Community Development and Public Policy, University of Massachusetts Boston.

U.S. Census. (1998a). "Table 3. Reported Voting and Registration, by Race, Hispanic Origin, and Age, for Divisions." *Voting and Registration in the Election of November 1996.* Downloaded on 17 April, 2000, from www.census.gov/prod/3/98pubs/p20-504u.pdf, p. 14.

———. (1998b). "Table 4. Reported Voting and Registration, by Sex, Race, and Hispanic Origin, for States." *Voting and Registration in the Election of November 1996.* Downloaded on 17 April, 2000, from www.census.gov/prod/3/98pubs/p20-504u.pdf, p. 26.

Uriarte-Gastón, Miren. (1988). "Organizing for Survival: The Emergence of a Puerto Rican Community." Ph.D. diss., Boston University.

Vargas, Arturo. (1998–1999). "A Decade in Review." *Harvard Journal of Hispanic Policy* 11: 3–7.

Vogler, Mark E. (1999). "City's future: Push on to Find Latino Voters." *Lawrence Eagle-Tribune*, 1 November, 9–10.

Watanabe, Paul, and Carol Hardy-Fanta. (1998). "Conflict and Convergence: Race, Public Opinion and Political Behavior in Massachusetts." An Occasional Paper of the John W. McCormack Institute of Public Affairs, University of Massachusetts Boston. Boston: McCormack Institute (June).

Wrinkle, Robert D., Joseph Stewart, Jr., J.L. Polinard, Kenneth J. Meier, and John R. Arvizu, (1996). "Ethnicity and Nonelectoral Political Participation." *Hispanic Journal of Behavioral Sciences* 18(2): 142–153.

CHAPTER 11

Black, Latino, and Asian Coalition Politics in Boston

Issues and Lessons for Urban Politics

JAMES JENNINGS

Political relationships between communities of color in the urban United States are key factors in understanding and analyzing the contours and content of local politics and racial/ethnic conflict today. Due to demographic and social developments the story of racial and ethnic conflict in cities will reflect increasingly the particular political relationships between blacks, Latinos, Asians, and other non-European groups in the United States. There are many variables that influence the state of racial and ethnic relations in U.S. society as is shown in other chapters in this volume. These include structural changes in the economy such as changing occupational and employment patterns that may contribute to conflict between communities of color. There may be cultural issues and values that represent potential variables for explaining political conflict between these groups. Historical factors are relevant to understanding political relationships between communities of color. And certainly immigration and foreign policy are relevant to this question. Although these explanations have validity, this topic is often discussed in ways that overlook a history of both conflict *and* coalition building between these groups. But understanding how the latter takes place and develops can be helpful in a greater understanding of racial and ethnic political conflict between these groups.

This chapter has two objectives: one is to review various frameworks for analyzing racial and ethnic conflict between communities of color. A second is to show that analysis of this issue requires attention to attempts aimed at building consensus among these groups, as well as conflict. Most of the literature and popular commentary has not only focused on conflict, but overlooked instances of consensus that offer insights about racial and ethnic conflict in the urban United States. Several cities in Massachusetts, including Boston, Lawrence, Springfield, and others, can be studied in order to understand how this issue influences local politics and public policy. Boston, however, offers numerous examples of attempts to build political alliances between these groups. In this city there is a long history of networks of activists who define themselves as progressive and are continually attempting to build multiracial and ethnic coalitions across black, Latino, and Asian communities. These individuals include elected officials and neighborhood activists such as Carmelo Iglesias, Mel King, Felix Arroyo, Michael Liu, Frieda García, Peter Hardie, Marilyn Anderson Chase, Alex Rodriguez, Meizchu Lui, Miren Uriarte, Chuck Turner, Byron Rushing, Jose Durán, and many others.

Demographic characteristics and trends in some urban places show that people of color, including blacks, Latinos, Asians, and others, are continuing to increase their relative share of the population. Housing patterns and residential segregation, furthermore, are contributing to greater concentrations of people of color in certain cities. At the same time that these groups are growing in terms of their share of the total population, studies show that social and economic conditions for masses of individuals and families in these groups are not improving significantly. This leads to political situations in which these groups compete with each other for basic economic resources and utilization of urban space. In certain cities these groups reside in close proximity to each other sharing space in terms of housing, education, and economic activities, thus contributing to the possibility for conflict (de la Garza 1992).

The growth and concentration of communities of color, as well as the relatively lower economic and social conditions for many people in these groups, are associated with periodic political and even violent eruptions in urban settings. A few political and policy issues can be identified as typical triggers for urban conflict between communities of color. These issues generally include police and community relations, legislative redistricting, bilingual education, and competition for jobs and appointments made by local government. Racial and ethnic conflict between these groups can take place in and outside electoral arenas.

Although episodic, this kind of racial and ethnic conflict is widespread enough to justify serious attention on the part of urban scholars and others. But although focus on conflict is justified, it is certainly not the complete story in assessing the history, current status, and future possibilities of how communities of color can work together in political arenas on behalf of progressive social policies. Boston, Massachusetts, offers a case study for learning about the factors that contribute to both conflict between communities of color, but very importantly, to consensus and coalitions as well.

A study published in 1983 by Yohel Camayd-Freixas and Russell Lopez (1983), *Gaps in Representative Democracy: Redistricting, Political Participation, and the Hispanic Vote,* was modeled after an earlier study that I authored, *The Black Voter in Boston, Massachusetts,* published in February 1982.[1] I completed this report for the Black Political Task Force, a prominent organization of black elected officials and community activists that was founded in 1978 and sought to exert influence on Boston elections and politics. The report was distributed widely as one of the first comprehensive investigations of black voter characteristics and patterns in the city in the post–World War II period. This report included demographic information, as well as voter registration rates and turnout rates in the precincts and wards that were predominantly black in 1980. Similarly, the study by Camayd-Freixas and Lopez was one of the first studies examining the characteristics of Latino voters. Both research reports identified the potential of electoral influence in two communities of color that were growing in size. Together these reports proposed, in effect, that the two communities of color can grow stronger politically as they increase in numbers, but possibly become weaker if their respective interests cancelled each other in the electoral arena rather than point toward the building of political coalitions.

These earlier reports suggest that today the weight and impact of voting on the part of both blacks and Latinos, and the rapidly growing Asian community, and resulting electoral influence for each group will be increasingly dependent on the quality and extent of their political relations. This is not to suggest that the ever present issue of racial relationships between blacks and whites is now moot in describing and studying local politics in Boston and other cities. Nor does it mean that other groups of color can be excluded from this critical topic in urban politics. But how these three groups and their activist and leadership strata decide to work together or not on a range of political issues in Boston will determine increasingly the contours of politics, as well as the content of public policies that are adopted by local government.

This reflects the situation in numerous other cities where communities of color are also growing in numbers and concentration, and where economic conditions reflect lower social status for these groups. The state of political relations between these groups, and whether it reflects conflict or consensus, has a direct effect on who enjoys power in the city. Examining New York City, for example, John Mollenkopf notes that the lack of political and ethnic cooperation between blacks and Latinos will tend to enhance the electoral strength of conservative politicians and regimes. Emphasizing the differences between these two communities of color, he writes, "these differences seem to divide and weaken the effort to mount a liberal reform challenge. They also provide the mayor favorable territory for a divide-and-conquer strategy" (Mollenkopf 1987, 495). Reiterating this idea I stated in an earlier article:

> Many social and political issues that urban mayors have to try to resolve are now colored by the political relationships between blacks and Latinos. For example, in places like Miami and Houston conflict between police and community reflects, in part, ethnic division and hostility between blacks and Latinos. In both these cities, instances of police brutality have involved Latino officers abusing black residents. In the area of education,

there are instances both of political conflict and of cooperation between blacks and Latinos in cities like Chicago and New York. Electoral redistricting struggles in places like Los Angeles and Boston have, to a certain degree, reflected black and Latino political solidarity. Police and community relations, education, and redistricting are but a few issues that have always confronted the mayor's office; today, these same issues become even more complex and pressing as a result of the growth and political maturing of two communities of color, neither of which has been accepted or integrated fully into the higher echelon of private and corporate wealth in urban America. (Jennings 1992a, 161)

I pointed out further in this article that how these issues are resolved, and in whose political favor, is influenced partially by the degree of racial and ethnic conflict between these groups. This means, in other words, that conflict between communities of color may be functional in maintaining the power base of dominant economic and political interests.

Numerous articles appearing in journals in political science, including the *American Political Science Review*, the *New England Journal of Public Policy*, the *Political Science Quarterly*, the *National Political Science Review*, and others, have highlighted conflict between these groups, as well as the causes for such conflict. Generally, the explanations utilized for analyzing this kind of conflict include a range of ideas that I have described in other articles as the *resentment explanation,* the *ethnic succession model,* the *social and economic status model,* and the *racial hierarchy model* (Jennings 1992b, esp. 15–27).

The resentment explanation contends that groups that have been living and working in a city for longer periods than newer groups resent the social and economic advances of the latter. This resentment is reflected in social conflict and tensions over housing, schools, control of public agencies, and electoral politics. In discussing political divisions between blacks and Latinos, Rodolfo O. de la Garza offers resentment as one factor. This includes, "resentment among many blacks over Latino access to affirmative action programs that blacks believe were designed for them," and "tensions because of the perception that immigration results in job displacement and the reallocation of public resources to Latinos rather than blacks" (de la Garza 1992, 141). According to this explanation, ethnic tension and conflict can be exacerbated by social and economic gains on the part of Latinos or Asians, for example. Blacks may resent such progress and interpret it as yet another reminder of society's historical treatment of them.

The ethnic succession model approaches ethnic and racial groups as primarily interest groups operating within a relatively open pluralist arena in the United States. According to this theory, blacks, Latinos, and Asians are interest groups and bump into each other as they all attempt to climb society's social and economic ladders. The model suggests that those groups residing in society the longest tend to have an important advantage over more recent groups. Historian Stephen Thernstrom (1973, 173–219) describes a facet of this model as the "last of the immigrants" thesis, where the economic status of a group is dependent on how long they have resided in the city. The second part of this thesis asserts that after paying some initial dues in the form of depressed economic conditions, new groups eventually realize progress and social mobility. Daniel P. Moynihan, regarding two groups in New York City, reflects the theory in a query: "How then are blacks and Puerto Ricans doing? If our theory holds up, they both ought to be moving up (and being pushed up) to be actively challenging the norms of previous groups, and also to be emulating them. If history holds up, they ought to be having some success" (Moynihan 1979, 5). Moynihan answers his query in the affirmative.

Related to this approach is the social and economic status model for analyzing racial and ethnic conflict. Stanley Steinberg (1981, 179) provides a brief description of this model when he writes: "If there is an iron law of ethnicity, it is that when ethnic groups are found in a hierarchy of power, wealth, and status, then conflict is inescapable." This means that groups that occupy similar social and economic positions, such as blacks, Latinos, and Asians in Boston, are natural group competitors as a result of their status, and numbers in the total population. As these groups seek to gain social and economic status they may find themselves, inevitably, in zero-sum political conflict with each other.

The racial hierarchy model is best described in an earlier work by Robert Blauner, *Racial Oppression in America*:

> In a racial order a dominant group, which thinks of itself as distinct and superior, raises its social position by exploiting, controlling and keeping down others who are categorized in racial or ethnic terms. When one or more groups are excluded from equal participation in society and from a fair share of its values, other groups not so excluded and dominated are correspondingly elevated in position. . . . Whether or not particular racist practices are followed consciously in order to benefit whites is not the issue. Whatever the intent, the system benefits all strata of the white population, at least in the short run—the lower and working classes as well as the middle and upper classes. (Blauner 1972, 16)

Thus, new groups arriving in cities, even African-descent groups, may seek to disassociate themselves from African Americans and their neighborhoods as much as possible, as this strategy may result in social and economic benefits for them. One benefit of this strategy on the part of new groups is that whites who hold prejudicial views do not stigmatize them by association with African Americans. This process is perpetuated by a widespread social stigmatization of African Americans as is reflected in many public opinion surveys, and evident in the popular medium, including newspapers, radio and television, and entertainment movies. The more a group can stay away from association or contact with African Americans, therefore, the greater its chances of taking advantage of racial hierarchy.

Another framework for understanding the nature of conflict between blacks and Latinos in the electoral arena is offered by Lani Guinier's (1995) taxonomy of stages of access and voting rights issues. She points out that there are three stages of politicking regarding the access and utility of voting rights for communities of color: "The first generation approach focused directly on access to the ballot. . . . Access issues, for the most part, have been replaced by the second-generation to voting rights, increasing the number of minority group members elected to office. . . . In the third generation, the marginalization of minority group interests is reproduced in the newly integrated legislature" (Guinier 1995, 32). As blacks and Latinos move toward second generation issues the likelihood of conflict based on contradictory group goals increases.

This approach is further explained by Seth Racusen's observation: "Indeed, one group's gain has come at the expense of another, a dynamic that becomes increasingly difficult as each group becomes larger. . . . The complexities are equally difficult in cities in which two equivalent-size minority groups are competing for political representation" (Racusen 1995, 165). Professors Paula McClain and Joseph Stewart (1994) add along this line of thought: "Another direction in which racial minority group politics may move is toward the formation of voting coalitions with other racial minorities. . . . The opposite may be true, however, in cities where a racial minority has become a numerical majority. In those instances, the majority minority no longer needs to form coalition." These two observations suggest the likelihood, as noted earlier, of zero-sum political situations in which the gains of one group are threatening to other groups.

A concern with some of these models is that they are built *solely* on instances and the possibilities of conflict without considering examples of collaboration between these groups. But as this chapter might suggest, there are important historical and contemporary efforts aimed at racial and ethnic collaboration. These can be instructive for building a progressive political coalition and agenda in cities. Another problem with some of these explanations is that scholars and the mainstream media, at times, approach the political relations between communities of color within an exclusively black–white racial paradigm. But this no longer reflects the current or projected demography of the nation. Race relations are still approached by many in the media as if it involved only blacks and whites. In many cases where people are polled by newspapers it is not unusual not to find mention of groups other than these two in discussions on race relations. This weakness is apparent in many scholarly and civic discussions on race throughout the 1980s and the 1990s.

Related to this weakness is the fact that some scholarship on racial and ethnic political conflict and coalition continues to be rooted in the classic work, *An American Dilemma* (1944), by Gunnar Myrdal. Here, the problem of race was defined as a social gap between the ideals of U.S. democracy and its practice in the area of race relations. This model is most applicable to social situations involving only blacks and whites. The nation, however, actually *never* reflected a demographic profile in which these were the only groups involved in the cauldron of racial and ethnic politics.[2]

There are some examples of how this paradigm continues to influence analysis of race and ethnic relations. One is the recent work, *Reaching Beyond Race*, by Paul M. Sniderman and Edward G. Carmines. These authors argue that the Myrdal framework is still relevant for understanding contemporary situations involving race relations. They write, for instance: "With the rise to prominence of the civil rights movement during the 1950s, followed by the passage of the historic civil rights laws in the middle of the 1960s, Gunnar Myrdal's classic work, *An American Dilemma*, seemed to have won the verdict of history. The American Creed, with its commitment to liberty, equality, and fair play would prevail" (Sniderman and Carmines 1997, 146). But here, too, other groups of color essentially are ignored, and how these groups relate to each other politically is not presented as a serious question.

They add that "[t]here are deeper moral considerations, having nothing intrinsically to do with race, that are responsible for the very fact that the issue of race has a moral claim upon us. Two of them are the values of equal opportunity and of equal treatment. It is by appealing to them that more support can be won in behalf of policies to assist the badly off" (Sniderman and Carmines 1999, 154). This claim may be irrelevant, however, to the issue of how communities of color respond to each other politically as they attempt to gain and compete against each other for economic resources and benefits. The oversight of how black, Latino, and Asian communities and interests might intersect in the political and policy arena is one reason that President William Clinton's race commission, also reflecting a Myrdal-oriented paradigm, was criticized by many grass roots activists and organizations. At least initially, the Commission seemed to have approached issues related to race and ethnic relations as primarily a social and economic dynamic between blacks and whites.

By emphasizing the Myrdal paradigm, Sniderman and Carmines tend to exclude the political relationships between communities of color as a significant matter. How this society approaches the issue of race, however, increasingly will reflect the kinds of relationships and discourse that arise as communities of color work together, and fight each other in the political arena. Under the framework offered by Sniderman and Carmines, it is how blacks and whites relate to each other that is the key issue in understanding urban and ethnic conflict in the contemporary period. Alas, however, Myrdal's framework is not comprehensive in terms of helping us to understand and analyze racial and ethnic politics at the local level in the contemporary period.

Another development that is overlooked in some scholarship germane to this topic is the increasing ethnic diversity in black, Latino, and Asian communities. This is important, however, in that ethnic groups within both these communities are overlapping the traditional racial classifications. Two political scientists identified changing ethnicization of these communities of color as a major factor affecting the nature and extent of political conflict or cooperation between these groups. Professors William Sales and Rod Bush write that "[a]t the national level barriers to Black and Latino coalition are considerable. The Black and Latino populations of New York City have experienced increasing ethnic differentiation since immigration from the Caribbean and Latin America." And "in discussing future possibilities for Black and Latino coalition, it is important to disaggregate the Latino population in terms of ethnicity, class, race, nationality, culture, specific histories associated with their homelands, and reasons for immigration" (Sales and Bush 1997, 137). These two scholars are claiming that ethnic categories within the broad racial classification of black, Latino, and Asian represent a significant factor in determining the nature and quality of political relations.

In Boston, increasing ethnicization in communities of color is certainly an issue that is part of the equation for understanding the future of coalitions between them. According to a study commissioned by The Boston Foundation, *A Dream Deferred: Changing Demographics, Challenges, and New Opportunities for Boston*, by Paul Watanabe et al. (1996), increasing ethnic differentiation is a prominent characteristic of these groups. As reported in this study: "There has been an influx of new ethnic groups such as Ethiopians, Haitians, Nigerians, Somalians, and black Latinos into Boston's traditionally African-American population. The Latino community in Boston is one of the most diverse Latino communities in the United States. And in the Asian American community substantial numbers of Southeast Asians have settled in the city augmenting the large and well-established Chinese population" (Watanabe et al. 1996, 42). Increasing ethnic diversity will tend to continue as a result of the population growth of these groups and immigration from Latin America and the Caribbean, Africa, and Asia.

A problem and impediment to analysis of racial and ethnic conflict today is the role of the media. Conflict between these groups is usually presented as sensational by the mainstream media. The media has played a negative role in reflecting simplistic approaches to questions related to political relations between communities of color. Unfortunately some scholars have adopted the ahistorical and sensational claims reported in the media about this issue without question.

This observation about the media is important to note because the media carries much influence in determining how communities of color perceive of each other, and consequently how they work or do not work together with each regarding political issues. Professor Karen Umemoto confirms this claim in a study of the role of media in black–Korean conflict in Los Angeles. In her article, "Blacks and Koreans in Los Angeles: The Case of LaTasha Harlins and Soon Da Ju," she explains that the media coverage was selective in the issues and perceptions that it generated among the public. Although there were attempts to provide a balanced view of the shooting of a Black victim by a Korean storeowner, according to her case study, the draw of sensational and divisive news coverage was evident here and in many similar instances (Umemoto 1994).

The media has played a negative role in enhancing the possibility of interethnic cooperation and work between communities of color as a result of how it covers incidents of conflict, and ignores instances of cooperation. This is why past instances of both conflict *and* cooperation between these groups should be reviewed and analyzed within the context of understanding the contemporary situation. In fact, as pointed out by the Puerto Rican educator and activist Luis Fuentes in "The Community Control Movement in New York City" (Fuentes 1999, in Torres and Velásquez 1999); Asian activist Yuri Kochiyama (1994) in "The Impact of Malcolm X on Asian-American Politics and Activism"; and Chicano activist Daniel Osuna (1994), in "Blacks and Chicanos: Parallels in Political and Historical Struggles," there are significant historical examples of political collaboration between communities of color (Jennings 1994a). In a key book about race and labor in the United States, *Black Workers*, historians Philip S. Foner and Ronald L. Lewis (1989) present several inspiring examples of workers in these communities, as well as whites, throughout U.S. history involved in organizing and struggling together to overcome the problem of racism directed against all of these groups.

The media's treatment of this topic has been divisive, and ahistorical, and excludes the experiences of grass roots activists working to build political bridges between communities of color as explained by John Anner. He observes that "Not much is being written these days about victorious popular movements in the Untied States. . . . [T]he gatherings of social justice organizations . . . are ignored or written about in terms hardly less condescending than those found in the pages of the *Wall Street Journal.* As a result, the current received wisdom on the left is that 'they' are strong, united, motivated, and purposeful while 'we' are weak, divided, fragmented, and too busy fighting amongst ourselves to accomplish anything" (Anner 1996, 5). In fact, as some of the examples in this chapter illustrate, there are historical instances of such bridge building (see Anner 1996; Jennings 1994).

Several foundation studies published in recent years provide numerous cases in which these communities are working together effectively for common political and economic purposes. These include Robert Bach et al. (1993), *Changing Relations: Newcomers and Established Residents in U.S. Communities*, a report issued by the Ford Foundation, and Grace Yun (1993), *Intergroup Cooperation in Cities: African, Asian, and Hispanic American Communities*, published by the Asian-American Federation in New York City. These reports document political collaboration but offer insight into the causes of conflict between these groups as well. This is key because, again, noting how *political cooperation* emerges is equally important to how it is discouraged in urban settings. Examining both sides of this issue allows us to understand the nature of power, and its relationship to race and ethnicity and communities of color in the contemporary period.

BLACK, LATINO, AND ASIAN POLITICAL RELATIONS IN BOSTON, MASSACHUSETTS

Although political relations between communities of color do reflect divisions and tensions at various times, the city of Boston offers several examples of political solidarity as well. The more prominent instances of alliances between communities of color in Boston include the electoral victory of mayoral candidate Mel King in the preliminary mayoral race of 1983 and the campaign of Carmen Pola for a seat in the Massachusetts State Legislature. Earlier than this campaign, South End activist Alex Rodriguez ran for the state legislature in 1967. Rodriguez's campaign was viewed by many in the black community as part of its own struggle for electoral empowerment. In 1982 and 1983, Latino, black, and Asian activists formed a coalition to challenge the constitutional legality of Boston's city and state electoral boundaries. The black and Latino communities of Boston, as well as the Asian community, as a matter of fact, have collaborated periodically in challenging the constitutionality of legislative district plans adopted by the city. The Latino Political Action Committee and the Black Political Task Force were political allies in a major coalition resulting in the redrawing of electoral boundaries more reflective of the city's population of color. It was this coalition that helped propel the election of Grace Romero in 1983, the first Latina to be elected to the Boston School Committee in the history of the city. She campaigned as both a member and endorsee of the Black Political Task Force. We can also include as an example of intergroup political cooperation between communities of color the Jesse Jackson presidential campaign in 1984 and 1988. (For a summary of some of these events, see Jennings and King 1983; Jennings 1994b.) The first Puerto Rican state representative in the history of Massachusetts was elected with significant black support. Nelson Merced's campaign manager was a black activist, Peter Hardie. Merced campaigned with strong endorsements from prominent black leaders and activists. The Black

Political Task Force endorsed his candidacy over several black candidates based on the multiethnic team he organized, as well as stating clearly progressive positions on issues dealing with affordable housing and local economic development.

I am not suggesting in this chapter that political relations between communities of color in Boston represent an ideal model of political solidarity. There are many instances of conflict between these groups. Issues dealing with legislative redistricting, public school reform, and funding of community-based organizations are areas in which the interests of these communities are sometimes defined competitively with each other. But there have been instances of these groups working together in order to support social and economic policies benefiting all neighborhoods, as well as in electing candidates considered progressive. This too is an important story, and a necessary one for developing a comprehensive understanding of how black, Latino, and Asian political relations in Boston are evolving.

Studying political relations between communities of color in other cities may help us to understand developments in Boston. For example, political scientists John J. Betancur and Douglas C. Gills have written a case study of Chicago highlighting both political collaboration and conflict between blacks and Latinos. They point out that there have been important events in the development of black and Latino political cooperation, primarily involving the elections of Harold Washington as Mayor in the mid-1980s. Their study is insightful not only because it provides information and analysis about the electoral impact of this coalition, but also because it looks at what happened after the successful electoral campaigns of Mayor Washington. They observe that after Mayor Washington's election the coalition became vulnerable to dissolution. They identify five factors that "contributed to the tenuous character of a Black-Latino collaboration during the administration of Harold Washington: 1) outside forces; 2) a limited tradition of coalition politics; 3) ethnocentrism; 4) limited efforts to create an agenda inclusive of all groups; and 5) the inability to resolve objective differences and contending interests between the two groups" (Betancur and Gills 1997, 92). These are factors that also mold the quality of political relations between communities of color in Boston. But in the latter case, as is suggested by some of the instances mentioned here, there is a "tradition of coalition politics" that should be analyzed by those interested in learning more about racial and ethnic conflict.

CONCLUSION

What do these instances of political solidarity among blacks, Latinos, and Asians teach us about this issue? And which of the explanations or models for understanding intergroup relations is most applicable to Boston? First, these examples illustrate that the focus of collaboration should be the development of urban policies that advance social and economic opportunities for people and neighborhoods. Such policies include the generation and maintenance of affordable housing, free and universal access to health care, investments in public schools, economic development for the city that is linked to the economic well-being of neighborhoods, public safety, and accountability of local government, especially the police. The recent political history of Boston shows that it is these kinds of issues that generate the greatest possibility of intergroup cooperation between communities of color.

A second lesson is that continual outreach and working together are important for maintaining cooperative political relationships. Nelson Merced's successful electoral campaign, for example, as well as his selection as Chair of the Massachusetts Black Legislative Caucus during part of his term as state representative, illustrates that continual communication is necessary for enhancing collaborative political possibilities. Activists and leaders from different communities have to be aggressive about communicating to each other about common and different interests. The social and political bonds that have emerged in some instances of political collaboration are easier when people talk to each other, and are concerned about the building of multiracial and multiethnic coalitions.

A challenge facing these communities is what Guinier refers to as third generation issues. She is suggesting that electoral victories related to the first two stages do not necessarily guarantee effectiveness; indeed victories in the first two stages may be Pyrrhic in the face of opposition from those in power. Political scientist, José E. Cruz, who in reviewing the status of Puerto Rican politics elaborates the point:

> The key challenge that Puerto Rican elected officials face is how to translate access into power in the context of small numbers, universalism in public policy, and slow growth. Getting elected is only half the game—governing being the other half. Puerto Rican elected officials have their public policy priorities right, but . . . they are not having an impact on Puerto Rican problems . . . [T]o be effective Puerto Ricans must become full partners in the process whereby government develops working relations with public and private centers of power. (Cruz 1995, 215)

A factor that contributes to the possibility of coalitions between these groups is the growing ethnicization in these communities. As mentioned earlier, the black community is no longer solely African American. Many different black groups, including some whose language is Spanish or French, are beginning to grow in numbers in this community. In the Latino community, the traditional pattern of rendering black Latinos invisible on the part of some elites will be more difficult as the number of African-descent Latinos who speak Spanish continues to grow in size. And certainly we can no longer speak simply of *the* Asian community as monolithic, given the many different ethnic and racial groups that comprise this category. These demographic developments will force attention to this issue. Meanwhile, there are basic elements to a progressive response to the issue of building a collaborative politics between communities of color. Activists and leaders interested in this matter must first seek to understand the social and cultural history of different groups of people in the city. People from many different cultural and ethnic settings may have far more commonalities in values than they may realize, and that can become evident in each community only by respecting the history and culture of the other. There should be attempts on the part of community-based leadership to investigate carefully the reasons that certain issues generate conflict in order to determine the possibilities of compromise that are supportive of progressive politics. And, finally, the leadership of communities of color in places such as Boston and other cities in Massachusetts must understand that significant improvement in living conditions in their communities requires fundamental social and economic changes. As long as racial and class hierarchies exist, communities of color cannot move forward safely and securely in this society. Therefore, there must be a focus on building political coalitions aimed not only at ensuring that the city and state treat all its citizens equally, but at ensuring that groups build their social and economic advances on the basis of challenging these racial and class hierarchies.

NOTES

1.   See Jennings (1982).
2.   See Myrdal's *An American Dilemma.* There are several national studies on race in the contemporary period that similarly utilize Myrdal's conceptual framework for analyzing and commenting on race relations and thereby overlook the issue of political relations between communities of color. For a review of some of these studies, see Jennings (1994b, 19–28).

REFERENCES

Anner, John. (1996). *Beyond Identity Politics: Emerging Social Justice Movements in Communities of Color.* Boston: South End Press.

Bach, Robert, et al. (1993). "Changing Relations: Newcomers and Established Residents in U.S. Communities." New York: Ford Foundation.

Betancur, John J., and Douglas C. Gills. (1997). "Black and Latino Political Conflict in Chicago." In *Race and Politics: New Challenges and Responses for Black Activism,* edited by James Jennings, 83–100. New York: Verso Press.

Blauner, Robert. (1972). *Racial Oppression in America.* New York: Harper & Row.

Camayd-Freixas, Yohel, and Russell López. (1983). "Gaps in Representative Democracy: Redistricting, Political Participation, and the Hispanic Vote in

Boston." Research Report. Boston: Hispanic Office of Planning and Evaluation.

Cruz, José E. (1995). "Puerto Rican Politics in the U.S.: A Preliminary Assessment." *New England Journal of Public Policy* 11(1): 199–220.

de la Garza, Rodolfo O. (1997). "Latino Politics: A Futuristic View." In *Pursuing Power: Latino, and the Political System*, edited by F. Chris Garcia, 458–466. Notre Dame, IN: University of Notre Dame Press.

Foner, Philip S., and Ronald L. Lewis. (1989). *Black Workers: A Documentary History from Colonial Times to the Present*. Philadelphia: Temple University Press.

Fuentes, Luis. (1999). "The Community Control Movement." In *The Puerto Rican Movement*, edited by Andrés Torres and José Velázquez, 280–295. Philadelphia: Temple University Press

Guinier, Lani. (1995). "The Representation of Minority Interests." In *Classifying by Race*, edited by Paul E. Peterson, 21–49. Princeton, NJ: Princeton University Press.

Jennings, James. (1982). "The Black Voter in Boston," *Research Report*. Boston: The Black Political Task Force.

———. (1992a). "Blacks and Latinos in the American City in the 1990s: Toward Political Alliances or Social Conflict?" In *Ethnic Politics and Civil Liberties*, edited by Lucius J. Barker, 158–163. New Brunswick, NJ: Transaction Publishers.

———. (1992b). "New Urban Racial and Ethnic Conflicts in United States Politics." *Sage Race Relations Abstracts* 13(3): 19–28.

———. (1994a). *Blacks, Latinos, and Asians in Urban America: Status and Prospects for Activism*. Westport, CT: Praeger.

———. (1994b). "New Demographic and Ethnic Challenges to Racial Hierarchy in the United States." *Sage Race Relations Abstracts* 19(3): 19–28.

Jennings, James, and Mel King. (1983). *From Access to Power: Black Politics In Boston*. Cambridge, MA: Schenkman Publishers.

Kochiyama, Yuri. (1994). "The Impact of Malcolm X on Asian-American Politics and Activism." In *Blacks, Latinos, and Asians in Urban America: Status and Prospects for Activism*, edited by James Jennings, 129–141. Westport, CT: Praeger.

McClain, Paula, and Joseph Stewart, Jr. (1994). *Can't We Get Along?* Boulder, CO: Westview Press.

Mollenkopf, John. (1987). "The Decay of Reform." *Dissent* (Fall): 492–495.

Moynihan, Daniel Patrick. (1979). "Patterns of Ethnic Succession: Blacks and Hispanics in NYC." *Political Science Quarterly* (Spring): 1–14.

Myrdal, Gunnar. (1944). *An American Dilemma: The Negro Problem and Modern Democracy*. New York: Harper & Row.

Osuna, Daniel. (1994). "Blacks and Chicanos: Parallels in Political and Historical Struggles." In In *Blacks, Latinos, and Asians in Urban America: Status and Prospects for Activism*, edited by James Jennings, 121–128. Westport, CT: Praeger.

Racusen, Seth. (1995). "'New' Civil Rights Strategies for Latino Political Empowerment." *New England Journal of Public Policy* 11(1): 161–182.

Sales, William W., Jr., and Roderick Bush. (1997). "Black and Latino Coalitions: Prospects for New Social Movements in New York City." In *Race and Politics: New Challenges and Responses for Black Activism*, edited by James Jennings. New York: Verso.

Sniderman, Paul M., and Edward G. Carmines. (1997). *Reaching Beyond Race.* Cambridge, MA: Harvard University Press.

Steinberg, Stanley. (1981). *The Ethnic Myth: Race, Ethnicity, and Class in America.* Boston: Beacon Press.

Thernstrom, Stephen. (1973). *The Other Bostonians.* Cambridge, MA: Harvard University Press.

Torres, Andrés, and José Velásquez. (1999). *The Puerto Rican Movement.* Philadelphia: Temple Univerisity Press.

Umemoto, Karen. (1994). "Blacks and Koreans in Los Angeles: The Case of LaTasha Harlins and Soon Da Ju." In *Blacks, Latinos, and Asians in Urban America: Status and Prospects for Activism*, edited by James Jennings. Westport, CT: Praeger Publishers.

Watanabe, Paul, et al. (1996). *A Dream Deferred: Changing Demographics, Challenges and New Opportunities for Boston.* Boston: The Boston Foundation.

Yun, Grace. (1994). *Intergroup Cooperation in Cities: African, Asian, and Hispanic American Communities.* New York: Asian-American Federation.

CHAPTER 12

Beyond Homeland Politics
Dominicans in Massachusetts

RAMONA HERNÁNDEZ AND GLENN JACOBS

ANTECEDENTS I: THE POLITICS OF RESISTANCE

From 1930 to 1961, the Dominican Republic was under the rule of Rafael Leonidas Trujillo, a dictator whose ruthlessness, bloodthirsty acts, and ambitious will, historians claim, could be compared only to the nineteenth-century Argentinean dictator Juan Manuel Rosas. Trujillo had been trained by American soldiers during their first occupation of the Dominican Republic (1916–1924) and, during his long dictatorship, he kept a hermetic control of the Dominican people.

Social control was executed in a political vacuum that had been produced during the American occupation. Americans imposed a political discipline that took away the rights of civilian Dominicans to possess or own weapons. It also allowed the persecution and elimination of all those who opposed the status quo. At the end of the occupation, Trujillo counted on a structurally disarticulated society, unarmed and politically beheaded, to impose his reign of terror.

Under Trujillo's regime, with the exception of a very small group closely connected to the government, Dominicans were not allowed to emigrate from the country; acts of protest and resistance were systematically suffocated; anyone who opposed his regime was violently incarcerated and tortured; and those who were found conspiring or were deemed dangerous and capable of bringing down his regime, were, in the best case scenario, exiled—in the worst, assassinated.

Though Trujillo's regime lasted for 31 years, terrorizing the Dominican people, strong resistance and militance against the government were common. Political activities against Trujillo were organized outside and inside the country by groups and individuals who included, among others, members of the middle class, the working class, the bourgeoisie, and students.

Foci of resistance were formally organized just 9 years after Trujillo came to power. In 1939, for instance, Dominicans exiled in Cuba formed

277

El Partido Revolucionario Dominicano, while others, exiled in Venezuela, launched *La Unión Democrática Dominicana. Juventud Revolucionaria Dominicana* was created by young students in the Dominican Republic in 1942 and, in 1959, a group of Dominicans attempted to overthrow the government through an invasion that had been organized in Cuba. Indeed, Trujillo's regime encountered resistance by Dominicans who, acting from a variety of ideological perspectives (i.e., liberal, Marxist, etc.), struggled against the regime with a common goal: to eliminate Trujillo.

After Trujillo's assassination in 1961, the Dominican Republic experienced a period of social instability that culminated in a revolution in 1965 and a second American military intervention in the same year. President Joaquin Balaguer, under the tutelage of the United States, was the "official" winner of the elections of 1966. He remained in power until 1978 when, pressured by civil disobedience and social unrest among Dominicans who angrily took to the streets protesting and threatening, he was forced to cede power to the opposition party many Dominicans felt had won the election.

Most historians in the country summarize Balaguer's 12 years of government as a continuation of Trujillo's dictatorship. During these 12 years, once again, social control of the Dominican people was secured through a rigid political discipline characterized by systematic incarcerations, torture, and murder. During Balaguer's successive governments, the opposition, particularly the leadership, was eliminated. According to historian Frank Moya Pons, "More than 3,000 Dominicans lost their lives in terrorist acts between 1966 and 1974. This situation only ended when the leadership of the leftist parties had been wiped out and the parties completely disorganized and when in 1972 the United States and other democratic countries demanded Balaguer to put an end to terrorism and the violations of human rights" (Moya Pons 1995, 392).

Yet, Balaguer's bloody and repressive twelve years of government faced systematic resistance from the Dominican people who undermined the regime with constant civil unrest, social disobedience, and daring attacks that emanated from most sectors of civil society. Indeed, repression does not develop in a vacuum and Balaguer's political repression responded to the need to undermine those who fiercely contested the imposition of a new social order that, though favored by certain sectors of Dominican society, was, by and large, resisted by others.

ANTECEDENTS II: THE POLITICS OF PARTICIPATION

One can easily argue that Dominicans are a highly political people who are proud to identify themselves publicly with their political parties. Some authors indicate that Dominicans have had a long tradition of public demonstration of political loyalty and political fervor, dating as far back as the very beginning of the Dominican state in 1844 (Hoetink 1985; Jiménez Polanco 1999). Often, affiliation to a political party implies that one would become militant, would show one's party affiliation with passion by following the party's leaders, rarely crossing party lines, and by demonstrating political fervor in public events such as caravans, walks, political rallies, and the like.

Likewise, sympathizing for a political party may imply the same commitment, enthusiasm, and involvement among people. In effect, during election times the entire Dominican Republic automatically turns into a political battlefield, where everyone participates. Taxi drivers and potential clients systematically avoid each other as the former decorate their vehicles with colorful paraphernalia representing the driver's political affiliation and the candidate for whom the driver will vote. Likewise, people will express their political affiliation enthusiastically by painting their homes with the colors of their political party or by placing symbols of their party on visible areas of their homes. The radio and other instruments of mass media become actively involved in the political process—often leading common people and experts to charge that a given radio station, television channel, or newspaper is clearly biased in favor of a given party's political candidate. Indeed, the entire country is adorned by colorful flags representing the different running parties, posters exhibiting the candidates' faces, and other paraphernalia typical of such events. In addition, whether publicly or in the privacy of their homes, people actively engage in debates about the candidates of their choice.

The level of public enthusiasm, activism, and involvement in the political process in the Dominican Republic is such that those who are unaccustomed to such public manifestations of political participation may feel fearful and intimidated in facing such an experience. Indeed, 45 days prior to the presidential elections of 1996, the president of the National Association of Hotels and Restaurants anxiously reported that the rate of hotel occupancy had declined approximately 15 percent compared to 1995, and attributed the decline to negative media propaganda in Europe and other developed countries about election time in the Dominican Republic. The president remarked that he was anxiously hoping that the months of July and August, when hotels exhibit the highest rate of occupancy, would not be affected by the negative impressions among tourists (*Rumbo* 1996, 37).

For the past two decades, the Dominican electorate has grown significantly due to the demographic growth of the population. From 1962 to 1998 the Dominican Republic has witnessed 12 election cycles. Participation in these elections has been high, though the level of abstention has systematically increased, particularly since 1978 (see Table 12.1).

In her recent analysis of political parties in the Dominican Republic, political scientist Jacqueline Jiménez Polanco (1999, 57) indicates that the holding of elections and encouraging people to vote have been historically salient features of the political culture among Dominican governments, including among those led by the first *caudillos* for whom "the celebration

Table 12.1 Voter Registration and Electoral Participation in the Dominican Republic, 1978–1998

	1978	%	1982	%	1986	%	1990	%
Registered Voters	2,283,748	100.0	2,601,684	100.0	3,275,570	100.0	3,275,570	100.0
Abstention	539,993	23.6	679,317	26.1	843,892	27.8	1,302,539	39.8
Number of Voters	1,743,791	76.4	1,922,367	73.9	2,195,455	72.2	1,973,031	60.2
Invalid Votes	97,555	5.6	91,637	4.8	83,710	3.8	39,190	2.0
Valid Votes	1,646,236	94.4	1,830,730	95.2	2,111,745	96.2	1,933,841	98.0

	1994	%	1996[a]	%	1996*	%	1998	%
Registered Voters	3,598,328	100.0	3,750,502	100.0	3,750,502	100.0	4,129,554	100.0
Abstention	451,618	12.6	801,404	21.4	870,077	23.2	2,036,868	49.3
Number of Voters	3,146,710	87.4	2,949,098	78.6	2,880,425	76.8	2,093,686	50.7
Invalid Votes	130,960	4.2	45,120	1.5	18,843	0.7	90,021	4.3
Valid Votes	3,015,750	95.8	2,901,579	98.4	2,861,023	99.3	2,003,665	95.7

Source: Jiménez Polanco (1999, 252)

[a] There are two elections reported for 1996, the first year the Dominican Republic held a run-off election.

of elections after successful 'revolutions' 'served to legitimize' the new status quo and settle, in an 'honest' manner, any internal conflicts with regards to the distribution of power" (author's translation).

Rather than simple apathy, abstention in each of the election cycles in the Dominican Republic has been connected to a number of reasons among which can be cited methodological problems in properly counting all those who are eligible to vote and securing information from all regions. In addition, situations of suspicion and distrust exist among registered voters who may act under the belief that the governing party will commit election fraud. Some observers have argued that high levels of abstention may be related to other structural problems such as keeping the names of Dominicans who live outside the Dominican Republic current and counting them among those eligible to vote (Baez and Duarte 1990).

When Dominicans leave their homeland, they leave influenced by a political culture in which involvement, manifested at various levels, is of paramount importance. Many may have left after resisting and challenging a tyrannical regime; others may have left with the understanding that political involvement provides social mobility. Everyone leaves influenced by a political culture in which political involvement is treated as part of the social mores, a socializing agent that exempts no one, whether one decides to remain passive or become actively involved. The question remains, however, as to how much this political culture influences the social behavior and actions undertaken by Dominicans once settled in a given receiving society.

MIGRATION AND SETTLEMENT: THE UNITED STATES AND MASSACHUSETTS

Since the 1960s international movement from the Dominican Republic has been primarily oriented to the United States. As Figure 12.1 indicates, the number of Dominicans admitted to the United States under permanent status has dramatically increased over the past 40 years. Indeed, current estimates based on the 1996 and 1997 Current Population Survey indicate that there were 832,000 Dominicans residing in the United States in 1997 (see Table 12.2). This constitutes a significant increase over the 520,121 Dominicans counted by the decennial census of population in 1990.

The major source of the rapid growth of the Dominican population in the United States in recent years has been immigration. As indicated in Table 12.2, 573,500 (69.9 percent) of the 832,200 Dominicans residing in the United States in 1997, were immigrants, of which 70 percent came to the country between 1980 and 1996. In 1990 among the top 10 countries which accounted for 52 percent of the legal immigrant flow to the United States, the Dominican Republic ranked number four in the list. (Mexico ranked number one.) (Hernández and Rivera-Batiz 1997).

Figure 12.1   Dominicans Admitted to the United States from 1961–1998

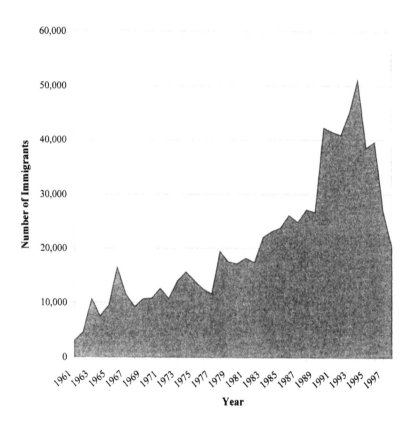

Table 12.2   Dominican Immigrants Residing in the United States

	Number	% of Immigrants
Total Dominicans	832,000	
Total Immigrants	573,500	
Arrived 1990 to 1996	184,000	32.1
Arrived 1980 to 1989	216,500	37.8
Arrived before 1980	173,000	30.0

Source: Hernández and Rivera Batiz (1997, 8).
Note: Percentages do not add up to 100 due to rounding

Table12.3   Intended Residence of Recent Dominican Immigrants

Dominican Immigrants Admitted to Selected Cities in the Continental U.S. in 1995		
Geographical Area	Number	Percent
Total Immigrants	32,265	100.0
New York City, NY	20,606	63.9
Boston-Lawrence, MA	1,877	5.8
Bergen-Passaic, NJ	1,547	4.8
Miami, FL	1,352	4.2
Jersey City, NJ	1,073	3.3

Source: U.S. Immigration and Naturalization Service, 1997

SETTING THE STAGE FOR POLITICAL ACTION: A SOCIOECONOMIC PORTRAIT OF DOMINICANS IN TWO MASSACHUSETTS CITIES

As of 1997, almost 60 percent of Dominican people in the United States lived in New York City, as they have for the past two decades or so. Recently, however, Dominicans have begun to move to other U.S. cities. Data indicate that the process of mobility has accelerated in the past decade, that Dominicans are migrating internally, and that such mobility may be encouraging a chain reaction with new Dominican immigrants coming directly from the Dominican Republic and settling in the new cities rather than in the traditional one of New York.

Dominicans are relatively new arrivals in several Massachusetts cities. Whereas in 1980, for instance, there were a total of 2,215 Dominicans residing in Lawrence, Massachusetts (U.S. Bureau of the Census 1988), by 1990, the number of Dominicans in this city had increased dramatically to 10,870. Patterns of mobility indicate that in 1990 more than one out of three Dominicans 5 years of age or older residing in Lawrence lived either abroad or outside the state of Massachusetts in 1985. In the case of the City of Lynn, which had a Latino population of about 12.2 percent in 1995 and houses a very small Dominican community, almost one out of two Dominicans 5 years of age or older residing there was reported to have lived outside the state or abroad in 1985 (U.S. Bureau of the Census 1993). As indicated in Table 12.3, in 1995 the cities of Boston and Lawrence were identified by the largest percentage of Dominicans as their intended place of residence, after New York City. In the same year, both cities combined received the second highest number of Dominicans admitted to the United States.

In Massachusetts, as in New York City, Dominicans face economic stress and social barriers. In 1990, 26.9 percent of Dominicans 16 years of age or older were unemployed in the city of Lynn, while in Lawrence the same age group had a 24.4 percent unemployment rate. In 1990, 35 percent of the Dominican families residing in Lawrence lived below the level of poverty, while in Lynn the proportion of Dominican families living below the level of poverty was 46.3 percent. In both cities the proportion of families headed by single women, with no husband present, was very high in 1990. In Lynn, for instance, one out of every two Dominican families was headed by a single woman, while in Lawrence the proportion was one in three (U.S. Bureau of the Census 1993).

Data on educational attainment and ability to speak English show that in 1990 almost 10 percent of Dominicans 25 years of age or older in Lawrence had less than a fifth-grade education, that 34 percent had a high school diploma or higher, and that only 7 percent had a bachelor's degree or higher. In the case of Lynn, the proportion of Dominicans with less than a fifth-grade education in 1990 was 17.1 percent, those with a high school diploma or higher, 38.9 percent, and those with a bachelor's degree or higher just 3.2 percent.

In both cities the proportion of Dominicans who did not speak English at all or who did not speak English very well was also high. In 1990, for instance, one out of every three Dominicans in both cities lived in a linguistically isolated household (U.S. Bureau of the Census 1993).

POLITICAL PARTICIPATION: THE TALE OF TWO CITIES

What follows is the result of face-to-face interviews with three prominent Dominicans, one who ran for office in the city of Lynn and two who currently hold offices in the city of Lawrence. The interviews were carried out in both cities and lasted between 3 and 4 hours. The interviews were preceded by several phone conversations that set the stage and broke the ice of not knowing the candidates personally. In each case candidates were interviewed in public places of their choice, including a Dominican restaurant and a community cultural club. On each occasion candidates were eager to be interviewed and emphasized the importance of letting others know about their political experience, difficulties, failures, successes, and expectations.

Two premises, perhaps hypotheses, guided the topics covered in the interviews. First, Dominicans running for political office in the United States were transplanting a political activism and know-how from their homeland; second, Dominicans were too involved in the politics of their homeland—hence their low level of citizenship—to pay serious attention to local politics. These premises reflect common beliefs concerning Dominicans in the United States. Ángelo Falcón's "Political Indigenous Index," devised to measure the ties that the emergent Puerto Rican leadership had to the New York City community in the 1970s, helped us to formulate the appropriate questions and provided a frame of reference in measuring Dominicans' political involvement in local politics, particularly in their communities (Falcón 1981). We adopted the index's components that identify indigenous ties to the community with the following variables: roots in the community, length of residence, schooling, and ability to speak English. The three Dominicans interviewed were Manuel Alcántara of Lynn, Julia Silverio of Lawrence, and Marcos A. Devers, also of Lawrence.

MANUEL ALCÁNTARA—LYNN

Manuel Alcántara came from the Dominican Republic to Boston in 1970 to study engineering at Northeastern University. He is from an upper-middle-class family, whose father was a high ranking officer in the Air Force. By 1971 he had married a second-generation Dominican woman who had came to the United States at the age of three. In 1979, after obtaining his degree, Alcántara returned home with his wife and a child and began to work as a civil engineer for the Dominican government. Though his family enjoyed a comfortable life, his wife complained of the many long hours outside home and the demands of his job. Tired of the multiple responsibilities his position demanded, combined with his difficulties at home, Alcántara decided to return to the United States in 1984. That year he became a citizen of the United States. In the same year also he became active in Boston politics, joining José Massó and Jovita Fontanez, two pioneering grass roots community leaders who were also active in the Democratic Party.

By 1986, divorced from his wife and pulled there by old friends from his school years, Alcántara moved to the city of Lynn. After moving to Lynn, Alcántara spent his days commuting to Boston to work at the Executive Office of Environmental Affairs and his evenings teaching English as a Second Language to adults at the North Shore Community College in Lynn. It was his teaching of English as a Second Language that put Alcántara in contact with the local Latino community, where he became aware of this community's most basic social needs. Between 1985 and

1989, Alcántara became active in the local community. In 1986 he moved permanently to Lynn after marrying one of his former students, a Dominican woman who had came from Florida with her two children after her divorce. During the same year, the Alcántaras established *The Lynn Language Institute* to teach English to working adults. He recalls:

> You see, we realized that working adults needed to learn English which they could use in their jobs; they needed to learn "everyday English," fast, and concrete. They could not afford months and years of learning grammar and punctuation, when what they really needed was to be able to communicate with their bosses in a simple and casual language required at their jobs. That was what we offered and guaranteed at the Institute.
> (Interview with Alcántara)

According to Alcántara, people loved it. The school gave him visibility in the Latino community and the opportunity to meet people.

In the meantime, his importance and involvement in the city grew along with a growing Latino community bereft of political representation. The mayor of the city of Lynn appointed him Commissioner on the Conservation Committee. He says, "There I became aware of the city's politics; who was who, and what they stand for. I have never studied politics and I do not come from a political family. None of my brothers and sisters have ever been involved in politics. You see, I had my sympathy for a given political party in the Dominican Republic.[1] But that was it. My political involvement began and developed here."

Alcántara had issues and he was vocal about them. There was no minority representation in the city government. In 1989 there was just one African-American man elected to office in the city. The Dominican community was growing, too:

> They were coming from Lawrence. You see, in 1985 Lynn was living an economic boom. Dominicans came looking for jobs in the milk and computer factories. Though many were involved in politics back home, they were showing indication of permanence by opening businesses and buying homes. By 1989 I had become very vocal about political issues in the city. My wife encouraged me to get more involved. I did not tell her anything, but one morning, I went and registered myself as a candidate to run for city council at large. Some people thought I was crazy. How could I? No Hispanic had ever run for any political office before in Lynn. Plus, I had no money and no political experience. It was suicidal! I thought that if I managed to even get three votes, I was okay. It meant that I had convinced effectively two other people and that was enough for the moment.
> (Interview with Alcántara)

Alcántara ran in 1989 for city council at large with seven other candidates. He ran on one issue: to provide better drinking water for Lynn. He says, "This was an issue that affected everyone. Not just Hispanic. You see, at that time, there were only 126 Hispanic registered voters. . . . But almost all of them voted. . . . 76 voted." He did not spend any money on his political campaign because he did not believe in spending money "to be known." Alcántara lost the election, but he felt satisfied: among the eight candidates, he finished in sixth place. In the meantime, Alcántara's activism and local involvement continued. In 1990, together with thirteen other activists (including eleven Dominicans, one Puerto Rican, one Costa Rican, and one Colombian), he created an organization, *Lynn Hispanic 2000*. According to Alcántara,

> The idea was to have an organization in which we all could discuss our political plans and visions; I do not like to talk about unity among Latinos. Unity without an organization is an empty word. One needs an organization where one can draw a plan. When the establishment talks about Latinos, it urges us to unite. . . . The whole thing is "Latinos unite"; yet, the establishment never encourages us to form organizations where we could come together and draw a plan to secure our common goals. An organization provides one with that opportunity. (Interview with Alcántara)

During the same year, Alcántara revitalized the moribund Lynn Hispanic Community Association, created in 1972 by a Puerto Rican man, José Vidal Méndez. Alcántara unsuccessfully ran for city council again in 1991. This time his issue was economic empowerment for the city of Lynn. He felt that if the economy was fine, everyone would benefit.

Today, Alcántara holds a high-ranking position, (Associate Commissioner of the Department of Public Works); has been appointed to a number of boards; has a close relationship with the mayor of the city; and enjoys the respect and admiration of most of his compatriots and other Latinos. He is unsure about future election campaigns: "I do not think I will run again. But who knows . . . I have such a good job! But who knows."

Alcántara unquestionably defies the two cited premises regarding Dominican political candidates and office holders. Early in the interview he denied political involvement in the Dominican Republic. However, one qualification intrudes here: the high rank of his father in the armed services bespeaks perhaps a parallel to such involvement, since his family background undoubtedly is an elite one. Still, he cannot be construed in the most narrow sense to have had political experience in his home country. Clearly, as far as the second premise is concerned, Alcántara also evades inclusion under it.

How then to explain his political involvement? The premises guiding the interviews as stated earlier become, in effect, straw men or null hypotheses. It behooves us to recall Falcón's index, which escapes the straitjacketing of leadership within narrow political boundaries. In other words, although Alcántara ran for office and lost, how do we know that his striving for and achievement of political influence ended with his "failed" campaign. In fact, it did not. One personal consequence is that he has achieved an important appointed position in municipal government. During the year of his defeat he created one and revived another community organization and now sits on important boards, has a close relationship with the mayor, and maintains strong ties to the community. One suspects that perhaps he has outgrown the status inducements of and need for political office. Thus Manuel Alcántara fulfills all of the aforementioned features of Falcón's ideal typical leader: he has strong and deep community ties; he has been in the United States for three decades; he is well educated; and clearly has excellent English and Spanish language skills.

JULIA SILVERIO—LAWRENCE

Julia Silverio moved to the City of Salem—located a few towns north of Boston on the coast—in 1969, at the age of 15. Her father, a sailor, had originally settled in New York City in 1962 when he first arrived in the United States. But in time he realized that it was not easy to find a good job in New York City. He also felt that the city was not a good place to raise his daughters. So, in 1967, Ms. Silverio's father moved to Salem. By 1972, Ms. Silverio had married her high school sweetheart who had come to Lawrence from the Dominican Republic. Enticed by her husband Ms. Silverio moved to Lawrence where she found a job in the personnel department of a shoe factory. It was there that Ms. Silverio developed an awareness of discrimination and exploitation in the United States. She relates:

> During vacation time the employers used to call the INS department. Dominicans, many of whom were undocumented and scared to be deported, used to abandon their jobs. After a while, ads looking for workers would be posted and Dominicans and others would be rehired as new workers. You see, by doing this, the factory avoided paying any vacation time or any other compensation accumulated through time to workers. Workers were always new and, when they were not needed, they were simply let go in this manner. That made me angry. It was an abuse against my people.

She continues:

> The abuses against workers continue. One day they called me at home. I was on medical leave. Since I was bilingual, they wanted me to spy on the workers to see who talked about bringing a union. I refused. That practically cost me my job. I was demoted; I was sent to work with papers, in a room in the back of the factory. (Interview with Silverio)

The shoe factory eventually closed and Ms. Silverio, pregnant with her first child, decided to work at home. She went to beauty school, completed the required training and opened up a business in her home. The business was doing well but demanded too many hours. Women wanted to do their hair on weekends and late at night, the time she wanted to spend with her daughter and her husband. She then decided to take a course in tax preparation. After completing this course, she went to work for H & R Block. By 1980, after completing another course in real state, Ms. Silverio embarked on a job at an agency—the Lawrence Neighborhood Housing Services—that provided a variety of services on housing, including help in buying a home. By 1981 she had been promoted to Coordinator of Housing but she eventually decided to leave because, as she says, "I began to notice too many injustices committed against people of color. In 1984 I opened up my own business, a multiservices agency—Julia's Consulting" (Interview with Silverio).

At the same time Ms. Sylverio was making these career moves, her involvement in the local community grew and became visible. In 1979, encouraged by a number of friends, she ran for the Parent Advisory Council. She won the seat. In 1981 she went as a delegate to the Democratic State Convention. Prior to that, she became involved with the celebration of the Spanish Week organized by the Hispanic Program Community Action Group. The idea was to hold a large celebration in Lawrence's main park to educate the larger society about the different Hispanic cultures and the contributions of the Hispanic community to the city. She recalls her motivation:

> You see, these were the times when there was a lot of racism and antagonism against us in the city. We had to fight the city to be able to get a permit to use the park. Some authorities claimed that we were going to use the park to get drunk and other bad things. We told them that we also wanted to have a voter registration drive there. We knew that many Hispanics were citizens but were intimidated to go to city hall to register to vote. Some opposed the idea, but we insisted. We knew what we wanted and we were not going to stop until we got it. In 1981 when we finally put the week together, after it had concluded, and we had finished cleaning—you see, the City did not assign a cleaning crew to clean after we had finished—we were told that we had to do the cleaning. . . . That year, after we had finished, someone from the newspaper managed to take a picture of a man who was near a pile of garbage we had put together. The photo gave the impression that we had left the park dirty, filled with garbage. That made me very angry. It was unfair. Hispanic people were miserably discriminated against . . . and they worked too hard!

In the meantime, Ms. Silverio's leadership in the local community continued to grow. By 1995 she had been appointed by the mayor to the zoning board. This was the first time a Dominican woman was appointed to a board in the City of Lawrence. That is also the year she decided to run for office for the first time: City Council from District B. Latinos in the community had been encouraging her to run for office for some time. Included among them were fellow Dominicans, many of whom she and other Latinos had registered to vote.

Data show that increasing numbers of Dominicans in Lawrence were becoming U.S. citizens. In 1980, for instance, only 17.5 percent of the Dominican people in Lawrence[2] had been naturalized. By 1990 the number had modestly increased to 23 percent (U.S. Bureau of the Census 1993).

Ms. Silverio ran a political campaign with two fundamental issues: she wanted to restore pride to the city of Lawrence and she wanted to create a bridge between the Latino and the Anglo communities. She lost the election in 1995 for a number of reasons including, as she says: "You see, I could not get the support of the elderly. They ran a dirty campaign against me. The elderly, which is the largest voting bloc in the city of Lawrence, and is located right in my district, were told that if I won, I was going to allow roaches and mice to get into their buildings. They got scared. I decided that I was not going to run a dirty campaign. I do not do that, so I lost, but I felt that I did not degrade myself or my family" (Interview with Silverio).

Ms. Silverio continued her local activism. She attended Mass in the local Catholic churches and continued to encourage people to vote in local elections though she was not running. At the same time, the Latino community continued to grow and mature. By 1999 there were 22,000 registered voters; about 8,000 were Latino and most were Dominicans. In 1999 Ms. Silverio ran again. Her campaign issues were the same, but this time she was politically more astute and collected enough money to run a wider campaign to reach a broader spectrum of the electorate. She says that people contributed; they wanted her to win: "People were so sad the first time I lost; they really could not believe it. . . . I felt we all lost that time. . . .This time they wanted to make sure that that did not happen again. You know, no one wins with the Hispanic votes alone; but over half of those who were registered voted in 1999. It felt good to have so many people behind you" (Interview with Silverio).

Ms. Silverio won the 1999 election. That year 11 Hispanics ran for office in the city of Lawrence, 7 of whom were Dominicans. Three of the seven won.[3] When asked if we could grant her a wish as a politician, she responded, "to make the city of Lawrence into a model city where all races and ethnicit[ies] can live together, learn to tolerate each other, respect each other, and learn from each other. I envision a city where all people feel that they can contribute to the city's well-being, where all children, regardless of their race or ethnic background, feel empowered and motivated to achieve the highest-ranking professions or political offices" (Interview with Silverio).

Here, again, we see the stereotype challenged. Ms. Silverio evinces quite strong ties to the local community, indeed a sense of duty and mission to assist not only her own people, but to combat racism as a strategy to improve intergroup relations in Lawrence. Thus, in a sense, she is moving in the direction of crossing boundaries. Again, she fulfils most of Falcón's leadership requirements. She has lived in the United States for more than three decades. Her English is impeccable. Although she has had only a high school education, she has cultivated her English and Spanish language skills because she feels that both are required to work effectively with all communities. In preliminary telephone conversations, for example, she came across as a person with an academic background. Again, here is an individual who has a strong social awareness that seems to transcend mere political ambition or what customarily passes for the qualifications for office-holding. For now it seems that it is this sort of uncompromising stance on social issues that provides a key to her political strength and contributes to make her into a leader and a politician.

MARCOS DEVERS—LAWRENCE

Marcos Devers first moved from the Dominican Republic to Puerto Rico in 1982. He held a degree in civil engineering from *Universidad Autónoma de Santo Domingo*. In 1984 he married a woman he had known in the Dominican Republic and who was also living in Puerto Rico. After working for a few years in Puerto Rico, he passed the qualifying examination and obtained his license as a civil engineer. In 1987 Dominican friends encouraged him to move to Lawrence. While in the Dominican Republic and Puerto Rico, he was rarely active in political activities or community organizations, although he admits that as a teenager in the Dominican Republic he used to distribute pamphlets for one of the local political parties active against Trujillo.

In Lawrence he began to work as an engineer in his own construction business. The company was doing well but the economic downturn at the end of the 1980s had a negative impact on his business. By 1991 he decided to take a job teaching science in a local high school. Bilingual teachers, particularly in science, were in high demand in the city since Latino children were the fastest-growing school population. That was the first year he ran for office, for city council at large. He explains his motivation:

> I was aware of the hostility and antagonism against Hispanics in the city. It was difficult. No Hispanic, let alone a Dominican, had ever tried to secure that office before. . . . I remember walking on the streets and encountering small homemade signs with the phrase "Spik go home." I thought that that was not right. At that time I had lived in the city for over twenty years; my children had all been born here. . . . I used to get so mad! (Interview with Devers)

Prior to running for the first time, Devers began to get involved in his local community. Just two years after his arrival in Lawrence in 1989 he formed an *Asociación de Profesionales Latinoamericanos*. The idea was to organize as many Latinos as possible. The year before, he had already become a member of an important and visible organization in the community, *Club Cultural Latinoamericano*. He also became active in *Club los Trinitarios* and *Asociación Cívica*, two Dominican cultural organizations.

His activism and local involvement grew. Devers was identified as a community leader and was appointed chairman of the Lawrence Community Partnership. He also was appointed to the board of the Family Health Center. Involved in the creation of *Agenda Latina*, a community-based organization that sought to empower the Latino community, he became its chair. Simultaneously, Devers strengthened his activism in the local Democratic Party. As a delegate, he attended four Democratic State Conventions where he met other Latino leaders and community activists.

In 1991, Marcos Devers became the first Latino ever to run for city council at large in Lawrence. He lost that election but persevered: he ran four more times, in 1993, 1995, and 1997, and was finally victorious in 1999. His participation marked a stage in the history of Dominican political candidates in the United States for he was the first to seek an office of such magnitude. Contrary to running for a seat on the city council from a district, where one can count on the participation of a given portion of the electorate distributed in a contained geographic location, running city council at large requires the crossing of geographic and social boundaries to secure enough votes to win the post.

Devers believes that in 1991 about 13 percent of the voters were Hispanic. In his estimation the proportion of Hispanic voters increased to 40 percent by the 1999 election. When he ran his campaign in 1999, he focused on the following issues: he wanted to present a fair, just and independent voice to the city council. He also wanted to restore and enhance public services to the people, particularly the schools and health centers, and to provide a safer Lawrence for everyone.

Devers believes that it was difficult for a minority candidate to win an election at-large in 1991:

> People were not used to minorities in high-ranking political posts. For me, a Dominican, it was virtually impossible to win. . . . I was not known. People did not trust Latinos or minority candidates for such a prestigious post. The Hispanic electorate was also small, and my political campaign was limited. . . . The way I saw it, every participation provided me with cleverness and political maturity. I knew that what I was seeking was not easy. I was attempting to represent people in the entire city and I was Hispanic! . . . What helped me in 1999 was my track record; name recognition—a larger group knew who I was. . . . Also, perseverance. . . . That was also a key in 1999. It was not easy!!! . . . But here I am.

As with our two prior cases, Marcos Devers does not conform to the stereotype concerning Dominican political involvement, but he did provide insight into both the stereotype and its debunking. In his mind the stereotype is, at best, a half truth. He agrees that Dominicans in the United States, in this case, Lawrence, do get involved in homeland politics. He even agrees that the political parties from the Dominican Republic solicit and receive financial support from fellow Dominicans in this country:

> During election times Dominicans in Lawrence are actively involved in political issues back home and local community leaders do raise funds for island parties. However, when the election times are over, the local activists turn their attention back to the community and local politics in the United States. . . . They support local politicians by printing pamphlets and flyers supporting candidates of their choosing; by encouraging their compatriots and militants of their parties to vote in local elections. When Dominicans are running they encourage their members to vote for Dominican candidates . . . and the party leaders also express their opinions about local politics to local radio stations. (Interview with Devers)

Political scientist Pamela Graham's study of Dominican politics in New York City documents the same phenomenon. She found that the leadership of the major Dominican political parties participated actively during local elections and publicly supported Dominican candidates (Graham 1996).

CONCLUSION

It is clear from our three cases that what appear to be tried and true adages about Dominican politics and politicians offer poor guides to the reality of Dominican political behavior in the United States. Furthermore, it might be wise to look at politics in this case as a subvariety of a larger phenomenon—leadership—for this notion provides a more accurate linkage between the candidate-activists and their rootedness in the community and, hence, their relationship, whether enunciated or not, with the social issues faced within and by their communities here.

In turning our attention to the first premise, however, we would like to problematize the equation concerning Dominicans' involvement in politics, their relatively rapid emergent leadership in the United States, and their presumptive transplanting of patterns of political behavior from one society to another. One cannot simply disregard the impact of the political culture of the Dominican Republic on Dominicans in the United States with respect to political activism, whether running for office, becoming an identified grass roots leader, or participating in political events.

Rather than positing that Dominicans exhibit a behavior produced by actual participation and involvement in politics back home, we suggest that their behavior may be the product of a cultural influence as opposed to an exact replication of political behavior on the island. The point is that the influence of the political culture may be attitudinal, producing a readiness to respond to influences radiating from the new environment. The issue is then not necessarily whether Dominicans were active in politics back home or came endowed with political "know-how," but more that they came here with culturally induced reflexes that equipped them for effective political action. Thus, seen from this perspective, political culture includes within its orbit citizen roles and behavior.

Turning back to the political science perspective, we find that a look at the literature on Latinos/as and politics in the United States would suggest that, in most cases, four conditions have been present at the time of their political involvement: leadership and activism, a growing community from their country of origin, growing and unmet socioeconomic needs, and marginalization of the Latino community. Thus, it should be evident from the aforementioned that Latinos, as Hardy-Fanta (1993) explains, contrary to another stereotype, are not politically apathetic, but rather confront strong sociopolitical barriers and obstructions to their participation.

It was precisely these barriers that pushed City Councilor Julia Silverio, along with others, to bring voter registration to the park and outside the walls of Lawrence City Hall. In looking at the development of Dominican political leadership we see an aggressive and rapid appropriation of political space in their local communities. Whether this appropriation turns into power for all still remains to be seen, suggesting that case studies such as this one shed light on the beginning or first stage of a process. There is a follow-up question: Will the second generation be assimilated and, in fact, become as "apathetic" as the general society, or will they continue the focus on the appropriation of power for the Dominican community and the Latino community at large in a way that will benefit the majority of the people in these communities rather than their own individual interests?

NOTES

1.   Alcántara did not specify the party.
2.   Data represent SMSA, Lawrence-Haverhill.
3.   The others were Ralph Carrero and Marcos Devers. Carrero was reelected to the School Committee post he has held since 1991; he was the first Dominican elected to a political post in the state of Massachusetts. Marcos Devers won after running a number of times in previous elections. (See also Chapter 3 in this volume.)

REFERENCES

Báez, C., and I. Duarte. (1990). "Geopolítica Electoral 1978–1986: Características y Tendencias." *El Siglo,* 3 de Mayo. Santo Domingo.
Duarte, Isis. (1996). "El Conteo Rápido de la Red." *Rumbo* del 22 al 28 de Mayo.

Falcón, Ángelo. (1981). *Ethnic Leadership, Community and the Capitalist State: The Puerto Rican Activist Stratum in New York City.* New York: Institute for Puerto Rican Policy.

Graham, Pamela M. (1996). "Re-imagining the Nation and Defining the District: The Simultaneous Political Incorporation of Dominican Transnational Migrants." Ph.D. diss., The University of North Carolina at Chapel Hill.

Hardy-Fanta, Carol. (1993). *Latina Politics, Latino Politics: Gender, Culture, and Political Participation in Boston.* Philadelphia: Temple University Press.

Hernández, Ramona, and Francisco Rivera-Batiz. (1997). "Dominican New Yorkers: A Socioeconomic Profile." *Dominican Research Monographs.* New York: CUNY Dominican Studies Institute.

Hoetink, H. (1985). "El Pueblo Dominicano (1859–1900)." *Apuntes para su Sociología Histórica.* Publicaciones de la UCMM. Santiago de los Caballeros.

Jiménez Polanco, Jacqueline. (1999). *Los Partidos Políticos en la República Dominicana.* Santo Domingo: Editora Centenario, S.A.

Moya Pons, Frank. (1995). *The Dominican Republic: A National History.* New Rochelle, NY: Hispaniola Books.

U.S. Bureau of the Census. (1983). 1980 Census of Population, Detailed Population Characteristics of Massachusetts. 5 percent Public Use Microdata Set. Washington, DC: Bureau of the Census.

———. (1993). 1990 Census of Population, Detailed Population Characteristics of Massachusetts. 5 percent Public Use Microdata Set. Washington, DC: Bureau of the Census.

U.S. Immigration and Naturalization Service. (1997). *1995 Statistical Yearbook of the INS.* Washington, DC: U.S. Government Printing Office (March).

CHAPTER 13

The Massachusetts Latin-American Caucus at One Year
An Assessment

JEFFREY N. GERSON

THE IMPORTANCE OF LATINOS IN STATE LEGISLATURES

A new wave of Latino representation on Beacon Hill was established with the election of three Latino legislators to the Massachusetts State legislature in November 1998.[1] The 200-seat Massachusetts State Legislature is comprised of 160 House seats plus 40 Senate seats. Three Latino legislators in a sea of representatives may seem like a miniscule number, but the political science literature reveals that there are concrete benefits that ethnic groups are likely to receive as a result of having a small but growing number of elected officials.

Elected officials have the potential of legitimizing and defending a group's interests in the official policy arena, whether it is in school boards, city councils, state legislatures, or the U.S. Congress (Pachon 1993, 2). In this capacity, minority elected officials have been linked to increased minority government employment (Eisenger 1982), increased numbers of Latino teachers in school districts, and more responsive public policies addressing minority community needs (e.g., minority contracting and minority representation on boards and commissions) (Fraga, Meier, and England 1986). Although electing minority candidates is no guarantee that socioeconomic progress for their constituents will follow, emphasis should be placed on electing candidates that will be effective in addressing the needs of Latinos along with those of the rest of the population.

THE MASSACHUSETTS LATIN-AMERICAN LEGISLATIVE CAUCUS

The election of three new Latino legislators to the Massachusetts State House in November 1998 and their creation of the Latin-American Caucus in February 1999, shortly after being sworn into office, has received little attention from either Massachusetts scholars who study legislative behavior and minority group politics or the journalists who cover legislative politics on Beacon Hill.[2] Studying freshmen Latino legislators and an infant Latin-American Legislature Caucus may be premature, yet it offers interested journalists, scholars, legislators, Latinos, and even the Latino legislators themselves a benchmark for future examination. The Caucus, one of several dozen at the State House,[3] is comprised of lawmakers Jarrett T. Barrios, a Democrat from Cambridge, representing the Twenty-Eighth Middlesex District[4]; Jose L. Santiago, a Democratic representative from Lawrence, representing the Sixteenth Essex District; and Cheryl Rivera, a Democrat from Springfield.

Since Latinos are the state's fastest growing minority group and the largest as well (6.8 percent—or one in fifteen—Massachusetts residents are Latino) it is easy to understand why Latino legislators would unite for common cause. According to the members of the Caucus their goals are to educate members of the state legislature and their staff, to provide a forum for the discussion of policy issues of concern to Latinos, to serve as a clearing house in the legislature for information on Latino issues, and be legislative advocates for Latinos at the State House.

Interestingly, the Latino representatives were invited by the outgoing Black Caucus Chair, Benjamin Swan of Springfield, to join the seven members of the Black Caucus. After careful consideration they decided not join their black colleagues and to form their own Latin-American Caucus. Their decision broke the tradition of former Latino Representative Nelson Merced, who joined the Black Caucus and served as chair for one term. African Americans have made progress in electing their own candidates for state office in Massachusetts—there are currently seven African-American legislators: six representatives and one senator (Massachusetts Black Legislative Caucus 2000)—representing 3.0 percent of the House seats.[5] Latinos lagged behind until 1998, having only elected Merced of Boston, who served two terms from 1989 to 1993.

Even though the Caucus is in its infant stage, this chapter raises several questions that may help to raise an awareness of the Caucus and contribute to a debate about its role in statewide Latino politics. Some of the following questions will be explored in this chapter.

Is this the right time for the Caucus to come into being? Is the Caucus a loose coalition or a united association when members vote on state legislation of concern to Latinos? If members of the Caucus do not look to it for cues on legislation and voting, whom do they take cues from: constituents, staff, personal opinion, committees, party members and leaders, interest groups, committee hearings, etc.? How much support do Caucus members offer to one another? Are Caucus members' interests and districts sufficiently similar to affect adherence to Caucus beliefs and values? Do Caucus members share the same power base in the legislature (access to leadership and all that flows from it, such as seats on power committees that bring access to resources and influence)? Do they hail from "safe districts," thus allowing them to focus on statewide issues in addition to local concerns? How effective is the Caucus, as viewed by Latino leaders around the state? How much can we expect of freshmen legislators in a political culture characterized by strong, centralized leadership from the Speaker's office? How does the Latin-American Legislative Caucus compare with already established state caucuses? And finally, what can the Latino community reasonably expect of the Latin-American Caucus?

TIMELINESS OF THE CAUCUS: THE PROBLEMS FACING LATINOS AND LATINO POLITICAL DEVELOPMENT

The Caucus has come along at an important time for Latino politics in Massachusetts. Some of the economic and social problems facing Latinos in the United States and Massachusetts are grave. A recent conference held in Worcester, Massachusetts, sponsored by the University of Massachusetts Boston's Mauricio Gastón Institute for Latino Community Development and Public Policy titled *"Un llamado a la acción política!"*—"A Call to Political Action!"—drew 450 elected officials, community leaders, and academics. Although they may not agree upon solutions, there is a consensus among the state's diverse Latino activists about the problems that do exist. Fifty-five percent of the state's Latino children live in poverty. Twenty-nine percent of Latino ninth graders will not finish high school (Grillo 2000)—three times the dropout rate for white students and the highest of any group in the state. In the new state standardized tests, known as the MCAS, only 2 percent of Latinos in the fourth grade passed (Grillo 2000). Latinos in the state are only one-third as likely as whites and one-fifth as likely as Asians to complete a four-year college degree.

On the other hand, there is reason for hope in the political development of Latinos in the state. A growing number of Latinos are registered to vote and actually vote and more Latino candidates are running and more have won seats in the halls of local and state government via elective and appointed positions (see Introduction). There is even some positive news on the economic front. There are more first time Latino homebuyers than ever before and the strong economy is bringing stability to the growing Latino middle class (Associated Press 2000). Latina women are moving into the workforce—and the business world—in greater numbers. They are more likely to work as professionals or managers than are Latino men. Government programs that help the working poor, such as the Earned Income Tax Credit, have helped lift Latinos out of poverty (Zaldivar 1997).

A UNITED FRONT: DEATH PENALTY, LANGUAGE INTERPRETER BILL AND VIEQUES

Is the Latin-American Caucus a loose association or a united front? The Caucus members interviewed for this chapter indicate that it is indeed their goal to become a united front whenever possible.[6] Since their election in 1998, the Caucus members have stood together to promote what they consider to be a Latino community agenda on three issues: voting against the death penalty, voting in support of a Language Interpreter Bill (sponsored by Rep. Barrios), and supporting a nonbinding resolution on the House floor calling upon the United States Navy to withdraw its forces from the island off Puerto Rico called Vieques.

DEATH PENALTY

One of the more controversial issues to come before the House of Representatives for a vote in 1999 was a bill to initiate capital punishment in Massachusetts. When the legislative year began it was quite uncertain whether Governor Paul Cellucci's bill in favor of the death penalty would pass the House. The previous year, Representative John Slattery of Peabody turned out to be the single decisive vote against the bill.

The Latino vote on this issue was, therefore, critical, but it was quite uncertain whether the Caucus would be able to unite against the death penalty. Representative José Santiago entered the legislature as a supporter of capital punishment (as had Slattery). His stance toward the death penalty is understandable given that he is a former police sergeant from Methuen, a city about 25 miles northwest of Boston (Santiago's district includes the cities of Lawrence and Methuen). Santiago received considerable support from the law enforcement community in his district. It became the task of Representatives Cheryl Rivera and Jarrett Barrios to convince Santiago that the death penalty disproportionately harms the Latino community. Rivera recalls:

> We talked about that issue when we had a training session for new legislators. We hadn't created the Caucus yet. Jarrett and I had discussed it but we knew that Mr. Santiago was undecided. We started to talk to him and lobby him and we knew it would make a difference, especially if that was the biggest vote in our first year. Three votes. But if we weren't united on that one, that would have set the tone. We were united and voted against the death penalty. It was defeated by around seven votes so our votes weren't the difference like Representative Slattery's vote the year before. That was one person who made a difference. (Rivera 2000)

Jarrett Barrios remembers:

> We convinced José to switch his position. I think the appeal for all of us of appearing united on this issue was great. Unity on this issue gives a sense of a community that is inordinately impacted through the Criminal Justice system by these sentencing guidelines. The fact that juries get it wrong and there is racism and bigotry. We would make that positive policy statement and give it some content, a spin: "This is what the Latino

community thinks." We testified together and that was great. (Barrios 2000)

The lobbying campaign by Barrios and Rivera, along with other death penalty opponents had an affect on Santiago, who began to study the issue intently and came around to see the damage capital punishment does to Latinos and members of other minority groups.[7] José Santiago explains how he came to change his position:

When I first came on I was undecided. I was a police officer for 14 years and I looked at it from both sides. I had to make an informed decision. By reading material that was available in the library, over the internet, and sent to me by anti-death penalty advocates, I learned that it has been shown in cities and towns that have the death penalty, it is not a deterrent to the crime of murder. So I looked at that. I read the material and saw that the people, who are poor, of minority descent, were the ones who received the death penalty because they weren't able to get the best defense possible to win their case. History has indicated that mostly minorities are the ones who get the death penalty.

I didn't catch criticism from the law enforcement community or from local constituents in Methuen and Lawrence, the way I expected. I thought more pressure would be put on me. But, when it comes down to issues of morality, the legislative leadership and some of the officers who were involved for 14 years in my career didn't put pressure on me to vote for the death penalty. Advocates against the death penalty put more pressure on me to vote against the bill. If that kind of pressure had come from my district it would have been harder.

We were thinking as a Caucus about gaining publicity for our votes. As you know, I was one of the votes that the media felt would decide whether it passed. The *Lawrence Eagle Tribune* and the *Boston Globe* highlighted Rep. William G. Reinstein from Revere and me. We were the potential deciding votes who had changed from pro- to anti-death penalty. I was looking at the publicity side of it. That gave the Caucus, coming down against the death penalty, more publicity as a united group. It did give us more of a hold on the leadership. They did take notice. (Santiago 2000)

Given the publicity that Slattery garnered for his crucial one vote, the Caucus expected to make a big splash in the media by uniting in their opposition to the Governor's bill. However, on March 29, 1999, Caucus members found themselves voting with the majority, 80 to 73, against the death penalty, for a difference of 7 votes. Their votes were not as decisive to the outcome as they had anticipated. Moreover, although Representative Santiago believes the House leadership took notice of their united front, a legislator interviewed off the record for this chapter, who is familiar with the death penalty issue, said that he and other legislators involved with this issue were not even aware of the Caucus's united votes. Nevertheless, although their votes were not, in the end, crucial to the defeat of the capital punishment legislation, and may have gone unnoticed, to the Latino Caucus members, their votes represented a good first test of what the Caucus could do if they were united in their legislative preferences.[8]

INTERPRETER SERVICES BILL

The years 1999 and 2000 also saw the Latino Caucus assist passage of the Interpreter's Service Bill, HR 4917. Under the bill, introduced by Barrios in 1999, passed by the House and Senate in 2000, and signed by Governor Cellucci on April 14, 2000, all acute-care hospitals are required to provide "competent" interpreter services in their emergency rooms; all acute-care mental health hospitals and other facilities are mandated to do the same (Hsu 1999).[9]

While Santiago and Rivera supported the Interpreter's bill as members of the Caucus, it was primarily the initiative of Representative Barrios. It was a means for Barrios to break out from the pack of freshman legislators, to address a statewide issue, and to make a name for himself in and out of the legislature. It worked. Barrios was the focus of a one-hour public affairs television show on Latino issues—"La Plaza." The program, titled "Freshman Year on Beacon Hill," shows how the neophyte legislator manages the world of Massachusetts State House politics. *Boston Globe* reviewer Don Aucoin wrote, "The 31-year-old Barrios exudes energy and likability, and he is voluble as many pols tend to be, but he also seems to possess that underrated and invaluable political skill: Knowing how to listen. Politicians don't get enough credit for this"[10] (Aucoin 2000). As a representative of the City of Cambridge, the most ideologically left leaning district in the state, Barrios believes that bills like Interpreter Services and low income housing are more important to his constituents than traditional service issues such as fixing pot holes and street lights (Barrios 2000).[11]

VIEQUES

The third issue that unified the Caucus was in an area of U.S. military policy: support for a House resolution sponsored by Representative Santiago on January 3, 2000 calling upon the U.S. Navy to discontinue weapons training on its base on the island of Vieques. The Vieques issue has united Puerto Ricans on the island as well as the mainland. All three legislators believe their constituents endorse the resolution. In April 1999 a civilian Puerto Rican guard was killed after Marine jets dropped bombs that unintentionally hit an observation tower. The death touched off protests that led to the occupation of the base by more than 100 people (Becker 2000).[12] As a result of the death, President Clinton suspended all military exercises on Vieques, a small island in the Commonwealth of Puerto Rico. On January 31, 2000 President Clinton and Puerto Rican officials reached an agreement that limited the Navy to using dummy shells during bombing practice. The Navy would have use of the island until 2003. In return, the United States would give $40 million in aid to the 9,400 islanders who live near the range. A referendum would be held in which residents could determine whether they wanted the Navy to leave.

The issue of Vieques involves more than the death of the Puerto Rican guard last year. As Representative Santiago explains, Vieques is an environmental issue of great concern to Puerto Ricans and to him:

> Vieques was a resolution I tried to pass, to have the House support the people of Vieques, to ask that the U.S. discontinue the operation of using live weapons on the island due to their polluting the environment—to stop. There is a group from Boston, at the Gastón Institute of the University of Massachusetts Boston—some folks who work there are very active with Vieques. A lot of leaders in Puerto Rico are against the Navy staying in Vieques. I moved to the mainland from Puerto Rico when I was six years old. I'm not too up to date on the issues over there, but I do have family in Puerto Rico. They informed me that the damage these weapons have done to the environment, water and air quality, indicates a 29 percent cancer illness rate on Vieques, which is higher than on the mainland of Puerto Rico. Evidence points out the issue of uranium in the weapons as probably the cause. The fishery and wildlife have diminished. Some of Vieques is contaminated due to firing in the waters. (Santiago 2000)

This was an issue that the Caucus and especially Representative Santiago expected to sail through the Massachusetts legislature. That was not to be. The resolution to this day remains bogged down on the floor of the House. Santiago explains that under House rules, if one representative objects to a floor resolution, the matter cannot proceed without an investigation and hearing:

> I introduced it and Representative Ronald Gauch of Shrewsbury has given me a tough time passing it. He was stationed there with the Navy during his military service. He says the Navy is keeping the island in the economic prosperity it has today. So he gave me a hard time. . . . Senator Stanley C. Rosenberg, Senator Dianne Wilkerson, and some other leaders from Boston went as a group, on a fact-finding mission, and I'm waiting for them so I can reintroduce the resolution. They have Puerto Rican constituents. Wilkerson has a large population of Latinos. It must go through the whole House, not through a committee. Since it was objected to, it has

to go to the House, where one representative can stop debate, if he objects to it. The Latin-American Caucus had a meeting with Mr. Gauch a month and a half to two months ago, just us three members. We worked out some language on the resolution. We were going to put it through but the fact-finding trip to Puerto Rico came up. Some of the Senators and Reps indicated, not to try to pass it but to wait till they get back. They did return three weeks ago. During these last three weeks we've been busy with the budget so the resolution is still on the floor; a hold is on it till we sit down with the senators and determine the best language to introduce in both Houses. (Santiago 2000) [13]

EFFECTIVENESS OF THE CAUCUS: PERSPECTIVES FROM COMMUNITY LEADERS

In sum, of the three legislative items on the Caucus agenda, one bill passed in a relatively short while—the Interpreter Service bill passed in 1 year. The second, a united vote with the House majority against the death penalty, turned out to have limited effect due to the seven vote margin of victory but proved to the Caucus members that they could unite on an issue that mattered to their constituents. The third legislative item—a resolution on Vieques—is currently stalled. Caucus members vow to continue to pursue the resolution, especially since the issue is far from being resolved.[14] Overall, Latino political observers of State House politics give the trio high ratings for less than a year and a half of service as freshmen on Beacon Hill.

Nelson Merced, their predecessor in the legislature, is encouraged by what the Caucus has accomplished after just 1 year. To him, the establishment of the Caucus was a great accomplishment in and of itself. "If they had agreed upon one issue, let alone passed legislation, that would be a significant accomplishment. Just the fact that members met regularly, three or four times over the year, was also an accomplishment. Regular meetings are an accomplishment" (Merced 2000).[15]

Juan Vega, the lone Latino city councilor from Chelsea, Massachusetts believes the Caucus has been wildly successful so far:

> It's amazing that we have three Latino legislators up there. I think they have the dual challenge of surviving as freshmen in the State House and showing the way for how Latinos can do their jobs, and laying the groundwork for those of us who have aspirations to higher office. I give them a grade of A. They just started. That is a huge advantage. A grade of A for effort. They got the Caucus up and running immediately. There was no power struggle. Decisively set it up. That speaks a lot. I have nothing specific to say about their agenda. The whole point of having them as representatives, playing the role of representing their district and Latinos in general. They are in a position to help us along in our community

groups and organizations, and keep us informed [about] what is going on up at the State House. Having that level of contacts is key. They're going to do a service to their colleagues as well, getting informed and educated on Latino issues. I have been in touch with Rep. Barrios, especially with the Interpreter Services bill for hospitals. I attended the training sessions the Caucus put together with NALEO. (Vega 2000)[16]

Gladys Rodríguez Parker, district manager for Congressman James McGovern of Worcester, and a member of the Political Action Committee (PAC) Jarrett Barrios has organized to encourage and assist Latinos interested in running for office at the state and local level, adds:

I didn't have any expectation of the Caucus. I know the limitations of what can be done in a year. A lot of relationship building: that is their biggest accomplishment. They have done that. For example, they have built bridges with the Black Caucus and have gotten Latino-friendly candidates and elected officials behind them. Having conversations with the Caucus has made me aware of statewide issues and, as insiders, they let us know if calls need to be made. All of this activity has put me at ease as to how fast things are moving. (Parker 2000)

OBSTACLES TO CAUCUS EFFECTIVENESS: FRESHMEN LEGISLATORS FOCUS ON REELECTION

There are many factors preventing the young Caucus and its freshmen legislators from having an immediate or even measurable impact on the legislative process including the very fact of their newness and the competitive nature of elections in Massachusetts. By having to work diligently to remain in the State House (members of the House serve 2 year terms, which means they run election campaigns every other year and constantly campaign and raise money), it is difficult for freshmen to concentrate on legislative matters, especially those with statewide importance. As the late Massachusetts Speaker of the U.S. House of Representatives, Thomas "Tip" O'Neill, Jr., born and raised in North Cambridge, Massachusetts, was fond of saying, "All politics is local." The legislator who fails to take care of his district's concerns first and foremost will feel the wrath of his constituents on election day.

Serving constituents is at the top of the agenda for all three freshmen members of the Latin-American Caucus. They are each paying close attention to their home district, focusing on providing excellent casework (doing favors for constituents) and making sure the state budget includes pork barrel projects in the district (highly visible construction projects such as highways, schools, and parks). As political scientist Morris Fiorina has written about the U.S. Congress, freshmen who do not reside in safe seats are far more likely to focus on constituent service rather than legislation because the former is a win-win situation for representatives, while the latter can involve controversy and result in dissatisfied voters (Fiorina 1977). Not many constituents will argue with favors carried out for them by their representative or the creation of new schools or bridges in the district. Votes on bilingual education, special education, welfare reform, and taxes are sure to reflect the diversity of opinion within the community and possibly result in lost votes at the polls. Who can argue with a new Charles River park at Magazine Beach in Cambridge, a new high school in downtown Lawrence, and a new mass transit system for Springfield and the Pioneer Valley?

HOW SAFE ARE THEY?

All three members of the Caucus have reason to be concerned about reelection.[17] The representative with perhaps most to fear is Cheryl Rivera. Representative Rivera came to office without having held a local elected position or having served in grass roots community organizations. Longtime (24-term) Representative Anthony Scibelli died 3 days after winning the September 15, 1998 primary, at the age of 86. Rivera, a newcomer to Springfield's factionalized politics, won a caucus vote of Democratic officials to become the party's nominee. She easily won the November 3 election, in a racially and ethnically diverse district. Because Rivera had not run a campaign of her own for office, she has stayed close to her district, making sure an electoral organization was in place for the fall 2000 elections. Cheryl Rivera explains:

> I could have traveled throughout the state, the country, to speak. I've been invited. I really didn't go to anything except what was in my district. I was very careful. I hope not to have a battle. I am working very, very hard, twenty-four hours a day, to reassure my constituents that I am accessible to them, paying attention to their needs. If someone runs against me, I will be successful—not to be cocky. I work very hard. My constituents notice. Results will be favorable to me. You can always get someone to run against you. The first year was a tough year because I had never run for office. (Rivera 2000)

Representative Rivera acknowledges that given her district's large elderly population (a population that turns out to vote in large numbers on election day), her service to seniors, in part through her seat on the Elderly Committee in the House, is paramount to her. In this respect, she is following in the footsteps of her predecessor, Representative Scibelli, who won reelection in part by caring for the elderly who reside in Springfield's Brightwood section in the city's North End. In the end, Rivera's hard work paid off as she ran unopposed in the 2000 primary and general election.

The Representative from Lawrence, José Santiago, has proven he is a politician not to be taken lightly. Santiago became the first Latino city councilor in Lawrence's history in November 1993, from a ward-based seat, District C. Santiago won that seat by cultivating a large Latino voting bloc, beginning with voter registration drives a year before his election and a strong get out the vote effort on election day. His victory over three term incumbent State Representative M. Paul Iannuccillo in October 1998 was unexpected, though aided in part by a court-ordered redrawing of legislative districts in 1994.[18] Although Santiago lost a bid to win an at-large seat on the Council last year (while he also held the post of state representative), he polled a surprisingly strong third place finish, losing to Francis J. Kivell by 19 voters (3,167 to 3,148). Two at-large councilors were elected, one of whom, Marcos Devers, is the first Latino to win at large in Lawrence history (Vogler 1999).[19] Santiago took nothing for granted, worked as hard as Rivera toward reelection in 2000 and was successful.

Jarrett Barrios has perhaps the safest seat of the three. He soundly defeated veteran legislator and incumbent, Alvia Thompson in 1998. He has remained extremely active in his district while maintaining a high profile in the Boston metropolitan area, raised a sizable sum of money, and like Rivera was free of an opponent for the 2000 primary and general election. According to Barrios, to ensure reelection, he has created

> [a] neighborhood advisory committee of 25–30 people. I cover every demographic niche in the district. They help me stay in touch with the community. Last summer I went—and I will again this summer go—door to door to stay available and learn a lot of what people want. It helps me set my own agenda. My own presence at different events helps me to keep on top of things. . . . So far, nobody has announced against me. I've raised money. You still have to raise money. The best defense is looking strong in your district. I continue to raise money. I have $40,000 in the bank, which is a decent amount for a representative to have in the beginning of an election year. I need to raise $60,000 to $70,000. (Barrios 2000)

THE IMPERIAL POWER OF THE MASSACHUSETTS SPEAKER: IMPLICATIONS FOR LATINO LEGISLATORS

One of the difficulties the Caucus of Latino freshmen legislators faces in Massachusetts is the strong and centralized leadership of the Massachusetts House of Representatives. Over the past decade, the political climate on Beacon Hill—site of the Massachusetts State House—has changed dramatically. Frank Phillips, long-time observer of legislative politics for the *Boston Globe*, has noted a decline in the level of debate, opposition, and sense of outrage in the Legislature. Phillips argues that in recent decades, legendary Speakers who ruled with an iron fist at least faced coalitions of GOP members and dissident Democrats who would gain some attention and once in a while rally enough support to break the leadership's grip. House Speaker Thomas M. Finneran and his leadership team today lack any real opposition, which is often attributed to Finneran's authoritarian style. "Indeed, his strong will, sharp intellect and ideological zeal bring an unusual force to his leadership and can overwhelm most opponents" (Phillips 2000).

Moreover, Phillips believes the decline in opposition is due to economic good times, and the lessening importance of state and local politics and public policy to Massachusetts's residents. Representative Jarrett Barrios told Phillips: "I think that any legislator will feel cautious about speaking up on an issue when they've already obtained something else through the budget process that they hold near and dear."[20]

The best any legislator can do in this political climate, let alone a trio of freshmen, is to "work with him [Finneran] as best we can," said Lexington Representative Jay Kaufman. A senior legislator who preferred not to be named told Phillips: "Little up here happens without the [S]peaker approval and that's the way it is" (Phillips 2000). In another show of Speaker Finneran's iron-fisted control of the House, representatives overwhelmingly voted (111 to 39) to lift the eight-year term limit on the speakership, allowing him to rule over the House chamber indefinitely (Cassidy 2001).

The Latino representatives are well aware of the culture of leadership that exists in the House and have taken steps to address their situation. For instance, Representative José Santiago revealed that both he and Representative Barrios make themselves available to the leadership when called upon to address Latino and immigrant constituents in the leaders' districts. When it became apparent that the rate of return of the Census 2000 forms in Massachusetts lagged behind the national average, Santiago and Barrios agreed to speak around the state in communities where Latino compliance was low. Their investment in this issue is based on the well-established fact that a low population count will hurt not only Latinos across the state but all of the state's residents in the eventual distribution of federal funds for highway, schools, housing, etc. In return for their speaking engagements, Representative Santiago is hopeful that leaders, such as Representative Kevin Fitzgerald and Representative John A. Stafanini of Framingham, who heads the all important Committee on Redistricting, can help them to obtain favored committee assignments and, in general, their fair share of legislative patronage. The Redistricting Committee is especially important since it has the power to make or break legislators. Caucus members hope to be remembered by Stefanini at the crucial moment new district boundaries are redrawn.[21]

DIFFERENT DISTRICTS, IDEOLOGIES, AND BACKGROUNDS

Another feature of the Latin-American Legislative Caucus is the diversity of members' districts. This demographic diversity suggests that their legislative concerns may be different as well. For instance, Rep. Barrios represents a district that comprises a section of the city of Cambridge that has a mere 7.4 percent Latino population out of its total of slightly more than 100,000. (Eight members of the House, including Barrios, represent parts of Cambridge.) Rep. Rivera's district is 30 percent Latino but she estimates that only 30 percent of the Latinos in her district vote. Rep. Santiago hails from Lawrence, a city with about 43,000 Latinos out of about 72,000, of which approximately 8,000 are registered to vote. Most of his constituents in Lawrence and Methuen's Arlington district are Latino.

Although all three Caucus members are Democrats, ideologically, their districts differ in their support for traditional Democratic Party concerns. In Cambridge, Representative Barrios's concern for affordable housing, opposition to the state welfare reform plan, advocacy for interpreter services in hospitals across the state, etc., reflects his constituents' concerns for greater government intervention in the economy to achieve social equity, a traditional liberal perspective. Cheryl Rivera, on the other hand, represents, in her estimation, an older and more conservative white ethnic district, where her support for the current welfare reform initiative of the Governor is welcomed. José Santiago's district is overwhelmingly poor and young, and this is reflected in his middle of the road position, in between Rivera and Barrios on welfare reform. As someone who grew up in poverty and lived on public assistance, Santiago believes the national as well as the state welfare reform measures are too punitive, yet he is not willing to defend the old welfare state laws that he believes encouraged dependency rather than offering transitional assistance that moves welfare recipients off the rolls.

The diverse backgrounds of Caucus members also helps to explain their lack of unity on some issues. Representative Barrios attended Yale as an undergraduate and Harvard Law School. His is also one of two openly gay legislators in the state and is of Cuban American descent. Representative Rivera attended local undergraduate and law schools, and most importantly is of Irish and Puerto Rican heritage. Her mixed ethnic background, she believes, has sensitized her to identity politics and leads her to favor a more inclusive definition of Latino, for membership in the Caucus, and for issues generally, such as the interpreter services legislation sponsored by Rep. Barrios. Rivera argued for interpreters for several language minority groups and not simply Spanish speakers. Representative Santiago was born in Puerto Rico and came to the mainland at the age of six. He attended Northern Essex Community College in Haverhill and was a Methuen police officer until last year. Because Representative Santiago had a personal experience with poverty and the bilingual education system, he believes he is in the best position of all three Caucus members to judge whether bilingual education or welfare reform is working. Interestingly, both Rivera and Barrios support the sink or swim, mainstreaming approach to bilingual education, while Santiago believes that would put an undue burden on a child from a non-English-speaking background. He favors a more gradual 2-year phase into mainstreaming.

What is most surprising to this author is the relative degree of unity among the Caucus despite their different backgrounds, ideologies, and districts. On a personal level, they appear to get along well and respect each other's positions, which may be more important at this stage of their careers than ideological and issue unity.

COMPARISON TO OTHER HOUSE CAUCUSES

One area in which the Caucus could use improvement is its lack of publicity or presence in the State House. When compared to other Massachusetts Caucuses, the Latin-American Caucus is far less well established. For example, thus far the Caucus has not printed a mission statement or any materials about the Caucus for Caucus members or associate members. Moreover, unlike the more established Black Caucus, Women's Caucus, and Children's Caucus,[22] for which the Speaker's office has secured budget line items to support staff, offices, and publications, the Latin-American Caucus has no resources or official recognition. A request by the Caucus to the House leadership for a staff person was denied. All of the endorsed Caucuses have publications that include a list of legislative victories and legislative tools (such as a resource library, fact book, etc.) as well as a newsletter sent to Caucus members. If the Caucus is to be taken seriously by other legislators as well as lobbyists and state officials, it needs to convince the House leadership that creating a staff would benefit not only Latinos but the leadership as well. Public and blunt criticism, that the House is unrepresentative of the changing demographic reality of Massachusetts, might get the leadership's attention.

CONCLUSION

The creation of the Caucus has come at an important juncture for Latinos in Massachusetts. An unprecedented three Latino legislators were elected to the State House and the number of Latino candidates, voter registrants, and voters at the local level has never been higher. On the other hand, some of the economic and social problems facing Latinos in the United States and Massachusetts are severe.

Given the stiff challenges they face as freshmen representatives, including an authoritarian leadership structure, the need to focus on wining reelection, their own different backgrounds, electoral districts, and political ideologies, the Caucus has taken several important steps forward to solidify its position in the legislature. As might be expected from a newly established Caucus, unification of interests and issues is elusive at this point. Surprisingly, the greatest unity of purpose was found in the death penalty, a contentious issue across the state and within the Latino communities as well. The weakest areas of consensus lie in the Latino community's hottest issues: bilingual education and welfare reform. It remains to be seen how much their efforts on behalf of the House leadership yield positive results. Redistricting, which takes place in 2001, will be a good test and fertile ground for scholars to examine in depth. The strength of the Caucus ultimately is dependent upon the election of new Latino activists to the state house. Leadership development workshops by national and state groups, such as NALEO and the Commonwealth Coalition, should be a high priority for the Caucus agenda in the next few years.

NOTES

1.   The election of three new Latinos to the Massachusetts legislature is part of a national trend. Hispanic membership in state legislatures across the nation continues to rise. In January 2000, the sum swelled to 190, according to NALEO, the National Association of Latino Elected and Appointed Officials. That is 32 more than the 158 who took their oaths in 1994. NALEO has counted the number of Latinos serving on all elective bodies nationwide to be more than 5,135 in 2000, up from 4,625 in 1994. Many of the newly elected had never won elective office before (Alma-Bonilla and Torres 1996).

2.   Although there are few scholarly studies of Massachusetts State legislative caucuses and state legislative caucuses around the nation, there is a literature on U.S. congressional caucuses. The best book on the subject is Hammond (1998). Hammond defines a caucus as "voluntary, organized associations of members of Congress, without recognition in chamber rules or line-item appropriations . . . that seek to play a role in the policy process." Hammond concludes, "caucus membership does affect members' voting." On balance, she sees caucuses as more integrating than fragmenting (Patterson 1999, 41–42). Other students of caucuses are less favorable. David Segal views the caucus as a destructive force in Congress because it "turns the members of Congress themselves into lobbyists. Caucuses are thus another facet of the everygroup-for-itself ethic that now pervades Washington, an ethic which has led to legions of perverse subsidies, dubious tax breaks and calcified government so besieged on all sides that it can barely creak into action when it attempts serious reforms." Where Massachusetts and the U.S. Congress differ in Segal's analysis is Segal believes the growth of congressional caucuses "occurred, not coincidentally, as power in Congress became more decentralized." No observer of Massachusetts's politics can find such a decentralizing tendency. Power has remained centralized in the hands of the offices of the House Speaker and the Senate President over the past few decades (Segal 1994, 19). Two other important contributions to the literature on congressional caucuses are Ainsworth and Akins (1997) and Singh (1999). Singh's work, a study of the Congressional Black Caucus, is particularly noteworthy. For state legislative caucuses see Cheryl M. Miller (1993), "Issue Selection by State Legislative Black Caucuses in the South," in *,Minority Group Influence: Agenda Setting, Formulation, and Public Policy,* edited

by Paula D. McClain, pp. 111–125. (Westport, CT: Greenwood); Beth Reingold, "Concepts of Representation Among Female and Male State Legislators," *Legislative Studies Quarterly* XVII 509–537; Sue Thomas (1991), "The Impact of Women on State Legislative Policies," *Journal of Politics* LIII 958–975; and Albert J. Nelson (1991), *Emerging Influentials in State Legislatures: Women, Blacks, and Hispanics* (Westport: Praeger). The author wishes to acknowlege the assistance of Professor John Berg of Suffolk University for helping locate the above citations.

3.   I say several dozen because nobody (clerk, librarian, counsel, speaker's office) at the State House has a hard figure on the number of caucuses in existence today.

4.   Cambridge is a city in eastern Massachusetts, across the Charles River from Boston. It is also the site of Harvard University, Radcliffe College and Lesley College, and the Massachusetts Institute of Technology. In 1990 its population was 95,802; approximately 6,000 were Latinos.

5.   The Black Caucus reached a peak of nine representatives in 1975.

6.   Each member of the Caucus was interviewed once. During the interview they were asked for the names of three individuals who were familiar with their work in the legislature: one critic, one supporter, and a member of the legislature, preferably a senior or high-ranking legislator. A few current legislators of the author's choosing (for their expertise in the policy areas discussed) were asked for their "off the record" assessment of the Caucus. Former representative Nelson Merced was also interviewed. Of note, senior legislators were not interviewed for this chapter, due to their professed scheduling difficulties or their failure to return phone calls.

7.   This particular case against the death penalty is made by many. Two examples are Amnesty International's study: "Race Drives Use of Death Penalty in the U.S. Judicial System," 18 May 1999. See www.amnesty-usa.org/news/1999/usa05181999.html, and the Death Penalty Information Center, which has numerous publications on the subject, including "The Death Penalty in Black & White: Who Lives, Who Dies, Who Decides" by Richard C. Dieter, Esq., Executive Director, Death Penalty Information Center, June 1998. See www.essential.org/dpic/

8.   The actual vote by the House (HR 3963) was to accept the vote of the House Criminal Justice Committee which rejected the pro-death penalty legislation proposed by Governor Paul Cellucci. Given that their message of unity was lost on their colleagues, especially the House leadership, it would be in the Caucus' interest to more effectively make their efforts known. A press conference or press release might have been in order. On the other hand, the Caucus may not have wished to draw too much attention to their vote, particularly Jose Santiago.

9.   See www.state.ma.us/legis/laws/seslaw00/sl000066.htm. The Bill was passed officially as Chapter 66 of the Acts of 2000: An Act Requiring Competent Interpreter Services In The Delivery Of Certain Acute Health Care Services. The act will take effect on July 1, 2001.

10.   Even the WGBH monthly program guide gushes: "Jarrett Barrios, an energetic new addition to the State House. Barrios boasts boundless energy, political savvy and a devoted staff."

11.   An example of Cambridge's liberalism came in November 1998 when voters approved three ballot initiatives that dealt with increased construction and availability of affordable housing statewide, universal health care and a patient bill of rights, and banishment of a small nuclear reactor from the Massachusetts Institute of Technology campus (Emery 1998).

12.   It should be noted that Santiago is in good company on this issue. Senators Charles Schumer of New York and Frank Murkowski of Alaska, along with the *New York Times* editorial board, have called on the Navy to immediately remove themselves from the island. The *New York Times* reports that a presidential panel created by Defense Secretary William Cohen found that "the Navy has not lived up to its earlier commitments to help with economic development, address safety and environmental hazards caused by the shelling and keep the use of live fire to an absolute minimum" (*New York Times*, 2000, 14).

13.   As of May 2000 the resolution had been tabled in the House. State Senator Dianne Wilkerson also sponsored a Vieques resolution in the Senate and it too has been postponed until the next legislative session which starts in January 2001. See http://www.state.ma.us/legis/history/s02183.htm, for information on "SENATE, NO. 2183: a resolution opposing United States Naval activities on the island of Vieques. 04/27/00."

14.   On May 4, 2000, U.S. Marshals and Federal Bureau of Investigation agents evicted 150 protestors from Vieques. In response to the eviction, demonstrations against the occupation of Vieques were held in several U.S. cities on May 5 (Wong 2000).

15.   Merced currently is the New England District Director of the Neighborhood Reinvestment Corporation, a national nonprofit organization created in 1978 by an act of Congress to revitalize America's older, distressed communities by establishing and supporting a national network of local nonprofit organizations. See www.nw.org/nrc. For a discussion of his election to the Massachusetts State Legislature in 1988 and 1992, see Chapter 2 in this volume.

16.   NALEO has held workshops to develop political leadership and teach the nuts and bolts of voter registration and running for office, in Boston, at the Caucus' request. They are scheduled to return sometime in the Fall 2000.

17.   In November 2000, 62 of the 150 Massachusetts House legislative districts offered voters a choice of candidates. José Santiago was the only Caucus member who faced a challenge. He defeated his Republican opponent, Israel Reyes, by a 2-to-1 margin (Rodriguez 2000, 10).

18.   The newly recreated Lawrence legislative district became the first in the state where Hispanics constituted a majority of voting-age residents (53 percent under the newly drawn district map in 1994).

19.   Santiago's GOP opponent in the Fall 2000 general election, Israel Reyes of Lawrence, garnered enough write-in votes in the September 2000 primary to make the ballot (Laidler 2000). Santiago, like Rivera, has not left himself open

for electoral challenges by following Rivera's lead, attending to constituents rather than going to regional and statewide functions.

20. Barrios (2000), unlike his Latino colleagues, won instant recognition from the Speaker in February 1999 when he, along with three incoming representatives, landed committee assignments they had coveted. Barrios was awarded a seat on the Housing and Urban Development Committee. This was a perfect match considering his specialization as an attorney in low cost housing cases and because his district is feeling the squeeze of skyrocketing housing costs (Jonas 1999).

21. The battle over redistricting is already underway in the legislature. Representative Santiago has proposed that Lawrence be apportioned a second representative, so that Latinos can elect a second representative in the near future. This is opposed by Santiago's neighboring representatives Barry Feingold and Robert Torrisi, who fear the loss of pieces of Lawrence currently in their district will push them into unfriendly or uncharted voters in neighboring Haverhill and Tewksbury, respectively.

22. The Black Caucus was formed in 1972, the Women's Caucus in 1975, and the Children's Caucus in 1985.

REFERENCES

Ainsworth, Scott H., and Frances Akins. (1997). "The Informational Role of Caucuses in the U.S. Congress." *American Politics Quarterly* 25(4), p. 407–431.

Alma-Bonilla, Yara I., and Joseph Torres. (1996). "Latinas Lead Way as Hispanics Gain 11 StateLegislative Seats." *Hispanic Link*, a NALEO Publication, Washington, DC, 1–3.

Associated Press. (2000). "Mass. Latinos looking to strengthen political voice." *Boston Globe.* 25 March. B, 3

Aucoin, Don. (2000). "'La Plaza' offers up a young pol's ups and downs." Boston Globe, 8 January, Living, F3.

Barrios, Jarrett. (2000). Interview with author, cassette recording, 20 January.

Becker, Elizabeth. (2000). "White House Talks Set in Dispute on Base." *New York Times.* National, 26 January, A13.

Cassidy, Tina. (2001). "House Vote Will Keep Finneran in Charge." *Boston Globe* 25 January, B1, 4.

Eisenger, Peter. (1982). "Black Employment in Municipal Jobs: The Impact of Black Political Power." *American Political Science Review* 76, 330–392.

Emery, Theo. (1998). "In the 28th, voters set an agenda for Barrios." *Boston Globe.* 8 November 1, 10.

Fiorina, Morris P. (1997). *Congress: Keystone of the Washington Establishment.* New Haven, CT: Yale University Press.

Fraga, Luis, Kenneth J. Meier, and Robert England. (1986). "Hispanic Americans and Educational Policy: Limits to Equal Access." *Journal of Politics* 48, 850–876.

Grillo, Thomas. (2000). "Educators, Others Tackle Hispanic Dropout Rate." *Boston Globe*. 20 November, B1, B4.

Hammond, Susan Webb. (1998). *Congressional Caucuses in National Policy Making*. Baltimore, MD: Johns Hopkins University Press.

Hsu, Karen. (1999). "Bill Would Require Hospital Interpreters." *Boston Globe*. 20 July, B1.

Jonas, Michael. (1999). *Boston Globe*. "Freshmen in the House Happy with Assignments." 14 February, City Edition, p. 2.

Laidler, John. (2000). *Boston Globe*. "Some Lively Races on Region's Ballots." 1 October, Northwest Weekly, 3.

Massachusetts Black Legislative Caucus. (n.d.). "History of Black Legislators in the State of Massachusetts."

Merced, Nelson. (2000). Telephone interview with author, 21 March.

New York TImes Editorial. (1999). "An Island Bombing Range." 31 October, Week in Review Section 4, 14.

Pachón, Harry. P. (1993). "Hispanic Elected Officials in 1992." 1992 National Roster of Hispanic Elected Officials. Washington, DC: National Association of Latino Elected and Appointed Officials (NALEO).

Parker, Gladys Rodríguez. (2000). Interview with author, telephone, 13 March

Patterson, Samuel C. (1999). "Review of Congressional Caucuses in National Policy Making." *Perspectives on Political Science* Winter, 28(1), 41–42.

Phillips, Frank. (2000). "When It Comes to House Debate, Silence Is Not Always Golden." *Boston Globe*. 20 April, B1, B6.

Rivera, Cheryl. (2000). Interview with author, cassette recording, 5 January.

Rodríguez, Nancy. (2000). "Bill Would Tighten Absentee Ballot Rules." Lawrence Eagle Tribune 10 December, 10.

Santiago José. (2000). Interview with author, cassette recording, 18 April.

Segal, David. (1994). "Caucus Crazy: Special Interests in Congress." *Washington Monthly* (May), 26(5), 18–24.

Singh, Robert. (1999). *The Congressional Black Caucus: Racial Politics in the U.S. Congress*. Thousand Oaks, CA: Sage.

Vega, Juan. (2000). Telephone interview with author, 11 January.

Vogler, Mark. E. (1999). "Four Veteran Councilors Ousted." *Lawrence Eagle Tribune*, 3 November, 15–18.

Wong, Edward. (2000). "Protesters Arrested on Vieques Bombing Range." *New York Times, on the Web*. 4 May. www.nytimes.com/yr/mo/day/late/04cnd-vieques-protest.html.

Zalidver, R.A. (1997). "Census Indicates Hispanics Falling Behind in Economy." *Boston Globe*. 12 October, A14.

Postscript
Thoughts on Increasing Latino Political Prospects

Our purpose in writing this book was not only the desire to expand the study of Latino politics to communities and states outside of the "big" Latino states—i.e., California, Texas, Florida, Arizona, New Mexico, Colorado, New York, New Jersey, and Illinois. We also hoped to share strategies learned from the struggles in one community with other communities—and activists—here in Massachusetts and in other states. We were interested in two major questions: What strategies and lessons do the contributing authors have to offer to Latino communities? How can the Latino political organizers of today make use of the experiences of the past described in this volume to shape a future political agenda that will increase Latino political representation and power?

First and foremost, Latino communities must continue their forward motion to develop civic organizations based on their diverse cultural traditions—they are indeed the repository of a great deal of "political capital." At the same time, to gain the representation needed to solve the social problems Latino communities face and to confront effectively the entrenched resistance posed by the dominant power structure, Latinos need to find a way to unite around a common Latino agenda and support Latino candidates. As the pluralist succession model suggests, American city politics is also ethnic interest group politics. Latinos must first see their interests as a community, despite the many factors that divide them ideologically or by reason of national origin. Only when differences between Puerto Ricans and Dominicans in Lawrence were resolved, if not yet overcome, for example, could organizational efforts to gain representation on the city council and in the state legislature succeed.

Second, due to their minority status in all cities across the Commonwealth except for Lawrence and Chelsea, coalitional politics is a must. Whether their numbers are a small fraction of a city's population, or the state for that matter, whenever it is possible to join forces with other minorities, especially African Americans, progressive or liberal whites, and, in some communities (such as Lowell), an emerging Southeast Asian political movement, coalitions should be created. Moreover, the lesson of Nelson Merced's pioneering electoral victory in Boston should not be lost on future aspirants for state and local office.

Third, the nagging problems of poverty, lower educational achievement and graduation rates, and high unemployment, to name just a few, must be addressed by all of the elected officials and candidates for office. The University of Massachusetts Boston's Mauricio Gastón Institute for Latino Community Development and Public Policy recently sponsored a conference in Worcester, titled *"Un llamado a la acción política!"*—"A call to political action!" The conference drew 450 Latino community leaders, elected officials and academics. The conference produced the "Latino Agenda 2000"—a report and call to action that can be used as a tool to influence statewide policy making (Gastón Institute 2000). This is certainly a good step in the right direction. Further leadership from the state's public and private universities is essential, since the virtual absence of support by the political parties in this state, especially at the local level, has left urban universities with the task of providing outside resources minority communities need to organize themselves to achieve political power. The example of CIRCLE (Center for Immigrant and Refugee Community Leadership Empowerment), coordinated by the University of Massachusetts Boston, should be studied and, where appropriate, emulated across the state (Arches et al. 1997). Though short-lived, CIRCLE showed what was possible when a serious university-community partnership was established and maintained by caring and dedicated faculty and community activists (Gamson 1997). Of course, as the chapters in this volume demonstrate, resources provided by local and national organizations (e.g., unions, NALEO, etc.) have proved to be critical elements in increased Latino political representation in this state. Success in the political arena is both the result—and cause—of the increased attention by these organizations.

Fourth, the role of religious institutions needs to be explored in depth. They are vital resources for Latinos in their daily lives. Even the Catholic Church, with its problematic record in ministering to recent immigrants, is sometimes the last institution that has remained in the *barrios* of Massachusetts, long after political parties, the federal government, and private and public health care institutions have left. Religious institutions, especially fundamental evangelical and Pentecostal ministries are central features in the lives of Latino families and communities—and they play a formative role in shaping attitudes. In Massachusetts, religious groups and interfaith councils must be enjoined to fight for the rights and quality of life issues of the Latino community. The same holds true for foundations, community economic development corporations, social service centers, and other institutions that remain in the inner cities.

Fifth, an investment in homeland politics should not be seen merely as a barrier to political participation in U.S. politics but rather a resource to be tapped. The issue of Vieques has united Puerto Ricans here and on the island in a way that no political pundit could have guessed. Dual citizenship for Dominicans has opened the door to political participation in both political systems. The fight for immigrant rights, as seen during the welfare reform battle in Massachusetts and the nation in 1997, and the immigrant community's response to Proposition 187 in California, have catalyzed all Latinos and brought Latino and non-Latino refugees and immigrants together in a common cause. The critical challenge is how to tap into this resource and channel the energies into a prospect for change in local and state-level politics. Finally, Latino communities need to build on the strengths of Latina women evidenced by their success in the electoral arena, voter registration, and grass roots community organizing.

In conclusion, a review of the chapters in this book suggests that prospects for Latino representation in cities across Massachusetts are hopeful. The prospects may depend, however, on establishing greater communication between Latino communities. Indeed, what may be most important politically for Latinos in Massachusetts is *un intercambio de ideas* (an exchange of ideas)—whereby the lessons Latinos have learned in one city or state are shared reciprocally with Latinos as they struggle and strategize in other cities and states across the nation.

REFERENCES

Arches, et al. (1997). "New Voices in University-Community Transformation by Joan Arches, Marian Darlington-Hope, Jefffrey Gerson, Joyce Gibson, Sally Habana-Hafner and Peter Kiang. *Change* 29(1): 36–41.

Gamson, Zelda F. (1997). "Higher Education and Rebuilding Civic Life." *Change* 29(1): 10–13.

Gastón Institute. (2000). "Latino Agenda 2000." Boston: Mauricio Gastón Institute for Latino Community Development and Public Policy, University of Massachusetts Boston.

About the Contributors

CAROL HARDY-FANTA is a Senior Fellow at the John W. McCormack Institute for Public Affairs, Chair of the Faculty at the McCormack Institute's Master of Science in Public Affairs, and Faculty Research Affiliate at the Mauricio Gastón Institute for Latino Community Development and Public Policy, University of Massachusetts Boston. She received her Ph.D. from Brandeis University's Heller School, an M.S.W. from Smith College, and a B.A. from Occidental College. Dr. Hardy-Fanta is author of *Latina Politics, Latino Politics: Gender, Culture, and Political Participation in Boston* (1993), *Latino Electoral Campaigns in Massachusetts: The Impact of Gender* (1997), and numerous articles on the subject of gender, race and ethnicity, and politics.

JEFFREY N. GERSON is an Assistant Professor in the Political Science Department at the University of Massachusetts Lowell and teaches courses in American Politics, urban politics and policy, ethnic and racial politics, and the politics of popular culture. His recent publications and studies have focused on the Southeast Asian and Latino communities of Lowell as well as state and regional politics. His current work in progress is a book that chronicles the political history of Latinos in Lowell. He is a member of the board of Latinos in Action in Lowell and has taught political leadership courses at the University's Center for Family, Work and Community, as part of the University of Massachusetts' CIRCLE program (Center for Immigrant and Refugee Community Leadership Empowerment). Two of his latest community collaborative projects are the Cambodian Holocaust Video Survivor's Project (an effort to preserve the memories of Cambodians who survived Pol Pot's murderous Khmer Rouge regime) and the Building Community Through Culture Program, which attempts to promote understanding and tolerance in Lowell's diverse community by focusing on the rich cultural expressions of Lowell's peoples.

ROSALBA BASSOLS-MARTÍNEZ was born in Mexico City and received her undergraduate degree from the *Instituto Tecnológico Autónomo de Mexico* (ITAM) in Mexico City and her master's degree in Urban Studies and Planning at the University of Maryland, College Park. During her stay in the United States she worked as a research assistant at the Gastón Institute for Latino Community Development and Public Policy at the University of Massachusetts Boston and earned a certificate in Management Community Organizations at Tufts University. Ms. Bassols-Martínez has also been involved with Action Langley Park, an organization that seeks to foster community development in a mostly Latino immigrant neighborhood located in the Washington, D.C., metropolitan area.

JOSÉ E. CRUZ is an Associate Professor of Political Science and Latino studies at SUNY–Albany. His research interests include the role ethnicity plays in the political mobilization of Latinos and racial and ethnic relations in urban and legislative settings. Currently he is working on a study of relations between the Congressional black and Hispanic caucuses. He is the author of *Identity and Power: Puerto Rican Politics and the Challenge of Ethnicity* (1998).

JUAN A. GÓMEZ is currently a member of the Worcester City Council. He was born in Santurce, Puerto Rico and has lived in Worcester for the past 21 years. After graduated from Doherty Memorial High School, he enlisted in the United States Marine Corps Reserve from which he received an Honorable Discharge. He received an Associate's degree from Quinsigamond Community College, and a B.A. from Assumption College. While in school, Gómez received the Martin Luther King Jr. Scholarship Award for outstanding Community Service, as well as the National Hispanic Scholarship Fund. He helped found several organizations to assist Latinos and minorities in the city, and has served on numerous boards of civic and charitable organizations in Worcester. He was the first Latino to be named to the Worcester Redevelopment Authority, and is a member of the board of Directors of Bay State Savings Bank. Gómez helped organize the first New England Puerto Rican Leadership Conference, and assisted in the First National Puerto Rican Summit in Washington, D.C., in 1994. Councilor Gómez credits his mother, his wife, and his sister with helping him reach his goals.

RAMONA HERNÁNDEZ, a native of the Dominican Republic, is Assistant Professor at the University of Massachusetts Boston and Associate Researcher at the Dominican Studies Institute at City College of the City University of New York. She received her B.A. in Latin American History from Lehman College, an M.A. in the Department of Latin American and Caribbean Studies from New York University, and a M. Phil. and a Ph.D.

in Sociology from the Graduate School of the City University of New York. Dr. Hernández is the co-author of *Dominican New Yorkers: A Socio-Economic Profile* (1998) and *Dominican Americans* (1998) and the author of *The Mobility of Workers under Advanced Capitalism: Dominican Migration to the United States* (forthcoming), as well as several chapters on Dominicans in the United States and the Caribbean.

GLENN JACOBS is Associate Professor of Sociology at the University of Massachusetts Boston. His current research interests and activities include a study of the causes and implications of low retention among Latinos in higher education; study and analysis of the work environments and social issues pertinent to under- and unrepresented Latino workers; comparison of the community contexts of *santería* in the United States and Cuba; and the sociological theory of Charles Horton Cooley, about which he is completing a volume for the University of Massachusetts Press.

JAMES JENNINGS is Professor of Urban and Environmental Policy and Planning at Tufts University. He has written several books and many articles on Black and Latino politics and urban issues, including, *Blacks, Latinos and Asians: Status and Prospects for Activism* (1994) and *The Politics of Black Empowerment* (1992, 2001). He has also published research and evaluation reports on various aspects of economic and community development in urban areas. Dr. Jennings is currently investigating the role and limitations of faith-based organizations in the civic arena and is also examining the institutional impact of welfare reform on neighborhood revitalization.

WILLIAM A. LINDEKE is Professor of Political Science at the University of Massachusetts Lowell. He has studied the Lawrence community and Dominican politics since the mid-1980s as an outgrowth of teaching Urban Politics and Politics of Central America and the Caribbean. Currently he is on extended leave lecturing on politics at the Polytechnic of Namibia and the University of Namibia. He has published widely in four countries, especially on democracy and development in Southern Africa.

RAMÓN OLIVENCIA obtained his bachelor's degree in political science at the University of Massachusetts Amherst, after initial studies at the University of Puerto Rico. He received a Master of Science in Public Affairs from the University of Massachusetts Boston, where he worked as a research assistant at the Gastón Institute for Latino Public Policy. In 1994 Olivencia moved from Chelsea to San Juan, Puerto Rico where he is currently studying towards his law degree. In 1997, he participated at the World Youth Festival in Habana, Cuba.

SETH RACUSEN, a doctoral candidate at the MIT Department of Political Science, is completing a dissertation on the role of racial ideology in the articulation and adjudication of racial discrimination complaints in Brazil: "The Brazilian Nation and the Legal Construction of Racial Discrimination." The chapter in this book developed from his research on the impact of electoral structure for Latino political representation in Massachusetts as a Faculty Associate at the Gaston Institute for Latino Affairs at the University of Massachusetts Boston. Racusen was formerly a visiting scholar at the W.E.B. Dubois Institute at Harvard University and the Center for Interdisciplinary Research and Study on the Brazilian Black at the University of São Paulo, where he conducted his fieldwork.

JAIME RODRÍGUEZ, a native of Puerto Rico, is President of the Massachusetts chapter of the National Congress for Puerto Rican Rights. He is also Research Coordinator at the William Joiner Center for the Study of War and its Consequences at the University of Massachusetts Boston. Jaime Rodríguez served as organizer of a massive 3-year statewide Latino voter registration campaign and has received a number of awards for his outstanding contributions to the Latino communities of Massachusetts, including the Action for Boston Community Development and Latino Democratic Committee Community Service Awards, the Massachusetts Hispanic Vietnam Veterans Award, and the Legislators Black Caucus Award.

Index

www.ingramcontent.com/pod-product-compliance
Ingram Content Group UK Ltd.
Pitfield, Milton Keynes, MK11 3LW, UK
UKHW020434010325
455677UK00029B/1150